RAISING THE AXE HEAD

Siam Bhayro

Philip Powell

Tony Pearce

Jacob Prasch

Philip Foster

First published in Great Britain in 2002
by
St Matthew Publishing Ltd

ISBN 1 901546 0 7 1

Acknowledgements:
Extracts from the Authorised Version of the Bible (The King James Bible), the rights in which are vested in the Crown, are reproduced by permission of the Crown's patentee, Cambridge University Press.

Extracts of Scripture taken from the Holy Bible, New International Version.
Copyright © 1973, 1978, 1984 by International Bible Society
Anglicisation copyright © 1979, 1984, 1989

Extracts of Scripture taken from the NEW AMERICAN STANDARD BIBLE © 1960, 1962, 1963, 1968, 1971, 1972, 1973, 1975, 1977, by The Lockman Foundation. Used by permission.

Publishing Ltd, 24 Geldart St, Cambridge CB1 2LX, UK
Tel: +44 (0)1223 504871, *Fax: +44 (0)1223 512304*
Email: PF.SMP@dial.pipex.com

Contents

RAISING

THE

AXE HEAD

And the man of God said, Where fell it? And he showed him the place. And he cut down a stick, and cast it in there; and made the axe head float.

2 Kings 6:6 KJV

Introduction

Raising the Axehead is a collection of messages preached at the first CWM conference to be held in the United Kingdom (Whitby, October 21-25 2002). The speakers who participated are regular contributors to CWM's publications. They demonstrate the true nature of the phrase "broad church". They come from a variety of backgrounds and attend a variety of fellowships. They do not agree on every point of doctrine. They do agree, however, that a certain style of preaching and writing is necessary if the church is to recover her mission and strength.

The messages are designed to encourage and equip the remnant church to build new fellowships. They cover a broad range of topics from eschatology to typology, from polemics to prophecy. It is hoped that this book will bless those who were not present at the conference, and serve as a reminder to those who attended.

Siam Bhayro lectures in the US and is the editor of *Vanguard.*

Tony Pearce heads up *Messianic Testimony* and edits *Light for the Last Days.*

Jacob Prasch heads up *MORIEL ministries* and is the author of two books: *The Final Words of Jesus* and *Grain for the Famine.*

Philip Powell heads up *Christian Witness Ministries* in Australia and New Zealand.

Philip Foster is the minister of a church in Cambridge and also runs St. Matthew Publishing Ltd which has released several books trying to deal with the current apostasy.

SECTION I

Raising the axe head

Siam Bhayro

I would like to begin by giving a quote from A W Tozer - *The Size of the Soul* (pp. 127-129).

"What is needed desperately today is prophetic insight. Scholars can interpret the past; it takes prophets to interpret the present. Learning will enable a man to pass judgment on our yesterdays, but it requires a gift of clear seeing to pass sentence on our own day. One hundred years from now historians will know what was taking place religiously in this year of our Lord 1956; but that will be too late for us. We should know right now.

If Christianity is to receive a rejuvenation, it must be by other means than any now being used. If the Church in the second half of this century is to recover from the injuries she suffered in the first half, there must appear a new type of preacher. The proper, ruler-of-the-synagogue type will never do. Neither will the priestly type of man who carries out his duties, takes his pay and asks no questions, nor the smooth-talking pastoral type who knows how to make the Christian religion acceptable to everyone. All these have been tried and found wanting.

Another Kind of religious leader must arise among us. He must be of the old prophet type, a man who has seen visions of God and has heard a voice from the Throne. When he comes (and I pray God there will be not one but many), he will stand in flat contradiction to everything our smirking, smooth civilization holds dear. He will contradict, denounce and protest in the name of God and will earn the hatred and opposition of a large segment of Christendom. Such a man is likely to be lean, rugged, blunt-spoken and a little bit angry with the world. He will love Christ and the souls of men to the point of willingness to die for the glory of One and the salvation of the other. But he will fear nothing that breathes with mortal breath.

This is only to say that we need to have gifts of the Spirit restored again to the Church. And it is my belief that the one gift we need most now is the gift of prophecy."

Tozer's words were themselves prophetic, and we are seeing them fulfilled to an extent in our days. But we are in dire need of a full realization of his vision the gifts of the Spirit are lacking in our fellowships, and especially prophecy is a rare thing.

The theme for this conference is "Raising the axe head", and it comes from a passage in the Bible that I believe reflects our situation in the church today. Before I explain this, let's first read 2 Kings 6:1-7

> And the sons of the prophets said unto Elisha, Behold now, the place where we dwell with thee is too strait for us. Let us go, we pray thee, and take thence every man a beam, and let us make us a place there, where we may dwell. And he answered, Go ye. And one said, Be content, I pray thee, and go with thy servants. And he answered, I will go. So he went with them. And when they came to Jordan, they cut down wood. But as one was felling a beam, the axe head fell into the water, and he cried, and said, Alas, master! For it was borrowed. And the man of God said, Where fell it? And he showed him the place. And he cut down a stick, and cast it in thither, and the iron did swim. Therefore said he, Take it up to thee. And he put out his hand and took it.

The context for this is very interesting, as it reflects the experience of many of us as we have grown accustomed to contending against the apostasy in the church. To appreciate this, let's go back to the appearance of Elijah, Elisha's mentor.

Elijah's experience reflects that of many of us. In 1 Kings 17, he appears as one making a lone stand against the corrupt leaders of God's people. He warns that a drought is coming something he would have learnt from the Law of Moses that promises that drought will follow disobedience (e.g. Deut. 28:24). Following his stand against the corrupt leaders of his day, Elijah's experience is one of isolation.

This is something that many of us have experienced. Having taken our stand against those corrupt men and women who lead our churches, we have been forced into isolation. Some of us have been banned from churches, ostracized from those we once called brothers and sisters in Christ. Judging from the letters we get, there are many believers who have suffered greatly because they have stood against error. This leads to emotional, psychological and spiritual suffering, and worst still, just as with Elijah, this is often experienced in isolation.

But just as the Lord was able to meet Elijah in his isolation and provide for him, He has done the same for many of us. The experience of the brook Cherith can be a precious one, as the Lord will meet us in our time of need. Furthermore, what follows this period of isolation is very interesting the prophet is gradually rehabilitated into fellowship once more, and it is a gradual process. First there is the widow at Zarephath (1 Kings 17:8-24), and then there is Obadiah (1 Kings 18). And gradually, Elijah becomes aware that he is not alone in his stand against the sinful leaders of Israel. Indeed, there are another one hundred prophets being hidden by Obadiah!

This is something many of us have also experienced. Being isolated, we have grown accustomed to being alone, yet the Lord would have us fellowship with like-minded believers. So tenderly and gradually, the Lord brings us into contact with like-minded believers and restores us to fellowship. This can be a traumatic experience, as Elijah's own story demonstrates.

In 1 Kings 19:10 & 14, Elijah is at his wits end, and complains to the Lord

> I have been very jealous for the LORD God of hosts: for the children of Israel have forsaken thy covenant, thrown down thine altars, and slain thy prophets with the sword; and I, even I only, am left; and they seek my life to take it away.

Yet the Lord points out that Elijah is not alone in fact there are seven thousand numbered faithful in Israel (1 Kings 19:18)!

We must be careful not to repeat Elijah's error. However isolated we feel, we must remember that there are in fact thousands like us scattered across the visible church, and that it is the Lord's will that we find fellowship with each other. By the end of his life, Elijah had found that fellowship. We see this clearly in the story of his translation into heaven. In 2 Kings 2, we see little fellowships of people of like-mind to Elijah the *sons of the prophets*. There is one group in Bethel (verse 3), and another in Jericho (verse 5). This Jericho group numbered at least fifty if not more (verse 7). So having begun his ministry in isolation, Elijah ended it in fellowship with those who had also remained faithful to God's word. It is this transition from isolation to fellowship that we must now experience. And it is this context that we should understand the story of the axe head in 2 Kings 6.

As we take our stand for the truth, others will join us. The Lord preserves His remnant in every generation. And as the fallout from each deception becomes apparent, those who were feeble will turn and once again seek out those who were faithful. In his time of need, even the corrupt Jehoram knew where he could find true counsel (2 Kings 3:10ff).

Over time, the company of the faithful grows and grows, until they need to change their surroundings and it is in this context that the company come to Elisha and initiate their building program. I believe that the remnant church will experience the same growth, to the point where it will need to step out in faith and establish new fellowships. And the detail in the lost axe head passage is very instructive for this situation. So let's work our way through this passage.

The first thing we notice is that they were responding to a clear need

Behold now, the place where we dwell with thee is too strait for us.

This in itself is instructive for the faithful church at this time. We must be prepared to respond to the needs of the body. For example, I know of one place where there are a number of believers who have clearly been called out of their fellowships because of the sin of their corrupt leaders and the accompanying deception. Immediately, this gives rise to a number of practical and spiritual needs. These people need to continue in fellowship together, so that they are not alone and vulnerable. This means that a venue is needed, so a willing brother has to open his house up regularly and faithfully to the others. There is also a need for commitment from spiritual brethren to continue to oversee such a work. Responding to such a need can be awkward, requiring a number of sacrifices on your part. You may have to change your current lifestyle and reconsider your priorities. But that is the nature of the beast and there is no point in complaining. The faithful church will respond to the need of the body. Let us not be under any illusions about this. I don't think the *sons of the prophets* were enthralled about the prospect of cutting down trees and building a house either it is hard work! It meant stopping their usual activities and walking a long way. It meant ceasing their prophetic activities and doing the mundane tree-cutting thing. But what needs to be done ... needs to be done.

But there is something else that is very important to notice here

Let us go ... and take every man a beam, and let us make us a place...

The *sons of the prophets* didn't turn round and dump the entire project on one man! They assumed a collective responsibility for it! It cannot be more explicit *let us go ... every man ... let us make.* And this point is of equal importance to the last responding to the need of the body is a task for the faithful church collectively. No one man should have to shoulder the burden of responsibility on his own. There should be many willing labourers. Indeed, each person should, metaphorically, cut his own beam.

Ask yourself this is someone else cutting your beam for you? If yes, then get involved! And if you are cutting someone else's, it is in their best interest to teach them to cut their own.

Verse three is very nice, and demonstrates something I think we are all aware of

Be content I pray thee and go with thy servant...

The *sons of the prophets* were acutely aware that such endeavours should be carried out under the care, oversight and supervision of an experienced and godly elder. Such men are rare. They were rare in tenth century Israel we read only of Elijah and then Elisha. And they are rare today also. But they are here the Lord will not leave us lacking in this respect. Mark out such men and enlist their help.

When I first started Vanguard, I had just turned 24 years old. My friend Neil Richardson was younger still, and we used to hang out with a very young crowd at University College London. Most of the leaders of the big London churches succumbed to one deception or another, so the elder-figures we needed were not there. In fact, some of them even turned on us. But I knew that such a work as Vanguard needed "grey hairs" (no offence intended to Philip Foster or Tony Pearce) so I sought older and more experienced contributors.

Later on, when the Lord caused our paths to cross with Philip Powell, I suggested that we combine our works. Why? OK we were doing the same work, for the same reasons etc. But more than that I knew that we needed an Elijah or Elisha figure there to accompany us on our "building program". Not only does wisdom dictate this, but in hindsight I see that 2 Kings 6:3 actually states it! So we praise God for His guiding hand.

I have no problem at all with saying that, in my opinion, Philip Powell is such a man in our time. The scarcity of men of his stature means that, all the more, such men should be marked out and enlisted just as the *sons of the prophets* did with Elisha.

So, as verse four tells us, the men journey to the Jordan, and begin the work. Again, let me say that it is hard work. I remember vividly the one time I wielded an axe to cut wood, and I wouldn't willingly do it again! It was a humiliating experience. The only way to succeed was to return to first principles, and learn to wield an axe from scratch. Gradually I became more proficient, but it took time. I reckon these *sons of the prophets* had to learn many new skills also. Cutting beams and building houses are not part of the everyday routine for prophets. Now this is instructive for us. As we begin to fulfil the need of the church, we may indeed have to be humble and learn new methods and skills. We may have to adopt an entirely new modus operandi. As the Tozer quote I began with says of the prophet, "he will stand in flat contradiction to everything our smirking, smooth civilization holds dear. He will contradict, denounce and protest in the name of God and will earn the hatred and opposition of a large segment of Christendom". Thus we may have to abandon much we have treasured in the past, and realign ourselves with the Holy Scriptures.

And don't think that such endeavours will be smooth. You will certainly come across problems

> But as one was felling a beam, the axe head fell into the water...

Part of the problem here is the location. If they had been cutting down trees away from water, there would have been no problem. He could have just picked the iron up from the ground and repaired the axe. But the problem is that trees grow next to water, so if you are going to cut trees, you have to go to the river, and this makes the task that bit more hazardous.

The same is true for what the Lord wills us to do. He will take you to the water, metaphorically, and this is a place fraught with danger. The currents of the Jordan run fast, and Israelites were not famed for their ability to swim! Similarly, the Lord may lead you to start a fellowship on a rough and unfashionable estate. You may be led to reach out to those the other fellowships won't touch because they are not good tithers. You may be called to open your home to people who will make your friend's eyebrows rise!

But if that is where the need takes you, then you have to go. That is where the Lord's blessing will be. And in the midst of trials and hitches, when your axe head flies off and is "irretrievable", there the miracle will occur.

I said that part of the problem is the location, but there is another problem here the dangerous nature of the tool. An axe is not a toy it is a potentially dangerous implement, especially when misused or abused. And in this respect, the axe is very much like the gifts of the Spirit.

Firstly, note that the axe is essential for the building of the house. Without it, the beams will not be cut, and the house will not be built. The same is the case for the gifts of the Spirit. Without them, we will accomplish nothing. They are the tools, the implements by which the Holy Spirit enables us to build up the body of Christ. Again, returning to the quote from Tozer, "This is only to say that we need to have gifts of the Spirit restored again to the Church. And it is my belief that the one gift we need most now is the gift of prophecy".

But the problem here is that there was a fault in the use of the axe, and it broke after all it was borrowed, so the young prophet may have not known what he was doing. I don't think the fault was with the axe, because it was retrieved, presumably to be repaired and used again (after all, iron is precious and not to be discarded).

Now, when the accident happened and the iron flew through the air into the Jordan, it would not have been entirely unreasonable for the prophet to panic. After all, a flying axe head is a very dangerous thing! It could have gone anywhere, causing injury or even death. Having witnessed this potentially fatal accident, I would not have blamed him if he had started shouting at the top of his voice, "Everybody stop! Put those dangerous axes down! Look what just happened to mine! These things are really dangerous and we should all stop using them!"

And this is what has happened with many damaged Christians indeed, the body of Christ herself has been damaged in this way. Seeing the danger that comes from misusing or abusing the gifts of the Spirit, she has downed tools and ceased work. So now we don't experience the gifts as we should. Indeed, many of us have ceased seeking them altogether. Remember, the apostle exhorted us to "covet earnestly" these things (1 Cor. 12:31). Ask yourself are you coveting earnestly the gifts of the Spirit? Because, in all honesty, you won't be able to build anything without them.

Before we note the proper course of action, as demonstrated by Elisha, there is another point to note

Alas master! For it was borrowed.

In other words, the axe wasn't his. It belonged to another, and this may explain its misuse and, hence, why it broke. Now there is an application of this to the gifts of the Spirit. Paul teaches that in the body, there are diversities of gifts, all of which are needed. These are given to each part of the body as the Holy Spirit sees fit in other words, they are not acquired by man. I think that, when man attempts to initiate such things, and play with things that don't belong to him, they brake just like with this axe. It wasn't his tool, and his ignorance of it caused it to break. Just so there are people in the church trying to exercise gifts they don't have, and the result is terrible. We have pastors who cannot pastor, preachers who cannot preach, apostles who accomplish nothing, prophets without inspiration, teachers who don't study the scriptures… the list goes on and on.

Much of this comes from us inheriting the Roman Catholic system of having a clergy and a laity, with one minister in each church. This poor man is then expected to do everything, and exercise all the gifts like a one-man-band performing in front of a passive church! But the Biblical pattern is entirely different. We should each possess our own toolkit, as presented to us by the Holy Spirit. And we should each know how to use our own tools.

Now, as a remnant church, we are left not exercising the gifts. Through abuse, misuse, ignorance, fear or plain downright laziness, we are left without the essential tools that God has provided for His church. And it is high time we recover these things.

The process for the recovery of the axe head is very revealing

And the man of God said, Where fell it?

This is the first step we need to go back and find out where the problem arose. If you once moved in a certain gift, such as prophecy, and then stopped, then you will need to sort this out. Repentance will be necessary, as neglecting a gift given by the Lord is something we are warned against. Also, talking through such things with an Elisha figure is a good idea, as this passage demonstrates.

At the place where it fell, where the gift was lost, Elisha and the prophet stood to recover the axe head

And he cut down a stick, and cast it thither and the iron did swim.

What is a stick, compared to the iron? It is certainly a good trade from the prophet's point of view. Think about this for a moment. They were there to cut down beams for a grand work a new house for the prophetic company.

Beams were needed for this venture. And to get a beam, you needed an axe.

But all they had was a small piece of wood in this context, this is the meaning of the Hebrew word translated "stick" by the KJV. Effectively, they had the axe handle, but no axe head so they had no axe!

I think many believers are in this situation they have a stick rather than an axe. Thus they have the pretence of possessing the gifts of the Spirit, but no cutting edge. So for all their activity, they actually achieve very little you won't cut many beams with a stick. You can wave it around and hit it against that tree, but you won't chop it down!

Now Elisha's action speaks clearly he threw it into the waters. Why? Because it was worthless. He needed the iron not the handle. And this is what the church needs to do. It needs to recover the iron, and to do this, it needs to throw away all that is worthless all those things that are distractions from what God has for us.

Being unable to use the gifts of the Spirit, and hence unable to do the work the Lord would have us do, we have satisfied ourselves with a little work of little consequence one that doesn't fulfil the needs of the body.

We should do what Elisha did and throw all these little sticks into the water, in order to recover the proper tools necessary to do God's will! There are many of these little sticks in the church today, which have proved a distraction from our lack of power and have comforted us in our loss of the gifts of the Spirit. All the church's extra-Biblical pursuits and agendas have proved great tonics for our loss! I can list pages of them, but for the sake of space here are a couple … Sabbath observance, whether it is trying to observe the Jewish Friday evening to Saturday evening, or campaigning to keep Sunday "special". I know Christians who have wasted hours on this vain pursuit, but why? It isn't Biblical and has only distracted them from what they should be doing.

Another "stick" is alcohol I have been banned from one pulpit and declared unfit to preach because I am not teetotal! This is another example of an impotent church using a non-issue to distract it from its true need. We don't need teetotal assemblies we need Spirit-filled ones.

I often marvel at how the "church" ascribes to God so many agendas that He is not interested in. I recently heard of a Christian official from Florida State who went on record condemning women who work outside the home. Do you think God really gets upset about women going to work? I just read in the New York Times (August 10, 2002) about a South African minister whose follower refuses to use condoms even though her husband has AIDS! Her reason for this is that she has been led to believe that taking the medically prescribed precaution compromises her faith in God. There are secular medics pleading with her to do the right thing for herself and her family, but her preacher claims to be able to heal people of AIDS, so she ignores the sound medical advice. Such things are not on God's agenda Christ did not bleed on the cross for this!

But it is not just the activities of the church that are our little sticks. It is also the structures, with one man at the top running everything rather than an eldership, having communion only once a week on a Sunday rather than whenever we meet together, making women cover their head and then stopping them praying out loud… the list goes on and on.

Elisha threw the little stick into the water, because he wanted to recover the implement necessary to cut down a beam, which would be used to fulfil the true need of the *sons of the prophets*. We too need to throw out everything that is superfluous to our calling, and beyond the body's true need, in order to recover the gifts of the Spirit that we lack.

I believe that the agenda of the remnant church is one of building it is time to move beyond the narrow confines of our present dwelling. But if we are to do so, we shall have to recover the necessary tools to build what the body needs. We need to seek the Lord wholeheartedly for a restoration of the gifts of the Spirit.

SECTION II

A Call to the Remnant

Philip Powell

Part 1 Elijah where are you?

CHAPTER 1

God always retains a remnant

GOD has always raised up and used the faithful remnant. It happened in Israel and in the Church throughout history and it's happening again. E.M. Bounds wisely said, *"God's method is men",* meaning that the divine initiative is reflected not in systems or programmes, but in His servants who receive His revelation, obey His Word and do His will. Sadly the human process creates a digression, which is reflected in the statement MEN produce MOVEMENTS, which end in MONUMENTS. The reality of this was brought home to me most powerfully on a ministry visit to UK in 1997. I preached at a place called Mow Cop, a village with a population of around 1,400 that is situated on a hill that towers 1,000 feet directly above the plains of Cheshire and Staffordshire in Great Britain. What an intriguing place! The Encyclopaedia Britannica refers to Mow Cop as the Mecca of Primitive Methodism, for it was here that the "Prims", as they were known, conducted their first Camp Meetings in 1807 in an attempt to revive the enthusiasm and fire of the earlier Wesleyan Methodists, who vehemently opposed them.

At the summit there is an unfinished tower locally called the "folly", which was built around 1754 as a summerhouse by the wealthy Wilbraham family to portray a ruined castle. It was at this precise site in 1907 that 100,000 people gathered to celebrate the centenary of those great Primitive Methodist camp meetings. Now both the Wesleyans and the Primitives are largely spent forces. As I stood and looked across the plains of Cheshire into North Wales on the west and turned to look over Staffordshire deep into England on the east, the unfinished summerhouse of the Wilbraham family, former citizens of that

Mecca of Methodism told its own story. MEN produce MOVEMENTS, which end as MONUMENTS. That's what calls forth the Faithful Remnant, for Christ said that His church would always prevail.

Consider another case scenario, which sadly tells the same tale and bites more deeply and closer to the bone as it relates to our own origins. Undoubtedly, the Pentecostal revival produced one of the greatest movements of church history being rightly described as the third arm of Christendom. Historically it can be identified in its origin as the Faithful REMNANT from Methodism. Clearly there were denials and departures and degrees of corruption from the inception, but no intelligent person who has travelled extensively can deny that the early Pentecostals influenced their world for good. However something has happened. One man put it this way: *"Revival movements start in the fire and end in the smoke"*. Now that's a picture that says a lot. Often the smoke is more impressive visually than the original fire.

As we look back (and it's not wrong to look back, for if we don't know where we've been then we can't know where we're going) there are two dangers each of which relates to the extremes to which humans tend to be driven. Firstly, it's possible to concentrate on the smoke and forget the fire. This tends to turn faith into doubt. Secondly some say that all the fire was false just because it got out of hand and they point to the smoke as the evidence. This however overlooks the nature of fire, which always produces more smoke after the flame has died down and the fire smoulders away. We have the Word of God to guide us with such statements as *"Let all things be done decently and in order"*. If we deviate from the mandate of the Word of God we're going to end up with a lot of smoke but that doesn't prove that all the fire was false.

At the outset of our first CWM Conference[1], I made two impassioned pleas: Firstly that we do not try to justify the bizarre as some have so foolishly attempted to do on either the notion that God's ways are not totally understandable to the rational mind or that God is doing something new for which we don't and can't have precedence in scripture. This is total nonsense for it strikes at the clear teaching of scripture that the truly spiritual people are able to judge ALL THINGS for they have the mind of Christ (1 Corinthians 2:15-16) and that the spiritual mind is rational, orderly and intelligent. It also attacks the basis of our faith in the authority and sufficiency of scripture, which is a most serious matter. Secondly and equally that we do not deny our godly heritage, which is very much related to our two major themes REVIVAL & TRUE HOLINESS and REVIVAL & GENUINE SUPERNATURALISM. These are not mutually exclusive. They are intrinsically joined and were in fact the major emphases of the founders of classic Pentecostalism. These two threads are essential in the fabric of any revival movement and must be stated and experienced at the commencement and restated and rediscovered among the faithful remnant. It was true in Elijah's time and it's true NOW as we ask the question, *"Elijah Where Are You?"* which is not just a question about Elijah, but about the God of Elijah, who as many interpret will in some mysterious manner be one of the final two witnesses of the end time spoken of in Revelation chapter 11:

"And I will give power to my two witnesses, and they shall prophesy for twelve-hundred and sixty days, clothed in sackcloth. These have power to shut heaven, that it not rain in the days of their prophecy: and have power over waters to turn them to blood, and to strike the earth with all plagues, as often as they will. And when they shall have finished their testimony, the beast that ascends out of the bottomless pit shall make war against them, and shall overcome them, and kill them. And their dead bodies shall lie in the street of the great city, which spiritually is called Sodom and Egypt, where also our Lord was crucified. ... And after three and a half days the Spirit of life from God entered into them, and they stood upon their feet; and great fear fell upon them, which saw them. And they heard a great voice from heaven saying to them, Come up here. And they ascended up to heaven in a cloud; and their enemies beheld them. And the same hour was there a great earthquake, and the tenth part of the city fell, and in the earthquake were slain seven thousand men: and the remnant were frightened, and gave glory to the God of heaven."

Revelation 11:3-13

This rather mystical and somewhat speculative allusion to Elijah as one of the two end time witnesses is worthy of brief comment. In response to the question about His identity the disciples answered Christ with, *"Some say that you are ... Elijah ..."* (Matthew 16:14). While on another occasion Jesus Himself testified of John the Baptist, *"But I say to you, that Elijah is come already, and they did not know him, but have done to him whatever they desired"* (Matthew 17:12) and yet again, *"... if you will receive it, this is Elijah, who was to come"* (Matthew 11:14). It was Elijah and Moses who joined Christ on the Mount of Transfiguration as witnesses to His forthcoming Crucifixion (Matthew 17:1-13) and it was Elijah whom the unbelieving Jews near the cross looked for to answer Christ's prayer in Aramaic, *"Eli, Eli, lama sabachthani"* which they misapplied as an appeal for Elijah to help Him (Matthew 27:46-49).

Clearly there was a general view among the Jews in New Testament times that Elijah would precede Christ their Messiah. Our Lord did not dispute the idea but rather confirmed it indicating that the fulfilment rested upon the faith and acceptance of the people at the time. This supports our view that prophecy frequently has more than one fulfilment. John the Baptist, to those who received his message, fulfilled the prophecy. He was indeed the forerunner of Christ who prepared the Way of the Lord and made His paths straight, BUT that does not preclude a future fulfilment. Malachi the last of the Old Testament prophets proclaimed, *"Behold, I will send you Elijah the prophet before the coming of the great and dreadful day of the LORD"* (Malachi 4:5) which is a clear reference to some future event that relates to God's judgment time of history.

Our topic, while relating in part to this prophetic aspect also has a practical application. When Elijah's mantle was taken up by his successor, the sons of the prophets observed, *"The spirit of Elijah rests upon Elisha"* (2 Kings 2:15). It is the spirit, attitude or disposition and the example of Elijah that I want to build upon in asking the question, *"Elijah Where Are You?"* and in considering how God always retains a faithful remnant as 1 Kings 19:9-18 implies.

"And he came to a cave, and lodged there; and, behold, the word of the LORD came to him, and he said to him, What are you doing here, Elijah? And he said, I have been very jealous for the LORD God of hosts: for the children of Israel have forsaken your covenant, thrown down your altars, and slain your prophets with the sword; and I only, am left; and they seek my life, to take it. And he said, Go forth, and stand upon the mountain before the LORD. And, behold, the LORD passed by, and a great and strong wind rent the mountains, and broke in pieces the rocks before the LORD; but the LORD was not in the wind: and after the wind an earthquake; but the LORD was not in the earthquake: And after the earthquake a fire; but the LORD was not in the fire: and after the fire a still small voice. And when Elijah heard it, he wrapped his face in his mantle, and went out, and stood in the entrance of the cave. And, there came a voice to him, and said, What are you doing here Elijah? And he said, I have been very jealous for the LORD God of hosts: because the children of Israel have forsaken your covenant, thrown down your altars, and slain your prophets with the sword; and I only am left; and they seek to take my life. ... (18) Yet I have left to me seven thousand in Israel, all the knees which have not bowed to Baal, and every mouth which has not kissed him."

1 Kings 19:9-18

There are four major stages in the Life and Ministry of Elijah:
I. The hidden years;
II. His public ministry;
III. The silent years; and
IV. Appointing his successor.

We do not know how long the first period lasted and would be entirely ignorant of it were it not mentioned by James in the New Testament. The public and silent years are interspersed. Elijah is a person that you cannot really tie down. He left for heaven in a whirlwind because he largely lived a whirlwind sort of life. Now you see him; now you don't. Here today and gone no one knows quite where tomorrow, but he'll be back soon when he's needed. That's how he lived his life and when he finally left this earth it wasn't clear to everyone where he'd gone or for that matter if he had finally left. He is one of only two who appear to have evaded death. Enoch was the other. Maybe all these facts about Elijah contribute to the mystery regarding his future appearance on this earth.

The final period was his link with Elisha, who was the third person God told Elijah to anoint:

"And the LORD s .d to him, Go, return on your way to the wilderness of Damascus: and anoint Hazael to be king over Syria: And Jehu the son of Nimshi you shall anoint to be king over Israel: and Elisha the son of Shaphat of Abelmeholah you shall anoint to be prophet in your place."

1 Kings 19:15-16

In fact there's no record that Elijah anointed anyone of the three in the normal sense of that word, which signifies the pouring of oil on the head of the anointed. All we know is that Elijah touched Elisha with his mantle as the latter was going about his business

"...and Elijah passed by him, and threw his mantle upon him. And he left the oxen, and ran after Elijah, and said, Let me kiss my father and my mother, and then I will follow you. And he said to him, Go back again: for what have I done to you?"

1 Kings 19:19-20

Elisha was never the same again and was not satisfied until he held the mantle in his hand. Yet Elijah didn't give Elisha his mantle as some wrongly teach. It fell from heaven and Elisha took it up.[2]

With the double portion of the spirit of Elijah upon him, Elisha is the one who prophesies that Hazael will be King of Syria (2 Kings 8:12-13) and later instructs one of the prophets of the faithful remnant to anoint Jehu King of Israel (2 Kings 9:1-3). There is no record that Elijah carried out the physical anointing of Elisha or of Jehu or of Hazael as God appears to have commanded him, so how do we explain what happened? The answer to that question lies in who and what Elijah represents and his link to the faithful remnant. Let's take a closer look.

CHAPTER 2

The hidden life of the remnant

Diamonds and real pearls are formed in dark and secret places

ELIJAH was clearly the most effective spiritual leader of his time yet the religious hierarchy marginalized him. One of the things that the New Testament emphasises about his "hidden life" was his human-ness. James says he was *"subject to like passions as we are"*. The Greek word[3] so translated signifies "like, similar, resembling" i.e. a thing or person corresponding to another. If we are part of the true and faithful remnant we both sympathise and empathise with Elijah for the word conveys the ideas of "suffering the like with another" and being "of like feelings or affections". Historically Elijah was the God-ordained leader of the faithful remnant though he was slow and reluctant to recognise it. In fact at one time he thought he was totally alone in his faithful stand for the truth and righteousness of Jehovah *"only I am left"*. In other words he didn't even recognise the people whom he had inspired and of whom he was the concealed leader. Paul identifies this negative confession of Elijah in the context of the over-riding grace and elective calling of God regarding the faithful remnant in Romans 11:3-5:

"Lord, they have killed your prophets, and torn down your altars; and I am left alone, and they seek my life. But what is the answer of God to him? I have reserved to myself seven thousand men, who have not bowed the knee to the image of Baal. Even so then at this present time also there is a remnant according to the election of grace."

Romans 11:3-5

In the historic setting Elijah twice protests to God his sense of isolation in his stand for Truth and that was after he called for a drought, prayed down fire and then prayed earnestly until the drought was broken

"And he said, I have been very jealous for the LORD God of hosts: for the children of Israel have forsaken your covenant, thrown down your altars, and slain your prophets with the sword; and only I am left; and they seek my life, to take it."

1 Kings 19:10

This statement is repeated in identical words in verse 14

"And he said, I have been very jealous for the LORD God of hosts: because the children of Israel have forsaken your covenant, thrown down your altars, and slain your prophets with the sword; and only I am left; and they seek my life, to take it."

1 Kings 19:14

James the apostle emphasises a very important truth about Elijah and by extension about the faithful remnant when he draws our attention to his human-ness. Remnant people are VERY human. However he emphasises another matter that is absolutely vital to our calling as God's people and not so naturally occurring as our human-ness. Here's the full quotation from James

"Elijah was a man subject to passions like we are, and he prayed earnestly that it might not rain: and it did not rain on the earth for three years and six months. *(18)* And he prayed again, and the heaven gave rain, and the earth produced its fruit."

James 5: 17-18

Interestingly Elijah prayed in private prior to his public proclamation and prayer. James tells us that he *"prayed earnestly"*. The Greek rendering is two words both of which signify "PRAYER". To express it literally, "Elijah PRAYED[4] in his PRAYER"[5]. The first is a verb and means, "to offer prayers, to pray". The second is a noun and signifies "prayer addressed to God". The double use of the same root word conveys the idea that Elijah deeply and intimately involved himself in the prayer that he offered. It was not something that was detached from him or from his manner of life. It was part and parcel of his passion and pursuit. Religious praying is mere verbiage and is an abomination to the Lord.

Both the historic setting and the New Testament application emphasise our two themes *Revival & True Holiness* and *Revival & Genuine Supernaturalism,* which are the two pillars on which all true revival movements are built. Picture Elijah in those HIDDEN YEARS dwelling as he did at Tishbeh on the east side of Jordan and earnestly seeking God regarding the wickedness of Ahab and Jezebel in their western idolatrous culture. What could he do? What was the mind of the Lord in the matter? Many years earlier as God's people stood on the verge of the Promised Land, Moses the servant of the Lord delivered the Word of the Lord to them in Deuteronomy chapter 11. It was both a command

and a warning and it included God's judgement on sin by withholding the rain.[6]

King Solomon confirmed the same thing in his great dedicatory prayer at the consecration of the Temple. 1 Kings 8:35 affirms: *"When heaven is shut up, and there is no rain, because they have sinned against you; if they pray toward this place, and confess your name, and turn from their sin, when you afflict them".*

James tells us that the *"effectual fervent* {Greek *energeo* (Strong 1754) from Greek *energes* (Strong 1756) i.e. "active" or "powerful") *prayer of a righteous man avails much* (literally PREVAILS i.e. has power shown by extraordinary deeds)" (v16).

Elijah could have been content in his rural lifestyle, dwelling among the people whose forebears had chosen less than God's best. For he was a descendant of the two and half tribes who settled on the east side of Jordan choosing not to go into the Promised Land permanently. But as he sought God he was motivated with a concern for HOLINESS and, mobilised by the clear teaching of the Word of God, he prophesied a SOVEREIGN and SUPERNATURAL intervention first in judgment, then in restoration, which is the ONLY way back. God's Word is always the light that shines forth prophetic direction. Those who persist in sin and idolatry deserve a drought. The Word of God pronounced judgement upon them so Elijah, with great confidence, "prayed earnestly" that it would not rain upon the earth and then, when he knew that God had heard and would grant his request, he strode across Jordan and into the palace of king Ahab and told that idolater that it wouldn't rain until he (Elijah) told it to. Then he turned on his heel, strode out of the palace, slammed the door in Ahab's face and returned to his home country, where he waited for the nearby Cherith brook to dry up as a consequence of the drought for which he had first earnestly prayed and then fearlessly prophesied.

A call for Elijah is a call for HOLINESS of life and a deep spiritual cry for the miracles of our fathers in the genuine SUPERNATURAL displays of the Almighty in JUDGEMENT and in RESTORATION. May God hear the cry of the faithful remnant from the hidden years. BUT that can only be if we get up off our knees and make a stand for righteousness. God's method is men and women whose hearts and minds He has touched. Prayer is more than kneeling in concern and reflection. It is an action, which always results in a stand for RIGHT against WRONG and a WALK, WORK and often a WAR on behalf of God and His righteous ways. Elijah's hidden life was the natural and spiritual precursor to his public life and ministry.

CHAPTER 3

The public life of the remnant

"Set the trumpet to your mouth. ... because they have transgressed my covenant, and trespassed against my law"
Hosea 8:1

As a public figure Elijah was most certainly a confrontationalist. His sudden appearance on the stage of holy writ was more dramatic than any other person and the consequences more far reaching than most. The first we read of him is in 1 Kings 17 verse 1

"And Elijah the Tishbite, who was of the inhabitants of Gilead, said to Ahab, As the LORD God of Israel lives, before whom I stand, there shall not be dew or rain these years, but according to my word."

1 Kings 17:1

Having delivered his message he returned to virtual obscurity for the next three and a half years but though "unseen" and cut off from public life, from then on it was Elijah who called the shots. King Ahab searched for him in vain as he dwelt in secret, first in the northern region of Gilead close to his home town of Tishbeh by the brook Cherith on the east side of Jordan and then at Zarephath or Sarepta[7] as it was called in New Testament times in the far northern area of Phoenicia on the Mediterranean coast. To get there he travelled a distance of some 80 kilometres as the crow flies, which could translate to twice or three times that distance due to the mountainous and difficult terrain that he traversed. Remember it was in the height of a drought when the streams and brooks had dried up. One can only conjecture as to how many miracles he experienced on the journey, but that is the nature of the hidden life of the faithful remnant and will be increasingly so for us in the future, but we must learn the lesson that miracles are not to be gloried in. They are the natural and normal expressions of God at work among and on the behalf of His people. They are to be expected BUT not sought after.

One foolish Bible teacher calculated that there were twice as many miracles performed by Elisha as were performed by Elijah and that this constituted "the double portion" blessing spoken of in 2 Kings 2:9 and 10.[8] Such a proposition is ridiculous despite the number of other Bible teachers who have echoed the notion. You can't count the miracles in Elijah's life. By the brook Cherith each morning and evening, ravens acted contrary to nature in bringing food to this most remarkable prophet. That's two miracles a day for who knows how long? Then clearly other aspects of his hidden and secret life are surrounded by miracles. Shutting up heaven so that it didn't rain was one thing, maintaining it in that condition for three and half years, was quite another. That required a miracle three and half years long and don't tell me that Elijah's "praying earnestly" ended with his call for the drought. The *"effectual fervent prayer of a righteous man"* that is *"powerful in its out-working"* is a persistent, patient, prevailing prayer that becomes a life-style and that, in the case of Elijah, produced miracles which were not always sensational but were too numerous to count. We will return to a consideration of this aspect later, as it is something that is most pertinent to the prophetic calling of the end time faithful remnant.

There were four dramatic public appearances of Elijah, each followed by a period when he went into hiding. This interspersing of the great public proclamations, involving the highest dignitaries in the land, followed by his disappearance into obscurity, is what marks out Elijah as being unique. They also have some allegorical application to the faithful remnant now.

Firstly, there was the time when he appeared before Ahab and called for a drought as we have read. Secondly, when, three and a half years later, he challenged the priests of Baal to a fire dual and then prayed for rain. Thirdly, when he confronted Ahab in the vineyard of Naboth and prophesied the utter destruction of Ahab's house. Fourthly, when he delivered God's message to the idolatrous king Ahaziah the son of Ahab, who had fallen through a lattice in his palace. On that occasion God protected his prophet against not one but two armies of men whom He destroyed with fire from heaven.

This inter-relation of the public expressions with the private aspects of Elijah's life adds interest and intrigue to his ministry. In fact they hang together as a whole, each contributing to the other and typifying the nature, call and ministry of the faithful remnant then, and throughout time, but especially in the End Time. What Elijah's life teaches above and beyond everything else is that the *"effectual fervent prayer of righteous people"* produces patience, perseverance and power in its effective out-working. This shines through in each of the time slots that surround his public declarations.

We know nothing about the hidden years of Elijah's birth, boyhood, youth and early manhood, except that he was of the tribe of Reuben, or Gad or half Manasseh and that Gilead on the east side of Jordan was his native country. In the original dividing of the land half the region of Gilead was allotted to Manasseh and the other half to Reuben and Gad, but Gilead itself became the possession of Manasseh's son Machir, who named his own son after the city and region. This gave rise to the term Gileadite, which features quite frequently in scripture. On this basis it is reasonable to presume that Elijah was a direct descendant from Manasseh through Machir his son and Gilead his grandson. (See Appendix 1).

Genealogy and inheritance are important issues in scripture. Both were jealously guarded by the devout and godly descendants of Israel the former especially in respect of the women folk and the latter especially by the men folk. (See Appendix 2) In respect of Elijah's origins there are two things that we can glean:

1) He came from the group of people who settled for less than God's best. They chose not to enter the promised land; and

2) He was probably a direct descendant from Manasseh, who was the older son of Joseph and who entered into half the birthright blessing of Israel by the default of Reuben who according to 1 Chronicles 5 verses 1 and 2 forfeited it through immorality.[9]

The practical application is, as REMNANT people, we will probably, like Elijah, have both good and bad in our background heritage. As he was not prepared to settle for less than the best after the example of his forebears, but was determined to retain his birthright blessing, so must we. One of the hallmarks of the calling and appointment of the faithful stand of the end time remnant will be that we will not excuse ourselves on the basis of genes or genealogy, but will press forward, recognising our true birthright as sons and daughters of the Living God. We have an inheritance to protect and to pass on.

CHAPTER 4

Drought, famine and the remnant

"Behold, days are coming, says the Lord GOD, that I will send a famine in the land, not a famine of bread, or a thirst for water, but of hearing the words of the LORD"
Amos 8:11

ELIJAH, the leader of the remnant, was directly responsible for the drought and the consequent serious famine throughout northern Israel as described in 1 Kings 18:2, *"And there was a severe famine in Samaria."* Deuteronomy chapter 11 and 1 Kings chapter 8 make it plain that drought and famine were to be part of the divine prescription to cure God's people of their waywardness. It was this Word of God about withholding the rain, which assured Elijah that he knew the mind and will of God through his earnest prayer. Judgment had to precede restoration, and that judgment affected both the wicked religious populace of Israel and the righteous remnant. Our Lord speaking of the beneficence of the Father in the normal acts of nature in His great sermon on the Mount said,

"He makes his sun to rise on the evil and on the good, and sends rain on the just and on the unjust."

Matthew 5:45

Conversely, when God acts judiciously through the forces of nature in a general manner, everyone will be affected in some way. Having called for a drought and having made it abundantly clear that it wouldn't be broken until he decided, Elijah became the most sought after man in all Israel. God uses drought and famine to turn or destroy the wicked and the rebellious and to get the attention of the righteous remnant, who have not bowed the knee to Baal, but who have not been doing much for the cause of Jehovah either. It's part of the Lord's method of dealing with us.

In Elijah's day, the remnant stood up only after he had made the running and I am sure in his day as in our time, there would have been those who said, "We agree with Elijah, BUT we wouldn't have done it that way". Consensus is only good among those who have the mind of Christ, but some situations call for a committee of one, who, like Nehemiah is not afraid to consult with himself and rebuke the nobles and set a great assembly against them.[10] Righteous remnants frequently call forth grass root movements, which is what is required in our time A GREAT ASSEMBLY to be set against them. Elijah and Nehemiah, each in different ways, recognised that an extreme situation calls for an extreme action, which is the quintessence of the faithful remnant. It is not required of everyone, BUT someone must do it to break the status quo, or to halt the slide into idolatry and immorality, which is the inevitable outcome of well meaning people confusing excitement and hype with godly revival.

We tend to forget that Baal worship within Israel was excused on the basis of a confusion of terms. Baal means "master", "possessor" or "husband" all of which were equally applied to Yahweh or Jehovah. The New Bible Dictionary (IVF) records,

"Yahweh was the 'master' and 'husband' of the Israelites and therefore they called Him 'Baal' in all innocence. But naturally this led to the confusion of the worship of Yahweh with the Baal rituals and it presently became essential to call Him by some different title ..." *(cf Hosea 2:16[11]).*

In Elijah's day another area of confusion had reached a crisis point and it related to the control of the natural elements. Again The New Bible Dictionary states,

"When the Israelites entered Canaan they found that every piece of land had its own deity, its 'owner'. There were thus many 'Baals' ... (English 'Baalim') ... the word gradually became a proper name to indicate the great fertility god of the Canaanites. ...The Baal cults affected and challenged the worship of Yahweh throughout Israelite history."[12]

The real reason, however, that Baal worship had impacted Israel was blatant disobedience to the Word of God. In Deuteronomy chapter seven, God commanded Israel to make no league with the nations by marriage or worship but to remain holy.[13]

This commandment and the consequence of disobeying were brought home to Israel in Judges chapter 2

"And an angel of the LORD came up from Gilgal to Bochim, and said, I made you to go up out of Egypt, and have brought you to the land which I swore to your fathers; and I said, I will never break my covenant with you. And you shall make no league with the inhabitants of this land; you shall throw down their altars: but you have not obeyed my voice: why have you done this?"

Judges 2:1-2

Sadly God's people are prone to rationalise away the clear instruction of His Word and sometimes semantics or similar superficial explanations are the excuse. This is what is happening again in our time and it always gives rise to the worship of Baal. In all probability the modern expression of Baalimism was introduced to Pentecostal circles through church-growth gurus Peter Wagner and his mentor John Wimber when they conceived their signs and wonders classes at Fuller in USA. Their practice was an adaptation of animism. They had the audacity to suggest that students could be taught how to perform miracles, which they had to redefine as being something "sensational" rather than something, which is essentially "supernatural" that only God performs out of His sovereignty.[14] Animism is part and parcel of the fertility cult once called the worship of Baal.

In Australia and some other countries, Assemblies of Baal have replaced Assemblies of God. Brian Houston president of AoG in Australia says, *You Need More Money*, which in some cases is a truism. Clearly some people, like Bill Gates for example, don't need more money. However when Brian Houston extends what may be a truism to claim that "money is the bottom line of everything" and applies that to the Kingdom of God, he is flying in the face of scripture and that is Baal worship pure and simple; and Hillsong with all its hype and excitement is little more than a repeat of the antics of the Prophets of Baal in Elijah's time. Our Lord said YOU CANNOT SERVE GOD AND MAMMON[15] so once you set out your stall with "money as the bottom line of everything"[16] the die is cast and the writing is on the wall and that calls for extreme action from the faithful remnant.

CHAPTER 5

The God who answers by fire

"... Come, and let us go up to the mountain of the LORD, and to the house of the God of Jacob; and he will teach us his ways, and we will walk in his paths: for the law shall go forth from Zion, and the word of the LORD from Jerusalem"
Micah 4:2

THE call for a drought was a necessary precursor to the fire dual for several reasons, not least that it made the faithful remnant start to stand up and be counted. From the widow of Zarephath, who came to a place of acknowledging her sin, whatever it was,[17] to Obadiah, who feared the Lord even though he was the governor of Ahab's house,[18] the faithful remnant were everywhere, but they needed the spark of an Elijah to encourage them to take a public stand. The hierarchy had to learn that it was not Elijah the prophet but Ahab the king and his wife Jezebel, who were the real troublemakers in Israel. The drought caused these things to surface, but another public confrontation was required to publicly identify the priests, who were the leaders of the cult of Baal, so that they could be removed from their positions. In a general way, though not all of them as individuals, the prophets of Baal (450) and the prophets of the groves (400) were known to Elijah (c/f 1 Kings 18:19[19]), but there had to be a public exposure. Thus the call to Carmel became the next step in the restoration of true worship and real revival among God's people.

The story of Elijah and the prophets of Baal is one of the most frequently told. Most of us have known it from school days and the lessons are plain. It is the story of the conflict between true and false religion and how the faithful servants of the Lord always restore the old and trustworthy system of worship. We learn that you can't measure truth by numbers. Those of the false system were 850 leaders who were thoughtlessly followed by a majority in Israel, while Elijah stood alone as the leader of a hidden faithful remnant. We learn that true religion can be tested. With the twelve barrels of water soaking the offering and surrounding trench there was no chance of trickery or any hocus-pocus. Elijah chose the cool of the evening so no natural explanation could account for the fire, which burned up the bullock, water and dust.

As we have suggested the alternation of the hidden and public ministry of

Elijah produced patience, perseverance and power, which is the pattern of all genuine ministry. The faithful remnant are not in a hurry but they do take action when it is required. Elijah was not afraid to let the prophets of Baal have their head. He gave them first choice of the bullocks and first go at getting an answer by fire. By way of contrast the wild antics of the prophets of Baal reveal how false religion always expresses itself in a frenzy. Today it usually employs the wild and loud music of the world to whip their followers up until they act like a riotous mob, who are then invited to make some religious commitment to a person called Jesus, the nature and character of whom is a million miles removed from the lowly Nazarene whom the Bible declares to be the Lord of Glory. Prophets of Baal preach another Jesus and a different gospel c/f 2 Corinthians 11:4 and Galatians 1:6.

Elijah was selective and simple in his action. He invited close inspection of what he was about to do and we read that when the people gathered around to closely observe,.

"... he repaired the altar of the LORD that was broken down. .... And it came to pass at the time of the offering of the evening sacrifice, that Elijah the prophet came near, and said, LORD God of Abraham, Isaac, and of Israel, let it be known this day that you are God in Israel, and that I am your servant, and that I have done all these things at your word. Hear me, O LORD, hear me, that this people may know that you are the LORD God, and that you have turned their hearts back to you again. Then the fire of the LORD fell, and consumed the burnt sacrifice, and the wood, and the stones, and the dust, and licked up the water that was in the trench. And when all the people saw it, they fell on their faces: and they said, The LORD, he is God; the LORD, he is God."

1 Kings 18:30-39

But that is by no means the end of the story. Elijah instructed the now convinced people to capture the false leaders and he personally slew them by the brook Kishon at the foot of Mount Carmel. Interestingly it was the prophets of Baal who were killed. Nothing is said about the 400 prophets of the groves, who may have escaped or maybe were deliberately left alive as a further test to Ahab and Israel. It is possibly not without significance that just prior to Ahab's death another prophet called Micaiah was withstood by about 400 of Ahab's prophets.[20] Maybe they were the same prophets of the groves who ate at Jezebel's table.

Having prayed down fire and having executed the false prophets of Baal Elijah told Ahab that rain was on its way and then, in the words of James the apostle, *"he prayed again and the heaven gave rain and the earth brought forth its fruit"*. Three and half years earlier Elijah prophesied a drought after he had *"prayed earnestly that it would not rain"*. On this occasion he first prophesies and then prays his prophecy into fulfilment. Either way the significant thing is that he was right on both occasions.

Today men and women are being touted as "prophets" when what they prophesy seldom comes to pass. John Lewis and Ben Gray who head up the Apostolic Revolution movement in Brisbane speak of Cindy Jacobs as a Prophet to the Nations. Cindy Jacobs recently prophesied a great economic up-turn in New Zealand. At the time the value of the NZ dollar was falling faster than the Fiji dollar during the military coup in that country and has continued in a depressed state ever since. Her prophesies are crazy see footnote below and note especially what Jacobs said about Y2K nine months before the event. Prophets don't make mistakes like that.[21]

Another person is Harold Caballeros who visited Wellington in New Zealand and took up an offering at the main Elim Church of $100,000 in gifts and pledges. He prophesied increase (10-12-95) and then took up the offering for a new building and falsely prophesied what the building would be like.[22] These people and those who promote them are nothing more than con-artists. Scripture commands that we do not fear or follow them.

During our sojourn in New Zealand, shortly after I had resigned as General Secretary of AoG in Australia (1992), I received a telephone call from Frank Houston who had been one of my former colleagues on the AoG National Executive. My wife answered the call and as I was indisposed at the time I suggested that she invite Frank to phone back later in say half an hour. When he called back we exchanged normal pleasantries and then Frank told me that God was going to cut me off. He claimed that he had some revelation from the Lord and that when he received these "words" he was never wrong and that whatever being cut off by God signified it was going to happen very soon, if not immediately. I let him talk for quite some time then I interrupted, "Frank I want you to know that my Bible tells me not to fear you and I don't fear you or what you have to say for I have proved you to be a false prophet. You may cut me off, BUT I don't think God will cut me off". He was obviously taken aback by my direct response and went on to accuse me of muckraking whatever that meant. I certainly was not engaged in anything that could equate to what he accused me of but there shouldn't be any muck to rake in any event.

Prophets of Baal build on doubtful reputations and they use hype and fear tactics to manipulate people. I could respond to Mr Houston as I did because I was in a meeting in Victoria, Australia where he called young ministers to the front to get a "prophetic word" normally referred to as a "word of knowledge", which is no such thing and nothing more than clairvoyance that is condemned in scripture.[23] Frank Houston told one young pastor that his church was going to see great growth. Within a very short period of time the young man in question had fallen morally and the church was in great financial difficulty resulting from a big building project which they had ventured forth on and which had been confirmed as being in the will of God by Frank Houston's "word of knowledge". We as remnant people MUST turn from this sort of nonsense entirely, even if these people are sometimes correct in what they predict. We must not be confused by the occasion when they appear to prophesy accurately. The test is not the number of times when they get it right, BUT when and how they can get it so wrong.

Watchman Nee's book entitled *The Latent Power of the Soul* explains a great deal about this sort of thing. He writes of Buddhist priests who practise the so-called "word of knowledge" antics of modern Pentecostals. Scripture clearly provides two tests that should be applied to any person who purports to predict things in the Name of the Lord. The closing verses of Deuteronomy chapter 18 tell us that any prediction that does NOT come to pass issues from a false prophet,[24] while the opening verses of Deuteronomy chapter 13 warn that even if a man predicts something that DOES come to pass he is not to be heeded in any way if he or his message counters the established Word and Ways of the Lord.[25] In both cases the "prophet" must NOT be feared or followed. To do so is SIN.

CHAPTER 6

Don't sell your inheritance

"Moreover the prince shall not take of the people's inheritance by oppression, to evict them from their property; but he shall give his sons inheritance out of his own property: that my people are not scattered from their property"
Ezekiel 46:18

THE penultimate public appearance of Elijah occurred in the vineyard of Naboth (1 Kings 21), who was clearly one of the faithful remnant. Following the fire dual and the breaking of the drought Elijah again sank into obscurity, this time under threat of death from Jezebel. This prince of prophets reveals his human-ness as he runs from the wicked wife of king Ahab and complains to God that he has had enough and would now prefer to die. I have heard some preachers explain that this was the end of Elijah, but they are mistaken. Some of his most important work lay ahead. God's grace covers human frailty. The Kingdom of God is not built upon the courage or correct conduct of His servants, but upon His own matchless grace and mercy, both of which shine brightly in the amazing story of Elijah.

It is ironic that the same prophet, who miraculously outran a horse-drawn chariot over a distance of 14 miles from Carmel to Jezreel, should run more than 200 miles from a woman who threatened to destroy him. It is even more ironic to think that this same man, who fearlessly challenged 450 prophets of Baal to an open fire dual and personally executed them all, would be afraid of Jezebel such is life! Perhaps he just knew when to run a powerful lesson! Despite his great exploits with rain and fire, Elijah had some more lessons to learn as we do too.

We must learn that individual members of the faithful remnant are NOT alone even though they may feel alone. A remnant mentality is something that we need to be rescued from. That was Elijah's second lesson in this section of his life. The first had to do with the notion of miracles and the voice of God. It is all contained in 1 Kings chapter 19. The worship of Baal was intrinsically interwoven with the notions of fertility, weather, the sun god and nature. Elijah had demonstrated that it is the true God and not the false idols that really control these things in the ultimate sense, but there is the ever-pressing danger of focusing on these things until God and nature merge in men's minds and we lose intimacy with the Lord, the almighty. Animism, pantheism, great sensational miracles, signs and wonders are not who or what our God is all about. The lesson in the cave and on the peak of Horeb as the strong wind, the earthquake and the fire vented their fury on the mountains was that God is not necessarily in any of these things. It was when Elijah heard the still small voice of revelation that he covered his face and stood before the Lord and again heard His voice of instruction. That and that alone can give us confidence to proceed.

A third and incidental lesson is that God doesn't mind listening to the complaints of His faithful remnant. He understands our frame. The remedy is for the Lord to clarify the fact that He is not finished with us. Elijah still had much to do in ensuring the continuity of the faithful remnant as well as national and international tasks. Then the Lord very quietly corrected Elijah's mistaken idea about his being alone. YES, God always reserves the 7,000 who have not bowed the knee to Baal and it is those, the faithful remnant, whom He will use to continue His work and to rebuild the walls that are broken down.

Refreshed and renewed by angel food and by a strengthened realisation of who God is and what He is about, Elijah passed by Elisha and touched the young ploughman with his mantle and the scene was set for the second and equally important half of Elijah's life and ministry. There were to be two more public confrontations: one involving king Ahab and the other Ahab's son king Ahaziah; then the passing of the baton to the next generation, after which Elijah could safely leave for heaven, there to patiently wait until he is needed in the end time to confront the Anti-Christ, of whom Ahab was but a figure. One of the problems with Ahab, and it's typical of religious hierarchies, was that he vacillated on the basis of perceived success and popular opinion. He was a weak man who married a strong woman. Jezebel was an idolater and exceedingly wicked. Ahab's obituary is given in 1 Kings chapter 21

"But there was none like Ahab, who sold himself to do wickedness in the sight of the LORD, whom Jezebel his wife stirred up."

1 Kings 21:25

The context of this text is the story of Naboth and his vineyard, which King Ahab coveted and which Naboth would not sell or exchange because it was the inheritance of his fathers and should, according to the law of inheritance, (see Appendix 2) remain in the family. No amount of money could buy it and no exchange was possible. Ahab knew that God's Word was on Naboth's side. A king's ransom would change nothing enter Jezebel, who by intrigue and deceit organised the murder of Naboth on a trumped up charge of blasphemy. (See Appendix 3). 2 Kings 9:25&26 indicate that Naboth's sons perished with him. Thus there was no one to claim the legal right of inheritance and so the title deed naturally passed to the reigning monarch. Wicked king Ahab went down to take possession of the inheritance, but he got more than he bargained for.

Enter Elijah he's always there when he's really needed. It's the still small voice, not the dramatic drought nor the furious fire; not even the refreshing rain that protects the inheritance of the righteous remnant. We must have the revelation of God in our preaching and in our actions if we are going to make a difference in our day and generation. Why did Elijah wait so long? Why was he not there to rebuke the sons of Belial who bore false testimony against Naboth? More significantly why didn't he confront Jezebel and thwart her wicked scheme? He might have saved Naboth and his family and prevented Ahab's take-over bid. The answer to our questions is very simple. Elijah couldn't act without God's instruction. The still small voice came after the death of Naboth and after Jezebel gloated over her apparent triumph and after Ahab had started in the direction of the vineyard to assume ownership. God decided that evil should run its course and Elijah acted within the sovereignty of God.

A confrontationalist to the end, this was the last meeting between Elijah and Ahab. The irony of the meeting is enormous. The prophet was the first to speak, *"Thus says the Lord..."* That is a most dangerous phrase to use unless you have the mind and the word of the Lord. True prophecy is the proof that one knows and correctly interprets the "still small voice". The king made one abortive attempt to interrupt the Word of the Lord, identifying the prophet as his enemy and recognising that it was always Elijah who found Ahab and not vice versa. *"Have you found me O my enemy?"* (1 Kings 21:20) were the last words spoken by the king to Elijah. The prophecy about the destruction of Ahab and his dynasty starts in verse 19 and continues to verse 24, so the description of the king's reaction and the prophet's response in verse 20 is an interlude.

The detail of the prophecy is incredible and was the consequence of what Jezebel, under Ahab's authority, did to Naboth and his house. Dogs would lick up the blood of the king in the place where Naboth's blood was spilt. Every male descendant of Ahab would be destroyed so that he would have no dynasty and no heritage. Dogs would eat Jezebel by the wall of Jezreel. None of Ahab's descendants would have a proper burial as their bodies would be eaten by dogs or by scavenging birds. It's pretty horrific stuff and the historic record confirms that it happened exactly as predicted. Such is the power of true prophecy and it makes a mockery of much of what passes for prophecy and words of knowledge in our time.

Andrew Evans told me that he accepted a sixty percent accuracy standard, meaning that a person may be wrong forty percent of the time and still be a true prophet. I reject that totally as does the scripture. If any man prophesies in the Name of the Lord i.e. he uses the phrase *"Thus says the Lord ..."* or similar, one hundred percent accuracy is required. The problem with so called prophets like David Cartledge and Cindy Jacobs et al is that they are what I call "euphoric prophets" i.e. those who like king Saul of old prophesy out of the atmosphere of the occasion c/f 1 Kings 10:11-12 with 1 Samuel 19:24, 18:10 and 1 Kings 22:12[26]. Much of this type of prophecy is based on wish fulfilment. If it fails, the speaker who predicted it is to be marked as a false prophet. Another thing that marks a "euphoric prophet" is that he/she prophesies ear-tickling pleasantries. These people seldom if ever give warnings or predict judgment unless of course you cut across them, then they prophesy out of their own spirits and their own imaginations. Usually they get very angry cf 1 Kings 22:24, 26-27.[27]

CHAPTER 7

Fire and removing idolatry

"He who marries the spirit of the age will soon become its widow."
Os Guinness in Dining with the Devil

"Resolution One: I will live for God. Resolution Two: If no one does, I still will."
Jonathan Edwards

THE impact of Ahab and Jezebel on their family and on Israel in general was pervasive. In spite of the clear judgment of the Lord upon them and their activity, idolatry remained entrenched in the national leadership and psyche of Israel. Ahaziah who succeeded Ahab must have known about the prophecy of Elijah regarding the death of his father and how it was fulfilled to the letter, yet he continued to embrace Baal worship in its most hideous form. When he fell sick as a result of an accident in his palace, instead of praying to the Lord he sought counsel from his mother's favourite deity Baalzebub the god of Ekron. This act called forth the final public appearance and denouncement of Elijah.

Through the ministration of an angel the prophet was instructed to deliver a message to the envoys of the king who were on their way to consult with the foreign god. Ahaziah would die, not because his injury was fatal but on account of his idolatry. The ambassadors turned back to their master the king, who inquired of them the nature and manner of the prophet who had confronted them. The fact that he immediately identified the man as being Elijah proves that Ahaziah was familiar with all that had proceeded under his father's rule.

Ahaziah was in open rebellion to God and to His word and demonstrated this by seeking to capture Elijah with a force of 50 men, who were destroyed by fire from heaven at the prophet's word. When this was repeated with a second army of 50 men the captain of the third group sent by the king to arrest Elijah fell on his face before the prophet to petition for his life and that of his army. The angel of the Lord, who appears to have stood by the prophet throughout this ordeal, gave him leave to go with the men to the king, who without apology was told in no uncertain terms that he would die for the treachery of his idolatry; and so it came to pass.

This is recorded in 2 Kings chapter 1 and, apart from the commissioning of Elisha, concludes the public and private ministry of the most remarkable Old Testament prophet. We can only conjecture as to the length of his life on earth. Almost certainly he prophesied throughout most of the 22 years of Ahab's reign (see 1 Kings 16:29[28]) plus the two years of Ahaziah's reign (see 1 Kings 22:51[29]). The Companion Bible dates this period from 822BC while The Thompson Chain Reference Bible dates it from 910 BC. We don't know how long he *"prayed earnestly"* before he appeared before Ahab. A number of things about Elijah remain hidden, but that is just the nature of the man and his calling.

CHAPTER 8

Appointing his successor

SOME years ago as I reflected on Elijah's life and especially on the last journey he made, which was not for his benefit but for that of Elisha, I began to see a number of parallels between Elijah and Christ and between Elisha and the true church, which in my view explains the ministry of the double portion into which the remnant church is always called. I don't say that Elijah is a type of Christ or that Elisha is a type of the church. Types have to carry through in every regard. For this reason no human being can rightly be described as a type of Christ. The closest you get to it is the life of Joseph but even there the type breaks down.

However, it is quite in order to describe a detail in the life of an Old Testament character as typifying an aspect of Christ's life. This is particularly true of Elijah, the miracles in whose life were mostly judgemental. In John 9:39 our Lord said, *"For judgment I am come into this world..."* and again in Matthew 10:34, *"Don't think that I am come to send peace on earth: I came not to send peace, but a sword"*. In this regard Elijah pre-figures Christ, while Elisha is representative of the church in that his ministry was more restorational than judgemental. There is some overlap in that Elisha was obviously "anointed" to continue the work of Elijah as the church is commissioned to continue the work of Christ.

Another parallel is to be seen in the final bequest of both Elijah and Christ. Elisha was promised the double portion if he saw Elijah when he departed to heaven. Our Lord promised that His followers would do "greater works" after He ascended to heaven (John 14:12[30]). Represented by those early disciples His people saw Him go (Acts 1:9[31]) and were in the right place at the right time to receive the enduement from on high (Luke 24:49 c/f Acts 1:8 & 2:1-4[32]). Interestingly, our Lord did not promise that His church would do "different works" but rather "greater works". The works were to be of the same nature as those of Christ as the previous clause clarifies *"the works that I do he shall do also"*. The adjective "greater" is very clearly linked to the new dimension of prayer in Christ's name. Here's the full quote:

"Truly truly I say to you, He that believes in me, the works that I do shall he do also; and greater works than these shall he do; because I go to my Father. And whatever you ask in my name, that will I do, that the Father may be glorified in the Son. If you ask anything in my name, I will do it"

John 14:12-14

No human being will do more or greater works than Christ. The promise is to the collective body, BUT it is still Christ who is doing the works from the throne, which He now shares with the Father (c/f John 21:25). The idea that Peter did something greater than Christ when the crowds gathered in the hope of his shadow "healing" them (Acts 5:15) is silly nonsense. There is no indication that anyone was healed by being overshadowed by Peter. It could be a superstitious idea that is alluded to in Acts 5. (See Appendix 4) Peter never claimed to heal anyone by his own power let alone through his shadow. Apart from that if we're thinking of "distance healing" our Lord on one occasion just sent His word and the person was healed[33], so even if folks were healed in the streets as Peter passed by, the "work" was not greater than that done by Christ. To suggest, as some do, that the nonsensical sensational tricks of men like Rodney Howard-Browne and Benny Hinn are part of the promised "greater works" is not only utter rubbish but also damnable blasphemy.

The key to understanding the "double portion" ministry, at least in degree,[34] is seen in the fact that Elijah saw just one person raised from the dead whereas there were two raised from the dead through Elisha. This, in my view, has great significance in the calling and ministry of the faithful remnant.

In the case of Elijah we read:

"And it came to pass after these things, that the son of the woman, the mistress of the house, fell sick; and his sickness was so serious, that there was no breath left in him. And she said to Elijah, What have I to do with you, O man of God? are you come to me to call my sin to remembrance, and to slay my son? And he said to her, Give me your son. And he took him out of her arms, and carried him up into a loft, where he dwelt, and laid him upon his own bed. And he cried to the LORD, and said, O LORD my God, have you also brought evil upon the widow with whom I lodge, by slaying her son? And he stretched himself upon the child three times, and cried to the LORD, and said, O LORD my God, I pray you, let this child's soul come into him again. And the LORD heard the voice of Elijah; and the soul of the child came into him again, and he revived."

1 Kings 17:17-22

In the case of Elisha we read:

"And when Elisha was come into the house, the child was dead, and laid upon his bed. He went in therefore, and shut the door upon them both, and prayed to the LORD. And he went up, and lay upon the child, and put his mouth upon his mouth, and his eyes upon his eyes, and his hands upon his hands: and he stretched himself upon the child; and the flesh of the child became warm. Then he returned, and walked in the house to and fro; and went up, and stretched himself upon him: and the child sneezed seven times, and the child opened his eyes. And he called Gehazi, and said, Call this Shunammite. So he called her. And when she was come in to him, he said, Take up your son. Then she went in, and fell at his feet, and bowed herself to the ground, and took up her son, and went out."

2 Kings 4:32-37

On the surface it would appear that Elijah and Elisha both did the same thing. They both "stretched" themselves over a dead body. A closer look however reveals that there are two different Hebrew words that are rendered "stretched" in our English version of the two passages. In the case of Elijah it is the Hebrew word *"madad"* (Strong 04058) which signifies "to extend oneself". In the case of Elisha it is the Hebrew word *"gahar"* which has the connotation of "casting oneself down" i.e. "reducing self". John the Baptist's magnificent tribute to Christ springs to mind *"He must increase, but I must decrease"* (John 3:30). The resurrection life of Christ is intrinsic and inherent. He alone has life in Himself. None but He can say, *"I am the resurrection and the life ..."* (John 11:25). Elisha representing the true church casts self down in order to experience resurrection life, but the truth goes yet further. There was another resurrection experience in the life, or rather death, and ministry of Elisha. We read about it in 2 Kings chapter 13 verses 20 and 21:

"And Elisha died, and they buried him. And the bands of the Moabites invaded the land in the spring of the year. And it came to pass, as they were burying a man, that, behold, they spied a band of men; and they put the man into the tomb of Elisha: and when the man was let down, and touched the bones of Elisha, he revived, and stood up on his feet."

2 Kings 13:20-21

As part of the faithful remnant the great truth that we must rediscover and put into operation is that stated by Paul the apostle to the gentiles:

"I am crucified with Christ: nevertheless I live; yet not I, but Christ lives in me: and the life which I now live in the flesh I live by faith in the Son of God, who loved me, and gave himself for me."

Galatians 2:20

That leads me to make two brief and final observations relating to the fact that, although God directly instructed Elijah to anoint his successor and the future kings of Syria and Israel, he appears not to have carried out the tasks allotted to him. All he did was touch Elisha with his mantle. Why? We have suggested that Elijah represents Christ and Elisha represents the church, which is the body of Christ through which our Lord is continuing to do His essential work. It was through the spirit of Elijah, which rested on Elisha that the work continued. When Elisha announced to Hazael that he would be king over Syria (2 Kings 8:13[35]) and when the unnamed son of the prophets, on Elisha's instruction, anointed Jehu king over Israel (2 Kings 9:1-10[36]) it was one and the same thing as Elijah doing the work. And for the record Elijah did not give his mantle to Elisha. It fell from heaven and Elisha took it up.

As part of God's faithful remnant there are two things that we must closely guard: Firstly, we must take care that we take no credit for anything that our Lord Jesus Christ is pleased to achieve through us. It is He that does the work and He alone MUST have the glory. This applies to all the works in which we have a part, including the miraculous. Secondly, we must not make the mistake of thinking that we can pass our mantle or anointing if we have any to anyone else. The two abominations that have entered the Pentecostal/Charismatic (see Appendix 5) "church" are the incredible amount of self-praise and self-promotion and the idea that ministers can operate under the anointing of another usually the senior pastor. Both things lead to all sorts of abuses, which ultimately corrupt the whole.

APPENDICES

1

Elijah's forebears

THE NEW BIBLE DICTIONARY (IVF) under the heading ELIJAH, states the following: "Apart from the reference to Elijah in 1 Kings xvii, 1 as *"the Tishbite, who was of the inhabitants of Gilead"*, no information about his background is available. Even this reference is obscure, The Massoretic Text suggests that while Elijah resided in Gilead ... his birthplace was elsewhere (perhaps Tishbe of Naphtali). The Septuagint reads *"ek thesb_n tîs galaad",* thus indicating a Tishbe of Gilead, Josephus seems to concur (Ant. Viii. 13.2). This has been traditionally identified with a site about 13 kilometres north of the Jabbok." (© IVF 1962 page 363).

Based solely on scripture taken at face value our inclination is to concur with the Septuagint and with Josephus. It is with a reasonable degree of probability based on the following scriptures and in the light of the above description of his background, that we conclude that Elijah was a direct descendant from Joseph through Manasseh and Machir.

"And this land, which we possessed at that time, from Aroer, which is by the river Arnon, and half mount Gilead, and the cities there, I gave to the Reubenites and to the Gadites. And the rest of Gilead, and all Bashan, being the kingdom of Og, I gave to the half tribe of Manasseh; all the region of Argob, with all Bashan, which was called the land of giants. Jair the son of Manasseh took all the country of Argob to the coasts of Geshuri and the Maachathites; and called them after his own name, Bashan Havothjair, to this day. And I gave Gilead to Machir."

Deuteronomy 3:12-15

"Of the sons of Manasseh: of Machir, the family of the Machirites: and Machir fathered Gilead: of Gilead come the family of the Gileadites."

Numbers 26:29

"And the children of Machir the son of Manasseh went to Gilead, and took it, and dispossessed the Amorites who were in it."

Numbers 32:39

"And Moses gave Gilead to Machir the son of Manasseh; and he dwelt there."

Numbers 32:40

APPENDIX 2

Genealogy and inheritance

GENEALOGY and inheritance are viewed as being of great importance in the Jewish context for two reasons: Firstly, on account of the obvious link with the Promised Messiah; and secondly, because of the unique association of Israel with the God of Israel.

The first Messianic prophecy speaks of the *"seed of the woman"* (Genesis 3:15), whereas Jewish genealogy as recorded in scripture normally refers to the male (not female) descendants in terms of a patriarchal (not matriarchal) line. In our time a Jew is reckoned as one whose mother is a Jewess, not one whose father is a Jew. In the polygamous setting of the Old Testament, prior to the Mosaic Law, which included the prohibition of adultery, sexual promiscuity was viewed as being more culpable when practised by women than by men. This is explainable at least in part on the basis that it was the secret hope of every Jewish girl that she should be the chosen vessel through whom the Messiah would be born. Even though the truths of the Incarnation and of the miraculous, divine conception of Christ were not foreseen, every godly Jewess saw her own sexual purity as important in the possibility of her being chosen to bring forth the Messiah. Ultimately Rahab (Matthew 1:5), who is called a harlot in Joshua 2:1 and 6:25, features in Messiah's line, which simply goes to show the over-riding grace of God.

Sexual sin is viewed in the New Testament as being different from all other sins, as Paul explains, *"Flee immorality. Every sin that a man does is outside the body; but he that commits immorality sins against his own body"* (1 Corinthians 6:18). In both Testaments immorality is sometimes used as a euphemism for idolatry. The message is clear. God requires of His people sexual and spiritual fidelity. The idea that leaders can commit immorality with impunity is contrary to the nature and character of God, Christ and of the true church, which is presented as the Bride of Christ who keeps herself pure. The marital and sexual infidelity of the many so called church leaders of our time is an indictment upon them, their doctrine and their followers who should revolt against such low standards.

Inheritance is linked to genealogy and is one of the major emphases of the Old Testament, which is to be viewed as being typical with New Testament teaching providing the anti-type. This is because in the ultimate sense God is the inheritance of His people and visa versa.

"And he (Moses) said, If now I have found grace in your sight, O Lord, let my

Lord, I pray, go among us; for it is a stiff-necked people; and pardon our iniquity and our sin, and take us for your inheritance."

Exodus 34:9

"But the LORD has taken you, and brought you forth out of the iron furnace, even out of Egypt, to be to him a people of inheritance, as you are this day."

Deuteronomy 4:20

"In whom also we have obtained an inheritance, being predestined according to the purpose of him who works all things after the counsel of his own will."

Ephesians 1:11

"The eyes of your understanding being enlightened; that you may know what is the hope of his calling, and what are riches of the glory of his inheritance in the saints."

Ephesians 1:18

Thus material possessions, such as lands, which were bequeathed by God as an inheritance, took on sacred significance.

While the right and responsibility of inheritance normally rested upon males, the passages of scripture which deal with the case of the daughters of Zelophehad (Numbers 26:33; 27:1-11; Numbers 36:1-13; Joshua 17:3; and 1 Chronicles 7:15) underscore the importance of refusing to surrender tribal and family inheritance even where the descendants were all female.

"So the inheritance of the children of Israel shall not move from tribe to tribe: for every one of the children of Israel shall keep himself to the inheritance of the tribe of his fathers. **(9)** Neither shall the inheritance move from one tribe to another tribe; but every one of the tribes of the children of Israel shall keep to its own inheritance."

Numbers 36:7, 9

It was this aspect of the Law of Inheritance, which dominated Naboth's thinking and action when he refused to give or sell his vineyard to Ahab. His action was enormously significant and has a huge application to the faithful remnant throughout the ages.

Significantly, the descendants of Aaron were given no inheritance in the land, because the Lord was their inheritance and He guaranteed their support and livelihood. This was so that they could devote their energies and efforts to matters relating to worship and service (ministry). They were to be committed to protecting the inheritance of the Lord among His people and the inheritance of the people in their worship of the Lord. The significance of this has been largely ignored in today's church, resulting in considerable abuse of the people by leaders, who lord it over God's heritage.

"The elders which are among you I exhort, who am also an elder, and a witness of the sufferings of Christ, and also a partaker of the glory that shall be revealed: Feed the flock of God which is among you, taking the oversight thereof, not by constraint, but willingly; not for money, but of a ready mind; Neither as being lords over God's heritage, but being examples to the flock. And when the chief Shepherd shall appear, you shall receive a crown of glory that does not fade away."

1 Peter 5:1-4

The subject warrants a full study. Variants of the word "inheritance" appear 273 times in the Bible. The Old Testament contains entire chapters dedicated to the topic.

"Some remove the landmarks; they violently take away flocks, and feed on them."

Job 24:2

"You shall not remove your neighbour's landmark, which they of old time have set in your inheritance, which you shall inherit in the land that the LORD your God gives you to possess it."

Deuteronomy 19:14

"Cursed is he that removes his neighbour's landmark. And all the people shall say, Amen."

Deuteronomy 27:17

"Do not remove the ancient landmark, which your fathers have set."

Proverbs 22:28

"Do not remove the old landmark; or enter into the fields of the fatherless."

Proverbs 23:10

"The princes of Judah are like those that remove the landmark: therefore I will pour out my wrath upon them like water."

Hosea 5:10

APPENDIX 3

The law of blasphemy

ACCORDING to The New Bible Dictionary the root meaning of the word "blasphemy" in the Old Testament is *"an act of effrontery in which the honour of God is insulted by man"* (page 159 © IVF 1962). According to the Encyclopaedia Britannica, *"St Thomas Aquinas described it as a sin against faith."* (© 1964 Vol 3 page 763) The Mosaic Law prescribed death by stoning and is predicated upon an incident recorded in Leviticus chapter 24 as follows:

"And the son of an Israelite woman, whose father was an Egyptian, went out among the children of Israel: and this son of the Israelite woman and a man of Israel fought together in the camp; And the Israelite woman's son blasphemed the name of the LORD, and cursed. And they brought him to Moses: (and his mother's name was Shelomith, the daughter of Dibri, of the tribe of Dan:) And they put him in custody, until the mind of the LORD might be shown them. And the LORD spoke to Moses, saying, Bring forth him that has cursed outside the camp; and let all that heard him lay their hands upon his head, and let all the congregation stone him. And you shall speak to the children of Israel, saying, Whoever curses his God shall bear his sin. **(16)** And he that blasphemes the name of the LORD, shall surely be put to death, and all the congregation shall certainly stone him: the stranger, as well as he that is born in the land, when he blasphemes the name of the LORD, shall be put to death."

Leviticus 24:10 16

While the death penalty was prescribed there were general safeguards against false accusations and false witnesses provided by the Mosaic Law as detailed in Deuteronomy 19:15 to 21. Providing those responsible for applying the law (i.e. the nominated leaders) remained unprejudiced, diligent and just in their examination and judgement, miscarriage of justice would be avoided. The legal process mentions four things:

1) There must be at least two witnesses against a person accused of INIQUITY (lit *"perversity"* or *"depravity"*) or SIN (lit *"miss the way"* or *"go wrong"*):

"One witness shall not rise up against a man for any iniquity, or for any sin, in any sin that he sins: at the mouth of two or three witnesses, shall the matter be established."

Deuteronomy 19:15

2) If there was doubt about the honesty and integrity of a witness then the accuser and the accused must be interrogated by the judges and the priests before the Lord;

"If a false witness rise up against any man to testify against him that which is wrong; Then both the men, between whom the controversy is, shall stand before the LORD, before the priests and the judges, who shall be in those days; And the judges shall make diligent inquisition..."

Deuteronomy 19:16-18

3) If a witness was found to be false then the judges were required to condemn the false witness in the precise terms that he intended for the accused:

"And the judges shall make diligent inquisition: and, if the witness is a false witness, and has testified falsely against his brother; Then you shall do to him, as he had thought to have done to his brother."

Deuteronomy 19:18-19

4) The purpose of the legal process was to put away evil and to bring the fear of God upon the people in respect of His judgments and ways:

"... so shall you put the evil away from among you. And those which remain shall hear, and fear, and shall never again commit any such evil among you."

Deuteronomy 19:19-20

The incident relating to Naboth was based on a trumped up charge with the connivance of two hired false witnesses. This parallels the case of Stephen in the New Testament (c/f Acts 6:11 & 13 with 1 Kings 21:10 & 13) and illustrates the way that wicked people abuse the Word of God to serve their own ends. Both Jezebel and the accusers of Stephen employed a similar tactic based on the above referred to biblical laws, viz. the Law of Blasphemy and the Law of False Witness. Because the elders in both cases were parties to the deception and the plan, wrong judgment proceeded, notwithstanding the fact there was an ostensible appeal to the Word of God. Deceived and wicked leaders are incapable of applying the Law and Word of God.

While blasphemy was an act normally committed in Old Testament times by foreigners or pagans (2 Kings 19:6, 22; Isaiah 37:6, 23; 52:5; Psalm 74:10, 18 etc), Leviticus 24:16 applies the law equally to Israelites as we have seen above. Furthermore the conduct of God's people is to be such that they do not cause others to blaspheme as did King David see 2 Samuel 12:14. Both Isaiah (65:7) and Ezekiel

(20:7) equate idolatry with blasphemy. If God's people fail to hallow His Name they become guilty of profanity and that is blasphemy.

"You shall not take the name of the LORD your God in vain; for the LORD will not hold him guiltless that takes his name in vain."

Exodus 20:7

APPENDIX 4

The Shadow of Peter

THE incident relating to healing and the shadow of Peter is detailed in Acts chapter five verses 12 to 16 of which the second half of verse 12 together with all of verses 13 and 14 are in parenthesis. The sense is maintained and made clearer by omitting the section that is bracketed to read as follows:

"And by the hands of the apostles many signs and wonders were done among the people; So much so that they brought out the sick into the streets, and laid them on beds and couches, that at least the shadow of Peter passing by might overshadow some of them. Also a multitude came out of the cities round about Jerusalem, bringing sick people, and those who were tormented with unclean spirits: and they were all healed."

Acts 5:12a, 15, 16

The opening comment suggests a special manifestation of God's power to perform miracles, referred to here as *"signs and wonders"*. Verse 16 specifically tells us that every sick or tormented person was healed irrespective of where they were situated in the crowd. Nowhere does the passage say that those who were overshadowed by Peter were affected more or less by the power of God in the healing process, than all the others. The clear implication of verse 15 is that some in the crowd had an expectation about being within the cast of Peter's shadow. This savours of a superstitious perception about an aura surrounding the apostles and Peter in particular. Such is never countenanced in scripture, in fact quite the opposite. Peter himself protested against any such idea developing among the people in respect of the performance of miracles.

"And when Peter saw it, he answered the people, you men of Israel, why do you marvel at this? Or why look so earnestly at us, as though by our own power or holiness we had made this man walk?"

Acts 3:12

Paul the apostle to the Gentiles made a similar protest in Acts 14:12-14. Only God performs true miracles. Men are just agents or instruments through which God is pleased to work. The idea that there is some power or virtue in the *"shadow"* of Peter or any other person has more to do with witchcraft than with the Christian gospel. Sadly, this misconception, which is based upon a failure to rightly divide the Word of God by comparing scripture with scripture, has been a basis for all sorts of wrong teaching particularly among Pentecostals and Charismatics.

Back in the 1950s W.F.P. Burton wrote to Oral Roberts about his *"point of contact"* doctrine, telling him that it had more in common with Roman Catholic dogma than with the Bible. Roberts' instruction to people, who were seeking healing, to reach out and touch the radio as a point of contact started a process, which has led people away from true faith in God to the place where they put faith in objects. In a recent TV programme in Australia, Marilyn Hickey offered people a trinket filled with oil, which had been blessed by herself and by Oral Roberts with the promise that the wearer would derive benefit and blessing. This is fetishism, pure and simple and has no place in the Christian faith.

The Oxford dictionary defines a FETISH as (1) *"an inanimate object worshipped by primitive peoples for its supposed inherent magical powers or as being inhabited by a spirit;"* or (2) *"A thing evoking irrational devotion or respect"*. The worst aspect of this sort of practice today is that people such as Marilyn Hickey and Oral Roberts commercialise the practice. Marilyn Hickey offered her trinkets of oil on the basis of a donation of $35 to her so called ministry.

There is a similar and somewhat controversial incident in the life and ministry of Christ, to that of Peter's shadow, referred to in John 5:1-9, which, if not properly understood can be appealed to as a basis for the superstitious belief that healing occurs at such places as Lourdes, as taught by the Roman Catholic Church. Here's the passage in full:

"After this there was a feast of the Jews; and Jesus went up to Jerusalem. Now there is at Jerusalem by the sheep market a pool, which is called in the Hebrew tongue Bethesda, having five porches. In these lay a great multitude of sick, blind, lame and withered, waiting for the moving of the water. For an angel went down at a certain time into the pool, and agitated the water: whoever then went in first after the agitation of the water was cured of whatever disease he had. And a certain man was there, who had a sickness for thirty-eight years. When Jesus saw him, and knew that he had been there a long time, he said to him, Do you want to be made well? The sick man answered him, Sir, I have no man, when the water is agitated, to put me into the pool: but while I am coming, another steps down before me. Jesus said to him, Rise, take up your bed, and walk. And immediately the man was made well, and took up his bed, and walked: and it was the Sabbath day."

John 5:1-9

The end of verse 3 and verse 4 raise the problem: *"...waiting for the moving of the water. For an angel went down at a certain time into the pool, and agitated the water: whoever then went in first after the agitation of the water was cured of whatever disease he had."*

Both the NIV and the NASB omit this part of the passage in the main text and insert it in the margin with a note to the effect that *"some less important manuscripts"* (NIV) and *"Many authorities insert, wholly or in part"* (NASB) what they marginalized. *The New Testament from 26 Translations* (© Zondervan Publishing 1967) provides the following note "The last phrase of verse 3 ("waiting...water") and verse 4 are now recognised as not adequately supported by original manuscripts". We prefer the note contained in *The Companion Bible* "The water was intermittent from the upper springs of the waters of Gihon. The common belief of the man expressed in verse 7 is hereby described. All will be clear if we insert a parenthesis, thus: 'For (it was said that) an angel ... etc".

As in the case of Peter's shadow, so in this incident in John 5 there is no mention of anyone being healed based on either superstitious notion. In the case of Acts 5 everyone was healed, no matter where they were positioned in the crowd. In the case of John 5, the only person healed was by a miracle performed by our Lord Jesus Christ.

APPENDIX 5

Pentecostals Classical, Neo and Charismatics.

Pentecostals may be broadly defined as those who teach and practise the present day reality of the Holy Spirit in gifts and fruit.

Classic Pentecostals otherwise referred to as "early" or "historic" Pentecostals are made up of those groups who formed around the turn of last century 1900 to 1906 and who organised themselves into "movements" or denominations in the 1920s and 1930s. While there were some extreme ideas and practices which took place early on, with these people, there was a ground swell uprising against bizarre happenings and false teaching. With the formation of the official "movements" such as Assemblies of God (AoG), Elim Four Square, Commonwealth Revival Crusade (CRC), Church of God

(CoG) and several similarly named associations there developed within Classic-Pentecostalism an emphasis on holiness and wholesome Bible doctrine, with distinctive tenets of faith that were historically orthodox and soundly Bible based. The test of whether a person was truly Pentecostal was not based on an experience of "charismata" alone but on sound doctrine and holy living.

Charismatic was the term applied to people in the 1950s and 1960s within the historic "Churches" such as Roman Catholics and Anglicans (Episcopalians) who "spoke in tongues". They remained within their denominations and continued with their basic forms of worship, teaching and practice. Doctrine became secondary to the experience of "charismata". For example, no classic-Pentecostal would question baptism by total immersion or the plenary inspiration of the scripture or the eternal damnation of the finally impenitent. Charismatics on the other hand had a variety of views on these and other clear biblical teachings.

Neo-Pentecostals is a term that is used to delineate between the early or classic-Pentecostals and those in more modern times who have been influenced by "charismatics" and others to jettison their emphasis on sound Bible doctrine in favour of a strong movement towards unity. With these as with Charismatics an over-emphasis is placed on "experience" at the expense of Bible truth.

Others such as good evangelical Baptists and sound Bible-based Brethren people as well as a minority or majority, as the case may be, of truth related born-again members of the many denominations that make up present day Christendom are being influenced to some extent by the so called "things of the Holy Spirit" espoused and promoted by Pentecostals and Charismatics. We consider that the message of this book is an important consideration by all these groups.

FOOTNOTES:

[1] March 8-10, 2002 in Melbourne, Australia.

[2] *"And Elijah took his mantle, and wrapped it together, and struck the waters, and they were divided this way and that, so that they went over on dry ground. And it came to pass, when they were gone over, that Elijah said to Elisha, Ask what I shall do for you, before I am taken away from you. And Elisha said, I pray you, let a double portion of your spirit be upon me. And he said, You have asked a hard thing: nevertheless, if you see me when I am taken from you ; it shall be so to you ; but if not, it shall not be so. And it came to pass, as they still went on, and talked, that, behold, there appeared a chariot of fire, and horses of fire, and parted them both asunder; and Elijah went up by a whirlwind into heaven. And Elisha saw it, and he cried, My father, my father, the chariot of Israel, and the horsemen thereof. And he saw him no more: and he took hold of his own clothes, and tore them in two pieces. He took up also the mantle of Elijah that fell from him, and went back, and stood by the bank of Jordan; And he took the mantle of Elijah that fell from him, and struck the waters, and said, Where is the LORD*

God of Elijah? and when he also had smitten the waters, they parted this way and that,: and Elisha went over. And when the sons of the prophets who were from Jericho saw him, they said, The spirit of Elijah does rest on Elisha. And they came to meet him, and bowed themselves to the ground before him" (2 Kings 2: 8-15).

[3] (Strong 3663) *homoiopathes* from (Strong 3664) *homoios*

[4] (Strong 4336) proseuchomai = to offer prayers, to pray

[5] (Strong 4335) proseuche = prayer addressed to God or a place set apart for the offering of prayer

[6] *"Therefore you shall keep all the commandments which I command you this day, that you may be strong, and go in and possess the land, which you go to possess; And that you may prolong your days in the land, which the LORD swore to your fathers to give to them and to their seed, a land that flows with milk and honey. For the land, where you go in to possess it, is not as the land of Egypt, from where you came out, where you sowed your seed, and watered it with your foot, as a garden of herbs: But the land, which you go to possess it, is a land of hills and valleys, and drinks water of the rain of heaven: A land which the LORD your God cares for: the eyes of the LORD your God are always upon it, from the beginning of the year even to the end. And it shall come to pass, if you shall listen diligently to my commandments which I command you this day, to love the LORD your God, and to serve him with all your heart and with all your soul, That I will give you the rain of your land in its due season, the first rain and the latter rain, that you may gather in your corn, and your wine, and your oil. And I will send grass in your fields for your cattle, that you may eat and be full. Take heed to yourselves, that your heart be not deceived, and you turn aside, and serve other gods, and worship them; And then the LORD'S wrath will be kindled against you, and he shut up the heaven, that there be no rain, and that the land not yield its fruit; and lest you perish quickly from off the good land which the LORD gave you."* (Deuteronomy 11:8-17)

[7] *"But Elijah was sent to none of them, except to Sarepta (Zarephath), a city of Sidon, to a woman that was a widow"* (Luke 4:26).

[8] "And it came to pass, when they crossed over, that Elijah said to Elisha, 'Ask what I shall do for you, before I am taken away from you'. And Elisha said, 'Please let a double portion of your spirit be upon me'. And he said, 'You have asked a hard thing: nevertheless, if you see me when I am taken from you, it shall be so to you; but if not, it shall not be so'" (2 Kings 2:9-10).

[9] *"Now the sons of Reuben the firstborn of Israel, (for he was the firstborn; but, because he defiled his father's bed, his birthright was given to the sons of Joseph the son of Israel: and the genealogy is not listed after the birthright. For Judah prevailed above his brethren, and from him came the chief ruler; but the birthright was Joseph's)"* (1 Chronicles 5:1-2).

[10] *"Then I consulted with myself, and I rebuked the nobles, and the rulers, and said to them, every one of you exact usury from his brother. And I set a great assembly against them"* (Nehemiah 5:7).

[11] *"And it shall be at that day, says the LORD, that you shall call me Ishi; and shall*

no longer call me Baali" (Hosea 2:16).

[12] *The New Bible Dictionary* (IVF- May 1962) p. 115 Article - BAAL

[13] *"When the LORD your God shall bring you into the land where you go to possess it, and has cast out many nations before you , the Hittites, and the Girgashites, and the Amorites, and the Canaanites, and the Perizzites, and the Hivites, and the Jebusites, seven nations greater and mightier than you; And when the LORD your God shall deliver them before you ; you shall strike them, and utterly destroy them; you shall make no covenant with them, nor show mercy to them: Neither shall you make marriages with them; your daughter you shall not give to his son, nor his daughter shall you take to your son. For they will turn away your son from following me that they may serve other gods: so will the anger of the LORD be kindled against you, and destroy you suddenly. But thus shall you deal with them; you shall destroy their altars, and break down their images, and cut down their groves, and burn their graven images with fire. For you are a holy people to the LORD your God: the LORD your God has chosen you to be a special people to himself, above all people that are upon the face of the earth. The LORD did not set his love upon you, nor choose you, because you were more in number than any people; for you were the fewest of all people: But because the LORD loved you, and because he would keep the oath, which he had sworn to your fathers, has the LORD brought you out with a mighty hand, and redeemed you out of the house of bondmen, from the hand of Pharaoh king of Egypt. Know therefore that the LORD your God, he is God, the faithful God, who keeps covenant and mercy with them that love him and keep his commandments to a thousand generations; And repays them that hate him to their face, to destroy them: he will not be slack to him that hate him, he will repay him to his face. Therefore you shall keep the commandments, and the statutes, and the judgments, which I command you this day, to do them"* (Deut 7:1-11).

[14] "In 1982, shortly after taking over the Vineyard, Wimber returned to the Fuller Theological Seminary to co-teach with C. Peter Wagner a course entitled MC:510, "The Miraculous and Church Growth." It was a laboratory for experiments in signs and wonders. There were many ways in which Wimber's attempts at signs and wonders differed from the simple, direct, and unfailing ministry of the Holy Spirit. With the Wimber/Vineyard method, in order to effect a healing one must "interview" the subject, often taking him or her back into the past to relive circumstances (inner healing) that may have lead to their problem. Casting out demons is likewise a process that may take days or even years. The byword for all Wimber/Vineyard ministry is *method*. In spite of Wimber's statements that seem to warn against the use of methodology, it is methodology that typifies the Vineyard form of ministry. Their methods include inner healing techniques, visualization, meditation, and psychological integration. Wimber's book *Power Evangelism* has even been updated to include a study guide on how to perform signs and wonders, replete with methodologies." *John Wimber & The Vineyard* by Albert James Dager, *Media Spotlight,* 1996.

[15] *"No man can serve two masters: for either he will hate the one, and love the other; or else he will hold to the one, and despise the other. You cannot serve God and*

mammon" (Matthew 6:24). *"No servant can serve two masters: for either he will hate the one, and love the other; or else he will hold to the one, and despise the other. You cannot serve God and mammon"* (Luke 16:13).

[16] *You Need More Money* © 1999 Brian Houston Ministries page 2.

[17] *"And she said to Elijah, What have I to do with you, O you man of God? Have you come to me to call my sin to remembrance, and to slay my son?"* (1 Kings 17:18).

[18] *"And Ahab called Obadiah, which was the governor of his house. (Now Obadiah feared the LORD greatly)"* (1 Kings 18:3).

[19] *"Now therefore send, and gather all Israel to me on mount Carmel, and the four hundred and fifty prophets of Baal, and the four hundred prophets of the groves who eat at Jezebel's table"* (1 Kings 18:19).

[20] *"Then the king of Israel gathered the prophets together, about four hundred men, and said to them, Shall I go against Ramothgilead to battle, or shall I refrain? And they said, Go up; for the Lord will deliver it into the hand of the king"* (1Kings 22:6).

[21] *New Wine Messages* Cindy Jacobs reading Transcript at National School of the Prophets **Randy & Ann Gingrich** (gingrich@uswest.net) Fri, 12 Mar 1999 17:14:23 -0700 Cindy Jacobs: And before I read this word, I'm going to ask my pastor if he will pray for me, okay? [Dutch Sheets] Lord, we just thank you now for Your strong anointing that is upon Cindy right now and upon each one of us, to flow with what she is doing, and to give her the ability to share these words, under a true and pure anointing of your Holy Spirit. And Lord, that we would have prophetic ears to hear, Lord, that there would be a canopy anointing that hovers over this entire room. So Lord, we claim that now, and I just speak release over Cindy in boldness, and even the tender heart of God and the bold heart of God, wrapped in one, to bring forth this word in the way you want it done. I just speak protection blessing over you and your household, and over your anointing in Jesus' name. [Cindy Jacobs] Jesus! [She took a deep breath and began.] A report of words that came to the gathering of elder prophets, January 27, 1999. An alliance will form between Communism and Islam. A second prophetic word came from 1988, which said there will be an alliance between Communism and Islam more evil than anything we have previously known. Europe particularly needs to cry out to God. If Europeans cry out, God will hear them in their day of trouble, and American intercessors are to be a great help to them in that time.

What is coming on the world is so serious that Y2K will pale in comparison. It's all right to prepare for Y2K provided that preparation is not a heaping up solely for our personal needs without considering the plight of neighbours. If storing is done selfishly, it will be like sifting sands that slip through our fingers. The Church is not to fall into fear and panic, but to seek His face and presence. Y2K issues will be different in various regions. Some will be harder hit than others. Each area needs to raise up a prayer shield and gather apostles, prophets, and intercessors to pray to hear from God.

[22] Documented on the CWM website at
<http://www.christian-witness.org/cwmf/cwmf.html#war>

[23] *"There shall not be found among you any one that makes his son or his daughter*

to pass through the fire, or that uses divination, or an observer of times, or an enchanter, or a witch, Or a charmer, or a consulter with familiar spirits, or a wizard, or a necromancer" (Deut 18:10-11).

[24] *"But the prophet, who shall presume to speak a word in my name, which I have not commanded him to speak, or that shall speak in the name of other gods, even that prophet shall die. And if you say in your heart, How shall we know the word, which the LORD has not spoken? When a prophet speaks in the name of the LORD, if the thing does not happen or come to pass, that is the thing which the LORD has not spoken, but the prophet has spoken it presumptuously: you shall not be afraid of him"* (Deuteronomy 18:20-22).

[25] *"If there arise among you a prophet, or a dreamer of dreams, and gives you a sign or a wonder, And the sign or the wonder come to pass, which he spoke to you , saying, Let us go after other gods, which you have not known, and let us serve them; you shall not listen to the words of that prophet, or that dreamer of dreams: for the LORD your God is proving you, to know whether you love the LORD your God with all your heart and with all your soul. You shall walk after the LORD your God, and fear him, and keep his commandments, and obey his voice, and you shall serve him, and cling to him. And that prophet, or that dreamer of dreams, shall be put to death; because he has spoken to turn you away from the LORD your God, who brought you out of the land of Egypt, and redeemed you out of the house of bondage, to entice you out of the way which the LORD your God commanded you to walk in. So shall you put the evil away from your midst"* (Deuteronomy 13:1-5).

[26] *"And it came to pass, when all that knew him before saw that, behold, he prophesied among the prophets, then the people said one to another, What is this that has happened to the son of Kish? Is Saul also among the prophets? And one of the same place answered and said, But who is their father? Therefore it became a proverb, Is Saul also among the prophets?"* (1 Kings 10:11-12).

"And he stripped off his clothes also, and prophesied before Samuel in like manner, and lay down naked all that day and all that night. Wherefore they say, Is Saul also among the prophets?" (1 Sam 19:24). *"And Saul sought to smite David even to the wall with the javelin; but he slipped away out of Saul's presence, and he smote the javelin into the wall: and David fled, and escaped that night"* (1 Sam 18:10). *"And all the prophets prophesied so, saying, Go up to Ramothgilead, and prosper: for the LORD shall deliver it into the king's hand"* (1 Kings 22:12).

[27] *"But Zedekiah the son of Chenaanah went near, and smote Micaiah on the cheek, and said, Which way went the Spirit of the LORD from me to speak to you? And the king of Israel said, Take Micaiah, and carry him back unto Amon the governor of the city, and to Joash the king's son; And say, Thus saith the king, Put this fellow in the prison, and feed him with bread of affliction and with water of affliction, until I come in peace"* (1 Kings 22:24, 26, 27).

[28] *"And in the thirty-eighth year of Asa king of Judah Ahab the son of Omri began to reign over Israel: and Ahab the son of Omri reigned over Israel in Samaria twenty-two years"* (1 Kings 16:29)

[29] *"Ahaziah the son of Ahab began to reign over Israel in Samaria the seventeenth year of Jehoshaphat king of Judah, and reigned two years over Israel"* (1 Kings 22:51).

[30] *"Truly, truly, I say unto you, He that believes in me, the works that I do he shall do also; and he shall do greater works than these; because I go to my Father"* (John 14:12).

[31] *"And when he had spoken these things, while they watched, he was taken up; and a cloud received him out of their sight"* (Acts 1:9).

[32] *"And, behold, I send the promise of my Father upon you: but wait in the city of Jerusalem, until you are endued with power from on high"* (Luke 24:49).

"And, being assembled together with them, commanded them that they should not depart from Jerusalem, but wait for the promise of the Father, which, he said, you have heard of me... (8) But you shall receive power, after the Holy Spirit is come upon you: and you shall be witnesses to me both in Jerusalem, and in all Judaea, and in Samaria, and to the uttermost part of the earth. (2:1) And when the day of Pentecost was fully come, they were all with one accord in one place. And suddenly there came a sound from heaven as of a rushing mighty wind, and it filled all the house where they were sitting. And there appeared to them divided tongues like as of fire, and it sat upon each of them. And they were all filled with the Holy Spirit, and began to speak with other tongues, as the Spirit gave them utterance" (Acts 1:4, 8 and 2:1-4).

[33] *"The centurion answered and said, Lord, I am not worthy that you should come under my roof: but only speak the word, and my servant shall be healed. ... (13) And Jesus said to the centurion, Go your way; and as you have believed, so be it done to you. And his servant was healed in the same hour"* (Matthew 8:8,13).

[34] *"And so it was, when they had crossed over, that Elijah said unto Elisha, Ask what I shall do for you, before I am taken away from you. And Elisha said, Please let a double portion of your spirit be upon me. (15) And when the sons of the prophets who were at Jericho saw him, they said, The spirit of Elijah rests on Elisha. And they came to meet him, and bowed themselves to the ground before him"* (2 Kings 2:9 c/f 15). The English "double portion" = in Hebrew (Strong 08147) *sh'nayim* meaning "two" i.e. the cardinal number plus (Strong 06310) *peh* which is most frequently translated in the KJV to "mouth" (340 of the 480 usages in the OT) is extremely difficult to translate, but may have more to do with uttering God's Word than performing miracles c/f 1 Cor 14:1 *"Follow after love, and desire spiritual gifts, but rather that you may prophesy."* The only other time the English translation of the same Hebrew words occurs is in Deut 21:17, where the "double portion" is applied to the birthright. In essence Elisha requested the double inheritance of the first-born. This is related to Elijah's spirit (Heb *ruarch* v.9) and to the power from on high, seeing the mantle fell down as Elijah was being translated see 2 Kings 2:15.

[35] *"And Hazael said, But what, is your servant a dog, that he should do this great thing? And Elisha answered, The LORD has shown me that you will be king over Syria"* (2 Kings 13:8).

[36] *"And Elisha the prophet called one of the children of the prophets, and said unto*

him, Prepare yourself, and take this flask of oil in your hand, and go to Ramoth Gilead: And when you arrive, look for Jehu the son of Jehoshaphat the son of Nimshi, and go in, and make him rise up from among his brethren, and go to an inner room; Then take the flask of oil, and pour it on his head, and say, Thus says the LORD, I have anointed you king over Israel. Then open the door, and run ... And he arose, and went into the house; and he poured the oil on his head, and said to him, Thus says the LORD God of Israel, I have anointed you king over the people of the LORD, even over Israel. .... And he opened the door, and ran" (2 Kings 9:1-10).

PART TWO

Our Supernatural Heritage

CHAPTER 1

Where are the Miracles? God restores divine reality

IN an article entitled *Messianic Muslims?* Dr Orrel Steinkamp formerly from Australia but now living in the USA wrote: "Last year it was reported that several international mission organizations, including Youth With A Mission (YWAM) are testing a new approach to missionary work in areas where Christianity is unwelcome. A March 24 *Charisma News Service* report said some missionaries are now making converts but are allowing them to "hold on to many of their traditional religious beliefs and practices," so as to refrain from offending others within their culture. The *Charisma* article noted: "Messianic Muslims, who continue to read the Koran, visit the mosque and say their daily prayers but accept Christ as their Saviour, are the products of the strategy which is being tried in several countries." A YWAM staff writer wrote: "They continue a life of following the Islamic requirements, including mosque attendance, fasting and Koranic reading, besides getting together as a fellowship of Muslims who acknowledge Christ as the source of God's mercy for them... YWAM is also adopting this approach in India, where a team is working with a Hindu holy man." (*Foundation*, May/June 2000, p39)."

So pastor Aeron Morgan was not being facetious when he asked, "I wonder when we will have *"charismatic Mormons... JW's..."* And in the current ecumenical climate, with its sentimentally sloppy and unresearched pronouncements on Islam, could it even be one of these days, *charismatic Muslims?"*[1]

Orrel Steinkamp continues, "Mosque attendance and Koranic reading endorses Allah as the only true God and Mohammed as his true prophet. The Koran sees Jesus as only a prophet and not God's Son. Can one be a Messianic Christian and a Muslim believer at the same time?"[1] *The Plumbline*, Vol. 6, No. 2, March/April 2001.[2]

The faithful remnant always answers such a question with an unequivocal

"NO" simply because they recognise the difference between true and false religion. This was what motivated the great deliverers of God's people in the Old Testament. As we have seen in the case of Elijah it was the absence of holy living and the encroachment of evil within Israel that focused his attention and prompted his action. But these things were a secondary cause. The primary cause was Elijah's knowledge of and association with the Most High, Jehovah the God of Israel. James the apostle testifying through the Spirit of Christ within him and looking back, just as did the Old Testament prophets when looking forward,[3] removes the veil that obscures this reality in the historic record, when he writes: *"he prayed earnestly and he prayed again"* (James 5:17-18). It was God at work in Elijah's time that called forth the faithful remnant and it is ever so.

Another Old Testament scenario springs to mind in line with our themes of HOLINESS and TRUE SUPERNATURALISM. It is that of Gideon who in Judges 6:13 asks, *"...if the LORD is with us, why then has all this befallen us? And where are all his miracles which our fathers told us of ..."*. The setting of the emergence of Gideon and the faithful remnant in his day could hardly be of greater contrast to that of Elijah whom he pre-dates, though the parallels are clear. Both were obscure until they encountered God. Both were deeply concerned about the current plight of God's people. Both were humble men who knew and bore testimony to the fact that it was the Lord, Jehovah, the Almighty and not them personally who could make the difference. Elijah's opening words to King Ahab were: *"As the Lord the God of Israel lives before whom I stand .."* (1 Kings 17:1). When the angel, who appeared to Gideon, stated that the LORD was with him Gideon responded in a corporate manner *"if the LORD be with us why then has all this befallen us?"* (Judges 6:13). These men were reluctant to draw attention to themselves and did so only in the context of the overriding sovereignty of God, to whom ALL glory should be given at all times.

The scripture is quite explicit on this point, establishing this characteristic as an important yardstick by which the faithful remnant is measured:

"Though the LORD is on high, yet he respects the lowly: but the proud he knows from afar."

Psalms 138:6

"Let this mind be in you, which was also in Christ Jesus: Who, being in the form of God, thought it not robbery to be equal with God: But made himself of no reputation, and took upon him the form of a servant, and was made in the likeness of men: And being found in fashion as a man, he humbled himself, and became obedient to death, even the death of the cross."

Philippians 2:5-8

"I am the LORD: that is my name: and my glory will I not give to another, neither my praise to graven images."

Isaiah 42:8

I would go so far as to say that modesty and self-effacing humility are hallmarks by which the righteous remnant are always known. Such characteristics are not easily offended and while being recognised in others are seldom perceived to be part of one's own constitution, at least NOT in the absolute sense. Those who follow the lowly Nazarene constantly strive to be more like Him.

In contrast those who promote or head up the current "Apostolic Prophetic" movement have a tendency to detract from the godly and genuine work and sacrifice of their predecessors in their arrogant self-promotion. They appropriate to themselves the propensities of the Almighty. I have glanced at some of their books *The New Apostolic Churches* and *Churchquake* by C. Peter Wagner, *The Apostolic Revolution* by David Cartledge and *The 21st Century Out There* by Ben Gray. Apart from stealing each other's words, which, according to Jeremiah 23:30[4] is characteristic of false teachers, and the constant superficial generalisations, the one thing that struck me was the amount of the blowing of their own trumpets that these men do. They seem to have forgotten the old adage "self-praise is NO recommendation." Sadly some who don't know their church history are taken in by the hype about this being the great new move of God, when it is simply the result of human orchestration and a reviving of an old fallacy. As Orrel Steinkamp correctly points out,

"The only thing that's new about it, is the personalities that promote it". He then goes on to document the links between this *new* end time Apostles and Prophets movement with the mid 20th century heretical Latter Rain and Manifest Sons of God movements, which were outlawed by the then godly Assemblies of God and other Pentecostal movements in the USA.[5]

True revival always leads to spiritual awakening, which invariably impacts upon the secular community for good and for God. This is the biblical and historic pattern. It happened with Elijah as we have seen and it happened with

Gideon as recorded in Judges chapters 6 to 8. The setting of his emergence could NOT have been more ironic.

"And an angel of the LORD, came and sat under an oak which was in Ophrah, that belonged to Joash the Abiezrite: and his son Gideon threshed wheat by the winepress, to hide it from the Midianites. And the angel of the LORD appeared to him, and said to him, The LORD is with you, mighty man of valour. And Gideon said to him, Oh my Lord, if the LORD is with us, why then has all this befallen us? And where are all his miracles, which our fathers told us of, saying, Did not the LORD bring us up from Egypt? But now the LORD has forsaken us, and delivered us into the hands of the Midianites. And the LORD looked at him, and said, Go in this your might, and you shall save Israel from the hand of the Midianites: have not I sent you? And he said to him, Oh my Lord, wherewith shall I save Israel? behold, my family is poorest in Manasseh, and I am the least in my father's house. And the LORD said to him, Surely I will be with you, and you shall strike the Midianites as one man."

Judges 6:11-16

As with Elijah so with Gideon there was a preliminary of persistent prayer that prompted a divine response. In this case it was not just one man but also an entire nation who cried out to God:

"And it came to pass, when the children of Israel cried to the LORD because of the Midianites, That the LORD sent a prophet to the children of Israel, who said to them, Thus says the LORD God of Israel, I brought you up from Egypt, and brought you forth out of the house of bondage; And I delivered you out of the hand of the Egyptians, and out of the hand of all that oppressed you, and drove them out from before you, and gave you their land; And I said to you, I am the LORD your God; do not fear the gods of the Amorites, in whose land you dwell: but you have not obeyed my voice."

Judges 6:7-10

All true prophets always speak warning and usually some form of rebuke. It is their *lingua franca*; their tools of trade; the hallmark of their calling! For this reason, if for no other, you can dismiss today's euphoric prophets such as David Cartledge, Peter Wagner, Cindy Jacobs, Frank Houston, and Steve Penny. Today's self acclaimed prophets seldom if ever speak warning unless someone withstands them and then they lose their tempers, while continuing to speak out of their own spirits, but now with a vitriol that reveals the nature of their motivator the father of lies. Some others such as Rick Joyner and Paul

Cain are craftier, so the measuring stick has to be more carefully applied. They are false nonetheless.

The most ironic aspects of this encounter of the Angel of the Lord, (see Appendix 1) in the light of Gideon's activity and attitude, are seen in the opening and concluding comments of the divine visitor, who appeared as a wayfaring man.[6] From a human perspective he was anything but *"a mighty man of valour"*, as the angel calls him (see Appendix 2) too scared to expose himself to the Midianites and then hiding the wheat that he threshed from the enemy, because he couldn't defend it (Judges 6:11&12). His attitude was totally negative, which, in human terms, does not indicate a *"mighty man"* who is cut out for any sort of success. Yet the Lord said that even this was the basis of the victory that would be achieved *"Go in this your might, and you shall save Israel from the hand of the Midianites:"* (v14). It's both ironic and paradoxical. The truth is carried through into the New Testament in such statements as, *"when I am weak, then am I strong"* (2 Corinthians 12:10), *"if a man thinks himself to be something, when he is nothing, he deceives himself"* (Galatians 6:3) and *"God has chosen the weak things of the world to confound the things which are mighty"* (1 Corinthians 1:27). The reason is given by Paul two verses later *"That no flesh should glory in his presence"* (1 Corinthians 1:29). As faithful remnant people we must rediscover and constantly bask in the truth of the fact that it is *"Not to us, O LORD, not to us, but to your name give glory, for your mercy, and for your truth's sake"* (Psalm 115:1).

Or to put it another way in the language of the New Testament,

"I am crucified with Christ: nevertheless I live; yet not I, but Christ lives in me: and the life which I now live in the flesh I live by faith in the Son of God, who loved me, and gave himself for me."

Galatians 2:20

CHAPTER 2

Miracles and Divine Sovereignty

IN the Gideon story it seems that the word of the unnamed prophet is interrupted by the appearance of the Angel of the Lord. Judges 6:6 tells us that the impoverishment of the children of Israel resulted in their crying to the Lord who sent His prophet to deliver a brief message, which ends abruptly with the rebuke, *"but you have not obeyed my voice."* (c/f Judges 6:6-10). Then the wayfaring theophany appears in the very next verse. The context presents a most instructive insight into the paradox we face when we reflect on the meeting point of the responsibility of man with the sovereignty of God in the divine human interaction. Consider the scenario the people disobey God, which is irresponsible on their part and obviously against the will of God for them. The immediate result of this is that they fall prey to the Midianites who oppress them, just as God warned. This results in their crying to the Lord, who sends a prophet and then comes Himself to their rescue. At no time does God override human responsibility though clearly in the ultimate sense He is sovereign, even using the circumstance of the impoverishment of the children of Israel to humble them to the point where they call upon the Name of the Lord.

A story told by the late A.W. Tozer regarding a private meeting that he had with Martyn Lloyd-Jones[7], when they discussed Calvinism and Arminianism illustrates the way we can reconcile the *"irreconcilables"* of this theological dilemma. After each of these godly men presented his ideas, coming as they did from opposing camps yet having a great respect for each other, Tozer reports that he suggested to Lloyd-Jones that God in His sovereignty had determined to allow man as a responsible being to exercise freedom of choice. It is said that the Dr smiled and nodded his head in his own inimitable manner. There really is no need for a moderate Calvinist such as Dr Martyn Lloyd-Jones to break fellowship with a moderate Arminianist such as A.W. Tozer providing of course that each recognises the overriding Sovereignty of God in the human divine interaction as the scriptures clearly portray.

Gideon asked two inter-related questions, which can be paraphrased as follows:

1) If the Lord is with us then why are we facing our present difficult circumstances? and

2) If the Lord is with us where are His sovereign supernatural interventions that occurred in the past?

Sometimes we try to answer the second question before considering the first. That is wrong and will lead to distorted ideas about miracles as well as to a failure to learn from history. The answer to Gideon's first question is clear and easy to grasp. Judges 6:1 records: *"And the children of Israel did evil in the sight of the LORD: and the LORD delivered them into the hand of Midian for seven years."* The prophet whom the Lord sent identifies the precise area of departure: *"I said to you, I am the LORD your God; do not fear the gods of the Amorites, in whose land you dwell: but you have not obeyed my voice"* (v 10). Idolatry brought judgment simply by God withdrawing His protection. So it wasn't just a matter of active miracles but also passive protection both of which, of course, are within the sovereignty of God.

The second question is both intriguing and instructive. It recognises the source and nature of true miracles:

"Where are all HIS miracles which OUR FATHERS TOLD US OF, saying, Did not the LORD bring us up from Egypt?" (Emphasis added). Gideon had no interest in some new miracle of questionable origin. The miracles that he inquired of were sourced in GOD HIMSELF and were regulated in their nature by what had preceded them in Israel's remarkable history. There was no confusion in his mind between mere sensationalism and true supernaturalism. He wasn't interested in hyped up psychological or hypnotic mysticism or exhibitionism. He was a seeker after TRUTH and REALITY, which are basic hallmarks of the faithful remnant. He bore testimony to the foundation of their very existence the *raison d'être* of God's own people in the extension to that question: *"Did not the LORD bring us up from Egypt?"* This is the central truth of both Testaments. Egypt was literal in the Old Testament and is figurative in the New, signifying the world, the flesh and the devil from which God's people are delivered through the shed blood of our Saviour. Unless that marvellous truth is maintained as being central and fundamental all miracle seeking and miracle claims are meaningless and empty.

The significance of all of this in the setting of the GATHERING of the FAITHFUL REMNANT in our time is enormous and before I proceed to a more detailed application of the basic question of my topic *"Where are the miracles?"* let me emphasise here in the story of Gideon as I did in the case of Elijah that everyone Gideon's band of 300 here and Elijah's 7,000 there (both were unbowed) everyone is affected when things go wrong within the Kingdom. Ultimately we are thrown upon God's grace to transact the change and make the difference. The remnant MUST and WILL remain faithful but the divine intervention is sourced in God NOT in man no matter how many or to what extent His people remain true to Him.

Gideon refers to miracles as belonging to God *"where are HIS miracles"*. Men do not perform supernatural displays. Biblically people are at best only vessels or instruments through which miracles flow. Significantly in the Judges we read of the activity of the Holy Spirit upon men whom God chose to bring deliverance to his people. The term that is used is *"the Spirit of the LORD came upon*[8]*"* Othniel (Judges 3:10), Gideon (6:34), Jephthah (11:24), Samson (14:26). Othniel was the first judge, so in a sense what happened to him is a prototype of what happened to all the judges whom God raised up as deliverers. The Spirit of the Lord came upon them. That is what made the difference. In the case of Gideon the expression *"came upon"* is the translation of the Hebrew (Strong 03847) *"labash"*, which appears 112 times in the Old Testament and is rendered by the KJV as *clothe* 51, *put on* 22, *put* 18, *array* 6, *wear* 4, *armed* 3, *came* 3, *apparel* 1, *apparelled* 1, *clothed them* 1, *came upon* 1, *variant* 1 Total 112. Judges 6:34 could well have been rendered *"But the Spirit of the LORD clothed Himself with Gideon, and he blew a trumpet; and the Abiezrites gathered behind him."*

This idea of the Holy Spirit coming upon individuals is carried forward into the New Testament, when our Lord promised *"But you shall receive power* (Strong 1411 = Greek *dunamis*), *after the Holy Spirit is come upon you* (Strong 1904 Greek *eperchomai*)*..."* (Acts 1:8). The expression *"come upon you"* does not have the same connotation or strength in the NT Greek as it does in the OT Hebrew but there is nonetheless the strong implication in the use of the Greek *"eperchomai"* that the Holy Spirit actually "overtakes" the individual, thus emphasising the sovereignty and force of God in the action, an idea that is further emphasised in the use of the Greek *"dunamis"*, which signifies more than just *"power"*. It contains the thought of our transliterated English word "dynamo" and would be more accurately translated "enabling" or "ability." In the coming of the Holy Spirit upon an individual in the New Testament sense, that person is given a divine enabling to meet all circumstances and challenges by virtue of the inbuilt energy that derives from the "*dunamis*" received. When the Spirit of the Lord clothed Himself with Gideon he *"blew a trumpet"*, which was not a bizarre but a purposeful act. When the Holy Spirit came upon the 120 disciples in the upper room they *"began to speak with other tongues, as the Spirit gave them utterance"* (= literally "to articulate") (Acts 2:4). Both were rallying cries that heralded the revival of the remnant and both were supernatural in their origin and operation and within the ambit of the sovereignty of God.

The following explanation may seem controversial, but if we see it in balance I think it will help us to avoid some extremes. The rallying call of the faithful remnant in Gideon's time involved the blowing of a trumpet once. In a sense that was the initial evidence of the work of the Holy Spirit at that time. Neither Gideon nor his followers kept on blowing the trumpet though the principle of the blowing of a trumpet is clearly entrenched within scripture, relating as it does to the sounding of an alarm,

"Blow the trumpet in Zion, and sound an alarm in my holy mountain: let all the inhabitants of the land tremble: for the day of the LORD is coming, for it is close at hand."

Joel 2:1

And the calling of a solemn assembly,

"Blow the trumpet in Zion, sanctify a fast, call a solemn assembly: Gather the people, sanctify the congregation, assemble the elders, gather the children..."

Joel 2:15

Compare Numbers 10:7 where the distinction is stated and explained in the entire context, which deals with the teaching of the blowing of trumpets.

"And the LORD spoke to Moses, 'Make two trumpets of silver; make them of a whole piece: for the calling of the assembly, and for the journeying of the camps. When they shall blow with them, all the assembly shall gather to you at the door of the tabernacle of the congregation. If they blow with only one trumpet, then the princes, who are heads of Israel, shall gather to you. When you blow an alarm, then the camps that lie on the east shall go forward. When you blow an alarm the second time, then the camps that lie on the south side shall take their journey: they shall blow an alarm for their journeys. But when the entire congregation is to be gathered together, you shall blow, but not sound an alarm. And the sons of Aaron, the priests, shall blow with the trumpets; and they shall be to you for an ordinance for ever throughout your generations. And if you go to war in your land against the enemy that oppresses you, then you shall blow an alarm with the trumpets; and you shall be remembered before the LORD your God, and you shall be saved from your enemies. Also in the day of your gladness, and in your solemn days, and in the beginnings of your months, you shall blow with the trumpets over your burnt offerings, and over the sacrifices of your peace offerings; that they may be to you for a memorial before your God: I am the LORD your God."

Numbers 10:1-10

In Gideon's case there was another significant occasion when the blowing of trumpets was required in the deliverance wrought by the faithful remnant,

"And he divided the three hundred men into three companies, and he put a trumpet in every man's hand, with empty pitchers, and lamps within the pitchers. And he said ... When I blow with a trumpet ... then you blow the trumpets ... and say, The sword of the LORD, and of Gideon. So Gideon, and the hundred men that were with him, came unto the outside of the camp in the beginning of the middle watch; ... and they blew the trumpets, and broke the pitchers that were in their hands. And the three companies blew the trumpets, and broke the pitchers, and held the lamps in their left hands, and the trumpets in their right hands to blow with them: and they cried, The sword of the LORD, and of Gideon."

Judges 7:16-20

The rallying call on the day of Pentecost was undoubtedly related to speaking in tongues BUT only and exclusively as the Holy Spirit *"gave them to articulate"*. In other words the initiation of their speaking in tongues was by the Spirit and not by themselves. Some 20th century Pentecostals, especially Assemblies of God, turned the biblical incidents of tongues speaking into a doctrine relating to the evidence of the Baptism *in* or *into* the Holy Spirit.

This inevitably focussed the expectation of Pentecostals on speaking in tongues in a rather unhealthy and I think unhelpful manner. With the possible exception of the Samaritan case (Acts 8) I do not fault the logic in their appeal to the four historic incidents recorded in Acts (chapters 2, 8, 10 and 19) to establish the common and initial "sign" or evidence of tongues speaking. I am sure that in the main, classic Pentecostals retained the important balance between the manifestation and what produced the manifestation viz a genuine operation of the Holy Spirit. My concern rests in what the humanly argued doctrine of the initial evidence tends to lead to. Now I know that this was not the intent of the formulators of it, nor is it the intention of those who cling to it. It is simply the natural and, to a large extent, the unavoidable result of stating it as a tenet of faith. Some leaders overemphasise it and thus tend to make it the thing that is sought after, while followers tend to make it their focus of experience and of testimony.

Those who do these things overlook the fact that in none of the Acts incidents was tongues speaking any sort of focus. In Acts 2 there is no indication that the disciples had any idea that they would speak in tongues certainly they were not instructed or *"taught"* how to receive the Holy Spirit. In Acts 8 there is no direct reference to any clearly established "evidence", though obviously there was some supernatural occurrence, which convinced Simon, who is described in that chapter as a sorcerer. In Acts 10 what happened to the gentiles was supernatural and spontaneous, as Peter was preaching about Christ and particularly about His resurrection. In Acts 19 there is no indication that Paul mentioned tongues or prophecy prior to his ministering the Holy Spirit to the disciples, whom he met at Ephesus. The point that I am making is that in all these cases tongues speaking was not a prior focus as it inevitably becomes when you formulate or state a doctrine of the initial evidence of the baptism in the Holy Spirit.

The problem with all of this is that it tends to humanise and thus relegate to the mundane and the ordinary what should be one of the greatest and mightiest spiritual experiences in the life and walk of the Christian. Even worse it can replace a spiritual encounter with the third person of the trinity with mere psychological tongues speaking. Two illustrations may serve to explain my point. Firstly from my own experience and secondly something based on a powerful illustration from the 19th Century Welsh revival, which shows how we must maintain this focus upon the sovereign choice and intervention of God Almighty, avoiding all humanistic attempts to produce certain fixed expectations or results.

I have been associated with the Pentecostal movement for almost sixty years having been saved in an Assembly of God fellowship in Great Britain when I was six years old and receiving what is generally called the Baptism "in" or "into" the Holy Spirit at the age of ten. At twelve years old I accompanied my parents and sister and brother to New Zealand and answered the call into the ministry when I left high school at the age of sixteen. I had the opportunity of entering university in New Zealand but declined, having a desire to serve God full-time. At the age of seventeen I entered an AoG Bible School in Brisbane, Australia (Commonwealth Bible College CBC) to train for the ministry. Throughout my life and ministry I have always had an antipathy towards the sort of "specialist" promoters of the Baptism in the Holy Spirit who have been given platform opportunity within the Pentecostal fold, because of their tendency to make tongues speaking fundamental when it is clearly presented in scripture as something that is incidental. My honest assessment is that among these so-called specialists have been some who have taken on the role from a basis of ignorance or naîvety. Others have been manipulators, who not only instruct people but also actually coerce them into speaking in tongues. This is dangerous and can result in a psychological or even a demonic counterfeit.

A case in point is the well-known Pentecostal preacher Frank Houston who was perceived as a man who could "get people through" into tongues speaking. He used all sorts of methods and manipulations. When he came to Britain in the late 1960s my paternal uncle, David Powell, stopped him praying for people at the Rotherham Assembly of God because Mr Houston evidenced this tendency and later my uncle explained his reasons to Frank. Instead of weighing the words of warning Mr Houston returned to New Zealand and denigrated my uncle and the Rotherham Assembly, stating publicly that this large AoG church in Britain and its pastor were not "Pentecostal". It now turns out that about that time, or a little later, Frank Houston had a "serious moral fall" [9] or as it is elsewhere referred to as "serious sexual offences that took place 30 years ago".[10] This has enormous implications in the light of Paul's instruction: *"Lay hands on no man suddenly, or share other men's sins: keep yourself pure"* (1 Timothy 5:22) See Appendix 3.

My major point is that relating to the sovereignty of God in respect of His ways and works and this leads me to my second illustration. Dr Martyn Lloyd-Jones in his magnificent book entitled *Preaching and Preachers* speaks of a number of cases where God worked uniquely and sovereignly in the setting of revival both in the book of Acts and throughout church history. The last chapter, entitled *Demonstrations of the Spirit and of Power,* is given over to this aspect. The true stories are thrilling indeed, but none more so than those concerning a man called David Morgan, who featured in the Welsh Revival in 1859. Mr Morgan was a very ordinary preacher before the Holy Spirit came upon him and after two years of being mightily used by God he became quite ordinary again for the final 15 years of his life. One night after listening to Humphrey Jones preach a powerful message David Morgan later reported,

"I went to bed that night just David Morgan as usual. I woke up the next morning feeling like a lion, feeling that I was filled with the power of the Holy Ghost."

Martyn Lloyd-Jones goes on to tell how for more than two years this man, David Morgan, had a profound influence on Wales and on some most influential people, who came under conviction and were converted through his reaching, among them "T C Edwards, the author of a well known ;ommentary on the First Epistle to the Corinthians" who went to hear the reacher with his mind "full of philosophical difficulties and perplexities. His aith had been shaken by his reading of philosophy and he was in trouble" bserves the Dr and then goes on to describe what happened.

"He had a red silk handkerchief in his pocket as was the habit of such young ıen in those days; and all he knew was this, that at the end of the meeting the ed silk handkerchief was torn in shreds on the floor of the pew in which he vas sitting in the gallery. He was quite unaware of the fact that he had done ıis, but the fact was that his entire life was changed, his philosophical doubts vere dispersed, all his uncertainties vanished like the morning mist, and this reat scholar was filled with the power of the Holy Spirit and became an utstanding preacher."

David Morgan later said, "I went to bed one night still feeling like a lion, illed with this strange power that I had enjoyed for the two years. I woke up he next morning and found that I had become David Morgan once more."

Dr Martyn-Lloyd Jones observes,

"The power came, and the power was withdrawn. Such is the lordship of the pirit! You cannot command this blessing, you cannot order it; it is entirely the ift of God. The examples I have given from the scriptures indicate this. 'Peter, illed with the Spirit.' The Spirit filled him. He did the same to David Morgan; nd then in His own inscrutable wisdom and sovereignty He took it from him. Revivals are not meant to be permanent. But at the same time I maintain that all f us who are preachers should be seeking this power every time we preach." [11]

The very language of the Bible bears this out in respect of the operations of he Holy Spirit, which are called *"the manifestation"* i.e. "the shining forth" *"of the* (Holy) *Spirit"* in the New Testament (c/f 1 Cor 12:7[12]). Pentecostals ave generally referred to these nine manifestations as the Gifts of the Spirit nd they are, but in an inclusive not an exclusive sense. There are other *"gifts"* isted in such passages as Romans 12:6-8 and implied in 1 Corinthians 2:14-31. The nine gifts listed in 1 Corinthians 12:7-11 are exclusively the *"manifestations of the Spirit"*. With the definition of a "shining forth" the ocus is again on the sovereign and supernatural work of God through these lisplays. There are nine of them and it is important to note that they do NOT nclude prostrations, jerking, laughter, roaring or any of the bizarre things vhich have passed as manifestations of the Spirit in the false revival associated vith Rodney Howard-Browne, Toronto and Pensacola etc.

These *manifestations* are complementary to the nine fruit (singular not plural) of the Spirit.[13] Scripture does not speak of the fruits of the Spirit for it is a cluster that is envisaged with the one dominant characteristic of love pervading the whole. So the fruit of the Spirit is LOVE, being the very nature of God that is expressed in all the other qualities listed. Love expressed in *"joy, peace, longsuffering, gentleness, goodness, faith"*. Fruit is the product and proof of life. This is why Paul says, *"Now if any man does not have the Spirit of Christ, he is none of His"* or as J.B. Phillips renders it *"he doesn't belong to Him at all"* (Romans 8:9). This is a statement about the disposition or nature of Christ, which is produced by the Holy Spirit in the individual.

We are considering here what is fundamental to the life of the Christian. Just as fruit grows and develops, so the nature of Christ is progressive throughout the life and experience of the Christian. The important fact to note is that the Fruit of the Spirit must be present in degree otherwise there is no real spiritual life. For this reason while the Fruit of the Spirit is complementary to the Gifts of the Spirit the former is infinitely more important than the latter in respect of a person's relationship with Christ and of his eternal destiny. As one man put it you can't have living fruit like gifts on a dead Christmas tree, which I suppose is a reasonable analogy except for the fact that in the realm of the Spirit *fruit* must precede *gift* so neither is possible on a dead tree! In other words if you do not have the life of Christ you will not have the true manifestation of the Holy Spirit life precedes gift.

This underscores one of the great concerns that has arisen within the Charismatic movement and inevitably points to the fact that those who receive *"tongues"* and are not truly born-again have had a counterfeit psychological or demonic experience. This highlights one of our major concerns about Alpha, the other being the clear links of Alpha and its major promoter, Nicky Gumbel, with the ecumenical drift that is headed up by the Roman Catholic Church. We have documented this in our CWM publications available in the archives section on our website and in the booklet *Alpha Unmasked* available from our CWM office in Australia.[14]

"But without faith it is impossible to please Him: for he who comes to God must believe that He is, and that He is a rewarder of those that diligently seek Him"

Hebrews 11:6

"Pursue peace with all men, and holiness, without which no man shall see the Lord"

Hebrews 12:14

CHAPTER 3

Supernatural Shinings Forth

THE word that is rendered *manifestation* in 1 Corinthians 12:7 is the Greek *"phanerosis"* (Strong 5321) which appears only twice in the New Testament in this noun form.

"But the manifestation of the Spirit is given to everyone to profit the entire body."

1 Corinthians 12:7

"But have renounced the hidden things of dishonesty, not walking in craftiness, nor handling the word of God deceitfully; but by manifestation of the truth commending ourselves to every man's conscience in the sight of God."

2 Corinthians 4:2

The Greek root *"phaino"* (Strong 5316) from which *"phanerosis"* is derived, signifies "to bring forth into the light, cause to shine, shed light; to shine, be bright or resplendent; to become evident, to come to view, appear; to be exposed to view; to meet the eyes, strike the sight, become clear or manifest." When we apply these ideas to the operations of the Holy Spirit (1 Corinthians 12:7) and to required human conduct and ministry (2 Corinthians 4:2) we are faced with our two themes HOLINESS and THE SUPERNATURAL.

Paul commences his teaching on the manifestations of the Holy Spirit with the statement: *"Now concerning spiritual gifts, brethren, I do not wish you to be ignorant"* (1 Corinthians 12:1).

The expression *"spiritual gifts"* is a rendition of the Greek *"pneumatikos"* (Strong 4152), which is rendered "spiritual" 26 times in the KJV of the NT. The word "*gifts*" was inserted by the translators to give what they thought was the sense of the passage. They were right to a degree, but not in total and in fact the use of the word may have produced some of the confusion, which surrounds this passage of scripture. Greater clarity occurs when the word "gifts" is replaced with the word "things". The topic being addressed is that of spirituality which includes, but is not limited to, the manifestations of the Holy

Spirit, otherwise called by some the gifts of the Holy Spirit.

During much of this epistle to the church at Corinth Paul has been developing the theme, which he introduced at the end of chapter 2 and the start of chapter 3, where he describes three types of people:

1) Those who are natural Grk *"psuchikos"* (Strong 5591) ch 2:14;
2) Those who are spiritual Grk *"pneumatikos"* (Strong 4152) ch 2:15;
3) Those who are carnal Grk *"sarkikos"* (Strong 4559) ch 3:1.

The first type, *Psuchikos* = "of or belonging to breath" i.e. natural or sensual are those who are outside of the Kingdom of God, being unregenerate, not born again. Such, Paul tells us, do not and cannot receive the things of the Spirit of God. Like Nicodemus they constantly ask, *"How can these things be?"*

The only valid answer is that given by Christ in John 3:3 *"Truly, truly I say to you, Except a man be born again, he cannot see* (i.e. understand or perceive) *the kingdom of God."* It is vain to try to explain spiritual things to natural people, BUT, and this is very important, "natural" *(psuchikos)* is NOT a description of any Christian. A person who is truly born-again is no longer a natural person with just a natural mind. Rodney Howard-Browne and those who follow his weird unbiblical teaching have got it all wrong when they apply this description to Christian men and women, all of whom have the "mind of Christ" (c/f 1 Corinthians 2:16) at least in degree and are therefore able to "judge" i.e. examine and make a conclusion regarding spiritual things.

The second type, *Pneumatikos* = "of or belonging to the spirit" are those who are related to, filled with or governed by the Holy Spirit. Such, Paul tells us, have the potential to judge all things and in the ultimate sense cannot be analysed (judged) by the purely natural person (implied in the text). Corporately, spiritual people have the mind of Christ. For a *"psuchikos"* person to become a *"pneumatikos"* person requires the action of the Holy Spirit in regeneration. Psychological pressure through music and other things in the long run is not only useless but it is also harmful as it is counter-productive. Youth Alive and its offspring called Planet Shakers, and Hillsong with their current drive to become relevant to win people to Christ are very wrong in their approach and method. These people, with their carnal leaders, have become so relevant in worldly terms that they are NOW irrelevant in terms of the Kingdom of God. The Holy Spirit has long since departed from their hyped-up, emotionally charged events that pass as worship or evangelistic outreaches in our time. The appeal and atmosphere are not something that He who is HOLY would choose to be associated with.

The third type, *Sarkikos* = "of or belonging to the flesh" are those who are governed by the nature of the flesh. This is a description of carnal Christians, who have had a born-again experience, but instead of pressing on to a higher plain spiritually, they have allowed the things of the world, the flesh and the devil viz worldliness to dominate their lives and conduct. It is this group that Paul addresses at Corinth in an attempt to bring them back on course.

Thus he addresses such things as carnal divisions over leadership (chs 1-3), perceived success (ch 4), immoral conduct (5), legal action, (6), marriage and divorce (7), eating things offered to idols (8), liberty, legalism and self-denial (9), idolatry and immorality (10), male and female activity in the House of the Lord and the Lord's table, as the great equaliser and regulator (11). This is merely an overview and of course there are overlaps within the 11 chapters covered. We need to recognise that there were no chapter divisions in the original. They were introduced for convenience of reference.

In coming to chapter 12 it is important to see that Paul returns to this matter of spiritual things or spirituality i.e. *"pneumatikos"* of which he says that we should not be ignorant. He then gives his reason as being the fact that the Corinthian Christians were saved out of a pagan idolatrous religion that was built upon spirit guides leading men and women to useless dumb idols. The Christian faith is vastly different being built upon the activity of the Holy Spirit witnessing to a living Christ, who is the supreme goal in every Christian's life and the sovereign object of all our worship. It is therefore impossible for anyone who is under the influence of the Holy Spirit to call Jesus accursed and this is a test to apply to all spiritual activity, which Paul then goes on to describe by first giving an outline of his teaching on the topic and then dealing with it in greater detail.

A. Verse 4 There are various kinds of Manifestations of the Holy Spirit;

B. Verse 5 There are various types of Ministries (literally services); and

C. Verse 6 There are various Appointments and Operations in the local church.

The section that deals with THE SUPERNATURAL GIFTS OF THE HOLY SPIRIT is verses 7 to 11 and, as we have seen the key word is *manifestation*. This is the major consideration of our topic *"Where are the Miracles? God Restores Divine Reality"* so we'll return to this after briefly looking at the other two sections of 1 Corinthians chapter 12. Remember we are discussing here the *Pneumatikos*, i.e. spiritual things or spirituality and this includes supernatural manifestations of the Holy Spirit.

Verse 5 provides us with the heading for the second section, which is contained in verses 12 to 27. Here the topic is service or ministry within the local body of believers. The emphasis is on unity, interdependence and the importance of not despising our own function or that of anyone else in the body. Paul is not dealing here with the supernatural gifts or manifestations of the Holy Spirit per se though they are not excluded. He is teaching about our function or service within the church, which may relate to natural ability that has been dedicated and consecrated to the Lord. A detailed consideration of this is not possible here.

The various appointments and operations within the local church are presented in verses 28 and 29 and it is important to note that their setting is local, i.e. resident within the church and not visiting. Here we have representative reference to the ministry gifts of Christ in their local expression. We plan to deal with this fully in the last chapter where we will consider how God re-enters His redemptive realm as we ask the question, *"Where are the true ministers?*

CHAPTER 4

Miraculous Grace & Gifts

THE word that is translated "gifts" in 1 Corinthians 12:4 is the Greek *"charisma"* (Strong 5486), which, as Jacob Prasch correctly points out, lays an emphasis upon "grace" rather than "gift". As Prasch explains elsewhere this indicates that the person through whom the manifestation occurs is not the possessor or performer but rather the instrument or vessel that receives the grace for the gift to flow.[15] If there is any notion of residency with respect to the nine manifestations (gifts) of the Holy Spirit it relates to the church, the local body of believers and not to any one individual. The beneficiary of the manifestation and not the instrument through whom it flows is the person with the gift. Seeing and accepting this immediately removes the super-star image in regard to healing, the performing of miracles, prophecy or a genuine word of knowledge etc. The problem with much of the past teaching on this subject is that it has tended to draw attention to the person who prays or performs rather than to the recipient as being the person with the gift. Paul's teaching is quite clear, each manifestation is at the discretion of the Holy Spirit and is given for the general benefit of the entire body of believers i.e. the local church, c/f 1 Corinthians 12:7*"But the manifestation of the Spirit is given to every man to profit everyone;"* with 1 Corinthians 14:12*"Even so you, since you are zealous for spiritual gifts, seek that you may excel to the edifying of the church."*

There are nine manifestations of the Holy Spirit. These are what we might call the supernatural gifts, meaning that they are outside of the scope of natural ability or normal expression. The early Pentecostals, who are sometimes referred to as "classic Pentecostals", tended to approach this topic from two angles. Firstly, they divided the nine into three groups of three a trinity of a trinity teaching that the three sections covered all realms of miraculous intervention. Secondly, they always appealed to the Bible for their doctrine about the receipt, operation and illustrations of these manifestations or supernatural gifts. This appeal to scripture became a great safeguard against the later errors, which developed in the wider charismatic scene, where experience, not the Bible dominated. An example is the dispute, which arose during the 1960s, when it was claimed that priests and nuns of the Roman Catholic Church had been baptised in the Holy Spirit with the sign of speaking in tongues. Classic Pentecostals opposed the idea simply because the Bible teaches that a person must be regenerated i.e. "born-again" by the Holy Spirit before he can be baptised into the Holy Spirit.

I recall that in the Assemblies of God in Great Britain there was much opposition to David du Plessis who had taken the "experience" to the Vatican. The concern was two fold: Firstly, biblical as I have just outlined. Secondly, there was great concern and caution over the well-known and recognised ability that Rome has to adapt to anything that is perceived to be of benefit to her. The Roman Catholic Church is a religious chameleon, as is being increasingly demonstrated. Now she is adapting to Islam in the huge ecumenical build up to the One World Church that Bible teachers have long since predicted would occur. The principle that classic Pentecostals applied to this dispute was one, which they sought to apply to the nine manifestations of the Spirit as outlined in 1 Corinthians chapter 12.

Three of the nine have to do with INFORMATION requiring supernatural REVELATION and the APPLICATION of such revealed information. These are designated by Paul as *"the word of wisdom"*, *"word of knowledge"* (1 Corinthians 12:8) and the *"discerning of spirits"* (v10). Three of them have to do with the INTERVENTION of the POWER of God in the physical, material and natural realms. These are called *"faith"*, *"gifts of healings"* (v9) and *"the working of miracles"* (v10). The final three are even more difficult than the previous to classify. Early Pentecostals made a number of attempts calling them the VOCAL or the INSPIRATIONAL gifts. But of course there are others among the nine, which are vocal and all are inspirational in the true meaning of that word. For the purposes of this study we will simply list them. They are *"prophecy"*, *"different kinds of tongues"* and *"the interpretation of tongues."*

CHAPTER 5

Three revelatory gifts

BY doing what the early Pentecostals did in appealing to scripture for our definitions and illustrations, we can very soon rule out many of the expressions of these "gifts" by modern leaders in the current Charismatic cum Pentecostal camp. Take for example the last of the three manifestations that may be listed under this heading that of the *"discerning of spirits"*, which many wrongly call the gift of discernment thus justifying all sorts of character and personality analysis. Biblically there is no such gift as "discernment", which really describes an ability, which some people are better able to exercise than others. The gift is called the *"discerning of spirits"*. So the area is established, being an enabling by the Holy Spirit to discern whether a person is operating by a false, wrong or evil spirit as opposed to the Spirit of God. Acts 16:16-1816 is a case in point, being the classic biblical example of the operation of this supernatural gift for the protection of the Gospel and of the church. Interestingly the expression "spirit of divination" (v16) is *"pneuma"* (Strong 4151) *"Puthon"* (Strong 4436) literally a "spirit of a python", which identifies the source of the spirit by which the girl from Philippi was operating. Divination and clairvoyance in its various forms e.g. fortune-telling is part of the devil's play-things and sadly, forms of it have invaded the church, sometimes under the guise of the so called gifts of the Holy Spirit. By clearly establishing your biblical definition *"discerning of spirits"* not discernment per se, you immediately establish a safeguard. That was one reason why I could be so certain about Frank Houston's false statement about me that I referred to earlier.17

The early Pentecostals frequently experienced the operation of this particular manifestation of the Holy Spirit. CWM published something relating to my own father in the early days of Pentecost in Wales, when he discerned that a man who was seeking leadership was in fact a spiritist18. A Welsh preacher told me how my paternal uncle, the late David Powell left the platform where he was due to preach and walked up to two women who sat in the congregation identifying them as witches, who had come to spy on God's people and how he (the young preacher) became confirmed in his calling into the ministry by the event and what transpired subsequently. When I related this to my uncle he said that he had many experiences like that in his early ministry. It is the shining forth of the Holy Spirit in His protective ministry within the church. This is a gift that has virtually disappeared from within the Pentecostal movement and the reason is two-fold: Firstly, we have glamorised the gifts when relating them to men to whom we have attributed a super-star image and secondly, we have accepted counterfeit operations, which have no biblical basis. The Holy Spirit who honours God's Word above God's Name19 is displeased and will withdraw if we fail to take God's Word seriously in respect of our service.

These principles apply to the other two revelatory gifts viz. *"the word of wisdom"* and *"the word of knowledge"* and in a sense to all of the gifts. At this point it is important to note that these are not "gifts" of wisdom and knowledge. The wording is important. God does not impart all of His wisdom or all of His knowledge both of which are infinite. Humans cannot contain either, so He gives just a fragment a *"word"* of His wonderful wisdom or His absolute knowledge. There is no such thing as a "gift of wisdom" or a "gift of knowledge". Early Pentecostals recognised and taught this well. Here are three quotes that will help in an understanding of my point:

"The Word of Knowledge is the supernatural revelation by the Holy Spirit of certain facts in the mind of God. God keeps ever before Him, in the storehouse of His mind all the facts of heaven and earth. He knows every person, place and thing in existence, and He is conscious of them all at the same time. It is not that He merely recalls them: that would be Memory. It is that He has them ever before Him: that is Knowledge. The Word of Knowledge is the revelation to man by His Spirit of some detail of His All-knowledge..."[20]

"The word of knowledge is a participation to some infinitesimal degree, in the omniscience of God...any fragment of His unlimited knowledge".[21]

"It is 'a' word of knowledge. There is no definite article in the Greek. It is therefore a fragmentary revelation, a minute portion of the vast treasures of knowledge that are in Christ (Colossians 2:3)....a manifestation of God's all-embracing comprehension, a particle of omniscience."22

We must always keep the biblical basis of examination before us. Sadly, in today's climate and church, it is far more popular to base things on experience especially if there is a degree of sensationalism associated with the experience. This is particularly so with the so-called *"word of knowledge"* as it is currently practised. People are instructed to let their imaginations loose regarding people and events and to experiment with so-called words of knowledge. This is highly dangerous and results in Pentecostal clairvoyance masquerading as a spiritual gift. The Bible, not experience, must be our guide and very significantly we have no sickness diagnosis by or through a manifestation of the Holy Spirit recounted in scripture. Certainly there are occasions where people are told by a word of knowledge, which is clearly not natural that they have been healed23 or will not be healed or are about to die.24 BUT there is not ONE case where the nature of a person's sickness is identified supernaturally. Yet this has been the major area of claims relating to the word of knowledge in our time.

Just one more illustration before we move on to the next section. During the 70s and 80s there was a popular preacher from America called Dick Mills, who was looked upon as a specialist in the area of the operation of what passed as the Word of Knowledge. His ability to quote texts from the Bible was remarkable. He would call people out from the congregation, or get others to call them out, and give them a series of verses with brief instruction relating to their "discerned" situation. The ostensible basis of this practice was the operation of the gifts of the word of knowledge and the word of wisdom wisdom being defined as applied knowledge it follows that the word of wisdom relates to guidance.

Dick Mills was guest speaker at an AoG Conference held in Canberra in the mid 1980s. One night he or the conference organisers nominated another preacher to call people out for a "word". My wife Kathleen and I were among a number so chosen. Mr Mills said some nice things about us, mixing his statement with verses from the Bible and then told us that someone would oppose us and that the Lord would deal with that person. Remarkably the Bible verses seemed to fit and what Dick Mills said appeared to be almost accurate but not quite. In hindsight what happened then did more harm than good though it produced no ultimate ill probably because we refused to put too much store by it.

Significantly Dick Mills told the conference one night that he would give words regarding financial blessing to people the next day, a row at a time so they needed to be careful where they sat. That night he contracted laryngitis and that was the last time he spoke at the conference, which left me with a question: How could Dick Mills see things relating to others when he didn't know his own lot the very next day and made a false promise about what he would do? Again I strongly recommend that you read Watchman Nee's *The Latent Power of the Soul*".

Nee claims he could practise this type of clairvoyance, but refused to do so, because it is occult and wrong.

CHAPTER 6

Demonstration and Power of the Spirit

ALL of the manifestations of the Holy Spirit are supernatural. From a human perspective, however, the gifts of FAITH, HEALINGS and MIRACLES are more spectacular than the others. A failure to differentiate between the truly supernatural and the merely sensational has contributed to the humanising and consequent degrading process that has occurred in respect of the "miracles" of our time. Other acts, attitudes and expectations have contributed to this situation. For example in the mid 1980s AoG sponsored a conference in Brisbane, Australia on the theme of Signs and Wonders with Paul (later changed to David) Cho Yongi of Korea, popularly called Dr Yongi Cho, as the publicised guest speaker.[25] After the event John Lewis, a member of the organising committee quipped, "There weren't any signs and everyone has been wondering ever since." There are a number of reasons why nothing happened. Apart from other things the emphasis and expectation were wrong. If we read and understand our Bibles we will know that Christ the head of the church won't provide a miracle sideshow to titillate or to satisfy inquisitive carnal seekers after sensational displays (see Appendix 4).

As a boy I recall the late Percy Brewster, well-known Elim preacher in the UK, telling how God dealt with him regarding this issue. He was the pastor of the City Temple in Cardiff, South Wales and a popular evangelist. One day, as he drove through a town where his crusade was being advertised on various hoardings, he was convicted about the wording, which offered signs and wonders and healings and miracles in the meetings. He said that from then on he changed his tack, advertising only the Gospel of Christ and the fact that the sick would be prayed for in the meetings. He bore testimony to the fact that this modest and modified approach produced genuine lasting fruit.

Interestingly the first manifestation of the Holy Spirit among these more spectacular gifts is called "faith". In effect Paul says, "To another is given by the Spirit FAITH ..." (1 Corinthians 12:8&9). This is what classic Pentecostals refer to as the Gift of Faith. It is foundational to the miracle displays of the gifts of healings and the working of miracles, just as the word of wisdom is foundational to the revelatory expressions of the word of knowledge and the discerning of spirits, wisdom being the principal thing as Proverbs 4:7[26] explains. Faith is basic to Christian living and is the one virtue on which all others are built. We read, "Now abides faith, hope love..." (1 Corinthians 13:13) and Hebrews 11:6 reminds us that "without faith it is impossible to please Him for he who comes to God must believe that He is and that He is a rewarder of them that diligently seek Him." Faith contains the element of trust and it is this passive aspect of faith, which is emphasised in the gift of faith, which early Pentecostals defined as the faith for miracles.

Howard Carter, a pioneer of Assemblies of God in Great Britain, although he was a man who did not conform to the structured denomination and frequently operated independently of it, explained the difference between the gift of faith and the working of miracles by referring to the Old Testament characters of Daniel and Samson. When the spirit came upon Samson there were spectacular shinings forth of His power in miraculous displays of strength. For example we read:

"Then Samson went down, with his father and his mother, to Timnah, and came to the vineyards of Timnah: and, a young lion roared at him. And the Spirit of the LORD came mightily upon him, and he tore it as he would have torn a kid, and he had nothing in his hand:"

Judges 14:5-6

This, says Howard Carter, is a biblical example of the "working of miracles." Daniel in the Lions' den, on the other hand, is a good example of the gift of faith, being the divinely bestowed enabling to trust the Lord in an extreme situation. I heard Mr Carter humorously suggest that if you put Samson in a den of lions there would be skin and hair flying everywhere, whereas with Daniel in there, all was calm and the lions were under complete control.

Scripture distinguishes between saving faith the gift of God for salvation in which all Christians are equal (Ephesians 2:8)[27], faith for service which differs according to calling (Romans 12:3)[28] and this gift of the Holy Spirit being extraordinary faith for miracles. Each is foundational in its particular realm.

Saving faith is basic to salvation and all associated with it. Hope and love are built on faith and not visa versa as some teach. It is because of faith that we have hope and love and everything else in the Christian life.

Faith is the rationale of the Kingdom and so each person is provided with adequate faith to serve in the capacity of his calling, which differs from one person to another. For this reason it is wrong to suggest, as some do, that a person can serve and act under the "anointing" of another person e.g. the so-called senior pastor. Just as God has no grandchildren in respect of life, so He has no second-class servants in respect of ministry. Each of us is directly responsible to the Great Shepherd who provides the grace and the gift to do His bidding.

Supernatural faith, the manifestation of the Holy Spirit, is governed by this same principle while operating at a higher level. It is sovereignly given and is a prerequisite to the operation of the miraculous displays of God in the gifts of healings and the working of miracles.

Sadly, the Word of Faith practitioners such as Kenneth Hagin and Kenneth Copeland have distorted the Bible view of faith so much that the elements of trust and endurance are perceived by some to be vices rather than virtues, but these are the essence of Christian life and service. Without the faith to endure there is no faith to perform miracles or anything else. Job declared, "Though he slay me, yet will I trust in him" (Job 13:15) and we read in Hebrews chapter 11 of others who,

"were tortured, not accepting deliverance; that they might obtain a better resurrection: And others had trial of cruel mockings and scourgings, yes, of bonds and imprisonment: They were stoned, they were sawn in two, were tempted, were slain with the sword: they wandered about in sheepskins and goatskins; being destitute, afflicted, tormented; (Of whom the world was not worthy:) they wandered in deserts, and in mountains, and in dens and caves of the earth. And all these, having obtained a testimony through faith, did not receive the promise"

Hebrews 11:35-39

This supernatural gift of faith prevails in all circumstances and is the prerequisite to the performance of miracles, which partially accounts for the fact that genuine miracles are normally experienced among people who are persecuted for their faith. These have received the "dunamis" of the Spirit promised by Christ in Acts chapter one to become His witnesses (martyrs) as He promised[29].

My observation after more than 40 years of full-time ministry experience, in a number of countries including the third world, is that we need to radically change our expectation and action in respect of the performance of miracles and the ministry of healing within the backslidden decadent church of the west by recognising five things:

Firstly, that the promise regarding the signs following spoken of by Christ in Mark 16[30] relates to the missionary mandate, so the fulfilment is to be expected at the real cutting edge of missionary endeavour and not in big crusade events in our largely gospel hardened and Christ rejecting countries.

Secondly, that the promise about healing and miracles, in the evangelistic setting, is predicated upon preaching the GOSPEL of Christ not the money message of our time.

Thirdly, that we need to get away from the superstar image in respect of the operation of the gifts of the Holy Spirit and return to the simple truth that these gifts are resident in the local church, where they should function in a quiet and natural manner.

Fourthly, that James chapter 5[31] provides for the healing of those who trust God and His Word and that to chase after the latest "evangelist" on the block is to despise the provision and Word of the Lord and to put faith in men.

Fifthly, that God is sovereign in all His workings and is NOT our servant to do our pleasure or meet our needs. We are His servants and that means we obey His Word in all things.

CHAPTER 7

Prophecy, Tongues and Interpretation

THE early Pentecostals made a definite distinction between what they referred to as the "simple" gift of prophecy and the function or office of the prophet. The purpose of the former is clearly established in 1 Corinthians 14:3 *"edification* (i.e. building up) *and exhortation* (i.e. stirring up) *and comfort* (i.e. cheering up)*"* whereas the position and purpose of the latter is explained in Ephesians 2:20 and 4:11,[32] which is a major part of the theme of part seven of this book.

Classic Pentecostalism taught that simple prophecy does not contain the predictive or directive elements, which are the province of the "prophet" who is open to examination or judgment as the scriptures require *"Let two or three prophets speak, and let the others judge"* (1 Corinthians 14:29). This distinction, which I think is valid in degree, does tend to open the simple gift of prophecy to abuse rendering it inane and innocuous. If scripture does in fact support the distinction, then a case can be made for the idea that simple prophecy is not subject to the judgment by *"the others"* that Paul refers to. This has resulted in a situation where many of us have experienced and recoiled at the senseless or useless things that are said in the name of "prophecy". Clearly it has not been a "shining forth" (manifestation) of the Holy Spirit. The safeguard here is that scripture encourages us to "judge" all things (c/f 1 Thessalonians 5:21 with 1 John 4:1-4). In the case of those who prophesy or think they do, this "judgment" should be done by the leader in the meeting.

On the other hand a recognising that "prophets" should be judged did help to protect a section of the early Pentecostal movement from the bizarre utterances and actions of those who adopted the Apostolic Prophetic model of the early to mid 20th century Pentecostal revival. A number of humorous stories are told of alleged happenings within the so-called apostolic movement of that time. One was about a local "prophet" who said, "Lo my people, you are before me as cabbages. Some of you have soft hearts; some of you have hard hearts; and some of you have no hearts at all."

Another is alleged to have arrived after the meeting had been going for quite some time. Being the "set' prophet in that particular church he was expected to say something. Unfortunately he got wind of what had been happening and so pronounced: "Lo my people I have heard that you have been dancing before me. If I had been here I would have danced with you."

The early 20th century Apostolic Church in Britain adopted the idea that apostles rule and prophets direct, so, in effect, they became the governing body of the local and/or national church. This has no biblical warrant as we hope to clearly show in Part 7. It has the potential to lead to all sorts of abuses and bizarre happenings. In truth everything should be judged i.e. examined or tested by everyone but especially by leaders to protect the Lord's people from the nonsensical and dangerous things that might be done or said in the Name of the Lord. This is probably why Paul's mention of the gift of prophecy is immediately followed by his reference to the discerning of spirits. It is also one reason why we have the Bible, the Word of God, which should always be our yardstick of examination.

Paul elevates prophecy to the top of the list of the manifestations of the Holy Spirit when he instructs: *"Pursue love, and desire spiritual gifts, but rather that you may prophesy"* (1 Corinthians 14:1). This can only be understood and is best explained in the overall context of Paul's argument in this chapter. He is emphasising the fact that all operations or manifestations in the local meeting of the church should be for the *"edifying"* (building up) of the body and not for selfish use. For this reason he permits tongues speaking ONLY if it is accompanied by interpretation (v28) and he regulates the number of occasions for the operation of these two gifts (v27)[33]. He tells us that the operation of the gift of prophecy is greater than that of speaking in tongues unless interpretation takes place (v5)[34]. His entire argument relates to understanding and edification as verse 12 explains: *"Even so since you are zealous for spiritual gifts, seek that you may excel for the edifying of the church."*

True prophecy is the best and most direct way to edify the church as that is its very purpose as verse 3 explains: *"But he that prophesies speaks edification, and exhortation, and comfort to all."* While preaching per se is not the same as prophesying all true preaching will contain prophecy and this is the main vehicle by which the gift of prophecy and the ministry of the prophet (see Part 7) operates. If a preacher truly represents the Lord then his preaching will leave little if any need for something additional by way of prophecy. However, and here's the point, there are those who do and should operate the gift of prophecy and in fact any of the nine manifestations of the Holy Spirit, who may not be the appointed or recognised preacher or leader in a given local church.

This matter of the edifying of the church being the principal point of Paul's discussion here, also explains the difficult sections of this chapter especially verses 15 to 20[35] and 21 to 26[36] where we have the interaction of tongues speaking with the gift of prophecy. Paul does not despise speaking in tongues, which some have dubbed the least of the gifts though scripture never refers to it in that way. Contrary to the claims of some 1 Corinthians chapter 14 does not condemn tongues speaking at any time. Paul is simply correcting its abuse and misuse. This is abundantly clear as witness the fact that when he tells the church that they should not pray or sing in tongues, unless the praying and singing is interpreted, he adds a commendation (not condemnation) about giving thanks in tongues and cites his own practice of tongues speaking in verses 17 and 18: *"truly you give thanks well, but the other is not edified. I thank my God, I speak with tongues more than you all."* He then goes on to say that he deliberately chooses to teach in a known language rather than engage in speaking in tongues in the church. Why? So that the entire church may be edified,

"Yet in the church I had rather speak five words with my understanding, that by my voice I might teach others also, than ten thousand words in an unknown tongue."

1 Corinthians 14:19

The great purpose of our gathering together as a local body of believers is that we may edify, i.e. build up each other for the benefit of the whole.

The most difficult section is verses 21 to 26, where we have an apparent contradiction. The latter part of verse 22 reads: *"prophesying serves not for them that do not believe, but for them which believe"* while verses 24 and 25 state,

"But if all prophesy, and there come in one that does not believe, or one uninformed, he is convinced by all, he is judged by all: And thus the secrets of his heart made manifest; and so falling down on his face he will worship God, and report that God is in you of a truth."

In the first verses of this section Paul clearly states that tongues speaking is a sign to unbelievers, while prophecy serves believers, then he gives an illustration where prophecy serves, and becomes a sign to, unbelievers. How do we reconcile this apparent contradiction? We must look at the whole of the teaching of Paul on the subject in this chapter.

In verse 6 we read: *"Now, brethren, if I come to you speaking with tongues, what shall I profit you, except I shall speak to you either by revelation, or by knowledge, or by prophesying, or by doctrine?"*

The inference is that the manifestation of the Holy Spirit in tongues speaking may contain other supernatural manifestations including prophecy. This clearly happened on the day of Pentecost when ordinary Galileans spoke in languages, which they had not learned and could not understand. To those who heard them and could understand the languages their speaking in tongues became prophecy. The Bible says that they were speaking the *"wonderful works of God"* (Acts 2:11), which could of course imply revelation, teaching and/or knowledge, all of the things that Paul lists in this verse. This became prophecy to those who sat in the place of the uninformed or who were unbelievers.

While it is important to establish our teaching by scripture alone, it is legitimate to illustrate our doctrine from experience. The early Pentecostals often referred to incidents, when the above occurred. My own mother, who, as I write this, is in her 91st year, tells how on an occasion when she was staying at a Christian camp in Belgium, was impressed to go for a walk while a meeting was in progress. In the fairly extensive grounds of that camp setting Mum came across a group of gypsies and began to loudly speak in tongues over them. As she continued to speak in a language she had not learned and did not understand, many of these people fell on their faces weeping and apparently seeking God. My mother was and is convinced that she prophesied to them. Shortly afterwards there were reports of revival breaking out among the gypsies of Europe.

My late paternal uncle, David Powell (1909-2001) told me how during the war years in Britain a Pentecostal minister from Europe visited the Hampstead Bible College in London during the time when he was a student there under the leadership of principal Howard Carter. Someone from the college was assigned to show this visitor, who could not speak English, the sites of London. They visited Westminster Bridge and the Houses of Parliament, St Paul's Cathedral etc, and all the time the only communication was by hand signs emphasising an occasional word, which it was hoped the visitor would somehow understand.

Suddenly the visitor burst forth in perfect English speaking of the marvels of God's wonders and ways.

This type of occurrence is exceptional, but there are a number of similar illustrations that I have heard about, several relating to speaking in Hebrew by those who had not learned and did not understand what was being spoken. This is the only valid basis to reconcile what otherwise would be a contradiction in Paul's teaching on the manifestations of speaking in tongues and prophecy in the local church. It is perfectly acceptable so long as it is recognised that these are exceptional occurrences under the sovereignty of God. They should not be expected as a normal expression of tongues speaking.

This leaves us with two additional questions that we should attempt to answer:

1) What is meant by the reference to the law in verse 21, *"In the law it is written, With men of other tongues and other lips I will speak to this people; and yet for all that will they not hear me, says the Lord"* (1 Corinthians 14:21)? and 2) When, if ever, is it permissible to speak, pray or sing in tongues without interpretation?

Verse 21 is a clear reference to Isaiah 28:11&12, where some argue that the appeal is to judgment, so tongues speaking was a sign of judgment upon Israel and having served its purpose has now ceased. We addressed this false notion in an earlier article which was published in CETF Vol 7.1 so rather than develop the entire argument again I will simply quote the relevant section:

"In Corinthians Paul is addressing a Gentile church, as the apostle to the Gentiles c/f Acts 13:46 and Romans 15:16. The fact that he quotes from Isaiah 28:11&12, which relates to the Jews does not preclude the Gentiles whom Paul addresses. We readily acknowledge that the sign miracles that Jesus performed both vindicated Him in His person and validated His claims and therefore need never be repeated. They were signs of His true identity and His great mission and purpose in His first advent. However that does not mean that the "sign" of tongues speaking and by implication that of prophecy is to be understood in the same sense, which some cessationists argue. Take a careful look at Isaiah chapter 28 in its full context. In 1 Corinthians 14:21 Paul quotes Isaiah 28:11 & 12 and applies it to his teaching about tongues speaking in Corinth. Now some are very quick to point out that the Isaiah reference is that of judgment and therefore they say the "sign" that Paul alludes to is also one of judgment? But is that really the case? The judgment spoken of in Isaiah is the result of refusing the message, *"We have made a covenant with death"* verse 15, but hot on the heels of the pronouncement of judgment comes the promise of salvation,

"And your covenant with death shall be disannulled" verse 18. The message of Isaiah 28 alternates between judgement and blessing, as does 1 Corinthians 14:21-25, where the "sign" is made to apply equally to Jew and Gentile.

To ignore this is to ignore the sense of Paul's teaching, which quite clearly had application to the Christians Jews and Gentiles at Corinth. What happened at Pentecost as recorded in Acts chapter 2 is essentially an illustration of what Paul is maintaining here. Tongues speaking that is initiated and motivated by the Holy Spirit will have a dual impact. To those "unbelievers" who recognise the language and are open to receive from God it becomes a sign that God is truly at work. Conversely, those who do not understand the language and are mere "mockers" (c/f Acts 2:13) are candidates for judgement, though they may be rescued through the preaching of the Gospel in the known common tongue, as were 3,000 on the Day of Pentecost. By applying the scripture in a national corporate sense you miss the individual application. Some see corporate "baptisms", corporate "judgments", and corporate "signs" while others see it all more from an individual perspective. It really does depend on what is your basic presupposition."[37]

The point is that we should be careful about a superficial dismissal of the relevance of any part of scripture on the basis of our accepted systematic theology or on the basis of dispensationalism[38], both of which are valid but need to be carefully examined if they tend to make sections of the Bible irrelevant to the current situation. God's Word being eternal is relevant for all time, situations and circumstances.

In 1 Corinthians 14:4 Paul writes: *"He that speaks in an unknown tongue edifies himself; but he that prophesies edifies the church."* This self-edification is not condemned by Paul on account of what it is in itself but on account of where it is being practised i.e. in the local church, where everything should be for the benefit of all. Some have tried to argue that the verb *"edify"* in this case is used in a bad sense, so it is wrong to speak in tongues without interpretation anywhere. But this is clearly false as witness Paul's later instructions not to forbid to speak in tongues (v39), his own example of speaking in tongues more than anyone else (v18) and his commendation of those who give thanks by tongues speaking (v17) *"...truly you give thanks well."*

Apart from that to argue this way is very poor exegesis[39] and bad hermeneutics[40]. The word "edify" may have various connotations in the New Testament and certainly it can be shown that on occasions it is used in a bad sense, while on other occasions it is used in a good sense, the context always supplying the true sense. To argue that the very same word when used in the very same sentence, let alone the entire context, may be used in both senses is stretching things a bit too far. If you are going to make it mean being puffed up in the first clause viz. *"he that speaks in an unknown tongue PUFFS HIMSELF UP"* and then make the very same word mean something not only different but the opposite in the next clause viz *"but he that prophesies BUILDS UP the church"* then it appears to me that you really are playing around with the Word of God and engaging in private interpretation to suit your own particular view.

On balance the classic Pentecostal position and teaching on this matter would appear to be the ONLY valid explanation of Paul's instruction viz that speaking, i.e. praying or singing in tongues, where there is no interpretation, is permissible in private but is not permissible in the public gathering of God's people, where the entire emphasis is on building up the church and not on self-edification. This of course means that the current practice by Pentecostal and Charismatic leaders of encouraging an entire congregation to speak or sing in tongues is definitely wrong. Paul says we can quite rightly say that such people are mad see verse 23.

When I was quite young in the ministry we befriended a student from the Assemblies of God Bible School at Kenley, UK. The principal was a good man and I doubt that he should be held responsible for this person's experience. It is an example of the way things can get out of hand even under good leadership. This young man told me how he and others would pray in tongues alone and then give a so-called interpretation. He maintained that they were encouraged to do this, either by senior Bible College students or by lecturers. He told me how he did this in respect of his proposed marital situation. Bad as that was he even shared his experiences with the person whom he desired to marry and when she turned him down he became totally disillusioned. Speaking in tongues as a form of prayer or praise appears to be permitted by Paul but clearly speaking in tongues followed by interpretation of tongues is ONLY for the public gathering of God's people where everything is open to examination by others. What this young man did was simply an exercise in wish fulfilment. It is unbiblical and dangerous.

One more illustration and then I will conclude this section. Again it relates to my youth. In fact I was about 12 years of age at the time. Our family was about to emigrate to New Zealand from Wales. We attended the general conference of Assemblies of God in Britain. I was very interested in spiritual matters and had a keen desire for the reality of the things of God. During the week I met up with a group of Bible College students who were of course several years my senior. They asked me if I spoke in tongues and they put on a performance of tongues speaking encouraging me to participate. I recoiled and refused. The manifestations of the Holy Spirit are not by our initiation but as the Bible teaches, *"dividing separately as HE (the Holy Spirit) wills"* (1 Corinthians 12:11).

The same Holy Spirit who sovereignly clothed Himself with Gideon, who endued the early church with divine enabling and who sovereignly and uniquely filled David Morgan with His power is the same Holy Spirit who is available to clothe Himself with the faithful remnant in our day and generation.

We need HIM more than most of us realise or are willing to acknowledge.

APPENDICES

1

Theophanies or Christophanies

A THEOPHANY is a visible manifestation of God to man. Theologians frequently apply the word to certain occasions in the Bible when an angel appeared to bring an important message or to perform a particular task, especially when the context indicates that the visitor is greater than an ordinary angel as, for example, when he accepts worship or speaks in the first person as being God. These appearances are generally attributed to the second person of the trinity based on Micah 5:2 *"But you Bethlehem Ephratah, though you are little among the thousands of Judah, yet out of you shall come forth to me he that is to be ruler in Israel; whose goings forth have been from of old, from everlasting"* and other passages. This idea based on the Bible gave rise to the term Christophany, which is viewed as an appearance of Christ before the incarnation.

Stephen the first Christian martyr says that *"an angel of the Lord"* appeared *"in a flame of fire in a bush"* and that the law was *"received ... by the disposition* (i.e. administration or ministry) *of angels"* (Acts 7:30&53) and identifies Moses as being *"in the assembly in the wilderness with the angel who spoke to him in the mount ..."* (v38). Yet the Old Testament passage, which describes God appearing in the burning bush, makes no mention of an angel and much later Moses himself declines to accept God's offer to *"send an angel"* before the Children of Israel, requiring that God Himself goes before them see Exodus 3:1-6 c/f chapter 33:1-17. Joshua encounters a personage who is identified as *"the captain of the LORD'S host"* to whom Joshua is commanded to pay homage in the same way as Moses was required at the burning bush c/f Joshua 5:13-15.

In Judges 2:1-4 we read,

"And an angel of the LORD came up from Gilgal to Bochim, and said, I made you to go up out of Egypt, and have brought you to the land which I swore to your fathers; and I said, I will never break my covenant with you. And you shall make no covenant with the inhabitants of this land; you shall throw down their altars: but you have not obeyed my voice: why have you done this? Therefore I also said, I will not drive them out from before you; but they shall be as thorns in your sides, and their gods shall be a snare to you. And it came to pass, when the angel of the LORD spoke these words to all the children of Israel, that the people lifted up their voice, and wept."

The language used here makes it very clear that it was no ordinary angel. The fact that he takes the credit for bringing the Israelites out from Egypt and making the covenant with them, indicates that here we have a theophany or christophany.

Based on this and the appearance of the angel to Samson's parents, where he identifies His name as being secret (Judges 13:18) i.e. Hebrew *"pele"* = "wonderful" or more accurately "miracle" being the same identical term that is applied to Christ in Isaiah 9:6 *"His name shall be called WONDERFUL (pele)"* it is felt by some that each of the four appearances of angels in the book of Judges (chapters 2, 5 (verse 23), 6 and 13) are in fact theophanies or christophanies. The matter is somewhat conjectural though not without reasonable substance.

In Judges 6:12 the theophany is identified as *"the angel of the LORD"* i.e. Jehovah the Covenant God in relation to Gideon. In verse 20 this same being is referred to as *"the angel of God"* i.e. *"elohiym"* = the Creator working miracles for His creatures and especially for His servant Gideon.

"And the angel of the LORD appeared to him, and said to him, The LORD is with you, you mighty man of valour"

Judges 6:12

APPENDIX 2

Mighty Man of Valour

THE Hebrew translated *"mighty man of valour"* is *"gibbor"* (noun *"geber"*) = "strong, mighty" + *"chayil"* = "strength, might, efficiency, wealth, army."

The Companion Bible (Bullinger Publications Trust © 1964, 1970, 1974) states,

"There are four principal words rendered "man", and these must be carefully discriminated. ... They represent him from four different points of view:

> *1.* *'Adam,* denotes his *origin* as being made from "the dust of *Adamah*" ground (Latin, *homo*);
>
> 2. *'Ish*, has regard to *sex*, a male (Latin, *vir*);
>
> *3.* *'Enosh,* has regard to his *infirmities*, as physically mortal, and as to character, *incurable*;
>
> *4.* *'Geber,* has respect to his *strength, a mighty man.*

Companion Bible, Appendix 14. iv *"Geber* First occurrence is Genesis 6:4,[1] *mighty men,* and denotes man in respect of his physical strength, as *'Enosh,* does in respect of the depravity of his nature. It is rendered "man" 67 times, "mighty" twice, "man-child' once, "every-one" once. In the Septuagint rendered 14 times *anthropos* and the rest by *aner.* For illustrative passages see Exodus 10:11, 12:37; 1 Samuel 16:18; 2 Samuel 23:1; Numbers 24:3 & 15; 1 Chronicles 26:12, 28:1; 2 Chronicles 13:3; Ezra 4:21, 5:4, 10; 6:8.

[1] In Genesis 6:4, we have three out of the above four words: *"daughters of MEN"* (= daughters of {the man} *'Adam*); *"mighty men"* (= *"geber*); *"men of renown"* (= Heb *men ('Enosh) of name* i.e. renowned for their moral depravity.

APPENDIX 3

Laying on Hands Impartation

THE NKJ rendering of 1 Timothy 5:22 reads, *"Do not lay hands on anyone hastily, or share in other people's sins; keep yourself pure."* Being set as it is in the context of the conduct of elders and of the attitude of young pastor Timothy towards them, no doubt the principal application of this instruction of Paul relates to the appointment to office. Timothy was told not to be hasty in his appointing elders in local churches, for if they subsequently sinned he would be to some extent implicated. However in the light of the whole counsel of God there is undoubtedly a wider interpretation and application, which relates to the communication of evil and to the doctrine of the laying on of hands c/f Hebrews 6:2.

Haggai the prophet is commanded to ask two questions of the priests:

"Thus says the LORD of hosts; Ask the priests concerning the law, saying, If one bear holy flesh in the fold of his garment, and with it touch bread, or stew, or wine, or oil, or any meat, shall it be holy? And the priests answered and said, No. Then said Haggai, If one that is unclean because of a dead body touch any of these, shall it be unclean? And the priests answered and said, It shall be unclean"
Haggai 2:11-13

The conclusion is clear. Holiness and righteousness cannot be communicated by touch but evil and wickedness can.

"Then Haggai answered, and said, So is this people, and so is this nation before me, says the LORD; and so is every work of their hands; and that which they offer there is unclean" (v 14).

In putting these two questions to the priests, the prophet emphasised their primary role and responsibility being that of interpreting and applying the law, so that they were able to distinguish between the holy and the profane. This is made clear by several passages in the Bible, for example Deuteronomy 33:10, *"They shall teach Jacob your judgments, and Israel your law"* and Malachi 2:7, *"For the priest's lips should keep knowledge, and they should seek the law at his mouth: for he is the messenger of the LORD of hosts."*

To maintain this, Aaron and his sons were not allowed to drink intoxicating beverage while on duty as Leviticus 10:8-10 explains,

"And the LORD spoke to Aaron, saying, Do not drink wine or strong drink, you or your sons with you, when you go into the tabernacle of the congregation, lest you die: it shall be a statute forever throughout your generations: And that you may differentiate between holy and unholy, and between unclean and clean."

It is not without significance that those who promoted the so-called laughing revival a la Rodney Howard-Browne constantly referred to being "drunk" or "intoxicated". One of the things that convinced me that it was unclean, was a testimony by Ken Gott, AoG pastor from Sunderland England, which was recorded at the IBTI (International Bible Training Institute), UK. He related how he became "drunk" at Toronto Airport Church and crawled across the car park and through the foyer of the hotel where he was staying. Sadly the congregation laughed thinking what he described was great fun. As a consequence of this curse that emanated from Toronto, ministers became confused about the holy and the profane. An evil unclean spirit influenced them and through them impacted the church. The prophet Haggai explains this danger.

The modern doctrine of IMPARTATION, which has been popularised by the Toronto and Pensacola Revival teachers and promoters, is extremely dangerous, especially in the light of the disgraceful exposures of the moral failures of some of its top advocates. The Bible, not experience must be our guide at all times. Paul wrote:

"Do not receive an accusation against an elder, except from two or three witnesses. Them that sin rebuke before all that others also may fear. I charge you before God, and the Lord Jesus Christ, and the elect angels, that you observe these things without preferring one before another, doing nothing by partiality. Lay hands suddenly on no man, neither be a partaker of other men's sins: keep yourself pure"

1 Timothy 5:19-22

APPENDIX 4

Miracles, Signs & Wonders

We need to recognise three things:

1. The Unique Position of Christ

Peter declared on the day of Pentecost:

"Men of Israel, hear these words; Jesus of Nazareth, a man approved of God among you by MIRACLES and WONDERS and SIGNS, which God did by Him in the midst of you, as you yourselves also know"

Acts 2:22

The word MIRACLES defines the supernatural workings of God. It is a general term that describes God's supernatural interventions in nature or in human affairs so that the process and/or end result is entirely different from what it would have been if no miracle had occurred. The word WONDERS describes the effect upon people who observe genuine miracles. It is the sense of awe that accompanies true supernatural interventions and is one test that can be applied to determine if the work is truly God's work. SIGNS are genuine miracles but they point to something outside of themselves e.g. a principle upon which God operates or, in the case of Christ, a proof of His identity and the nature of His ministry.

In the above text Peter tells us that miracles, wonders and signs in the life and ministry of Christ witnessed to His authenticity and the accuracy of His claims. These facts are true of Christ and not of any other human being. Miracles do not authenticate other people either as to their character or to the genuineness of their message. They have been granted by God to follow the preaching of the Gospel and so in our case if and when they occur they approve the message and not the man or his ministry.

2. Supernatural or Sensational

Miracles are more than unusual occurrences. When attributed to God or to the servants of God they are to be defined as supernatural interventions in nature or in human affairs so that the process and/or end result is entirely different from what it would have been if no miracle had occurred. Miracles may or may not be sensational, but they are always supernatural. Today many people are conned into thinking that sensational happenings such as prostrations or what people call being slain in the spirit are supernatural. They are not. Unfortunately the word "miracle" is used very loosely today both by the world and by the church. The antics of televangelists add more confusion. No genuine miracle has ever been documented from Benny Hinn's worldwide ministry in spite of his many claims. One person died as a result of his so called "slaying in the spirit" activity. The family sued the Benny Hinn ministries for $15 million dollars. There was an out-of-court settlement. These facts and many more are documented in *The Confusing World of Benny Hinn* and *Benny Hinn Unmasked* both of which are available from Christian Witness Ministries, P.O. Box 353, Loch Sport Vic 3851, Australia. Phone + 61 3 5146 0280; fax + 61 3 5146 0270. Email: maureen@christian-witness.org

3. Signs and Wonders in Scripture

Of the 14 times the expression "signs and wonders" appear in scripture (5 in the OT and 9 in the NT see list of texts below) half of them (seven) have clear reference to judgment or to deception, while the idea of judgment is not absent from the other seven. The point that I am making is that the expression "signs and wonders" frequently involves what we might call a negative connotation. If you add the fact that during His life and ministry Jesus deliberately discouraged sign seeking and sign seekers, then the picture is very different from the one that has generally been presented to us by Pentecostals and Charismatics c/f Matthew 16:1-4 with John 4:48:

"The Pharisees also came with the Sadducees, and testing him requested that he would show them a sign from heaven. He answered and said to them, When it is evening, you say, It will be fair weather: for the sky is red. And in the morning, It will be foul weather today: for the sky is red and threatening. O you hypocrites, you can discern the face of the sky; but you cannot discern the signs of the times A wicked and adulterous generation seeks after a sign; and no sign shall be given to it, but the sign of the prophet *Jonah. And he left them, and departed"*

Matthew 16:1-4 (John 4:48 see below)

It is this ungodly and unscriptural pursuit of sensationalism that has contributed to much of the false teaching and practices of our time. On the one hand it has contributed to the drift towards Rome with her emphasis upon mystical experiences such as healing at Lourdes and the visions of Fatima etc. On the other it has led to the enormous amount of confusion in the Pentecostal and Charismatic camp through the practices of men such as Benny Hinn and Rodney Howard-Browne with their hypnotic antics that have masqueraded as miracles. Now the two ecumenism and charismania have joined forces in a relentless drive towards the one-world church. That the early church prayed for signs and wonders (see the Acts references below) demonstrates the fact that all genuine miraculous expressions are under the Sovereignty of God.

*"And the LORD showed signs and wonders before our eyes, great and severe, upon Egypt, Pharaoh, and all his household" (*Deuteronomy 6:22).

*"You showed signs and wonders upon Pharaoh, his servants, and on all the people of his land: for you knew that they acted proudly against them. So you made a name for yourself, as it is to this day" (*Nehemiah 9:10).

"You have set signs and wonders in the land of Egypt, to this day, and in Israel, and among other men; and have made a name for yourself, as it is to this day" (Jeremiah 32:20).

"I thought it good to declare the signs and wonders that the most high God has worked for me" (Daniel 4:2).

"He delivers and rescues and he works signs and wonders in heaven and in earth, who has delivered Daniel from the power of the lions" (Daniel 6:27).

"For there shall arise false christs, and false prophets, and shall show great signs and wonders; so that, if possible, they shall deceive even the elect" (Matthew 24:24).

"For false christs and false prophets shall rise, and shall show signs and wonders, to deceive, if possible, even the elect" (Mark 13:22).

"Then said Jesus to him, unless you see signs and wonders, you will not believe" (John 4:48).

"By stretching forth your hand to heal; that signs and wonders may be done through the name of your holy servant Jesus" (Acts 4:30).

"And by the hands of the apostles were many signs and wonders were done among the people; and they were all with one accord in Solomon's porch" (Acts 5:12).

"They stayed a long time speaking boldly in the Lord, who bore witness to the word of his grace, and granted signs and wonders to be done by their hands" (Acts 14:3).

"Through mighty signs and wonders, by the power of the Spirit of God; so that from Jerusalem, and as far as Illyricum, I have fully preached the gospel of Christ" (Romans 15:19).

"Truly the signs of an apostle were worked among you in all endurance, in signs and wonders and works of power" (2 Corinthians 12:12).

"God also bearing them witness, both with signs and wonders and with various acts of power, and gifts of the Holy Spirit, according to his own will?" (Hebrews 2:4).

APPENDIX 5

Systematic Theology and Dispensationalism

Spencer Gear, a great friend and supporter of CWM, provided me with the following definitions:

Systematic Theology

"Systematic theology is any study that answers the question, 'What does the whole Bible teach us today?' about any given topic."

Wayne Grudem, *Systematic Theology*(England: Inter-Varsity Press, 1994, p21)

Grudem said that he obtained this definition from one of his professors in Westminster Seminary, California, John Frame. Grudem goes on:

"This definition indicates that systematic theology involves collecting and understanding all the relevant passages in the Bible on various topics and then summarizing their teachings clearly so that we know what to believe about each topic." (p21)

Dispensationalism

The following is a summary by Spencer Gear.

"Dispensationalism is a system of theology that explains God's unfolding administration of the world in various dispensations (usually seven) or stewardship arrangements. God has two distinct plans for the redeemed in Israel and in the church. There will be blessings on earth for Israel and heavenly blessings for the church. The distinction will be evident especially during the millennium.

In recent years, 'progressive dispensationalism' has been influential. Instead of two separate purposes for Israel and the church, there is a single purpose in which the kingdom of God is established, with both Israel and the church participating.

Both kinds of dispensationalism see the Old Testament prophecies concerning Israel to be fulfilled in the millennium by the ethnic Jews who will believe in Christ and live as a model nation in the land of Israel."

Henry Thiessen, a dispensationalist, sees the seven dispensations as follows:

A. **In the Past:** (1) The Edenic Period; (2) The Ante-Deluvian Period (pre-Noah's Flood); (3) The Post-Deluvian Period; (4 The Period of Mosaic Law;

B. **In the Present** (the Church Period);

C. **In the Future** (the Kingdom Period)

Henry C. Thiessen, *Introductory Lectures in Systematic Theology,* Eerdmans, 1949, pp 279-282

Charles Ryrie, a dispensationalist, described the dispensations as follows:

"At least three dispensations (as commonly understood in dispensationalism) are mentioned by Paul: one preceding the present time (Colossians 1:25-26), the present arrangement (Ephesians 3:2), and the future administration (Ephesians. 1:10). These three require a fourth one before the law, and a prelaw dispensation would seem to need to be divided into pre and post fall economies. Thus five administrations seem clearly distinguishable (at least within a premillennial understanding of scripture). The usual seven-fold scheme includes a new economy after the Noahic flood and another with the call of Abraham"

Evangelical Dictionary of Theology, Walter A. Elwell (Ed.). Baker Book House, 1984, p322

FOOTNOTES:

[1] *Gathering the Faithful Remnant* © CWM 2002 pg 51

[2] Orrel Steinkamp publisher of *The Plumbline* Newsletter may be contacted at 74425 Co. Rd. 21, Renville, MN 56284, USA email Orrel Steinkamp <onst@tds.net>

[3] *"Searching what, or what manner of time the Spirit of Christ which was in them did signify, when it testified beforehand the sufferings of Christ, and the glory that should follow"* (1 Peter 1:11).

[4] *"The prophet that has a dream, let him tell a dream; and he that has my word, let him speak my word faithfully. What is the chaff to the wheat? says the LORD. (Is not my word like as a fire? says the LORD; and like a hammer that breaks the rock in pieces? Therefore, behold, I am against the prophets, says the LORD, who steal my words every one from his neighbour. Behold, I am against the prophets, says the LORD, that use their tongues, and say, He says. Behold, I am against them that prophesy false dreams, says the LORD, and tell them, and cause my people to err by their lies, and by their recklessness; yet I did not send them, or commanded them: therefore they shall not profit this people at all, says the LORD"* (Jeremiah 23-28-32).

[5] *The Plumbline* - Vol 4, No 1 Feb/March 1999 page 1 - *"A Second Pentecost"*

[6] "The angel of the Lord came in the guise of a wayfaring man and sat under the oak of Ophrah. Angelic theophanies (see Appendix 1) occur elsewhere (Jud 2:1-4; 13:2 ff; c/f the oracle in 5:3). The locale of the appearance was the oak of Ophrah, somewhere in the vicinity of Shechem. It belonged to Joash the Manassehite of the clan of Abiezer (c/f Josh 17:2; Num 26:21)" *The Broadman Bible Commentary* Vol 2 page 414 © Broadman Press *First British Edition 1971* Marshall Morgan and Scott Ltd.

[7] Audio Taped messages by A.W. Tozer CWM Resource Catalogue - PO Box 341, Healesville, Vic, 3777, Australia phone +61 (0)3 5962 5426; fax +61 (0)3 5962 2615.

[8] *"And when the children of Israel cried to the LORD, the LORD raised up a deliverer to the children of Israel, who delivered them, Othniel the son of Kenaz, Caleb's younger brother. And the Spirit of the LORD came upon him, and he judged Israel, and went out to war: and the LORD delivered Chushanrishathaim king of Mesopotamia into his hand; and his hand prevailed against Chushanrishathaim"*(Judges 3:9-10). *"But the Spirit of the LORD came upon Gideon, and he blew a trumpet; and Abiezrites were gathered behind him"* (Judges 6:34). *"Then the Spirit of the LORD came upon Jephthah, and he passed through Gilead, and Manasseh, and passed through Mizpah of Gilead, and from Mizpah of Gilead he passed through to the children of Ammon"* (Judges 11:29) *"Then Samson went down,*

with his father and his mother, to Timnah, and came to the vineyards of Timnah: and, a young lion roared at him. And the Spirit of the LORD came mightily upon him, and he tore it as he would have torn a kid, and he had nothing in his hand: but he did not tell his father or mother what he had done" (Judges 14:5-6).

[9] Letter (24/12/01) from John Lewis AoG Assistant President, Australia.

[10] Letter (21/1201) from Wayne Hughes Gen Super AoG, New Zealand.

[11] *Preaching and Preachers* Hodder and Stoughton © 1971 D. Martyn Lloyd-Jones p 321-324.

[12] *"But the manifestation of the Spirit is given to every man for all to profit. For to one is given by the Spirit the word of wisdom; to another the word of knowledge by the same Spirit; To another faith by the same Spirit; to another the gifts of healing by the same Spirit; To another the working of miracles; to another prophecy; to another discerning of spirits; to another different kinds of tongues; to another the interpretation of tongues: But all these are operations of the one and the same Spirit, distributing to every man according to his will"* (1 Corinthians 12:7-11).

[13] *"But the fruit of the Spirit is love, joy, peace, longsuffering, kindness, goodness, faith, Meekness, self-control: against such there is no law"* (Galatians 5:22-23).

[14] CWM website
<http://www.christian-witness.org/archives/van1997/alpha1_97.html>
Book available from CWM see back cover for contact details.

[15] For further study on this theme, we recommend Jacob Prasch's 5-tape audio series [Ordering code: AJP3027-3031] entitled *The Gifts of the Spirit* available from Moriel Ministries Australia, P.O. Box 112, Trafalgar, Victoria 3824, Australia. Tel/Fax: +61 (0) 3 5633 2300. Email: moriel@vic.australis.com.au

[16] *"And as we went to prayer, a slave girl possessed with a spirit of divination met us, who brought her masters much gain by fortune telling: She followed Paul and us, and cried, saying, These men are the servants of the most high God, who show to us the way of salvation. And she this did for many days. But Paul, being very annoyed, turned and said to the spirit, I command you in the name of Jesus Christ to come out of her. And it came out the same hour"* (Acts 16:16-18).

[17] *Elijah Where Are You?* Section one, page 23.

[18] URL http://www.christian-witness.org/archives/cetf1998/homeatlast.html

[19] *"I will worship toward your holy temple, and praise your name for your loving kindness and for your truth: for you have magnified your word above all your name"* (Psalm 138:2).

[20] *The Gifts of the Spirit* by Harold Horton, London: Assemblies of God Publishing House, sixth edition 1960; p.48.

[21] *Questions and Answers on Spiritual Gifts* by Howard Carter, London: Assemblies of God Publishing House, 1946; p.33.

[22] *Spiritual Gifts;* by Aaron Linford, London: Assemblies of God Publishing House, no date; pp.63-64.

[23] *"And Jesus said to the centurion, Go your way; and as you have believed, so it*

shall be done to you. And his servant was healed that hour" (Matthew 8:13).

[24] *"Now therefore thus says the LORD, You shall not come down from that bed on which you are gone up, but you shall surely die. And Elijah departed"* (2 Kings 1:4).

[25] Cho's doctorate is questionable as are all those on whom he has bequeathed similar titles, including Andrew Evans. Their bona fides should be examined.

[26] "*Wisdom is the principal thing; therefore get wisdom: ....* " (Proverbs 4:7).

[27] *"For by grace you are saved through faith; and that not of yourselves: it is the gift of God"* (Eph 2:8).

[28] *"For I say, through the grace given to me, to every man that is among you, not to think of himself more highly than he ought to think; but to think soberly, according as God has dealt to every man the measure of faith"* (Romans 12:3).

[29] *"But you shall receive power* (dunamis), *after the Holy Spirit is come upon you: and you shall be witnesses* {Greek "martus"} to *me both in Jerusalem, and in all Judaea, and in Samaria, and to the uttermost part of the earth"* (Acts 1:8).

[30] *"And he said to them, Go into all the world, and preach the gospel to every creature. He that believes and is baptized shall be saved; but he that does not believe shall be damned. And these signs shall follow them that believe; In my name shall they cast out demons; they shall speak with new tongues; They shall take up serpents; and if they drink any deadly thing, it shall not hurt them; they shall lay hands on the sick, and they shall recover"* (Mark 16:15-18).

[31] *"Is any among you suffering? Let him pray. Is any merry? Let him sing psalms. Is any sick among you? Let him call for the elders of the church; and let them pray over him, anointing him with oil in the name of the Lord: And the prayer of faith shall save the sick, and the Lord shall raise him up; and if he has committed sins, they shall be forgiven him. Confess your offences one to another, and pray one for another, that you may be healed. The effectual fervent prayer of a righteous man avails much"* (James 5:13-16).

[32] *"And are built upon the foundation of the apostles and prophets, Jesus Christ himself being the chief cornerstone"* (Ephesians 2:20). *"And he gave some, apostles; and some, prophets; and some, evangelists; and some, pastors and teachers"* (Ephesians 4:11).

[33] *"If any man speak in an unknown tongue, let it be two, or at the most three, and each in turn; and let one interpret. But if there is no interpreter, let him keep silent in the church; and let him speak to himself, and to God"* (1 Corinthians 14:27-28).

[34] *"I wish that you all spoke with tongues, but rather that you prophesied: for greater is he that prophesies than he that speaks with tongues, except he interpret, that the church may receive edification"* (1 Corinthians 14:5).

[35] *"What is it then? I will pray with the spirit, and I will also pray with the understanding: I will sing with the spirit, and I will also sing with the understanding. Or else when you bless with the spirit, how shall he that occupies the place of the uninformed say amen at your giving of thanks, since he does not understand what you say? For truly you give thanks well, but the other is not edified. I thank my God, I speak with tongues more than you all: Yet in the church I would rather speak five*

words with my understanding, that I might teach others also, than ten thousand words in an unknown tongue. Brethren, do not be children in understanding: however in malice be children, but in understanding be mature" (1 Corinthians 14:15-20).

[36] *"In the law it is written, With men of other tongues and other lips I will speak to this people; and yet for all that will they not hear me, says the Lord. Therefore tongues are for a sign, not to them that believe, but to unbelievers: but prophesying is not for unbelievers, but for those who believe. If therefore the whole church comes together in one place, and all speak with tongues, if those that are uninformed, or unbelievers come in, will they not say that you are mad? But if all prophesy, and there come in an unbeliever, or uninformed, he is convinced by all, he is judged by all: And thus the secrets of his heart are manifest; and so falling down on his face he will worship God, and report that God is truly among you. How is it then, brethren? When you come together, every one of you has a psalm, has a teaching, has a tongue, has a revelation, has an interpretation. Let all things be done to build up"* (1 Corinthians 14:21-26).

[37] *CETF*, Vol 7:1 *Why the Fuss About Tongues*

[38] See Appendix 5 on *SYSTEMATIC THEOLOGY* and *DISPENSATIONALISM*.

[39] "Exegesis: critical explanation of a text, especially of Scripture" *Concise Oxford Dictionary*.

[40] "Hermeneutics: the branch of knowledge that deals with interpretation, especially of Scripture" ibid

PART THREE

Our Evangelistic Mandate

CHAPTER 1

What is Evangelism?
God releases redeemed reapers

EVANGELISM has been simply defined as, *"One beggar telling another beggar where to find food and drink."* Such recognises three things: 1) The human condition we are all beggars; 2) The human need we all need food and drink the bread and water of life; and 3) Human dependence upon God to reveal and to provide.

Sadly men have complicated the message and the process, which are not just modern failures, though probably the situation is worse now than ever before. Confusion rages about the message of the Gospel as well as the method by which we should seek to reach our generation. The church is confused, if not in total disarray, in respect of evangelism. This situation has arisen on three fronts, but there is one principal cause and reason, which has to do with the sovereignty of God. C.H. Spurgeon knew this well and addressed it in one of his early sermons. Here is what he said on January 7, 1855 in the New Park Street Chapel in Southwark, London, Great Britain.

"It has been said by someone that the 'proper study of mankind is man'. I will not oppose the idea, but I believe it is equally true that the proper study of God's elect is God; the proper study of a Christian is the Godhead. The highest science, the loftiest speculation, the mightiest philosophy, which can ever engage the attention of a child of God, is the name, the nature, the person, the work, the doings and the existence of the great God whom he calls the Father.

There is something exceedingly improving to the mind in a contemplation of the Divinity. It is a subject so vast, that all our thoughts are lost in its immensity; so deep, that our pride is drowned in its infinity. Other subjects we can compass and grapple with; in them we feel a kind of self-content, and can go our way with the thought, 'Behold I am wise'. But when we come to this master-science, finding that our plumb-line cannot sound its depth, and our eagle eye cannot see its height, we turn away with the thought that vain man would be wise, but he is like a wild ass's colt; and with solemn exclamation, 'I am but of yesterday and know nothing'. No subject of contemplation will tend more to humble the mind, than thoughts of God ...

But while the subject humbles the mind, it also expands it. He, who often thinks of God, will have a larger mind that the man who simply plods around this narrow globe .... The most excellent study for expanding the soul is the science of Christ, and Him crucified, and the knowledge of the Godhead in the glorious Trinity. Nothing will so enlarge the intellect, nothing so magnify the whole soul of man, as a devout, earnest, continued investigation of the great subject of the Deity.

And whilst humbling and expanding, this subject is eminently *consolatory*. Oh, there is, in contemplating Christ, a balm for every wound; in musing on the Father, there is a quietus for every grief; and in the influence of the Holy Ghost, there is a balsam for every sore. Would you lose your sorrow? Would you drown your cares? Then go, plunge yourself in the Godhead's deepest sea; be lost in His immensity; and you shall come forth as from a couch of rest, refreshed and invigorated. I know nothing which can so comfort the soul; so calm the swelling billows of sorrow and grief; so speak peace to the winds of trial, as a devout musing upon the subject of the Godhead. It is to that subject that I invite you this morning ..."[1]

These words, spoken nearly 150 years ago by C.H. Spurgeon, at the time only 20 years old, are just as true now as then, but our problem is that we have lost the art of thinking and meditating upon God. As a result our preaching and our evangelism have become man based and man related instead of God based and God related. We have exchanged a study of God, and a contemplation of the Godhead for a study of man and a preoccupation with mankind and have ended up with a humanistic gospel. By starting with man we end in a mess. If we begin with God we have a chance of ending in glory. With respect to evangelism it really is a question of the starting point anthropology or theology?

There was a time when things began to change in the preaching emphasis within evangelicalism from a declaration about God's power to meet man's plight to a pandering to the "felt" human need. Clichés like we must learn to *"scratch where the people are itching"* were coined or popularised by Christian leaders such as David Watson of Britain and others who were looked upon as "good" evangelists. The overall perception of "success" added to the process. For example David Watson took on a run-down Anglican parish in the city of York, UK, and by his particular form of preaching and his use of music and drama transformed it into a thriving and exciting scene with the once virtually empty building bursting at the seems with a mix of ages but mainly young people. Not only the national church, but also the nation itself sat up and took notice.

I was part of an evangelical body in Manchester at the time called ECMA the Evangelical Council for the Manchester Area. We decided to invite David Watson to lead a crusade in our 3.3 million-population city. We filled the 3,000 seater Free Trade hall night after night with many community based ministry opportunities during each day. The event was perceived as a huge success. Not only were people added to the churches, but it also brought the various evangelical churches closer together, including some Pentecostal churches. In hindsight what we experienced was illustrative of a major paradigm switch in respect of preaching the gospel. History may record that it was the commencement of the great rot in our time in respect of the evangel that is committed to our trust, for the method that we adopt to some degree affects the message that we proclaim.

To address the felt human need rather than declare the divine standard and requirement is what the New Testament warns against in a number of places. In one place Paul actually uses the analogy of "itching and scratching" in his warning about the nature of the messengers and the message in the end time,

"For the time will come when they will not endure sound doctrine; but after their own desires because they have itching ears they will heap up for themselves teachers,"

2 Timothy 4:3

If you read the full chapter you will see that Paul places his warning in the context of evangelism. He commands *"Preach the word... do the work of an evangelist, fully carry out your ministry."* The gospel of our Lord Jesus Christ does meet man in his need, as the great manifesto of the Kingdom announced by Christ in the synagogue at Nazareth makes clear.

"And he came to Nazareth, where he had been brought up: and, as his custom was, he went into the synagogue on the sabbath day, and stood up to read. And there was given to him the book of the prophet Isaiah. And when he had opened the book, he found the place where it was written, The Spirit of the Lord is upon me, because he has anointed me to preach the gospel to the poor; he has sent me to heal the broken-hearted, to preach deliverance to the captives, and recovering of sight to the blind, to set at liberty them that are bruised, To proclaim the acceptable year of the Lord."

Luke 4:16-19·

All of human need is represented in that powerful proclamation. Our Lord was anointed by the Holy Spirit to meet that need through the preaching of His gospel, which is now entrusted to the church.

The confusion stems from our inability or reluctance to differentiate between psychology and reality. The "felt" need is based on perception, which relates all too frequently to psychology; the real need has to do with the physical, literal, and actual condition of human kind, and it is this reality that the gospel addresses and remedies. Because it is real, it does not change in any basic way. A poor person is just as needy in the 21st century as in the 1st century. The broken-hearted are no less so in the age of electronic emails than they were in the age of the horse and cart. Captives are captives whatever we call them victims of terror, the response to it, or asylum seekers. It really makes no difference. Blind, bound, and bruised people all need to hear about the liberty and acceptance they can find in turning to Christ and to God. The gospel relates to *The Acceptable Year of the Lord,* and the preaching of it is based upon the Sovereignty of God, and must not be changed according to the whim and fancy of man, or it will be rendered ineffective.

CHAPTER 2

Confusion, More Confused

I HAVE suggested that confusion has arisen on three fronts and for three reasons. Firstly on account of what I will call the *SUCCESS SYNDROME*: As human beings, we are motivated by three natural needs:

1) Satisfaction i.e. physical, material and intellectual satisfaction, the drives of which relate to hunger and food eating and drinking; possessions, goods, wealth; education, knowledge, learning, and so on.

2) Security i.e. in relation to housing, jobs, and insurance protection. The need for a sense of security is one of the great human drives.

3) Significance i.e. influence, reputation, status.

In this latter regard, one of the great considerations is how others perceive us viz peer pressure. These three human areas of need are interrelated and interdependent. From a purely natural perspective, the person who has the greatest significance is the person who has the most of the things listed.

What is missing in all of this is the spiritual element, and because man is essentially "spirit", deep inside himself he will know if he is satisfied, secure, and truly significant no matter how others may perceive him, or what he may possess. This analysis can and should be applied to the Christian message and method. In today's western culture and climate most judge that a church is successful if it is large, prosperous, and influential. If it is small and financially poor it is dismissed as being insignificant. Thus the humanistic measuring rod is applied to the church in much the same way that it is applied to mankind. However, scripture challenges this basis of analysis and assessment.

The resurrected Christ testified to the Laodiceans:

"Because you say, I am rich, and increased with goods, and have need of nothing; and you do not know that you are wretched, and miserable, and poor, and blind, and naked: I counsel you to buy from me gold purified in the fire, that you may be rich; and white garments, that you may be clothed, and that the shame of your nakedness does not appear; and anoint your eyes with eye-salve, that you may see."

Revelation 3:17-18

It is possible to have every natural benefit and blessing and yet have nothing spiritually and that applies both inside and outside the church. It was to the church of the Laodiceans that the message came and it was to them that our Lord said,

"Behold, I stand at the door, and knock: if any man hear my voice, and open the door, I will come in to him, and will dine with him, and he with me."

Revelation 3:20

The second cause of the confusion that we face in the area of evangelism is what I call the *PERSONALITY PARADE*.

Hollywood and international sport have contributed a great deal to our perception of people. We live in the age of the superstar and the hero, and while this problem stretches back to the early church, when Christians living at Corinth factionalised over the leaders of their time, as Paul describes: "*...every* *one of you says, I am of Paul; and I of Apollos; and I of Cephas ..."* (1 Corinthians 1:12) it is certainly more pronounced and complicated in our time. It even reflects on our view of Christ, who came into our world to be a saviour not a superstar.

The third contributing factor to the confusion that I have described is that produced by the *FORMULA FREAKS,* who so frequently flaunt their folly in the name of evangelism.

Scripture deals with the success syndrome unequivocally in Paul's corrective instructions to the Corinthians when he points out that he doesn't know if he is a success or not and won't know until he stands before Christ the righteous judge. The only thing he can do is remain faithful to His Lord and to His calling:

"Let a man consider us, as of the ministers of Christ, and stewards of the mysteries of God. Moreover it is required in stewards that a man is found faithful. But with me it is a very small thing that I should be judged by you, or of man's judgment: yes, I do not even judge myself. For I know nothing by myself; yet am I not hereby justified: but he that judges me is the Lord. Therefore judge nothing before the time, until the Lord come, who will both bring to light the hidden things of darkness, and will manifest the counsels of the hearts: and then shall every man have praise from God. And these things, brethren, I have in a figure transferred to myself and to Apollos for your sakes; that you might learn in us not to think of men above that which is written, that no one of you be puffed up for one against another."

1 Corinthians 4:1-4

The judgment that Paul refers to here, which he says should not be engaged in, relates to the measurement of success in service not to judging character or doctrine, both of which are open to examination and should be judged on the basis provided in scripture as 1 Thessalonians 5:21, 1 John 4:1 and John 7:24 require and Acts 17:10-12 illustrates.

"Prove all things; hold fast that which is right."

1 Thessalonians 5:21)

"Beloved, do not believe every spirit, but prove the spirits whether they are of God: because many false prophets have gone out into the world."

1 John 4:1

"Judge not according to appearance, but judge righteous judgment."

John 7:24

"And the brethren immediately sent away Paul and Silas by night to Berea: who, on arrival, went into the synagogue of the Jews. These were nobler than those in Thessalonica, in that they received the word with all readiness of mind, and examined the scriptures daily, whether those things were so. Therefore many of them believed; also honourable women who were Greeks, and not a few men."

Acts 17:10-12

It is largely this drive for success, which from a biblical perspective can never be certainly assessed in this life, that has caused the church to look for modern role models and formulae as guides. One of my spiritual mentors, the late Denis Clark, frequently pointed out that humans operate on the basis of formulae, whereas God works on the basis of principle. Very early in the charismatic experiment, he detected the danger and spoke out against it. I recall his mentioning how Joy Dawson of YWAM had this tendency to teach formula based practices. No wonder YWAM is among those who are experimenting with a new mission approach to accommodate "Messianic Muslims"[2]. The true gospel of Christ cannot be adapted to modern or any other man. It is man who must change not the Gospel.

Another modern illustration of what I am trying to say here relates to the practice of so called Spiritual Warfare. Our appeal must always be to the Bible and not to human experience no matter how successful or sensational it sounds. That there is such a thing as *Spiritual Warfare* is made abundantly clear by passages like Ephesians 6 which teach about our contending *"against spiritual wickedness in the heavens"* (v12), 1 Peter 5 where Satan is likened to a lion whom we must *"resist steadfast in faith"* (v9 c/f James 4:7), and 1 Corinthians 15 where Paul uses the euphemism of fighting against wild animals in His witness at Ephesus (v32 c/f Acts 19:21-41). These passages present us with Spiritual Warfare in the local church or group (The Corporate Level Ephesians 6); at The Individual Level (1 Peter 5:9 and James 4:7); and in Evangelism (1 Corinthians 15:32).

However, nowhere in the Bible are we told to go to mountains or hotels to discover and bind some imaginary wicked prince who has charge of a city or region, so that we can become effective in evangelism. Such a practice was unknown to the early church and apostles, who taught us the *"whole counsel of God."* So my question is, "If it's not God's counsel then whose counsel is it that these people bring to us?" Sadly, what happens with this sort of thing is that seeing it is based on deception to start with, the end result is outrageous lies in an attempt to maintain the deception as we have documented in our Vanguard article entitled *Reflections on the Transformations Video* written by Olympia Barczynska.[3]

CHAPTER 3

Follow ME and I will MAKE You...

THE call of Jesus to discipleship is most aptly expressed in Matthew chapter four, while the commission to evangelism is most fully given in Matthew chapter 28. Between the two events the first century disciples sat at the feet of the greatest teacher of all time and *"learned from"* Him, who was *"meek and lowly"* and thereby they found *"rest to* (their) *souls"* (Matthew 11:28-29)[4]. Restless people cannot minister rest to the souls of others. So have we missed something?

In Mark 3 we read:

"And He went up into a mountain, and called to him whom he wanted: and they came to him. (14) And he appointed twelve, that they should be with him, and that he might send them forth to preach, (15) And to have authority to heal sicknesses and to cast out demons."

Mark 3:13-15

Ordination was for the purpose of intimacy of relationship with Jesus. He ordained twelve so that they might be *WITH Him*. The call to discipleship, which preceded ordination, expresses the same idea.

"And Jesus, walking by the sea of Galilee, saw two brothers, Simon called Peter, and Andrew his brother, casting a net into the sea: for they were fishermen. And he said to them, Follow me, and I will make you fishers of men. And straight away they left their nets, and followed him."

Matthew 4:18-20

Jesus said, *"Follow me* (literally IMITATE ME) *and I will MAKE you"*. Our business is to FOLLOW; His responsibility is to MAKE us and ultimately He *"will make"* us to become *"fishers of men."* That is evangelism, pure and simple, flowing out of our relationship with Christ. It has nothing to do with setting goals or operating on the basis of formulae as taught by well meaning church growth gurus. Programmed evangelism frequently fails at this point, not that there is anything wrong with a programme per se. The problem is with people trying to communicate a living Christ, whom they have never come to know in any degree of intimacy.

Last year (2001) we planted our first Christian Witness Ministries (CWM) Fellowship. Seeing people frequently inquire about a church's Faith and Mission Statements, we thought it would be prudent to adopt both. After some discussion the following was entrenched in the Constitution of the CWM-Fellowship in Brisbane:

VISION AND MISSION: *"to KNOW Christ and to make HIM known." "And he appointed twelve, that they should be with him ..."* (Mark 3:14). *"And Jesus said to them, Come after ME, and I will make you to become fishers of men"* (Mark 1:17). *"Go therefore, and make disciples of all nations"* (Matthew 28:19).

The vision and goal of the Fellowship shall always remain that of Paul the apostle as expressed in Philippians chapter 3 verses 10 and 11, *"That I may know HIM, and the power of His resurrection, and the fellowship of His sufferings, being made conformable to His death; If by any means I might attain to the resurrection of the dead."* No humanly conceived goal or ambition shall replace or override this goal which shall remain the vision of the Fellowship at all times. Thus the Mission of the Fellowship is to KNOW Christ and to make HIM known. This is our MISSION STATEMENT."

We were convinced that we didn't need anything more than that and made a conscious commitment not to extend it or alter it in any way or at any time.

In Christ's initial call to discipleship, there is a promise and a warning. If we keep following Christ, then He will keep making us. If we quit following, then He will quit making. The ultimate purpose is that He will influence others through us. He will make us to become fishers of men. The ordination of the apostles, who were selected from among the disciples, was with the same purpose in view. They were chosen so that they would get closer to and become intimate with Jesus, who would eventually send them out to proclaim and demonstrate the good news of the Kingdom.

Evangelism is the extension of Christ's life, character, and nature through His people. An apostle is essentially a representative, literally an ambassador, who carries the authority of the one who sent him. In the Christian sense no man can rightfully claim to be an apostle (literally a sent one) of the Lord Jesus Christ if he does not have character and disposition, which are commensurate with that of his Master. Romans 8:9 warns us: *"Now if any man has not the Spirit* (i.e. disposition) *of Christ, he is not his."* Or as J.B. Phillips expresses it, *"he does not belong to Him at all."* It was really at this point that Judas Iscariot, though named an apostle, proved himself unworthy and was, like many others through church history who have assumed or accepted the title, excluded. What's in a name or a title? NOTHING.

When we grasp the fact that the call to discipleship is principally an invitation, to join Christ in a lifelong adventure of discovering HIM, and we respond positively to that invitation then the progression from learning to communicating is automatic. Paul illustrates this in his instruction, *"Be followers of me, even as I also am of Christ"* (1 Corinthians 11:1). The Greek word *"mimetes"* (Strong 3402) translated *"followers"* signifies "imitators". Mentoring is only safe as long as the mentor imitates Christ. Both discipling and evangelising come back to this same thing knowing Christ and making Him known, and of course the matter is progressive.

Writing about the Old Testament fathers and the wilderness wanderings of the Israelites Paul declares,

"Now all these things happened to them as examples: and they are written for our admonition, upon whom the ends of the ages have come."

1 Corinthians 10:11

In other words, while the settings and circumstances of the Old Testament events were literal, they also convey spiritual lessons to us. This of course is the basis of much of true biblical preaching from New Testament times to our own. The only legitimate form of allegorical application is that which builds on the literal event without replacing it. The word allegory is used in that sense in Galatians 4:24 where we have the only biblical use of the word.

"Tell me, you that desire to be under the law, do you not hear the law? For it is written, that Abraham had two sons, the one by a bondmaid, the other by a freewoman. But he who was of the bondwoman was born after the flesh; but he of the freewoman was by promise. Which things are an allegory: for these are the two covenants; the one from the mount Sinai, which genders to bondage, which is Hagar. For this Hagar is Mount Sinai in Arabia, and answers to Jerusalem, which now is, and is in bondage with her children. But Jerusalem above is free, which is the mother of us all."

Galatians 4:21-25

In the context Paul speaks of the two sons of Abraham Ishmael, who was the son of a slave woman and the product of human reasoning and design, and Isaac who was the son of a free woman and the product of promise and divine provision. He then applies this true and factual story to the problem that the Galatian church faced with the Judaizers, who attempted to bring those early Christians under the bondage of the law. At no time is there even a hint of any change with regard to the racial distinction between Arabs (descendants of Ishmael) and Jews (descendants of Isaac). Nor is there any thought that the Old Testament story was fictitious and only an allegory quite the contrary. The allegorical teaching is predicated upon the reality and accuracy of the original account.

In a similar manner, we can illustrate the walk and life of the Christian from Old Testament characters and events. Abraham is a good example. His first response was to the call to discipleship

"Now the LORD had said to Abram, Get out of your country, and from your kindred, and from your father's house, to a land that I will show you And I will make you a great nation, and I will bless you and make your name great; and you shall be a blessing."

Genesis 12:1-2

The key here is OBEDIENCE. This is paralleled in the New Testament by the call that came to Andrew and Peter *"Follow ME..."* In Hebrews chapter 11 verse 8 we are told *"By faith Abraham ... obeyed..."* and in Romans 4:3 that this faith, which expressed itself in obedience *"was counted to him for righteousness."*

The first aspect of the walk of faith is that of FOLLOWING, which suggests the ideas of observation, imitation, and learning by doing what your leader is doing. In effect our Lord says to us, "You watch where I walk and put your feet in the same place. Keep following (imitating) me and ultimately I will turn you into evangelists. Your life will influence others", Compare this with Genesis 12:1-2, and you will see that Abraham was given a similar mission and promise. So we can discover in Abraham's life an illustration of this first stage of the walk of faith.

Then there is also an illustration of the second stage conveyed in Genesis chapter 17,

"And when Abram was ninety nine years old, the LORD appeared to Abram, and said to him, I am the Almighty God; walk before me, and be blameless. And I will make my covenant between me and you and will multiply you exceedingly."

Genesis 17:1-2

The key here is INSTRUCTION. Psalms 32:8 states, *"I will instruct you and teach you in the way which you shall go: I will guide you with my eye."* Literally, this means that God guides His people while keeping His eye upon them. The two stages are, of course, inter related, and to some extent concurrent, even though there is a progress towards intimacy conveyed by the two ideas. In the first stage, the emphasis is on our observing Christ. In the second, it is Christ observing us. This second stage may be called the walk of adjusting or perfecting, which signifies the maturing process. When the Bible speaks of Christian perfection e.g. 2 Corinthians 13:9 and Hebrews 6:1, it does not mean perfection in the absolute sense. The real meaning is maturity.[5]

James in the New Testament presents the third stage.

"And the scripture was fulfilled which said, Abraham believed God, and it was imputed to him for righteousness: and he was called the Friend of God."

James 2:23

Here the key is COMMUNION friends walking together, side-by-side. This is the third stage with an emphasis on INTIMACY. Amos asks, *"Can two walk together, except they are agreed?"* (ch 3:3). The prophet is referring to the agreement to walk together not in agreement in everything. Friends disagree, but in their walk they agree to differ seeing they have agreed to WALK TOGETHER. This can be applied to our walk of discipleship, but the wonderful fact is that through our intimacy with Christ, we come to the place where we submit to his Lordship recognising that where there are differences it is ALWAYS we who are wrong and HE who is right. He is right at all times!

If you look at the three stages together they operate concurrently as well as progressively with an ever deepening application to our lives we learn that we are shaped by FOLLOWING, refined by INSTRUCTION, and matured through COMMUNION. The ultimate is an intimacy, which constantly desires each others company, and here we have to go to another Old Testament character for the best example:

"And Enoch walked with God after he fathered Methuselah three hundred years, and fathered sons and daughters: And all the days of Enoch were three hundred sixty and five years: And Enoch walked with God: and he was not; for God took him."

Genesis 5:22-24

Pardon a bit of Welsh melodrama. One day as Enoch was out walking with God he turned to his companion and inquired, "How long have we been walking together?"

"Three hundred years," replied God, "but it seems like no time at all for I dwell in eternity."

"What's it like where you dwell?"

"It is indescribable to humans like you. You can't know it. You can only experience it and for that you must be changed so that you move away from what you are to what you will become."

Enoch thought about that every waking minute as he longed for the returning of his companion of the previous day who had walked with him for 300 years. And then it happened! As Enoch was looking for Him *"he was NOT for God took him."*

No wonder it was Enoch who prophesied Christ's return in language, which presupposes the rapture. He knew the reality. He foreshadows it.

"By faith Enoch was translated that he should not see death; and was not found, because God had translated him: for before his translation he had this testimony, that he pleased God."

Hebrews 11:5

"And Enoch also, the seventh from Adam, prophesied of these, saying, Behold, the Lord comes with ten thousands of his saints."

Jude 14

CHAPTER 4

I will send another Comforter

A CAREFUL study of the life of the Lord Jesus Christ reveals that there were stages when He conveyed specific truths by His conduct and through His teaching. At the point at which the truth was grasped or rejected He moved on to another emphasis. A classic illustration of this type of progression is contained in Matthew chapter 16 where we read:

"From that time Jesus began to show to his disciples, that he must go to Jerusalem, and suffer many things of the elders and chief priests and scribes, and be killed, and be raised again the third day."
Matthew 16:21

The immediate precursor to this statement is the revelation of the true identity of Jesus to His disciples. Having shared in the truth of this revolutionary disclosure *"You are the Christ the Son of the living God"*, which was communicated through Peter by revelation, the disciples were ready to face the truths relating to Christ's crucifixion and resurrection, which involved their Lord leaving them. Thus Christ's new emphasis includes His teaching about the Holy Spirit.

"I will not leave you comfortless (Grk "orphanos" = orphaned): I will come to you"

John 14:18

"Jesus answered and said to him, If a man loves me, he will keep my word and my Father will love him, and we will come to him, and make our home with him."

John 14:23

"And I will pray the Father, and he shall give you another Comforter, that he may abide with you for ever. Even the Spirit of truth; whom the world cannot receive, because it does not see him, neither knows him: but you know him; for he dwells with you, and shall be in you."

John 14:16-17

The NIV renders "comforter" as "counsellor" in John 14:16 and elsewhere. It is the Greek *"parakletos"* (Strong 3875) and is translated "advocate" in the KJ rendering of 1 John 2:2.[6] The basic thought of the Greek is that of being summoned or called to one's side, and especially called to one's aid. The word is capitalised to *"Paraclete"* in the Concise Oxford Dictionary and defined as "the Holy Spirit as advocate or counsellor (John 14:16, 26 etc.) [Middle English via Old French *paraclet* and Late Latin *paracletus* from Greek *"parakltos"* 'called in aid' (as PARA-, *kltos* from *kalo* 'call')]." In its usage and definition there is a legal connotation with the thought of defence and support. This is the work of the Holy Spirit in His man-ward operations and is the basis on which Christ instructed His followers

"But when they shall lead you away, and deliver you up, take no thought beforehand what you shall speak, neither premeditate: but whatever shall be given you in that hour, speak: for it is not you that speak, but the Holy Spirit."

Mark 13:11

The implication of scripture is very clear. The promised Holy Spirit would be the same in nature as the Father and the Son. This is further emphasised by the Greek word which is translated *"another"* in John 14:16. It is *"allos"* (Strong 243), which denotes numerical distinction only. Its synonym *"heteros"* (Strong 2087) involves the secondary idea of difference of kind, i.e. a qualitative difference. Jesus' teaching regarding the Holy Spirit is that He is the same in kind as the Lord Jesus Christ Himself. Thus, when our Lord says that the third person of the trinity will replace Him in His presence and ministry, He tells us that the Holy Spirit will do what He Himself did while here on earth:

"I have yet many things to say to you, but you cannot bear them now. But when he, the Spirit of truth, is come, he will guide you into all truth: for he shall not speak of himself (i.e. about Himself from His own authority base); but whatever he shall hear, that shall he speak: and he will show you things to come. He shall glorify me: for he shall receive of mine, and shall show it to you. All things that the Father has are mine: therefore I said, that he shall take of mine, and shall show it to you."

John 16:12-15

In His Christ-ward or God-ward operations the Holy Spirit is called the Spirit of Truth or the Spirit of Christ. Jesus claimed, *"I am ... the TRUTH"* (John 14:6) so the terms are interchangeable as to their application. Four times

He is called the Spirit of Truth, and twice He is referred to as the Spirit of Christ. The context of each bears witness to the fact that the principal ministry of the Holy Spirit is to witness to the Person of the Lord Jesus Christ.

"If you love me, keep my commandments. And I will pray the Father, and he shall give you another Comforter, that he may abide with you for ever; Even the Spirit of truth; whom the world cannot receive, because it sees him not, neither knows him: but you know him; for he dwells with you, and shall be in you. I will not leave you comfortless: I will come to you."

John 14:15-18

"But when the Comforter is come, whom I will send to you from the Father, even the Spirit of truth, which proceeds from the Father, he shall testify of me: And you also shall bear witness, because you have been with me from the beginning."

John 15:26

"However when he, the Spirit of truth, has come, he will guide you into all truth: for he shall not speak of himself; but whatever he shall hear, that shall he speak: and he will show you things to come. He shall glorify me: for he shall receive of mine, and shall show it to you. All things that the Father has are mine: therefore I said, that he shall take of mine, and shall declare it to you."

John 16:13-15

"Beloved, do not believe every spirit, but try the spirits whether they are of God: because many false prophets are gone out into the world. By this you know the Spirit of God: Every spirit that confesses that Jesus Christ is come in the flesh is of God: And every spirit that does not confess that Jesus Christ is come in the flesh is not of God: and this is that spirit of antichrist, which you have heard should come; and even now is in the world. You are of God, little children, and have overcome them: because greater is he that is in you, than he that is in the world. They are of the world: therefore they speak of the world, and the world hears them. We are of God: he that knows God hears us; he who is not of God does not hear us. By this we know the spirit of truth, and the spirit of error."

1 John 4:1-6

"But you are not in the flesh, but in the Spirit, if the Spirit of God dwells in you. Now if any man has not the Spirit of Christ, he is not his. And if Christ is in you, the body is dead because of sin; but the spirit is alive because of righteousness. But if the Spirit of him that raised up Jesus from the dead dwells in you, he that raised Christ from the dead shall also give life to your mortal bodies by his Spirit that dwells in you."

Romans 8:9-11

"Of this salvation the prophets have enquired and searched diligently, who prophesied of the grace that should come to you: Searching what, or what manner of time the Spirit of Christ which was in them did signify, when it testified beforehand the sufferings of Christ, and the glory that should follow. To whom it was revealed that, not to themselves, but to us they ministered the things, which are now reported to you by them that have preached the gospel to you by the Holy Spirit sent down from heaven; things which the angels desire to look into."

1 Peter 1:10-12

This dual function of the Holy Spirit, as the great *Paraclete* on behalf of Christ's followers and as the Spirit of Truth in His witness to the work and worth of our Lord Jesus, is a truth that is overlooked in the modern setting of sensation seeking that prevails today. We so easily forget that our Lord entrusted the church with only three things when He departed:

Firstly, a group of trained men whom we considered in the previous chapter; secondly His own blood the blood of the New Covenant; and thirdly, the Holy Spirit executor of the Godhead and the new teacher and protector of God's people, who was the complete and perfect replacement of Christ Himself.

Jesus was available to His disciples for only a limited time. He said the Holy Spirit would be with us forever,

"And I will ask the Father, and he shall give you another Comforter, that he may remain with you for ever; the Spirit of truth."

John 14:16-17

Being of the same nature, character, and disposition as Christ, and having the same objective in leading men and women into truth in the revealing of Christ, it is clear that the Holy Spirit's primary and principal work is to do with us what Christ did with His disciples. In other words, He invites us to follow Christ and ordains us to be with Him and to learn of the One who is meek and lowly and so to find rest to our souls and by that process to turn us into evangelists.

I suggest that we are in danger of overlooking this essential work of the Holy Spirit and that this is the one thing that the faithful remnant will rediscover and emphasise. This is basic to everything within the church and our ideas about revival and evangelism. It is also a standard by which we can discern whether what men call revival is in fact true revival.

Some years ago, I was horrified to read about a man called Marc Du Pont who was associated with the Toronto movement, and who had preached a message entitled *The Holy Ghost Train.* I listened to his recorded ideas in which he characterised the Holy Spirit as some relentless force, who controlled preachers and ordinary people against their wills forcing them to do all sorts of bizarre things. I knew that he was not speaking of the Spirit of Truth whose nature and character are portrayed in the Bible. He was talking about another spirit.

Bad as this was, the thing that so profoundly disturbed me was that these totally unbiblical notions were taken up by so many including David Cartledge, a former colleague of mine. Mr Cartledge, who confessed that he had studied the person, ministry, and work of the Holy Spirit for more than thirty years, testified that his experience at Toronto Airport Church (TAC) had changed his whole theology on the Holy Spirit. He used the very same language, including at least one of the illustrations that Du Pont used in his *Holy Ghost Train.* This in itself should alert us to the fact that something is wrong. Men stealing each other's words is, according to Jeremiah, a sure sign of a false prophet:

"The prophet that has a dream, let him tell a dream; and he that has my word, let him speak my word faithfully. What is the chaff to the wheat? says the LORD. Is not my word like a fire? says the LORD; and like a hammer that breaks the rock in pieces? Therefore, behold, I am against the prophets, says the LORD, that steal my words every one from his neighbour. Behold, I am against the prophets, says the LORD, that use their tongues, and say, He says. Behold, I am against them that prophesy false dreams, says the LORD, and tell them, and cause my people to err by their lies, and by their recklessness; yet I did not send them, or command them: therefore they shall not profit this people at all, says the LORD."

Jeremiah 23:28-32

David Cartledge, who was at the time President of the Australian National AoG Southern Cross Bible College, went on to say that since his Toronto experience, when he was praying for people he sometimes found himself transfixed on one spot being unable to move for up to fifteen minutes. Then he told of one occasion when he was picked up from the platform where he was standing and thrown against the front wall of the church. I would say unequivocally, that is not a description of the activity of the Holy Spirit whom I know and have read about in scripture.

Of course in order to justify these sorts of weird happenings, whether real or imaginary, some people will refer to the incident where Christ took a whip and drove the moneychangers from the temple. What they overlook is that these were wicked desecrators of God's House and not sincere followers of the Lord Jesus Christ. So something's wrong whichever way you apply it.

The dual function of the Holy Spirit, as *"Paraclete"* and the *"Spirit of Truth"* is marvellously exemplified in Stephen's sermon to the Jewish council and his subsequent martyrdom recorded in Acts chapters six and seven. At the commencement of his defence, his face shone like an angel's (6:15), and at the end, he was full of the Holy Spirit (7:55) as his murderers dragged him away to be stoned. We read that he was *"full of faith and power* (*dunamis* c/f Acts 1:8)*"* (6:8) as a result of which his opponents from the Jewish synagogues *"were not able to resist the wisdom and the spirit by which he spoke"* (6:10). It was this energy and power of the Holy Spirit that was evident in Stephen's life and witness that sparked the conflict. So in what way was the Holy Spirit, the *Paraclete* (one who came along side to help) and the Spirit of Truth, active in Stephen's experience, since from a purely human perspective it appears that evil triumphed? The answer to that question is one of the great paradoxes of evangelism that reflects on the humanistic perception of success that we have previously discussed. It also relates to the next chapter of this section of the call to the faithful remnant.

Suffice it to note here just two things: Firstly, that the Christ, whom Stephen stood for and witnessed to, stood to welcome the first martyr home.

"But he, being full of the Holy Spirit, looked up steadfastly into heaven, and saw the glory of God, and Jesus standing on the right hand of God, And said, Behold, I see the heavens opened, and the Son of man standing on the right hand of God."

Acts 7:55-56

Secondly, that God had noticed another standing there, who thought he was in charge of the entire proceedings:

"Then they cried out with a loud voice, and blocked their ears, and ran upon him with one accord, And drove him out of the city, and stoned him: and the witnesses laid down their clothes at a young man's feet, whose name was Saul. And they stoned Stephen, as he was calling upon God, and saying, Lord Jesus, receive my spirit. And he kneeled down, and cried with a loud voice, Lord, do not lay this sin against them. And when he had said this, he fell asleep."

Acts 7:57-60

To His early followers the Lord had promised, *"you shall be witnesses* (Greek *"martus"*) *to ME"* (Acts 1:8). Stephen was the first to do that in the ultimate sense and possibly made the greatest contribution of all those living at that time, to the spread of the gospel.

"And when the blood of your martyr (Greek *"martus"*) Stephen was shed, I also was standing by, and consenting to his death, and kept the garments of them that killed him."

Acts 22:20

The blood of the martyr is the seed of the church.

CHAPTER 5

You will receive Dunamis

W.T.H. Richards, a pioneer of Assemblies of God in Great Britain, wrote a booklet entitled *Pentecost is Dynamite.* While I greatly respect Mr Richards, his memory, and the many good things that he wrote in that book, I have always felt that the title was a mistake. The Greek word *"dunamis"* is more correctly transliterated to "dynamo" than to "dynamite", as the idea is that of "built in energy", which was produced by the coming of the Holy Spirit upon the early disciples on the Day of Pentecost. Prior to His ascension, the Lord issued a command and a promise to His apostles:

"And, being assembled together with them, commanded them that they should not depart from Jerusalem, but wait for the promise of the Father, which, said he, you have heard of me. For John truly baptized with water; but you shall be baptized with the Holy Spirit not many days from now. Therefore when they had come together, they asked him, saying, Lord, will you at this time restore the kingdom to Israel? And he said to them, It is not for you to know the times or the seasons, which the Father has put in his own authority. But you shall receive power, after the Holy Spirit is come upon you: and you shall be witnesses to me both in Jerusalem, and in all Judaea, and in Samaria, and to the uttermost part of the earth."

Acts 1:4-8

The command was quite easy to follow. All they had to do was wait in Jerusalem until they were, to use Luke's words, *"endued with power from on high"* (Luke 24:49). The word translated *"power"* in both Acts 1:8 and Luke 24:49 is the Greek *"dunamis"*, which signifies strength, power, and ability with the principal idea of these expressions being inherent i.e. residing in a person or a thing by virtue of its nature. Thus, as we have suggested, the better illustration is that of a dynamo than of dynamite. The latter conveys an idea of power out of control. Dynamite can blow your head off, and sadly some who have claimed an experience with the Holy Spirit have in fact lost their minds. Their experience was not genuine. When the Holy Spirit comes upon a person, he does not act irrationally. He may do unusual things, but they are not idiotic things.

The *"dunamis",* which a person receives by virtue of the Baptism in the Holy Spirit, is with a view to witnessing to Christ. As we have seen, the principal work of the Holy Spirit is to lead us into Truth and to bear witness to the worth and work of Christ. It logically follows, therefore, that if He endues men and women with His power it is always with this same objective in view. Men who claim to be filled with the Holy Spirit and teach false doctrine or promote bizarre activity are making a false claim. This is a test that must be applied by the faithful remnant in these days to all those who claim to speak or act by the energy and power of the Holy Spirit.

Again I want to emphasise the fact that the coming of the Holy Spirit was with evangelism in view. Those who received or were filled or baptised into the Holy Spirit whatever term we use were to be witnesses to Christ in life and if necessary in death. They received the ability to evangelise, to become fishers of men, and in the case of the early Christians to *"turn the world upside down"* (c/f Acts 17:6). The three signs, which accompanied the coming of the Holy Spirit on the day of Pentecost the *"sound from heaven as of a rushing mighty wind",* the *"divided tongues like as of fire"* and the speaking *"with other tongues as the Spirit gave them utterance"* (Acts 2:2-4), were incidental. The sound like wind and the sign like fire were symbolic. The *"other tongues"* were not directly predicted and thus were not anticipated. The fundamental thing was the enabling to witness powerfully to the Lord Jesus Christ and thus to evangelise their world.

It seems to me that in this context and regard there are two very important things that we must not overlook and cannot overemphasise. They have to do with the two things that the Holy Spirit is in His relationship to us the *Paraclete* who aids us and the Spirit of Truth who leads us. These two ideas are amplified in the promise of Acts 1:8 where our Lord said His followers would receive the divine enabling *"dunamis"*, and they would, as a direct consequence of that enabling, be His witnesses (Greek *"martus"*).

It was the very same Holy Spirit who stood by Stephen, aiding him in his witness to Christ, which led to his death, who stood by Paul counselling him through vision to depart from Jerusalem because the Jews wouldn't receive his testimony (Acts 22:17-21[7]). Why was the latter protected and the former martyred? The answer has to do with the overall purpose of God to reach a world by evangelism.

In the case of Stephen we read:

"And Saul was consenting to his death. And at that time there was a great persecution against the church, which was at Jerusalem; and all, except the apostles, were scattered throughout the regions of Judaea and Samaria. And devout men carried Stephen to his burial, and made great lamentation over him. As for Saul, he made havoc of the church, entering into every house, and dragging off men and women committing them to prison. Therefore those who were scattered went everywhere preaching the word. Then Philip went down to the city of Samaria, and preached Christ to them."

Acts 8:1-4

"Now those who were scattered after the persecution that arose about Stephen travelled as far as Phenice, and Cyprus, and Antioch, preaching the word to no one but the Jews only."

Acts 11:19

In the case of Paul it is recorded:

"And he said to me, Depart: for I will send you far from here to the Gentiles."

Acts 22:21

God's evangelistic purpose that His people should witness to Christ in new territory was achieved in both cases, and that is the principal work and ministry of the Holy Spirit. Superficially, from a humanistic perspective, it seemed that Stephen's martyrdom was a waste of a young life, but it wasn't. It was a major contributing factor to the overall evangelistic mandate to witness to Christ *"in Jerusalem, and in all Judea, and in Samaria, and to the uttermost part of the earth"* (Acts 1:8). The lot of Saul of Tarsus, later called Paul the apostle, was far more onerous than that of Stephen. In the overall scheme of things the first martyr had it very easy even though he evidenced enormous courage and steadfastness. The same "Paraclete" and the same "dunamis" were at work in the witness of both of those early giants of the faith. Paul was directly responsible for the death of Stephen, whose martyrdom sparked the persecution and scattering of the church and contributed in a major way to his conversion. He in turn was martyred after an incredible life of evangelistic and missionary endeavour. God knows what He is doing, hallelujah!

So what are the lessons to the faithful remnant in our time? (1) We must redefine the word "power". It is not this notion of humanistic achievement in the demonstrable and the hugely successful that the church has tended to adopt. We must think in New Testament terms and see that the life of faith is always a mix of the observable and the unseen. The apparent victories and the apparent defeats may in fact be the opposite of what they appear to be. Let us not forget that the great men and women of faith listed in Hebrews chapter 11 includes those who chose *"to suffer affliction with the people of God"* and who considered *"the reproach of Christ greater riches than the treasures in Egypt"* (Hebrews 11:25 & 26) and others who (v35) *"were tortured, not accepting deliverance"* and who (v36) *"had trial of mocking and scourgings, yes, and of chains and imprisonment: (37) They were stoned, they were sawn in half, were tempted, were slain with the sword: they wandered about in sheepskins and goatskins; being destitute, afflicted, tormented; (38) Of whom the world was not worthy:) they wandered in deserts, and in mountains, and in dens and caves of the earth."*

(2) We must rediscover the true nature, character, and ministry of the Holy Spirit, recognising that He is the same in disposition as our Lord Jesus Christ, and that His essential work is to reveal Christ to His followers, to lead us into all truth and away from error, and to extend that witness throughout the world. The word "witness" (Greek *"martus"* Strong 3144) implies a testimony and a stand for truth in three respects:

1) In a legal sense, which reflects the nature of the *"Paraclete"*, being that of counsellor or advocate. We witness to THE TRUTH as opposed to error;

2) In a historical sense as one who observes a contest or is a witness to an event; and

3) In an ethical sense as a "martyr" i.e. one who after the example of *"the faithful and true witness"*[8] has proved the strength and genuineness of his faith

in Christ by undergoing a violent death for that faith.

This brings us right back to one of the opening remarks by E.M. Bounds contained earlier in this book *"God's method is men."*

It also leads to my final question Where are the true ministers? which this book attempts to answer.

FOOTNOTES:

[1] Quoted in *Knowing God* © J I Packer Hodder and Stoughton 1973 pages 13-14.

[2] See page 74

[3] URL http://www.christian-witness.org/archives/van2001/video13.html

[4] *"At that time Jesus answered and said, I thank you O Father, Lord of heaven and earth, because you have hidden these things from the wise and prudent, and have revealed them to babes. Even so, Father: for so it seemed good in your sight. All things have been delivered to me by my Father: and no man knows the Son, but the Father; neither knows any man the Father, but the Son, and whoever the Son will reveal him to. Come to me, all you that labour and are burdened, and I will give you rest. Take my yoke upon you, and learn from me; for I am meek and lowly in heart: and you shall find rest to your souls. For my yoke is easy, and my burden is light"* (Matthew 11:25-29).

[5] *"For we are glad, when we are weak, and you are strong: and this also we wish, even your completion"* (2 Corinthians 13:9). *"Therefore leaving the principles of the doctrine of Christ, let us go on to maturity; not laying again the foundation of repentance from dead works, and of faith toward God"* (Hebrews 6:1).

[6] *"My little children, these things I write to you, that you may not sin. And if any man sin, we have an advocate with the Father, Jesus Christ the righteous"* (1 John 2:1).

[7] *"...when I came again to Jerusalem, even while I prayed in the temple, I was in a trance; And saw him saying to me, Make haste, and get out of Jerusalem quickly: for they will not receive your testimony concerning me. And I said, Lord, they know that I imprisoned and beat in every synagogue those that believed on you. "And when the blood of your martyr Stephen was shed, I also was standing by, and consenting to his death, and kept the garments of them that killed him." "And he said to me, Depart: for I will send you far from here to the Gentiles"* (Acts 22:17-21).

8 *"These things says the Amen, the faithful and true witness, the beginning of the creation of God" (Revelation 3:14).*

PART FOUR

Commissioned to Serve

CHAPTER 1

Where are the Ministers? God Re-enters His Redemptive Realm

"Therefore he says, when he ascended on high, he led captivity captive, and gave gifts to men."
Ephesians 4:8

THE expression *"gave gifts"* is Greek *"didomi"* (Strong 1325) = "gave" plus *"doma"* (Strong 1390) = "gifts". *"Doma"* the noun is derived from the base of the verb *"didomi"* and is rendered "gift" in the KJV in each of its four usages:

"Ask, and it shall be given you; seek and you shall find; knock and it shall be opened to you: For every one who asks receives; and he who seeks finds; and to him that knocks it shall be opened. Or what man is there of you, whom if his son asks bread, will he give him a stone? Or if he asks for a fish, will he give him a snake? If you then, being evil, know how to give good gifts (Greek "doma") to your children, how much more will your Father who is in heaven give good things to them that ask him?"

Matthew 7:8-11

Luke repeats this with a slight variation in his gospel:

"And I say to you, ask, and it shall be given you; seek, and you shall find; knock, and it shall be opened to you. For every one who asks receives; and he who seeks finds; and to him that knocks it shall be opened. If a son shall ask for bread of any of you that is a father, will he give him a stone? Or if he asks a fish, will he for a fish give him a snake? Or if he shall ask for an egg, will he offer him a scorpion? If you then, being evil, know how to give good gifts (Greek "doma") to your children: how much more will your heavenly Father give the Holy Spirit to them that ask him?

Luke 11:9-13

The other two usages are by Paul in the Ephesians passage, which we are discussing and in Philippians chapter 4:

"Now you Philippians also know, that in the beginning of the gospel, when I departed from Macedonia, no church had fellowship with me concerning giving and receiving, but only you. For even in Thessalonica you sent once and then again for my needs. Not that I seek a gift (Greek "doma"): but I seek fruit that abounds to your account. But I have all, and abound ."

Philippians 4:15-18

Unlike the Greek "*charisma*" (Strong 5486) translated "gifts" in 1 Corinthians 12:4 where the root of the word is "grace" not "gift",[1] here in Ephesians chapter 4 the emphasis is most definitely on "gift" with no intrinsic idea of "grace". In fact we are told that grace is an additional requirement for the correct function of the gift:

"But to each one of us grace is given {Greek "charis" (Strong 5485)} *according to the measure of the gift* {Greek "dorea" (Strong 1431) = "present"} *of Christ."*

Ephesians 4:7

Verse 11 reads: *"...He gave* (Greek "didomi") *some* [Greek "men" (Strong 3303) = a participle meaning "truly, certainly, surely, indeed"] *apostles; and* [Greek "de" (Strong 1161) = normal conjunction "and"] *prophets; and evangelists; and pastors* (the English *"some"* is inserted in the KJV on each of these three occasions) *and* [Greek "kai" (Strong 2532) = "and also"] *teachers."*

Thus the verse could be rendered, *"And He* (Christ) *truly gave apostles; and prophets; and evangelists; and pastors and also teachers."*

The passage indicates that the apostle, prophet, evangelist, pastor or teacher is the gift. It is not emphasising the "gift or gifts", which each of these ministers may possess, but rather that the minister himself is the gift to the church. The idea here is quite different from that conveyed in 1 Corinthians chapter 12, where we are taught about the "manifestations" or supernatural gifts of the Holy Spirit, as we saw in Part three. The emphasis there was upon grace and the shining forth of the Holy Spirit in the manifestations of His power and presence. In Ephesians chapter four, we have what is generally referred to as the "ascension ministry gifts" of Christ to His church.

The trinity is involved in God's redemptive program to the world. The following brief summary may help to convey my point:

God the Father gave His Son

"For God so loved the world, that HE GAVE HIS only begotten Son, that whoever believes in him should not perish, but have everlasting life."

John 3:16

The Father and the Son gave the Holy Spirit.

"And I will pray the Father, and HE SHALL GIVE you another Comforter, that he may abide with you for ever."

John 14:16

"But when the Comforter is come, whom I WILL SEND to you from the Father, even the Spirit of truth, who PROCEEDS FROM THE FATHER, he will testify of me."

John 15:26

"But I tell you the truth; It is profitable for you that I go away: for if I do not go away, the Comforter will not come to you; but if I depart, I WILL SEND him to you."

John 16:7 "Jesus answered and said to him, If a man love me, he will keep my words: and my Father will love him, and WE WILL COME to him, and make our home with him."

John 14:23

God the Holy Spirit gave gifts to the church of the Lord Jesus Christ.

"For to one is given BY THE SPIRIT the word of wisdom; to another ... BY THE SAME SPIRIT; to another etc... (verse 11)...that ONE AND THE SAME SPIRIT, operates all these dividing to every man separately AS HE WILLS."

1 Corinthians 12:8-11

God the Son also gave gifts to His church, which is what we are considering here.

"But to each one of us grace is given according to the measure of THE GIFT OF CHRIST. Therefore he says When HE ASCENDED UP on high, HE LED CAPTIVITY CAPTIVE, AND GAVE GIFTS to men."

Ephesians 4:7-8

(Emphasis added in each case to the above references.)

Of course the Holy Spirit is involved in the inspiring and guiding of the gifts mentioned viz apostles, prophets, evangelists, pastors, and teachers, but it is Christ, not the Holy Spirit, who gives these gifts to men. He does so in His capacity as Head of His church, that through them God's people may be matured to serve in their various capacities so that the body of Christ is "edified" i.e. built up.

"And He gave some to be apostles; some prophets, some evangelists and some pastors and teachers; For the equipping of the saints, for the work of the ministry, for the edifying of the body of Christ: Till we all come to the unity of the faith and of the knowledge of the Son of God, to a perfect man, to the measure of the stature of the fulness of Christ."

Ephesians 4:11-13

According to verse 13, this maturing process will continue until the unity of the faith and conformity to Christ are achieved, which quite clearly is not yet. If, for no other reason, we may safely conclude from this that these five ascension ministry gifts of Christ are valid for all time. In addition, consistency of interpretation and application demand that if we accept the validity of some of these ministry gifts, evangelists, pastors and teachers, then we should accept the others, viz apostles and prophets. The important questions that we face as part of the faithful remnant are:

1) Is the present Apostolic/ Prophetic movement a true or even reasonable reflection of what scripture teaches?

2) If not then how are these ministry gifts intended to function in the church today?

CHAPTER 2

The New Apostles & Prophets

The Lord Jesus Christ said:
"I will build my church; and the gates of hades shall not prevail against it."
Matthew 16:18

C. Peter Wagner and Ben F Gray[2] wrote:

"The New Apostolic Reformation is an extraordinary work of the Holy Spirit that is changing the shape of Christianity globally. It is truly a new day! The church is changing. New names! New methods! New worship expressions. The Lord is establishing the foundations of the church for the new millennium. This foundation is built upon Apostles and Prophets..."[3]

On examination the two statements are in stark contrast the one to the other. Our Lord's simple statement contains two unconditional promises: (1) That He Himself will build His church and (2) That no force or power will overcome it, which really means that it will not change fundamentally. Wagner, Gray and their associates project changes, which are more than cosmetic, when they refer to the new "shape of Christianity" and a new foundation, which "is built upon Apostles and Prophets".

These are fundamental departures from the teaching of the New Testament regarding the church of the Lord Jesus Christ. So we are forced to one of two conclusions. (1) These men are wrong in their projections, or (2) The church to which they refer is not the church of Jesus Christ. I will develop this argument later but first let us consider another contrasting set of statements from Paul, a true apostle, and Bill Hybels, senior pastor of Willow Creek Community Church in South Barrington, Illinois, USA. Wagner, the church growth guru, touts this church as a new apostolic church, so presumably he views Hybels as an apostle.

Paul wrote:

"That I may know him, and the power of his resurrection, and the fellowship of his sufferings, being conformed to his death; ... this one thing I do... I press toward the goal for the prize of the high calling of God in Christ Jesus."

Philippians 3:10-14

"For I determined not to know any thing among you, except Jesus Christ, and him crucified."

1 Corinthians 2:2

Bill Hybels wrote:

"The church is the hope of the world, and its renewal rests in the hands of its leaders. I believe that statement to the core of my being. It has two parts, and they sum up the whole of what I have devoted my life to."[4]

This idea that the "church" is the hope of the world is a fallacy that leads to heresy. It sounds all right on the surface, but it's false and leads to the preaching of a false message that ultimately embraces ecumenism. It is contrary to scripture. This is deeper than mere semantics and, in my opinion, is one of the major mistakes made by church growth practitioners such as C. Peter Wagner.

Some years ago, when we launched Christian Witness Ministries (CWM), I decided to do a series of messages based on the theme of *The Bride of Christ The Emerging Church.*[5] The group that met in the city of Hamilton in New Zealand to listen to the talks every Sunday afternoon for ten weeks, was quite small 22 maximum. Offerings to defray expenses did not meet the cost of renting the hall, as I recall. The audio tapes from those meetings have circulated in a number of countries and have been listened to by hundreds, if not thousands, of people. One of the messages was entitled *Don't Replace the Bridegroom with the Bride.* If the church replaces Christ in any way, it ends up with a compromised message and a corrupted purpose, simply because the focus has been changed.

The thing that drives church growth advocates is numbers. Mr Wagner has made a career out of studying and writing about church growth. The facts and figures that he publishes are impressive, but his rationale and conclusions at times are very superficial. He reminds me, better than anyone else that I know, of the description I once heard the late principal of the Prairie Bible Institute of Canada apply to some men of his time as being "educated beyond their intelligence!" In contrast to the church growth men, who are driven by data and sterilised by statistics, the early Christians and those others, who have most impacted history, were driven by a passion for Christ a desire to KNOW Him and to make Him KNOWN. The fact that they impacted history establishes their influence, but this was incidental. Their commitment was to Christ and to no one and nothing else, and that kept them rooted in truth; for Christ is TRUTH.

Bill Hybels is a very good example of where something that looks like a very small deviation can lead. Crosswalk.com <newssummaries@lists.crosswalk.com> in *Religion Today Summaries* for Wednesday, October 17, 2001 reports the following under the heading,

Willow Creek Church Welcomes Muslim Cleric's Perspective

"Following the September 11 attacks, Pastor Bill Hybels, of the Willow Creek Community Church, was increasingly bothered by reports of hate crimes and misinformation about Islam. 'I was so concerned by the gap between Muslims and Christians that I thought Willow could do something about that,' he said, according to the Chicago Tribune.

That "something" was to have his church invite a local Muslim leader, Fisal Hammouda, to talk about Islam to a total of 17,000 churchgoers, spread out over four services. 'There are some Christians spreading half-truths that the Koran encourages violence,' Hybels told his congregation. '(When) you take some stuff out of context ... we've got major problems.'

Hammouda, a U.S. citizen, an engineer and religious leader in the Islamic Centre in Naperville, first visited Willow Creek as part of the church's world religions weekend in March. In one of his current appearances, Hammouda was questioned by Hybels, on stage in the 4,500-person auditorium. Hybels asked, 'It appears that Osama bin Laden directed the attack (on September 11) ... What do you think?'

Hammouda said at first he thought 'it couldn't be a Muslim,' explaining that the Koran does not allow violence against innocent people ... 'We believe in Jesus, more than you do, in fact,' Hammouda said, drawing laughter when Hybels, smiling, ventured to disagree.

'Muslims consider Jesus and other biblical figures to be Islamic prophets though not as important as Muhammad and we have all the prophets from the Bible,' Hammouda said."[6]

It may be suggested by some that there's nothing wrong with what Hybels did as some who were interviewed at Willow Creek after the event suggested (see Appendix 1). However we need to ask three questions:

1) Is this what Christian meetings are meant to be someone from another religion presenting what was clearly his religious views?

2) Why was there no Christian response to the Muslim view of Jesus and of the Old Testament prophets? Maybe you can justify a debate on the topic but not this one sided presentation by an imam, or religious leader, from an Islamic Centre see Appendix 1.

3) Why was there no response to the claim about the Koran's teaching on violence and Hybels' limited understanding of "context"? Those who have studied the Koran testify to the fact that it is deliberately contradictory in its position regarding violence so that the teaching can be variously applied depending on whether Muslims comprise a majority or minority of the community or country. Islam is like Roman Catholicism a lamb when in a minority; a wolf when equal; and a lion when in a majority.

4) What message is Hybels sending to the world and to the international Christian church especially in the light of the well publicised persecution of Christians that is taking place in Islamic countries? Christians are being martyred under Islamic regimes.

In *A REVIEW OF WILLOW CREEK SEEKER SERVICES: Evaluating A New Way Of Doing Church* by G. A. Pritchard (As Reviewed by Lance Ralston) we read:

"Anyone who seeks to be able to cogently address the larger seeker sensitive way of doing church should read this section of the book. It provides valuable insight into how the methodology of Willow Creek was developed over time. One surprise to be gleaned is the large impact Robert Schuller has had on Hybels and Willow Creek. Schuller even takes a significant measure of credit for the success of Willow Creek. Pritchard reports that the staff of Willow Creek seems somewhat embarrassed by this affiliation and rarely mention it today, though the influence of Dr Bob is undeniable."

Some time prior to December 2000, Robert Schuller hosted the son of the Grand Mufti of Syria as a platform guest in the Crystal Cathedral along with a number of other notable Muslims, whom he named and welcomed as part of the congregation. He told his audience that his guest and Robert Schuller's own son were destined to be two of the dominant spiritual leaders of the world in the 21st century. I have seen the video recording the occasion and can assure you that it is very disturbing in the light of Schuller's influence. In view of these facts the above quote regarding Hybels' links with Schuller raises a certain amount of cynicism as well as much concern

Significantly, in his book *Churchquake*[7] at the top of page 40, author C. Peter Wagner links Robert Schuller's *CRYSTAL CATHEDRAL* with Bill Hybels *WILLOW CREEK COMMUNITY CHURCH* as two examples of non-charismatic apostolic congregations, so presumably Wagner views both men as "apostles". This is alarming to the faithful remnant and should most certainly indicate to us that the great apostasy prophesied by Paul in 2 Thessalonians chapter 2 is upon us and is being supported and promoted by this so called Apostolic Revolution.

Recently, Wagner has exercised great influence in Australian Pentecostal and Charismatic circles being the person behind *The Apostolic Revolution* by David Cartledge and *The 21st Century Out There* by Ben Gray. Others who have joined forces with Wagner in Australia are John Lewis, AoG Assistant President, Danny Guglielmucci, AoG National Executive member, and Mark Conners, senior pastor of Waverley Christian Fellowship, Melbourne.

Before moving on to consider the biblical expression of the five ministry gifts of Christ including apostles and prophets, I need to give examples from Wagner's writings to support my contention that his rationale, conclusions, and, in fact, his basic *modus operandi* at times are superficial. I will also quote from a man who dubs himself an apostle, and who is promoted by Wagner as such, just to show the danger of what we are being presented with in this so called New Apostolic Movement, which has a lot to do with human manipulation and very little if anything to do with the work of the Holy Spirit.

Dr C. Peter Wagner wrote the foreword to David Cartledge's book, which is entitled *The Apostolic Revolution*. Cartledge claims a restoration of apostles and prophets in the Assemblies of God in Australia since 1977. So as to avoid a charge of making selective quotes out of context, I have decided to quote the entire Foreword, and then repeat pertinent statements to show Wagner's superficiality, which is certainly not a hallmark of a good researcher.

"FOREWORD: Be prepared. This is not an average book. David Cartledge has produced a veritable tour de force with the release of *The Apostolic Revolution*!

Few Christian leaders in these early years of the 21st century could remain unaware that an epochal new wineskin is being fashioned by God for the future of the church, in all probability as a preparation for the second coming of Christ. Those, here and there, who remain in denial, do so mostly because they possess a deeply rooted emotional attachment to the status quo.

Among those who are hearing what the Spirit is saying to the churches these days, many, predictably, are yet unsure as to the configuration of the new wineskin. When they hear terms like "apostolic revolution," they wonder, with not a little apprehension, where this movement might lead. If structural and organizational ecclesiastical standbys such as bureaucratic, hierarchical, and democratic principles of government are being relegated to the old wineskin, where do we go from here? Could the alternatives lead to dictatorships, personal empire building, ego trips, and prima donnaism?

No one I know is more aware of and sensitive to these questions than David Cartledge. He has held leadership positions in both wineskins. David understands that the old wineskin was the best wineskin for its times. At one time the old wineskin was a divinely ordained new wineskin, used for powerful advances of the kingdom of God. The difference between the two is not one of good and bad. Both, if they are within the plan of God, are good. The difference is that, while one was the best for the past, the other is the best for the future.

I call this new wineskin the "New Apostolic Reformation." I have been researching and writing on it since 1993. The New Apostolic Reformation now comprises the fastest growing segment of churches on every continent of the world. This fact is causing many traditional church leaders to ask, "What would we have to do to transition from the old to the new?"

Jesus said that significant transitions into the future will require new wineskins (see Mt 9:17). While everyone in Jesus' culture recognised that to be true, history tells us that there was also a procedure for reconditioning some old wineskins so that their usefulness could be extended. My research, as a matter of fact, did uncover some local churches which had once been traditional, but which now were under apostolic-type leadership. But I had not been able to locate any traditional denominations, which had made the transition. Several that I know of had declared that they wanted to transition, but the changes that they proceeded to institute were at best cosmetic changes. Their efforts fell short largely because they really had no idea of what profound structural realignments would be necessary in order to recondition their old wineskin.

I am grateful that before I released my textbook on the New Apostolic Reformation, *Churchquake*! (Regal Books), a conversation with my friend, David Cartledge, revealed that the Australian Assemblies of God had, in fact, made the elusive transition to the new wineskin years ago. He then provided information that I was able to include in Churchquake! along with a graph showing the dramatic acceleration in the growth of the Australian Assemblies of God immediately after the change.

This little section of my book has been a huge encouragement to many church leaders who want to remain on the cutting edge. At least I was able to let them know that it could be done. But I didn't answer their next question, "How was it actually done?" A major reason that I am so excited about this book is that David Cartledge now tells us how it was done.

And this book is not a simple case study, although it is certainly that. David also addresses, and not superficially, the profound biblical and historical questions that the apostolic revolution poses. This is a book that both engages the mind and stirs the soul.

In early 2000 I gave a prophetic word from the Lord that "Australia has the potential to become the first nation in the world to model, as a nation, the new wineskins that I am shaping for My church." The publication of *The Apostolic Revolution* before the end of the same year seems to be one tangible validation of that word. Without any question, this book takes its place, alongside of very few others, at the top of the list of the literature on God's new wineskin for the church of the 21st century!

C. Peter Wagner, Chancellor
Wagner Leadership Institute."

STATEMENT BY WAGNER (taken from the above Foreword):

"No one I know is more aware of and sensitive to these questions than David Cartledge. He has held leadership positions in both wineskins. David understands that the old wineskin was the best wineskin for its times."

Bearing in mind the setting of David Cartledge's book viz *"The Restoration of Apostles and Prophets in the Assemblies of God in Australia",* Wagner is saying that David accepted that the old system within AoG was the best for that time. However the order form advertising the book states, "This movement (AoG in Australia) made the transition from AN INEFFECTIVE DEMOCRATIC RELIGIOUS SYSTEM to leadership by Apostles. Since 1977 the Australian Assemblies has (sic) multiplied many times over AFTER 40 YEARS IN THE WILDERNESS. There is a reason why..." (emphasis added).

Clearly David Cartledge did not consider the *"old wineskin ... the best ... for its times."* In fact his book, for which Wagner provided the FOREWORD, contains a whole chapter of some ten pages devoted to this so called "Forty Years in the Wilderness." Cartledge denigrates the Pentecostal pioneers and early leaders of AoG in Australia. That Wagner should miss this reveals the deficiency in his research and defectiveness of his conclusions. This really calls into question all of C. Peter Wagner's work.

STATEMENT BY WAGNER:

"Jesus said that significant transitions into the future will require new wineskins (see Mt 9:17). While everyone in Jesus' culture recognized that to be true, history tells us that there was also a procedure for reconditioning some old wineskins so that their usefulness could be extended."

Presumably, what Wagner meant to say was that people living at the time of Jesus understood the significance of putting new wine into old wineskins. That however is not what he says. I very much doubt if "everyone in Jesus' culture" recognised that "transitions into the future will require new wineskins," which is what he asserts. The application of our Lord's statement to denominational or church structures is very dubious. So the entire premise on which this idea of the New Apostolic Reformation is built is questionable. Let's look at the record and do what all good researchers should do in respect of our Lord's teaching, viz examine it synoptically.

"Then the disciples of John came to him, saying, Why do we and the Pharisees often fast, but your disciples do not? And Jesus said to them, Can the children of the bride chamber mourn, as long as the bridegroom is with them? but the days will come, when the bridegroom shall be taken from them, and then they will fast. No man puts a piece of new cloth to an old garment, for that which is put in to repair it up shrinks from the garment, and the tear is made worse. Neither do men put new wine into old wineskins: or else the wineskins break, and the wine runs out, and the wineskins are ruined: but they put new wine into new wineskins, and both are preserved."

Matthew 9:14-17

"And the disciples of John and of the Pharisees used to fast: and they come and say to him, Why do the disciples of John and of the Pharisees fast, but your disciples do not? And Jesus said to them, Can the children of the bride chamber fast, while the bridegroom is with them? as long as they have the bridegroom with them, they cannot fast. But the days will come, when the bridegroom will be taken away from them, and then they will fast in those days. No man sews a piece of new cloth on an old garment: or else the new piece that repaired it up shrinks away from the old, and the tear is made worse. And no man puts new wine into old wineskins: or else the new wine will burst the wineskins, and the wine is spilled, and the wineskins will be ruined: but new wine must be put into new wineskins."

Mark 2:18-22

"And they said to him, Why do the disciples of John often fast, and make prayers, and likewise the disciples of the Pharisees; but yours eat and drink? And he said to them, Can you make the children of the bride chamber fast, while the bridegroom is with them? But the days will come, when the bridegroom shall be taken away from them, and then they shall fast in those days. And he spake a parable to them; No man puts a piece of a new garment upon an old one; otherwise, the new makes a tear, and the piece that was taken out of the new does not match the old. And no man puts new wine into old wineskins ;or else the new wine will burst the wineskins, and be spilled, and the wineskins ruined. But new wine must be put into new wineskins; and both are preserved. No man having drunk old wine immediately desires new: for he says The old is better."

Luke 5:33-39

All three writers agree that the matter arose out of a question put to Jesus because His disciples did not fast, whereas the disciples of John and of the Pharisees fasted often. Christ answered directly by saying that His disciples would fast when He, the bridegroom, was taken away from them. He then illustrates His answer with two short parables, which were well understood by His hearers. No sensible person will try to patch up a torn garment with new flannel i.e. as the Companion Bible explains "that which is undressed or unfilled as in this condition it is less supple and will tear away." Equally, no knowledgeable person will put new (unfermented) wine into an old wineskin, which, being dried and hard, cannot contain the expansion and action of the fermenting process.

Contextually, the illustrations have nothing at all to do with structures or corporate gatherings let alone denominations. They relate to rules and practices regarding fasting. Logically, you must conclude that Christ is likening the non-fasting of the disciples to the new, but He says they will return to the old when He is taken away from them. The transition that He proposes has an obvious reference to His crucifixion. The Companion Bible says the terminology implies a violent death as "lifted up" in John 3:14. Interestingly, Luke tells us that the old wine is "better" (literally "good"). New wine is not good. This is a point which the entire argument of Wagner and his associates conveniently ignores.

If the analogy can be applied as meaning that John the Baptist and the Pharisees represent the old wineskins, and Jesus and His disciples represent the new wineskins, which is stretching things a bit to say the least, the extrapolation of that idea to the parallels about denominations and structures throughout church history is still an incredible leap in logic. Wagner is incredibly superficial in his study and application of the Bible. Sadly so many follow him without thinking the issues through.

STATEMENT BY WAGNER:

"I am grateful that before I released my textbook on the New Apostolic Reformation, *Churchquake!* (Regal Books), a conversation with my friend, David Cartledge, revealed that the Australian Assemblies of God had, in fact, made the elusive transition to the new wineskin years ago. He then provided information that I was able to include in *Churchquake!* along with a graph showing the dramatic acceleration in the growth of the Australian Assemblies of God immediately after the change."

There are two things that are claimed here. Firstly, that AoG in Australia moved to a new apostolic leadership system. Is this true? Secondly, that there was a dramatic acceleration in growth immediately after the change. Do the facts support this claim? The year indicated by the graph and promoted by David Cartledge as the date of the transition is 1977.

It would appear that Peter Wagner accepted what "his friend", David Cartledge, claimed without checking it out carefully or very widely. Did he check the claim with anyone else associated with Assemblies of God in Australia, I wonder? Apart from the dubious analogy of the new and old wine and wineskins to suggest that AoG in Australia shifted from a democratic denomination to an Apostolic structure in 1977 is just not true.

My family and I came to Australia from Great Britain in 1978, and I know that the same democratic election process continued at state and national conference levels as had occurred previously. In fact, the democratic process of voting still pertains. There was no fundamental change in the *modus operandi.* While a good case can be made for the fact that new "boys" on the executive became increasingly dictatorial, self assertive, and self serving, which even Wagner sees as being disqualifications for true apostolic character and ministry[8], to claim that AoG was led by apostles and prophets after 1977 and by an ineffective democratic religious system previously is not only the height of arrogance, but it is also arrant nonsense.

We should also examine the claim about the dramatic acceleration in growth immediately after 1977, which involves our looking at the graph provided by Wagner on page 150 of *Churchquake!* and by David Cartledge in his *The Apostolic Revolution* (page 414).

Even a cursory examination reveals that the graph indicates a considerable increase during the four years 1959 to 1963. In fact, the number of Assemblies tripled during that period, as reflected in the biggest percentage jump on the entire graph. That took place during the so called ineffective democratic religious system of what was AoG until Wagner's "friend", David Cartledge, and his gang took control and became the great apostles and prophets in 1977. The increase according to the graph from 1977 to 1981 was a mere 33 percent in comparison and it never reached 300 percent growth during any subsequent four-year period that is graphed. If the rate of increase that occurred during the four year period 1959 to 1963 had been maintained from 1977, the time of the so called "new wineskin", to 1997, the end of the graph, the number of churches would have been 36,450 not a mere 825 as the graph indicates.

Graphs and statistics are very convincing to superficial researchers who all too often forget the adage, "There are three types of lies around white lies, black lies and statistical returns." It has been claimed that you can prove just about anything you want from statistics! My basis of calculation listed above should convince you of that if it doesn't convince you of anything else.

I looked at the graph provided by Mr Cartledge, and I quickly noticed that it is very inconsistent until 1981, when it proceeds in two-year increments throughout. Obviously, this says something about the care of documenting and retaining records during the period of what I will call the new regime 1977 to 1997. Prior to that we have gaps of varying lengths especially during the period 1937 to 1963, when I suspect some of the records were missing requiring in some cases educated guesses to fill the gaps. The early Pentecostals didn't put much store on statistics. In fact, some thought that to engage in counting was to commit the second sin of King David when he numbered Israel.

There are two things that are essential in respect of statistics, if that is the way you want to evaluate things. It seems that men like Peter Wagner and David Cartledge make that their major measuring line, which is suspect in my opinion. The two essentials are:

1) Great care to ensure that your records are correct; and

2) Rational evaluation with respect to contributing factors and circumstances etc.

In regard to the first I speak from experience as I was, for three years, General Secretary of Assemblies of God in Australia (1989 to 1992). During that period, the National Office was required to document returns provided by the various AoG State Superintendents or their offices. It was a constant headache and a virtual impossibility to ensure that the returns that came into the office were correct and in order. I and my colleague, who was more responsible than me in this regard, often spoke of it and in the end gave up in despair of ever being certain that the returns were accurate. On one occasion, I recall checking on some churches in Queensland, which were listed as being current that had ceased to function six years previously. We certainly didn't have the time, nor were we encouraged to carry out the exercise necessary to ensure that the records were accurate. Some listed Assemblies were so small as to be virtually non-existent. In addition, there was a keen sense of competition between the States in respect of growth achievements and this did not always augur well with respect to accuracy of records. The point I am making is that unless the returns are accurate the calculation won't be correct. In my opinion, this throws a huge question mark against the statistics on which the graph is based. I suspect that this also applies to the current records maintained by AoG in Australia.

If the records are correct, the next issue is rational evaluation. In this respect, it is important to recognise that the type of leaders and leadership is only one factor in the equation. This is the biggest mistake made by Wagner and Cartledge. and. of course. in principle it reflects on all statistical returns. You may have a 5 percent growth in a particular situation and reach more people than a 100 percent growth in another. If you start with one and end with two you have achieved a 100 percent increase (200 percent growth), even though you have increased by only one. The number of Assemblies in 1959, if the graph is accurate, was approximately 50. The number in 1964 was about 150 i.e. triple the number, but it is still only 100 more churches. According to the graph, there was no overall increase from 1964 until 1977, when the AoG moved into a growth period. This may be attributable in part to the change of leaders and leadership. There could well be other contributing facts, such as a greater openness on the part of secular people to the gospel. To claim credit for the increase, as David Cartledge does, is quite arrogant as well as questionable.

One should also take into account the matter of momentum. The nature of numbers and growth is that they are sparked by an initial increase, which will frequently continue until an optimum is reached. Australia is not the most populous of countries; nevertheless it has some very sizeable cities where the growth potential is considerable. The fact that AoG had seen little growth in its early years was a positive, not a negative, for it to expand at a reasonable rate when increase started to occur. But let us not get carried away, or we will be deceived by those who would impose upon us their notions of church government and the control of people upon an entirely false premise. To experience an increase from 150 churches in 1977 to 825 churches in 1997 may be better than the past, but by no stretch of the imagination can it be called "a dramatic acceleration in the growth" that renders the previous 40 years ineffective wandering in the wilderness in comparison. Neither Wagner nor Cartledge shapes up very well under scrutiny.

Here's another amazing statement made by C. Peter Wagner which makes me wonder what Bible he reads:

"This is one of the first books (i.e. Peter Wagner's book) I have seen that includes a chapter by one who designates himself "Apostle John Kelly," much like the APOSTLE PAUL did in MOST OF HIS EPISTLES."[9] (Emphasis added)

I did a search on the term "Apostle Paul" in my On-Line Bible and it does not appear even once anywhere in the Bible. The word "apostle" (singular) appears 19 times of which it applies to Paul 16 times, but never as a title. In fact the only time it is used as a title in the singular is in reference to Christ when the initial letter is capitalised.

"Therefore, holy brethren, partakers of the heavenly calling, consider the Apostle and High Priest of our confession, Christ Jesus."

Hebrews 3:1

The word "apostle" derives by transliteration from the Greek "*apostolos*" (Strong 652) signifying one who is sent forth on a mission i.e. a delegate, messenger, or an ambassador, who represents another and carries out His orders. Notwithstanding the fact that our Lord named the twelve as "apostles" (c/f Luke 6:13[10]) not one of them ever referred to himself as "Apostle so and so". In fact, it was only Paul and Peter who used the term "apostle" in respect of themselves and then only as a function never as a title.

Even in Romans 11:13, where we have the reference to the "office" of an apostle the term is "*diakonia*" (Strong 1248) from "*diakonos*" (Strong 1249) signifying ministry or service. The basic idea is that of a person on an errand i.e. one who executes the commands of another, especially of a master, as a servant, attendant, or minister would do. Contrary to what Peter Wagner says, Paul never designated himself "The Apostle Paul" in any of his epistles. It was always "Paul an apostle... " i.e. "Paul a sent-one... " except in the case where he defined his distinctive commission, viz Romans 11:13 *"For I speak to you Gentiles, inasmuch as I am an apostle of the Gentiles, I glorify my service"*. The biblical use of the indefinite rather than the definite article in the overwhelming majority of cases is instructive.

Peter Wagner records an incident in the early "ministry" of John Kelly, when the group that he was accountable to in ministry wanted to dismiss him over some activity in which he had engaged with the outcome being,

"John, a former officer in the Marine Corps special services division, called the board together and summarily informed them: "You don't fire me, I fire you!" It rather quickly transitioned to a new apostolic church."[11]

In his other book, Wagner inserts a page written by Kelly on Accountability, which commences with the following two sentences:

"Accountability is a cry we are hearing from many ministers today, but I regard much of it as more "talk than walk." For accountability to be truly effective, it must be based on strong personal relationships with other men and women in ministry."[12]

I couldn't agree more. So why didn't *"Apostle John Kelly"* "walk the talk" and build a relationship with those to whom he was accountable in his early ministry instead of dismissing them? This man reminds me of the person with the attitude, "I believe in Theocracy my name is Theo!" This type of inconsistency surfaces so consistently within the framework of the new apostolic movement advocated by Wagner, that it should press numerous alarm bells with the discerning.

On the topic of "Church Government" and what he had observed in the USA situation Kelly writes,

"They were either a one man show or they were governed by a church board. ... I began to realise that many of us were copying a corporate American paradigm or a paradigm that came out of Greco-Roman philosophy rather than building on the biblical paradigm."[13]

Two sections later under the heading of WHO IS IN CHARGE he states,

"We do not have a central hierarchical headship. When we understand family, we understand how apostolic ministry is meant to function. For example, when a father goes to his son's house he does not take charge, he submits. The son is in charge of that house. When the son goes to his father's house, the father is in charge. Within the context of a person's ministry, mission or church, that person has the ULTIMATE AUTHORITY (emphasis added).[14]

Sounds awfully like a one-man show to me! That aside, the analogy that

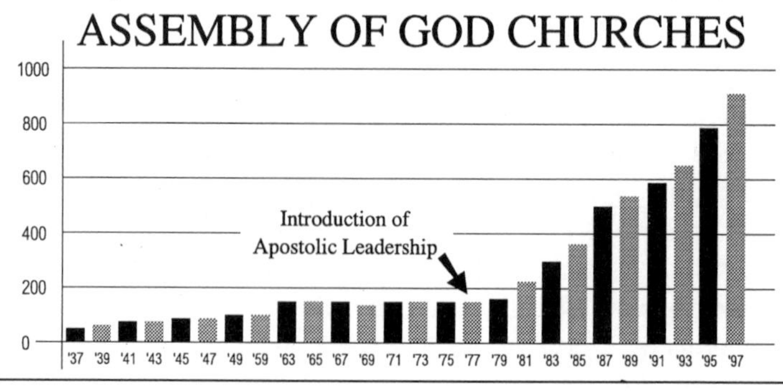

Kelly uses is based on Western culture, which does not pertain in all cultures e.g. some Indian and other cultures where the son remains part of the father's household. However, the most dangerous aspect of this teaching is that it's not biblical to transfer ownership of any expression of the household of faith from Christ to a man, no matter what you call him. Christ is the head of His church and will always remain so, and He promised that He would build His church not the church of Apostle John Kelly or whatever he or others may consider him to be.

Again I quote, and this is probably the most glaring example of inconsistency becoming a downright contradiction,

"In Antioch Churches and Ministries (ACM) we build relationally, person to person, rather than through CONFERENCES, publications and advertisements."[15] "Let me further explain our mission strategy by sharing an example. In 1991 we held a MINISTERIAL CONFERENCE in Mexico city"[16] (emphasis added).

Yet "Apostle John P. Kelly" has the effrontery to write, "... many men who read what the scriptures say about church government may not remember what they have read."[17] This man can't even remember what he has written! What does that say about the great C. Peter Wagner and his expertise as a researcher?

I suspect that the bottom line to this whole thing is MONEY, which may explain why Kelly got into it in the first place. Wagner profiles him in his book in the following terms,

"He draws on a varied background that includes service in the United States Marines, real estate sales and management, professional education and athletics as well as 15 years in New Testament ministry. Apostle Kelly has earned a Bachelor of Arts degree in Education and Business, a master's degree in Human Potential and Development and holds an honorary doctorate of divinity."[18]

With such a profile I have no doubt that Kelly is admirably fitted to talk about holding "a loaded revolver to the head of the average pastor"[19] and about the hand becoming a fist so "we can then experience true knockout power",[20] but I have no idea what it has to do with real Christian ministry as projected by Paul, a true apostle.

"But what things were gain to me, those I counted loss for Christ. Yes rather, and I count all things but loss for the excellency of the knowledge of Christ Jesus my Lord: for whom I have suffered the loss of all things, and do count them but refuse, that I may win Christ, And be found in him, not having my own righteousness, which is of the law, but that which is by the faith of Christ, the righteousness which is of God by faith: That I may know him, and the power of his resurrection, and the fellowship of his sufferings, being conformed to his death; If by any means I might arrive at the resurrection of the dead."

Philippians 3:7-11

At the risk of being accused of cynicism, I again suggest that it has something to do with money. Maybe that's why Kelly devised the system of which he writes as follows,

"Many pastors will declare they have a covering, but the question is, do they tithe to that covering? By tracking the tithe, WE can literally track the order in the house of God" [21] (emphasis added).

During my time as National Secretary of AoG in Australia, I frequently ministered at a place called Balaclava not far from Adelaide, where the National AoG office was based. The pastor of this church had adopted an idea of apostolic oversight, which was spreading within AoG at that time. He referred publicly to me as "their apostle" though I quickly pointed out my rejection of such a designation. After I resigned my position over the many conflicts that I had with my colleagues in respect of the direction in which they were taking the movement, the pastor of this church chose to relate to a man called Dudley Daniel who was also viewed by some as an apostle. Shortly after I left Adelaide for New Zealand, there was a fracas with Daniel and AoG over property, which resulted in Dudley Daniel leaving AoG and eventually removing to USA, which I suspect was his long term intention when he left South Africa a few years earlier. As far as I know, Mr Daniel continues his pursuit as an "apostle" over some regime of churches within USA and possibly elsewhere.[22]

As for AoG, the hierarchy continued to move down the apostolic route so much so, that when the controversy surrounding Rodney Howard-Browne and the laughing revival surfaced the so-called leaders of the Pentecostal/ Charismatic section of the Australian church convened a meeting to discuss the issue. I listened to a message preached by Andrew Evans, then General Superintendent of AoG in Australia and senior pastor of the Paradise Assembly of God. I was amazed to hear him claim that the "apostles and elders" of the Australian church had met to discuss the matter, and they had given the ruling that this new "laughing revival" was of God. He appealed to Acts 15 as the biblical precedent for what they did, making no reference to and giving no explanation of the teaching of Acts 15. His sole recourse was to the fact that the early church leaders came together to rule on a dispute, and the Australian leadership group had done the same thing. This was his justification for the arbitrary conclusion that the then current bizarre practices of Browne and others were legitimate.

This is crazy, and it illustrates where this whole "authority based" leadership structure can lead. It cuts across one of the major teachings of the Protestant Reformation, viz 'SOLA SCRIPTURA" (Scripture Alone). In fact, it is simply a reintroduction of popery under another guise. My strong recommendation is get away from it. It is flawed in its foundation, and I say that as one who believes in the five fold ministry gifts of Christ, including those of apostles and prophets.

CHAPTER 3

Overarching Grace & Undergirding Faith

"For I am the least of the apostles, and am not fit to be called an apostle, because I persecuted the church of God. But by the grace of God I am what I am: and His grace which was bestowed upon me was not in vain; but I laboured more abundantly than all of them: yet not I, but the grace of God that was with me."

1 Corinthians 15:9-10

"But having different gifts according to the grace that is given to us, whether prophecy, let us prophesy according to the proportion of faith; Or ministry, let us use it in our ministering: or he who teaches, in teaching; Or he who exhorts, in exhortation."

Romans 12:6-8

GRACE is more than a "charming sound" as the hymn writer expresses and much more than "unmerited favour" as it is popularly defined. Grace is the divine enabling which negotiates a change. Grace does not leave the recipient where it found him. There is a supernatural lift in God's grace. That's why I say it's more than unmerited favour, which is a correct definition of mercy, the passive aspect of grace. Grace has an active part. It is the basis of everything within the Kingdom of God.

"But to each one of us is given (Greek "didomi" Strong 1325) grace (Greek "charis" Strong 5485) according to the measure of the gift (Greek "dorea" Strong 1431) of Christ."

Ephesians 4:7

The implication is that with every "gift"[23] that is spoken of in this context, Christ, as the Head of His Church, makes provision for grace to be received so that the gift can function and be accepted. This is fundamental to ministry. We are not talking about the manifestations or supernatural gifts of the Holy Spirit here, where grace is intrinsic i.e. part, in fact, the essential part of the manifestation. With the ministry gifts of Christ, the "gift" of grace is something separate or additional. It requires a human response. Each ministry gift is spiritually effective to the extent that grace is present and increasing in the life of the minister.

Thus Paul was able to write:

"For I am the least of the apostles, and am not fit to be called an apostle, because I persecuted the church of God. But by the grace of God I am what I am: and His grace which was bestowed upon me was not in vain; but I laboured more abundantly than all of them: yet not I, but the grace of God that was with me."

1 Corinthians 15:9-10

Paul was undoubtedly a ministry gift of Christ as an "apostle" i.e. "a sent one". In addition, he was bestowed with grace so that he was able to labour in the capacity of his calling. It was this grace, which enabled him to perform (minister) and to endure.

"And lest I should be exalted above measure by the abundance of the revelations, a thorn in the flesh was given to me, a messenger of Satan to buffet me, lest I should be exalted above measure. For this thing I pleaded with the Lord three times that it might depart from me. And he said to me, My grace is sufficient for you: for my strength is made perfect in weakness. Therefore most gladly I will rather boast in my infirmities, that the power of Christ may rest upon me. Therefore I take pleasure in infirmities, in insults, in needs, in persecutions, in distresses for Christ's sake: for when I am weak, then I am strong."

2 Corinthians 12:7-1

Grace must also be present in varying degree in those who are ministered to. A rejection of the true ministry gift of Christ can quickly lead to a situation where those who have rejected the genuine *"raise to themselves teachers having itching ears"*.[24] During my more than 40 years in full time ministry I have observed this happen several times. This is a very serious matter, but not one which should stop us examining those who claim to be ministers of the Lord Jesus Christ. Once more the grace of God is the key.

"We then, as workers together with Him (Christ), exhort you that you do not receive the grace of God in vain." ..2 Corinthians 6:1

Faith is the other element that is essential to true ministry. The faith that is basic to Christian living,[25] being the one virtue on which all others are built, is also essential in ministry, but at a different level. When Christ gives a man as a ministry gift to the church, He gives to that man faith to function. However the minister must maintain and develop the faith that was given to him for the operation of his ministry.

"I beseech you therefore, brethren, by the mercies of God, that you present your bodies a living sacrifice, holy, acceptable to God, which is your reasonable service. And do not be conformed to this world: but be transformed by the renewing of your mind, that you may prove what is that good, and acceptable, and perfect, will of God. For I say, through the grace given to me, to every one that is among you, not to think of himself more highly than he ought to think; but to think soberly, as God has dealt to every man a measure of faith."

Romans 12:1-3

Biblical faith is presented at three levels, each being a gift:

(1) Faith For Salvation Ephesians 2:8,

"For by grace you are saved through faith; and this is not of yourselves: it is the gift of God: Not of works, lest any one should boast."

Ephesians 2:8-9

(2) Faith For Service Romans 12:3-7; and

"For I say, through the grace given to me, to everyone that is among you, not to think of himself more highly than he ought to think; but to think soberly, according as God has dealt to every man a measure of faith. ...according to the proportion of faith."

Romans 12:3 & 6

(3) Faith For Miracles 1 Corinthians 12:9,

"For to one is given through the Spirit the word of wisdom; to another the word of knowledge by the same Spirit; To another faith by the same Spirit;"

1 Corinthians 12:8-9

Grace and faith are the two spiritual prerequisites for the proper function of each of the five ministry gifts of Christ. Both are divine bestowals in their inception requiring attention, application, and development for the ongoing function of any one of the five.

CHAPTER 4

The Five-fold Ministry Gifts of Christ

"And he truly gave APOSTLES; and PROPHETS; and EVANGELISTS; and PASTORS and also TEACHERS"
Ephesians 4:11

APOSTLES

C. Peter Wagner claims that the New Testament refers to at least 12 apostles other than those named by Jesus, "including Andronicus, Apollos, Barnabas, Epaphroditus, James (the brother of Jesus) Junia, Mathias, Paul, Silas, Timothy and two others referred to but not specifically named."[26] The claim as a whole however is open to challenge. Andronicus and Junia (a woman) are linked together in just one verse in the New Testament on the basis of which some have argued for women apostles.

"Salute Andronicus and Junia, my kinsmen, and my fellow prisoners, who are of note among the apostles, who also were in Christ before me."

Romans 16:7

Those who support Wagner's view argue that the expression *"of note among the apostles"* signifies that Andronicus and Junia[27] were recognised as apostles, but this is questionable. The expression could simply mean that the apostles recognised these two people as worthy (i.e. noteworthy) Christians. To allow for women "apostles" on the basis of this one verse is certainly poor hermeneutics, especially in the light of Paul's teaching about women in ministry e.g. *"But I do not allow a woman to teach, nor to exercise authority over a man, but to be in silence"* (1 Timothy 2:12).

Epaphroditus is mentioned three times, (including the salutation at the end of Philippians see below), but not once is he clearly identified as an "apostle" in the accepted sense. Presumably Wagner's idea is built upon the fact that

Epaphroditus is closely associated with Paul and is identified as a "sent one" to the Philippians, but the matter is by no means clear:

"Yet I considered it necessary to send to you Epaphroditus, my brother, and companion in labour, and fellow soldier, but your messenger (Greek "apostolos"), and he who ministered to my need."

Philippians 2:25

"But I have all things and abound: I am full, having received from Epaphroditus the things which were sent from you, an odour of a sweet smell, an acceptable sacrifice, well pleasing to God."

Philippians 4:18

"The grace of our Lord Jesus Christ be with you all. Amen. (To the Philippians written from Rome, by Epaphroditus.)"

Philippians 4:23

I have always held Timothy in doubt as being called an "apostle". The idea would appear to be built upon verses such as,

"Paul, an apostle of Jesus Christ by the will of God, and Timothy our brother, to the church of God which is at Corinth, with all the saints who are in all Achaia."

2 Corinthians 1:1

"Paul, Silvanus, and Timothy, to the church of the Thessalonians ... Nor did we seek glory from men or from you, or others, when we might have been burdensome, as other apostles of Christ."

1 Thessalonians 1:1 & 2:6

"Paul, a prisoner of Jesus Christ, and Timothy our brother, to Philemon our dearly beloved, and fellow labourer."

Philemon 1

"Know you that our brother Timothy has been released; with whom, if he comes shortly, I will see you."

Hebrews 13:23

The matter is by no means certain. However, I have no problem with the idea that Timothy was an "apostle" in the general sense of one being sent forth with a commission. My point is that we cannot list him in the way Mr Wagner lists him with any real biblical evidence.

However, having said that, I must agree that it is quite clear from the New Testament that there were more than the original twelve who were recognised as "apostles". The very fact that there is a reference to "false apostles" signifies that the list was quite open. If it were a closed list then no false apostle would hold sway for long. All that would be required would be to check the names on the list.

"For such are false apostles, deceitful workers, transforming themselves into the apostles of Christ."

2 Corinthians 11:13

Paul refers to the "signs" (Greek "*semeion*" Strong 4592) and the "seal" (Greek *sphragis* Strong 4973) of his apostleship (both words capitalised below):

"I am become a fool in boasting; you have compelled me: for I ought to have been commended by you: for in nothing was I behind the very eminent apostles, though I am nothing. Truly the SIGNS of an apostle were done among you in all perseverance, in signs and wonders, and mighty deeds. For what is it in which you were inferior to other churches, except it be that I myself was not a burden to you? forgive me this wrong."

2 Corinthians 12:11-13

"Am I not an apostle? am I not free? have I not seen Jesus Christ our Lord? are not you my work in the Lord? If I be not an apostle to others, yet doubtless I am to you: for you are the SEAL of my apostleship in the Lord."

1 Corinthians 9:1-2

The majority sense of the word "sign" in the New Testament usage relates to the supernatural. However, it is not used exclusively in this sense. For example, Paul uses the same Greek word to refer to his identifying mark (sign) much as we refer to a signature at the end of a letter:

"The salutation of Paul with my own hand, which is the sign in every epistle I write. The grace of our Lord Jesus Christ be with you all. Amen."

2 Thessalonians 3:17-18

By applying the above ideas in our modern setting, the conclusion is unavoidable. A true "apostle", in the sense in which Paul applies the word, is someone who has personally seen the Lord (1 Corinthians 9:1), has a proven record of genuine church planting in virgin (missionary) territory (1 Corinthians 9:2), and ministers with patience and humility in the power and energy of the Holy Spirit with genuine miracles and with no thought of personal advantage (2 Corinthians 12:11-13 c/f verse 14). By applying these, none of the "would-be" apostles qualify. In fact, the very first requirement (a personal encounter with the resurrected Christ) disqualifies everyone after Paul. (See Appendix 2).

For this and some other reasons, it is claimed that there are two categories of Apostles portrayed in the New Testament. I agree with this proviso that, apart from the specific requirement of seeing the Lord Jesus Christ, all the other qualifications implied and directly stated by Paul must apply.

Paul justifies his calling as an apostle in 1 Corinthians chapter 9 and in 2 Corinthians chapter 12. Here we have the character and conduct of an apostle portrayed. The following verses (quoted below) are most instructive. They helped guide me during a contentious time in my ministry, when I was asked by the Australian National Executive of AoG, of which I was a member at the time, to give a paper on Apostles and Prophets. I concentrated on the former emphasising the point that as a general standard we must apply not only the positive features that Paul refers to as "marks" of an apostle, but also the negative things that he speaks about e.g. his sufferings, beatings, shipwrecks and so on. I suggested that we should take into account his reference to the apostles being last and not first (see 1 Corinthians 4:9)[28]. During the discussion that ensued, one of my colleagues suggested that a certain man was an apostle in Australia.

This man had come from New Zealand and had planted a number of churches, with claims of "signs and wonders". It was on this basis that he was touted as an apostle and in fact he is named in that context in Mr Wagner's *Churchquake*. I told the National Executive that he was not an apostle as far as I was concerned because he did not meet the requirements implied by Paul. I had discovered that this man rather than appointing godly leaders to a particular church in New South Wales had sent them a man who fell in adultery and another who fell into homosexuality. My point was, and is, that a true apostle will appoint men of good character and conduct as leaders of churches.

Since that time it has been recently revealed that this so-called apostle was himself guilty of sexual offences as an ordained pastor thirty years ago. Our CWM files contain official letters from the New Zealand and the Australian

Assemblies of God to support this information. We cannot be wiser than the Bible and we are very foolish when we ignore the standards set. Here are the verses that were a guide to me (emphasis added):

"Did I make a gain from you by any of them I sent to you? I urged Titus, and with him I sent a brother. Did Titus gain anything from you? Didn't we walk in the SAME SPIRIT? Didn't we walk in the SAME STEPS? Again, do you think that we need excuse ourselves to you? We speak before God in Christ: but we do all things, dearly beloved, for your edification."

2 Corinthians 12:17-19

The twelve apostles appointed by Christ, also called the apostles of the Lamb (Revelation 21:14[29]), are unique as a group. Judas fell from his apostleship (called a *"bishopric"*[30]) and was replaced either by Matthias, as some think, or by Paul as others argue based on the premise that the election of Matthias was something that occurred outside of the direct instructions of Christ and was done out of convenience and on the basis of humanistic reasoning. Personally, I favour this argument, but I am not pedantic about it. What is clear is that this group of men is unique in their status and function. John, the revelator, sees them as foundational to the New Jerusalem, and it is in this sense that they are referred to in Ephesians chapter two.

Scripture implies two unique features about the "twelve".

1. They ALL saw the Lord Jesus in the flesh and were directly appointed by Him see Appendix 2, and

2. They, together with prophets, laid the foundation of the church for ALL time.

"Now therefore you are no more strangers and foreigners, but fellow citizens with the saints, and of the household of God; And are built upon the foundation of the apostles and prophets, Jesus Christ himself being the chief cornerstone; In whom all the building joined together grows into a holy temple in the Lord: In whom you also are built together for a habitation of God through the Spirit."

Ephesians 2:19-22

One of the most important hermeneutic principles is that of comparing scripture with scripture. Nuances of English and Greek words are important, but they must be seen as subservient to this vital rule of Bible interpretation. If we do not put this into practice at all times we will fail to *"rightly divide the word of truth[31]"*. This cannot be over-emphasised as a guiding light to the faithful remnant. God has magnified His Word above His name, and we must treat it with the respect and care that it deserves. When we talk about the work and ministry of the Holy Spirit, the thing that should dominate our thinking and consideration is as I once heard the late David Newington say, "The Holy Spirit lives residentially within God's Word." He inspired it, and He won't operate outside of it. Let us never buy the idea that God is bigger than His Word, which is one of the nonsense expressions that circulates among Christians today. God and His Word are one.

When we apply this principle to the above text, we must conclude that the apostles and prophets are not the FOUNDATION of the church per se because another verse clearly tells us that Christ is the foundation, which fact is conveyed in Ephesians by the reference to "the chief cornerstone". The implication of Ephesians 2:20 is that the apostles and prophets i.e. the exclusive group of "the twelve" together with the prophets of the Old Testament and the New actually laid the foundation, and they did it once and for all time. The foundation itself is Jesus Christ, whom scripture identifies as being "all and in all[32]", for He is the "alpha and the omega ... the beginning and the ending.[33]"

"For no other foundation can any man lay than is laid, which is Jesus Christ."

1 Corinthians 3:11

The doctrine that we are discussing here reflects on the basic difference between Roman Catholicism and Protestantism. Admittedly, there are those within the Protestant camp who sincerely believe that the apostles and prophets in some way form part of the foundation of the church. They build their ideas on a perceived link between what Christ said about building His church upon *"this rock[34]"* and Isaiah's reference to Abraham:

"Listen to me, you who follow after righteousness, you who seek the LORD: look to the rock from which you were hewn, and to the hole of the pit from which you were dug. Look to Abraham your father, and to Sarah who bore you: for I called him alone, and blessed him, and increased him."

Isaiah 51:1 and 2

The argument at best is superficial and is undoubtedly Romish in its basis. In fact, I listened to a Roman Catholic apologist expound at length on this particular view and found it quite fanciful. The Protestant position has always been that Christ not Peter is the rock upon which the church is built.

Anything or anyone who replaces Christ should be viewed with suspicion, and this is probably the most concerning feature of much that is passing as

Christian in our time. There is much grandstanding that is linked to the use of grandiose terms and titles. Basically, it is all personality based, which Paul warns us against in the early part of his epistle to the Corinthians. Scripture very clearly declares that God will not give His glory to anyone else, and that, in itself,is a wonderful guide in examining the projections and practices of our time when so many men seem to be motivated by a desire for position to such an extent that they actually corrupt the Word of God.

"I am the LORD: that is my name: and my glory I will not give to another, or my praise to graven images."

Isaiah 42:8

"For we are not as many, making a gain by corrupting the word of God: but as of sincerity, but as from God, we speak in the sight of God in Christ."

2 Corinthians 2:17

So we see the first two ministry gifts listed in Ephesians chapter 4 as being quite different from those referred to in Ephesians chapter 2. The former are continuing. The latter are exclusive as to who they are and what they performed. Their laying of the foundation of the church equates to what Jude tells us,

"Beloved, when I was very diligent to write to you of our common salvation, it was necessary for me to write to you, and exhort you that you should earnestly contend for the faith which was once for all delivered to the saints."

Jude 3

Note the following parallels between our delivered faith and the church's foundation:

1. The foundation of the church has been laid We have a delivered not a developing faith;

2. Christ builds His church upon that foundation through His servants We contend for the faith and proclaim an uncorrupted message; and

3. The scriptures instruct us in both see APPENDIX 3 for a balanced summary.

PROPHETS

Christ identified John the Baptist as a prophet:

"But what did you go out to see? A prophet? Yes, I say to you, and more than a prophet."

Matthew 11:9

Our Lord was called a prophet, and He tacitly accepts the designation when he refers to a prophet not being accepted in his own country.

"And the multitude said, This is Jesus the prophet of Nazareth of Galilee."

Matthew 21:11

"And they were offended at him. But Jesus said to them, A prophet is not without honour, except in his own country, and in his own house."

Matthew 13:57

Apart from John and Jesus, the only person who is clearly identified in the Bible as a prophet in New Testament times is Agabus, though obviously there were others as the plural use of the word in the first of the following verses signifies...

"And in those days prophets came from Jerusalem to Antioch. And one of them stood up named Agabus, and showed by the Spirit that there should be a great famine throughout all the world: which happened in the days of Claudius Caesar."

Acts 11:27-28

"And as we stayed there many days, a prophet, named Agabus came down from Judaea."

Acts 21:10

The list of those named in Acts 13 fails to differentiate between prophets and teachers. Some have named additional New Testament prophets from the list either by guessing or from extra biblical sources.

"Now there were in the church at Antioch certain prophets and teachers; Barnabas, and Simeon who was called Niger, and Lucius of Cyrene, and

Manaen, who had been brought up with Herod the tetrarch, and Saul."

Acts 13:1

From what occurred with Agabus, we can safely conclude that New Testament prophets actually predicted events 100 percent accurately and always issued a warning. This immediately throws into question the claim made by so called "Apostle John P. Kelly".

"Apostolic ministry focuses on building ministry; prophetic ministry focuses on blessing."
The New Apostolic Churches, page 24.

It must have been a huge blessing to Paul to learn from Agabus that he would be bound and beaten in Jerusalem. Where in the world do these men get their ideas?

With the completion of the cannon of scripture, true prophets continue to function, but now their major ministry is to act as a voice of direction to the church by taking God's Word and applying it powerfully in the current situation. Revelation is the key to true prophetic ministry. A.W. Tozer and D. Martyn Lloyd-Jones were true prophets.

One of the most horrible things that has happened to the current church is the intrusion of the School of the Prophets, linked to so called Bishop Bill Hamon, who also features in Wagner's *The New Apostolic Churches.* The bizarre things that are associated with that movement beggar description. Chris and Debby Gaborit led the Australian expression of it. We have documented the strange things that they taught and promoted in our CETF journal. Gaborit is mentioned at http://www.christian-witness.org/archives/cetf1996/noah.html. Hamon is mentioned in

http://www.christian-witness.org/archives/van1998/twomysteries98.html, http://www.christian-witness.org/archives/cetf2000/NewReform61.html.

I listened to a taped message by Bill Hamon's son, in which he suggested that parents would recover their sons and daughters into the Kingdom of God if they paid $1000 to the School of the Prophets for each child who was away from the Lord. This is the doctrine of indulgences in a Protestant garb. That aside, it is deceitful. The fact that Hamon's son corrupted the Old Testament story about the godly woman from Shunem told in 2 Kings chapter 4 is desperately wicked. (See Appendix 4).

EVANGELISTS

The word "evangelist" appears twice in addition to the Ephesians reference. Philip is the only person who is called an evangelist. However, in its verb form, the Greek "*euaggelizo*" (Strong 2097) is used 55 times being variously translated to "preach" 23, "preach the Gospel" 22, "bring good tidings" 2, "show glad tidings" 2, "bring glad tidings" 1, "declare" 1, "declare glad tidings" 1, miscellaneous 3; Total 55.

The three references to evangelist(s) are as follows.

"And the next day we that were of Paul's company departed, and came to Caesarea: and we entered into the house of Philip the evangelist, who was one of the seven; and stayed with him."

Acts 21:8

"And he gave some to be apostles; some prophets; some evangelists; and some pastors and teachers."

Ephesians 4:11

"But be watchful, endure afflictions, do the work of an evangelist, fulfil your ministry."

2 Timothy 4:5

An evangelist (Greek "*euaggelistes*" Strong 2099) is specifically commissioned to preach Christ as witness the example of Philip in Acts.

"Then Philip went down to the city of Samaria, and preached Christ to them. ... Then Philip opened his mouth, and began at this scripture, and preached Jesus to him."

Acts 8:5 &35

However, part of proving one's call to the ministry, whatever the commission, is to do the work of an evangelist. It is the responsibility of an "*apostolos*" = a "sent one" as witness all of those named as apostles in the New Testament. It is equally part of the task of a "prophet" (Greek "*prophetes*" Strong 4396). A good definition of a prophet is "one who, moved by the Spirit of God and hence His organ or spokesman, solemnly declares to men what he has received by inspiration, especially concerning future events, and in particular such as relate to the cause and kingdom of God and to human salvation."[35] Pastor and teacher Timothy was so instructed to do the work of an evangelist. No one can escape this responsibility seeing it is part of the great commission.

"And Jesus came and spoke to them, saying, All authority has been given to me in heaven and on earth. Therefore go, and disciple all nations, baptizing them in the name of the Father, and of the Son, and of the Holy Spirit: Teaching them to observe all things that I have commanded you: and, lo, I am with you always, even to the end of the age. Amen."

Matthew 28:18-20

"Therefore those that were scattered went everywhere preaching the word."

Acts 8:4

PASTORS AND TEACHERS

The English "pastor" appears only in Ephesians chapter 4. However, the Greek equivalent "*poimen*" (Strong 4166) appears a total of 18 times, being rendered "shepherd" on all other occasions. The Online Bible makes this instructive observation:

"The tasks of a Middle Eastern shepherd were...
- To watch for enemies trying to attack the sheep;
- To defend the sheep from attackers;
- To heal the wounded and sick sheep;
- To find and save lost or trapped sheep; and
- To love them, share their lives and so earn their trust.

During World War II, a shepherd was a pilot who guided another pilot whose plane was partially disabled back to the base or carrier by flying alongside him to maintain visual contact."

Due to the construction of the English version of Ephesians 4: 11, it has been argued by some that there are four not five ministry gifts of Christ, that of pastor and teacher being a dual calling. This basically would not allow for the isolated ministry of a travelling or resident teacher. However, the Greek construction favours the idea of five not four ministry gifts. A Shepherd i.e. pastor does three things:

1. He leads or guides the sheep;
2. He feeds or provides for the sheep; and
3. He guards and protects the sheep.

Clearly then as a feeder, he must be also a teacher. The point, however, is that while a pastor (shepherd) must be able to teach, a teacher may not always be able to "shepherd". However, he must share the responsibility of guarding and protecting the sheep by virtue of his calling as a teacher.

As Jacob Prasch has well pointed out, the New Testament links false prophets with false teachers, and the Old Testament condemns the false "pastors" for the situation of declension which exists. If the false apostles, false prophets, hirelings, and false teachers are replaced with those who are genuine and true that will be a sign of God re-entering His redemptive realm. True revival will result, and the world will be evangelised in the way that God has sovereignly decreed.

"But there were also false prophets among the people, even as there shall be false teachers among you, who will secretly bring in destructive heresies, even denying the Lord who bought them, and bring on themselves swift destruction."

2 Peter 2:1

"Woe to the shepherds that destroy and scatter the sheep of my pasture! says the LORD. Therefore thus says the LORD God of Israel against the shepherds that feed my people; You have scattered my flock, and driven them away, and have not attended to them: behold, I will attend to you for the evil of your doings, says the LORD. And I will gather the remnant of my flock out of all countries where I have driven them, and will bring them again to their folds; and they shall be fruitful and increase. And I will set up shepherds over them who shall feed them: and they shall fear no more, or be dismayed, nor shall they be lacking, says the LORD."

Jeremiah 23:1-4

APPENDICES

1

Islam and Christianity

THE following is a summary of an article written by Sean D. Hammill, staff reporter of the Chicago Tribune which was entitled, *Pastor, Imam have dialogue at suburban church* dated October 12, 2001.

For the first few weeks after the September 11 terrorist attacks, senior pastor Bill Hybels of Willow Creek Community Church was increasingly bothered by reports of hate crimes and misinformation about Islam.

Hammill reports Hybels as saying, "I am so concerned by the gap between Muslims and Christians that is growing week by week by week and I thought Willow could do something about that." So Hybels' church in South Barrington, one of the larger Christian churches in the country, invited a local Muslim leader, Fisal Hammouda, to talk last weekend (October 6/7, 2001) about Islam to an aggregate of 17,000 churchgoers. Hybels told his congregation, "There are some Americans and some Christians spreading rumours and half-truths that the Koran encourages violence," then added, "Well, you take some stuff out of context and we've got major problems."

Hammouda is a U.S. citizen who emigrated from Egypt in 1969. He is an engineer and an imam, or religious leader, in the Islamic Centre in Naperville. He had visited Willow Creek in March as part of the church's world religions weekend, and had continued to talk to Bill Hybels in the period before the September 11 attacks. Because of their past association the discussion was at times light-hearted. They even joked about converting each other. It became sombre as it turned to politics and violence.

Hybels talked with Hammouda on stage in a 4,500-person auditorium for about 45 minutes, asking questions that he said were drawn from hundreds of emails. "As it started to look like it might be Osama bin Laden ... who directed the attack, what did you think?" Hybels asked. Hammouda said that at first he thought, "It couldn't be a Muslim," explaining that the holy book of Islam, the Koran, does not allow violence against innocent people. "The Koran says: `Who kills an innocent life, it's as if he killed all humanity.'"

The imam discussed the links between Christianity and Islam. "We believe in Jesus, more than you do in fact," said Hammouda. When Hybels ventured to disagree the audience laughed. Hammouda explained that Islam teaches that Jesus and other biblical figures are Islamic prophets though of lesser importance than Muhammad, the faith's main prophet. "We call you 'the people of book.' We have all the prophets from the Bible," he said.

That fact alone surprised many in the audience. Church member Elizabeth Perez, 60, later commented, "I didn't know they believed in Jesus. I thought it was interesting how much we have in common". Hammouda claimed that the true definition of a "jihad," or holy war could refer to "overcoming" a desire to eat more candy. When

Hybels asked Hammouda, "Why do some Muslims hate the U.S. as much as they do?" Hammouda said many Muslims see U.S. decisions about Israel, Iraq and Yugoslavia as "inconsistencies in our foreign policy" that favour non-Muslims.

Later Marilyn Stoken, 69, a church member for two years who was visiting the church with her daughter, Leslie, 38 said Hammouda "still professes hate for Israel". After the service, Hybels commented that the goal of the event wasn't to change longstanding views. "I don't know that many views needed to be changed," he said. "I think questions were answered." Judy Barrie, 30, said the interview "opened up doors to communicate and showed [Muslims are] people just like we are."

That is the kind of impact Hybels had hoped for. "It gave us a greater sense of assurance that maybe, despite all of our differences, we can get along," he said."

APPENDIX 2

Have I Not Seen Jesus Christ

IN Paul's classic defence of the truth of the resurrection he claims that he saw Christ and that he was the last to see Him. Set as it is in the context of the definition of the Gospel of Christ Christ died for our sins as the Bible predicts and records; He was buried i.e. He was truly dead; He rose again from the dead; and finally He was seen by witnesses (1 Corinthians 15:1-8) it is quite clear that Paul is linking himself as a witness to the resurrection. And he claims to be the last to so witness Christ. Clearly then this is more than a mere vision to which he is referring. He says that he saw Christ as literally and with the reality of Peter and all the rest, including about 500 at one time. Traditionally it has been understood that here, Paul is actually stating that he is the last witness to Christ's resurrection. No one else will ever see Christ in that capacity again. So much for all the claims about Christ appearing in the flesh to modern day televangelists.

This fact Paul later claims is one of the requirements (marks, signs, seals) of an apostle of the first order viz one of the twelve. Paul puts this forward as distinctive evidence that a claim to being an apostle of the Lamb in association with the "twelve" is genuine.

"And last of all he was seen by me also, as of one born out of due time"

1 Corinthians 15:8

"Am I not an apostle?... have I not seen Jesus Christ our Lord?"

1 Corinthians 9:1

APPENDIX 3

Doctrinal Purity Commission

From a member of AoG USA Doctrinal Purity Commission:

Dear Bro. Philip,

I received your paper (see Part 9) for which you had asked comment. I am grateful to God for what you are doing. I am especially glad you are continuing to press the issues with the national A/G leadership. I appreciated much your paper. I thought there might be some additional clarification you may or may not want to add to your section on Apostles.

We addressed the subject with our Doctrinal Purity Commission. Allow me for whatever it may be worth to you to throw in a few thoughts:

The Pulpit Commentary has an excellent dissertation on this in Volume 20 in the introduction to the Book of Galatians beginning on pg. xxiii. Allow me to summarize.

The uses of the word apostle.

1. It is first used of Christ (Hebrews 3:1 & 2).
2. It was used of the "apostles of the Lamb"those immediately delegated by Christ.
3. Matthias is likewise chosen by Christ himself to fill the place among the twelve vacated by Judas's fall.
4. It is used of Paul who claimed Christ appointed him.

All of these were given for the founding of the church and fixing the faith which was then "once for all delivered unto the saints," their function, after the analogy of the earthly work of Christ himself, neither needed nor was designed to be perpetuated through successors, whether in one line or in several.

5. But last of all there were apostles delegated by the church. These are not rulers of the church. This word was frequently applied to messengers who were sent upon some religious errand (including preaching the gospel) with credentials of a public missionary from this or that church.

With this in mind, when the word was translated into the Latin it was given the Latin word from which we get our word "missionary." And as R.E. McAlister who wrote about this matter back in 1949, when this was such a problem during the "Latter Rain" error, "...it would be in keeping with true humility to avoid presumptuous titles, which are easily misunderstood, and which place the user in a position of superiority complex.

No person today could be an apostle in the class with Jesus Christ. No person today could be an apostle in the class with the twelve "Apostles of the Lamb." No person today could be an apostle in the class with the apostle Paul. But thousands today could be and are in the fourth class with Barnabas, who was a mission, evangelist an helper...Missionary is the generally understood and accepted term throughout th English speaking world."

Our early forefathers opted to use the name Pentecostal instead of apostolic becaus of these implications. Brumback says, while they knew that the faith which they hel was apostolic doctrine, they felt that "Pentecostal" did not make them appear t arrogate unto themselves apostolic office, and yet continued to identify them with th outpouring of the Spirit."

The restorationists make a big deal about the restoration of apostles. The church ha never been without them. People sent on special mission for the Lord's work. Withou getting into great detail, we also have prophets. But the N.T. prophet is not the same a the O.T. prophet who was looking forward to the coming of Messiah and who gave th Word of God. Let me paraphrase,

"In the past God spoke in many times in many ways to our fathers through th prophets, but in these last days he has spoken to us through His Son - the ultimat prophet beyond whose revelation none of us can speak. The job description of presen prophets is spelled out in 1 Corinthians 14."

May God bless you richly,

Carl Guiney,
Woonsocket, R.I.
U.S.A

APPENDIX 4

Apostles, Prophets & Money

THE following is just one section from a historic document called *The Teaching o the Lord to the Gentiles by the Twelve Apostles* (also known as Didache). It wa translated by J.B. Lightfoot and later adapted and modified. © 1990 Athena Dat Products.

Didache 11:1 *Whosoever therefore shall come and teac you all these things that have been said before, receive him;*

Didache 11:2 *but if the teacher himself be perverted an teach a different doctrine to the destruction thereof, hear him no but if to the increase of righteousness and the knowledge of th Lord, receive him as the Lord.*

Didache 11:3 *But concerning the apostles and prophets, s*

do you according to the ordinance of the Gospel.

Didache 11:4 *Let every apostle, when he cometh to you, be received as the Lord;*

Didache 11:5 *but he shall not abide more than a single day, or if there be need, a second likewise; but if he abide three days, he is a false prophet.*

Didache 11:6 *And when he departeth let the apostle receive nothing save bread, until he findeth shelter; but if he ask money, he is a false prophet.*

Didache 11:7 *And any prophet speaking in the Spirit you shall not try neither discern; for every sin shall be forgiven, but this sin shall not be forgiven.*

Didache 11:8 *Yet not every one that speaketh in the Spirit is a prophet, but only if he have the ways of the Lord. From his ways therefore the false prophet and the prophet shall be recognized.*

Didache 11:9 *And no prophet when he ordereth a table in the Spirit shall eat of it; otherwise he is a false prophet.*

Didache 11:10 *And every prophet teaching the truth, if he doeth not what he teacheth, is a false prophet.*

Didache 11:11 *And every prophet approved and found true, if he doeth ought as an outward mystery typical of the Church, and yet teacheth you not to do all that he himself doeth, shall not be judged before you; he hath his judgment in the presence of God; for in like manner also did the prophets of old time.*

Didache 11:12 *And whosoever shall say in the Spirit, Give me silver or anything else, you shall not listen to him; but if he tell you to give on behalf of others that are in want, let no man judge him.*

FOOTNOTES:

[1] Refer section 3 chapter ?? page ??

[2] The organisers of the Apostles and Prophets Conference (APC) Brisbane - February 2000

[3] The advertising literature of the APC held in Brisbane in February 2000.

[4] *The New Apostolic Churches* © 1998 by C. Peter Wagner published by Regal Books, p 73.

[5] *The Bride of Christ Series* is available from your nearest CWM Office see back cover or address.

[6] http://link.crosswalk.com/UM/T.ASP?A3.15.3057.1.272087 link may no longer be available; www.christian-witness.org/not_in_pubs/willowc_islam.htm

[7] *Churchquake,* Regal Books, California © 1999, C. Peter Wagner.

[8] Refer *CHURCHQUAKE* pages 118 and 119 APOSTLES HAVE GODLY CHARACTER see ref to humility on these pages.

[9] *The New Apostolic Churches,* Regal Books © 1998 C. Peter Wagner, p20.

[10] *"And when it was day, he called to him his disciples: and of them he chose twelve, whom also he named apostles"* Luke 6:13.

[11] *Churchquake!* page 90

[12] *The New Apostolic Churches* page 36.

[13] Ibid page 32

[14] Ibid page 34

[15] Ibid - page 33.

[16] Ibid - page 38.

[17] Ibid page 40.

[18] Ibid page 29.

[19] Ibid page 40.

[20] Ibid page 35.

[21] Ibid page 38.

[22] Dudley Daniel has returned to Australia for health reasons, pending a possible operation which has been described as too costly in the USA.

[23] *Dorea* denotes " a gift which is also a gratuity, hence of the gift of a sovereign".

[24] *"Therefore I charge you before God, and the Lord Jesus Christ, who will judge the living and the dead at his appearing and his kingdom; Preach the word; be ready in season, out of season; convict, rebuke, exhort with all patience and teaching. "For the time will come when they will not endure sound doctrine; but after their own desires because they have itching ears they will heap up for themselves teachers," And they will turn away their ears from the truth, and will be turned aside to fables"* (2 Timothy 4:1-4).

[25] See Section 3 page 98-100.

[26] *Churchquake!* page 104.

[27] The Companion Bible argues that the Greek allows for Junias i.e. male.

[28] *"For I think that God has displayed us the apostles last, as men condemned to death: for we are made a spectacle to the world, to angels, and to men"* (1 Corinthians 4:9).

[29] *"And the wall of the city had twelve foundations, and in them the names of the twelve apostles of the Lamb"* (Revelation 21:14).

[30] *"For it is written in the book of Psalms, Let his habitation be desolate, and let no one live in it: and let another take his bishopric* (office)*"* (Acts 1:20).

[31] *"Be diligent to show yourself approved to God, a workman that doesn't need to be ashamed, rightly dividing the word of truth"* (2 Timothy 2:1).

[32] *"Where there is neither Greek nor Jew, circumcised nor uncircumcised, barbarian, Scythian, bond nor free: but Christ is all, and in all"* (Colossians 3:11).

[33] *"I am the Alpha and Omega, the beginning and the end, says the Lord, who is, and who was, and who is to come, the Almighty"* (Revelation 1:8). *"Saying, I am the Alpha and the Omega, the first and the last: and, What you see, write in a book, and*

send it to the seven churches which are in Asia; to Ephesus, to Smyrna, to Pergamos, to Thyatira, to Sardis, to Philadelphia, and to Laodicea" (Revelation 1:11). "And he said to me, It is done. I am the Alpha and the Omega, the beginning and the end. I will give to him that thirsts freely of the fountain of the water of life" (Revelation 21:6). *"I am the Alpha and the Omega, the beginning and the end, the first and the last"* (Revelation 22:13).

34 *"And I say also to you, That you are Peter, and upon this rock I will build my church; and the gates of hades shall not prevail against it"* (Matthew 16:18).

35 *On Line Bible definition.*

PART FIVE

Cessationism versus Biblicism
Cessationism under the biblical spotlight

Can the Cessationist and the moderate Pentecostal reach agreement over spiritual gifts?

This was published as a separate paper, which appeared in CWM Journal Contending Earnestly for The Faith (CETF). Your comments on this, and any other part of the book are welcomed.

CHAPTER ONE

A Universal Issue

Introduction

An earlier draft of this article was sent by email to a number of men from both the cessationist and non-cessationist camps. Barry Chant, Peter Barnes, Jacob Prasch, Andre van der Linden and Spencer Gear made the most comprehensive responses, some of which have been incorporated. However I stand responsible for what is published below, which I know will not be the final word on the subject. Your comments are very welcome. Spencer Gear made the suggestion that a biblical response to cessationism warrants a more detailed look at such questions as: *What supernatural gifts are available for today's church? Can "tongues" in the Book of Acts be compared with I Corinthians 12-14? Why the fuss about tongues? Is the hassle concerning the supernatural gifts in the church today in any way related to the church's lack of power and impact on society (in the Western world)? Is there any way of reconciling cessationists with moderate (biblical) charismatic/pentecostals? If apostles continue today, what should their function look like?* These are all valid questions and no doubt there are more.

In what follows I have simply sought to open the subject and give a reasonably comprehensive overview. Somewhere along the line we will endeavour to act on Spencer's suggestion and possibly publish a booklet addressing these issues or maybe one of our readers will take up the challenge. Already we have received some very helpful comments about the modern "apostle" idea from Carl Guiney, who is a member of an AG (USA) committee who are looking at the vexed question of doctrinal purity associated with the revival of the latter rain errors linked to Pensacola and Toronto, which have been taken on board by so many. Douglas Dean of Florida, suggested that there is a huge conflict in the USA and he, like so many, encouraged us to go forward in the battle for truth. We value your prayers and your thoughts on the subject.

Philip L. Powell

CHAPTER TWO

Definitions and Perspectives

THIS might prove to be the major issue confronting part of the church in our time. Bible-believing Christians find themselves in a tension between the extremes of charismania and Pentecostalism on the one hand and their steadfast commitment to a God who never changes, as presented in scripture and throughout history, on the other.

What confronts us here is the old *"baby and bath-water"* analogy, which has been much over-used and at times can be dismissed as being too simplistic. In some cases there may be more than one bathtub or there's no baby, just dirty water, which needs to be thrown out! But the analogy does apply in this case as we are dealing with an honest dilemma that has produced a pendulum swing. Good people, who won't endorse the false, do, at times, end up rejecting the real.

To examine the issue dispassionately and fairly we must start with a right premise and proceed with clear logic, humbly looking to the Lord that the Holy

Spirit will guide us into all truth. So let's begin with definitions and then establish a foundation for our rationale:

CESSATION: "a stopping, permanent or temporary discontinuance"
The World Book Dictionary by Thorndike Barnhart.

From a theological perspective "*Cessationist* refers to someone who thinks that certain miraculous gifts *ceased* long ago, when the apostles died and scripture was complete."[1]

When the word *CESSATIONISM* is applied in a biblical or theological setting it signifies a body of belief which asserts a permanent or temporary discontinuance of the supernatural displays of God and/or of the manifestations or gifts of the Holy Spirit as listed in 1 Corinthians 12:7-11 and/or of some of the ministry gifts of Christ referred to in Ephesians 4:11. Just as there are degrees of charismatic and Pentecostal teaching and emphases so there are degrees of CESSATIONISM.

The extreme position of the latter asserts that everything supernatural ended with the establishment of the canon of scripture and the passing of the twelve Apostles. Dr Jack Deere[2] shows how serious the cessationist position can become. He writes:

"I was once arguing with a well-known theologian over the subject of the gifts of the Spirit. I made the comment that there was not a shred of evidence in the Bible that the gifts of the Spirit had passed away. He said, 'I wouldn't go that far, but I know that you cannot prove the cessation of the gifts by scripture. However, we do not clearly see them in the later history of the church, and they are not part of our own theological tradition."

This man taught at a seminary that was dogmatically cessationist in its approach to miraculous gifts, but in private conversation he freely admitted that this doctrine could not be proved by scripture.[3]

Dr Peter Masters of Spurgeon's Metropolitan Tabernacle, London, is a cessationist. He wrote:

"In these days of charismatic confusion we need constantly to draw attention [to] the texts which prove that signs and wonders were peculiar to the apostolic band, and were not bestowed generally."[4]

Very few Christians, let alone denominations and local churches, accept this extreme teaching today. Most will acknowledge that at the very least supernatural divine healings do sometimes (occasionally) occur; that inexplicable miracles do take place; that God does still answer prayer, otherwise why pray? This view seems to be widespread,

"The more spectacular gifts (tongues, healings, miracles) necessitated some degree of order that would prevent their indiscriminate use (1 Corinthians 14:40). The spirits of the prophets must be subjected to the prophets (vs 32). Paul clearly insists that spectacular gifts were inferior to those that instructed believers in faith and morals and evangelised non-Christians. Tongue speaking was not forbidden (vs 39), but intelligent exposition of the word, instruction in faith and morals, and preaching the gospel were infinitely superior. The criteria used to judge the relative values of spiritual gifts were doctrinal (1 Corinthians 12:3), moral (1 Corinthians 13), and practical (1 Corinthians 14)."[5]

The more moderate and reasonable cessationist teaching focuses upon some, if not all, of the nine gifts of the Holy Spirit mentioned in 1 Corinthians 12:7-11 and upon two of the ascension ministry gifts of Christ viz that of apostle and prophet c/f Ephesians 4:11. In short, moderate CESSATIONISM believes and teaches that the ministries of apostle and prophet are not valid since the completion of the canon of scripture and that those gifts of the Holy Spirit, which were essential to their function, have ceased. How many of the nine gifts of the Holy Spirit are thus affected is not always clear. There are varieties of opinions among those who take the cessationist position on this point. Most will deny three of the *vocal* gifts speaking in tongues, interpretation of tongues and prophecy, unless prophecy is interpreted as preaching, as it is by many cessationists. John MacArthur is such an example.[6]

Some will deny the *sign* gifts viz working of miracles and some aspects of the gifts of healings and of the gift of faith. Often cessationists adopt a view about the three *revelatory* gifts the word of wisdom, word of knowledge and discerning of spirits so as to diminish or destroy the supernatural nature of their displays. Thomson & Elwell provide an example of this kind of interpretation:

"Speaking the word of knowledge suggests a word spoken only after long and careful consideration. This would be a word that the Christian teacher would ordinarily speak."[7]

"The greatest problem with my former point of view [as a cessationist] is

that it is not even remotely close to the experience of the people of the Bibl
God did speak to them apart from the scripture. He warned, encouraged, an
gave specific geographical leading to his people. In order to support my ol
view, I had to find a way to *explain away* all the biblical examples of God'
regular special revelation and guidance for his children."[8]

BIBLICISM: "strict or literal adherence to the Bible"
The World Book Dictionary by Thorndike Barnhart.

Theologically, biblicism "refers primarily to an excessively literal method o interpretation. It emphasizes individual words, rejects any form of th historical-critical method, and frequently employs some form of fre association or taking verses out of their context to prove a point (hence, proo texts). Some evangelicals may use biblicism to indicate their commitment t the absolute authority of the Bible in all matters of faith and practice."[9]

In every theological discussion we must start with scripture, so let's do it an return to the basic argument and an examination of the presuppositions an "modus operandi" of both sides later.

"Bind up the testimony, seal the law among my disciples. And I will wai upon the LORD, who hides his face from the house of Jacob, and I will lool for him. Behold, I and the children, whom the LORD has given me are fo signs and for wonders in Israel from the LORD of hosts, who dwells in moun Zion. And when they shall say to you, Seek unto them that have familia spirits, and unto wizards that whisper, and that mutter: should not a people seel unto their God? for the living to the dead? To the law and to the testimony: i they speak not according to this word, it is because there is no light in them."

Isaiah 8:16-2(

When Isaiah penned those words the expression *"to the law and to th testimony"* was an appeal to the Word of the Lord as it then stood as Ale Motyer in his Tyndale OT Commentary[10] on Isaiah and H.C. Leupold in hi Exposition of Isaiah: Volume 1, Chapters 1-39 (one vol. edition) prove se footnote 10, below. We must of course remember that the Israelites had strong and accurate oral culture at this time.[11]

The Law and the Testimony included everything and precluded nothing o the whole counsel of God at that time. Interestingly Isaiah in this passag condemns all those who go outside of the Word of God for their instruction o teaching as being in total darkness even though v19 makes it clear that he i opposing those who are into spiritism. Sola Scriptura is a doctrine that stretches right back to the Garden of Eden and is supported by the balance of the Old Testament e.g. Micah 3:5-7, Jeremiah 27:12-22 and 29:4-9.

The New Testament affirms the same thing,

"For I testify to every man who hears the words of the prophecy of this book, If any man shall add to these things, God shall add to him the plagues that are written in this book: And if any man shall take away from the words of the book of this prophecy, God shall take away his part out of the book of life, and out of the holy city, and from the things which are written in this book"

Revelation 22:18-19

While the words "this book" may indeed be primarily a reference only to the Book of the Revelation as some assert[12] there are many other New Testament scriptures, which affirm the unique authority of the Bible in matters of spiritual life and doctrine as the following bear testimony by way of example.

"And that from a child you have known the holy scriptures, which are able to make you wise unto salvation through faith which is in Christ Jesus. All scripture is given by inspiration of God, and is profitable for doctrine, for reproof, for correction, for instruction in righteousness"

2 Timothy 3:15-16

"Search the scriptures; for in them you think you have eternal life: and they are they, which testify of me. And you will not come to me, that you might have life"

John 5:39-40

At this point we can reasonably conclude, with some reservation that in theory, at least, both sides think they are standing on common ground, but in practice each tends to stray and sometimes for a very noble reason on the part of both viz a commitment to the *Sola Scriptura* principle. On the one hand some who belong to the Pentecostal or charismatic camps, in their honest attempt to support the biblicism that includes the present day reality of the Holy Spirit, end up trying to defend the indefensible in justifying some or all of the aberrations of their history and/or current bizarre practices. On the other hand some of those who adopt the cessationist position, by starting from the premise of these obvious unscriptural and non biblical occurrences sometimes end up undermining their most cherished doctrine Sola Scriptura by actually appealing to extra biblical sources in an attempt to establish their point.

John MacArthur has done this by his examples from experience. See chapter 7 of *Charismatic Chaos*, "How do spiritual gifts operate?" and the experiential examples he gives. One example is that of parents who wrote to his church about their daughter who "had become involved in a large, well-known Third Wave church. Her mother wrote about the daughter's experience with speaking in tongues, angels and demons. One demon 'sat on her husband's head one night and hissed at her. She sees others riding on top of cars or standing on rooftops and some in battle with the angels. She sometimes sees darkness around people. She believes seeing this is a God-given gift'."[13]

In fairness to MacArthur, we must remember that Paul appealed to the experience of the Judaizers when he confronted Peter in Galatians 2. I'm sure we could find other examples from experience in scripture. We cannot confront error without appealing to current examples.

Jack Deere observes,

"There is one basic reason why Bible-believing Christians do not believe in the miraculous gifts of the Spirit today. It is simply this: they have not seen them [his emphasis]. Their tradition, of course, supports their lack of belief, but their tradition would have no chance of success if it were not coupled with their lack of experience of the miraculous. . . No cessationist writer that I am aware of tries to make his case on scripture alone. All of these writers appeal both to scripture and to either present or past history to support their case. It often goes unnoticed that this appeal to history, either past or present, is actually an argument from experience, or better, an argument from lack of experience."[14]

Jack Deere pointedly says "Even the greatest of the cessationist scholars, Benjamin Breckenridge Warfield, could not make his case on scripture alone. He appealed both to the scriptures and to "the testimony of later ages."[15]

In effect each arrives at the one point a denial of the sufficiency and adequacy of scripture why? I suggest that it is because their premise is wrong. I am not saying that we must not appeal to church history or to experience far from it. All valid as well as false doctrines find their outworking in real life. What I am saying is that if we start with history instead of with our doctrine of God from the Bible we will go astray and come to wrong conclusions. We must build our argument upon the basis of scripture alone. Having done that, then we should examine history and current happenings in the light of the doctrine that we have established from the Bible. This is the only safe way to proceed.

Is Cessationism Biblical?

Here we must once more emphasise the fact that there are degrees of cessationism see the examples above. To say, as was common among a number of branches of conservative evangelicals several decades ago, that supernaturalism ended with the passing of the original apostles is without any biblical support. Statements such as, *"Jesus Christ the same yesterday, and to day, and forever"* (Hebrews 13:8), whether interpreted solely in relation to the context or taken as a great principle of the gospel, clearly denies the idea. There are many biblical statements that teach the same thing.

"For I am the LORD, I do not change; therefore you sons of Jacob are not consumed."

Malachi 3:6

"Every good gift and every perfect gift is from above, and comes down from the Father of lights, with whom is no variableness, neither shadow of turning."

James 1:17

What we are discussing here is what theologians call the immutability of God. The extreme cessationist view is so clearly contrary to the doctrine of the changelessness of God as taught in scripture that we would only labour the point if we quoted more passages from the Bible against it.

The more moderate view is not so easily dismissed as it impinges upon another equally important theological truth, which we call the sovereignty of God and which needs to be held in tension with God's immutability. Cessationists tend to focus on the former whereas most Pentecostals and charismatics focus on the latter. Correct teaching about each will not deny or undermine either. This is where the art of rightly dividing the Word of Truth by comparing scripture with scripture, is so important. Sovereignty says that God can choose to withdraw the displays of His supernatural powers. Immutability says that He will only do so in accordance with His nature and character as revealed in His Word, the Bible.

Far from sovereignty denying and undermining immutability, the fact that God is SOVEREIGN means that He is able to maintain the changelessness of His ways and works. Now this is the principal part of the premise on which we must build our argument in respect of our topic.

Cessationism affirms that God in His sovereignty has determined to cause certain things that He gave to the early New Testament church to cease or come to an end. We say that such a position must not be arrived at arbitrarily by conjecture, nor simply on the basis of history as we perceive it, but by scripture. Does the Word of God establish (prove) it?

To those in the Pentecostal and charismatic camps we would issue the same challenge. Let the Word of God decide and let history and experience illustrate what the Bible teaches. To the one we say, "Take out your Bibles and show us clearly where scripture teaches that the supernatural displays of God, including the nine gifts of the Holy Spirit and the five ascension ministry gifts of Christ, are said or prophesied to cease and we will support your view. Do this before you make your appeal to church history."

To the other we say, "Take out your Bibles and show us clearly where your strange and sometimes bizarre so called manifestations of the Holy Spirit find support. Do this in a reasonable and convincing manner before appealing to experience or history and we will go along with you".

At the risk of labouring the matter I suggest that this is where some who have already spoken or written on this topic have been in error. I have read a number of Cessationists, of varying degree, who have started out by attacking their opponents, not on the basis of Bible doctrine but on the basis of what is perceived to be their bad record or suspect origins. This is a false starting point and will inevitably result in misleading conclusions, especially when men make huge leaps of logic purportedly based on scripture.

For example several opponents of those who are of a Pentecostal persuasion have started their discussion by pointing to the extremes of Azusa Street and W.J. Seymour or of Charles Parham at the beginning of this century. Or they have attacked prominent Pentecostal ministers, such as Smith Wigglesworth, on the basis of the alleged extremes, which no sensible Bible-believing person would endorse. Others who are anti-charismatic have begun by exposing the pro-Roman Catholic leanings of the leaders of the so-called Charismatic Renewal of the 1950s and 1960s, such as David du Plessis, who took *"charismania"* to the Roman Catholic Church (RCC). They ignore the fact that du Plessis' action was condemned by a number of his Pentecostal colleagues at the time. Bible-believing Christians from both camps cannot justify these extremes or the actions, which have contributed to ecumenism. BUT I say that this whole approach of starting with history instead of with scripture is wrong and will inevitably lead to suspect conclusions. The argument is founded upon a wrong premise. Sadly, some good people who were committed to the immutability of God in respect of the present day reality of the Holy Spirit in fruit and gifts have cast away their first love and their faith and now wander in the wilderness of doubt.

Both sides do it and both are equally wrong. Pentecostals and charismatics, in some regards are worse than those in the Cessationist camp, for they frequently revise history and claim or imply that many of the great heroes of the "church" support their position. All too frequently they do this on the basis of very flimsy evidence and in some cases no evidence at all. These are the sorts of consequences that inevitably flow out from an argument that is built on history and not on scripture. Let us appeal to history and to experience, by all means, but let us do so only after we have established our case clearly on the Word of God.

To illustrate my point I refer to two cases: One of my former colleagues appealed to Charles Wesley's great hymn , *"Oh For A Thousand Tongues To Sing My Great Redeemer's Praise"* as evidence that John and Charles Wesley and the early Methodists supported speaking in tongues as taught by Pentecostals. He said that the thousand tongues of the hymn were *"diverse kinds of tongues"* referred to in 1 Corinthians 12:10. On another occasion a former associate in that particular camp suggested to me that the late Dr Martyn Lloyd Jones (MLJ) would support the bizarre happenings of Toronto and Pensacola. He based his assertion simply on the doctor's many spoken and written statements in support of revival.

Having known MLJ to some extent during my time as a preacher in Great Britain and being aware of his great suspicion of the charismatic movement, I of course knew that my friend was quite wrong in his conclusions. Despite his well-known criticisms of the extremes of both Pentecostalism and charismania, it is worth noting that MLJ was still very friendly with well-known Assemblies of God leaders including the late WTH Richards and the late David Powell.

Maybe Jack Deere puts his finger on the problem,

"When Christians from the Western world hear stories like this [Corrie ten Boom's vitamin bottle that did not run out], they sometimes ask, 'Why don't we have more supernatural revelation in our churches?' I think it's because the Western church often has more in common with the Laodicean church than with the faith of those like Corrie ten Boom. "Why should we expect God to speak to us when we spend so little time with him?

The question is not, 'Why don't we see more miracles and have more supernatural revelation in the church today?' Rather, given the apathy and the lack of godliness in the church today, the question is, 'Why do we have any supernatural experiences at all in the American church?'"[16]

To the LAW and the TESTIMONY

Isaiah's appeal to the Word of God in terms of His law on the one hand and the record of His acts on the other (c/f Is 8:20 explained above) finds a counterpart in DOCTRINE (mainly the epistles) and HISTORY (mainly the four gospels and the book of Acts) in the New Testament. Isaiah actually implies what will happen to those who depart from a Sola Scriptura position dead formality i.e. a religious experience and practice, which lacks the supernatural element that is essential to make God's people "signs and wonders" (Isaiah 8:18) on the one hand; or on the other hand an occult situation among the "mediums and wizards, who whisper and mutter" (Is 8:19). This is precisely what is happening.

John MacArthur gives an example,

"I talked to a man who is a leader in the modern Pentecostal movement, and he said to me, 'You cannot deny my experience.'

I responded by saying, 'Well, let me ask you this. When an experience occurs, do you always, without question, know that it is of God? Be honest.' He answered, 'No.'

'Could it be of Satan?' I asked. He reluctantly replied, 'Yes.' My charismatic friend had no answer. This is exactly where the Corinthians were. They did not know what was of God and what was not. The work of the Spirit was confused with pagan ecstasies. They needed help."[17]

MacArthur is of the view that "only what is valuable is counterfeited". He explains,"It seems obvious that if people in the Corinthian assembly were calling Jesus accursed, the gifts they claimed to have received from the Holy Spirit were counterfeit. My father had a saying, 'No one counterfeits what isn't valuable.' One never hears about counterfeit brown paper. People do not counterfeit trash. But they do counterfeit money, diamonds, and jewellery. Counterfeits copy what is valuable because that is the only point in counterfeiting. Satan was busy in the Corinthian church imitating spiritual gifts, and he is busy doing the same thing today."[18]

Wayne Grudem warns about associating tongues' speaking with the demonic,

"Paul says, 'I want you all to speak in tongues' (1 Corinthians 14:5 RSV). He gives no warning that they should beware of demonic counterfeit or even think that this would be a possibility when they use this gift."[19]

On balance I favour MacArthur here as 1 Corinthians 12:3 implies the possibility of a demonic counterfeit.

CHAPTER THREE

Spiritual Gifts & Callings

Apostles & Prophets

"Now therefore you are no more strangers and foreigners, but fellow-citizens with the saints, and of the household of God; And are built upon the foundation of the apostles and prophets, Jesus Christ himself being the chief corner stone; In whom all the building fitly framed together grows into a holy temple in the Lord: In whom you also are built together for a habitation of God through the Spirit"

Ephesians 2:19-22

In another place Paul tells us that Christ Himself is the foundation (1 Corinthians 3:11). Here, in Ephesians, he explains that this foundation is already laid and that Christ is also the *"chief corner stone"* viz that which holds the whole building together. The apostles and the prophets of Ephesians 2:20 have done the job once and for all time (c/f Jude 3). They were an exclusive group who were committed to a unique work. Neither will ever be repeated. The work of the apostles of the Lamb and the prophets of the scripture, through the enabling of the Holy Spirit, was foundational to the establishment and continuous building of the church of our Lord Jesus Christ.

This is common ground for both parties Sola Scriptura! Extreme Pentecostals and Charismatics depart from the sufficiency of scripture when they fail to see this and like Peter Wagner and his associates go into a non-biblical authoritative heavy shepherding teaching that end times "apostles and prophets" lay the foundation of the present day church.

For example, Peter Wagner says,

"I am giving considerable emphasis to prophecy on these pages because I sense we are living in the midst of an extraordinary move of God. It has recently become evident that the fastest growing segment of Christianity on six continents is a movement I call the New Apostolic Reformation. It includes, among many others, African Independent Churches, Chinese house churches, Latin American grassroots churches, independent charismatics and many local congregations still operating within traditional denominational structures. One of the most innovative characteristics of this movement (although several exceptions might exist) is the reinstatement of the New Testament offices of prophet and apostle."[20]

The idea that modern "apostles and prophets" are the foundation of the church is rank error and leads to an apostasy of THE FAITH once delivered to the saints. But and here's the dividing line between those who take a cessationist position and those of us who don't while the Ephesians 2:20 "apostles and prophets" and their work were unique, those mentioned two chapters later are not just the twelve or the Old Testament prophets, as an examination of the context and a detailed study of the New Testament make plain.

"And He gave some, apostles; and some, prophets; and some, evangelists; and some, pastors and teachers; For the perfecting of the saints, for the work of the ministry, for the edifying of the body of Christ: Till we all come to the unity of the faith, and of the knowledge of the Son of God, to a perfect man, to the measure of the stature of the fullness of Christ."

Ephesians 4:11-13

Here is the New Testamemt reference to the five (some say four) ascension ministry gifts of Christ. Each person is himself a "gift" of Christ to His church. Naturally each will have "gifts" to enable him to perform his function, but that is not the emphasis of this passage. Christ gave each ministry gift to His body for all time until *"we all come to the unity of the faith"*. The fact that "evangelists" and "pastor/teachers" or "pastors and teachers" are mentioned alongside of "apostles and prophets" points to the fallacy of the idea that the ministry gifts of apostles and prophets ended with the canon of the New Testament or the passing of the Apostles of the Lamb. Paul teaches that Christ gave all five (four) for the *"equipping of the saints for the work of ministry"*, which is required throughout the church age.

The incident of Acts 1:15-26 indicates that the *apostles* chosen by Christ did not view themselves as exclusive. They were prepared to elect someone to replace Judas. Irrespective of whether we view Matthias or Paul as the true replacement we are faced with an extension to the original twelve apostles. Acts 14:14 mentions Barnabas as another. It is possible, though not certain that Judas, Barsabas and Silas (see Acts 15:22, 23 & 33) were also apostles. Some have pointed to Romans 16:7 as including Andronichus and Junia (a woman), but the evidence is flimsy to say the least.[21] Wayne Grudem writes, "The verse has too little clear information to allow us to draw a conclusion."[22] It is far more likely that the apostles recognised them as notable faithful followers of

Christ. The idea of a woman being a New Testament apostle is contradicted by Paul in 1 Timothy 2:12 and 1 Corinthians 14:34. These considerations, plus texts such as 2 Corinthians 11:13 and Revelation 2:2 indicate that the term apostle was fairly liberally applied to leaders in New Testament times, so much so that there arose false apostles, who were in danger of deceiving God's people. All of this points strongly to the idea that we are not looking at an exclusive group that was as numerically limited as some have led us to believe.

"Now you are the body of Christ, and members in particular. And God has set some in the church, first apostles, secondarily prophets, thirdly teachers, after that miracles, then gifts of healings, helps, governments, diversities of tongues. Are all apostles? Are all prophets? Are all teachers? Are all workers of miracles? Have all the gifts of healing? Do all speak with tongues? Do all interpret? But covet earnestly the best gifts: and yet I show you a more excellent way"

1 Corinthians 12: 27-31

In 1 Corinthians chapters 12 to 14 Paul is basically dealing with conduct within the local church especially as it applies to spiritual activity. He commences with the injunction "Now concerning spirituality" literally "spirituals" [Greek *pneumatikos* (Strong 4152) the word *gifts* is not in the original of verse 1]. In verses 4-7 he outlines his subject:

1) Verse 4different gifts - taught in verses 7-11;
2) Verse 5different parts - taught in verses 12-27; and
3) Verse 6different appointments - taught in verses 28-30.

Contrary to what is implied by some Pentecostals, Paul is dealing with spirituality and spiritual function as a whole within the context of a local church and not only with the gifts of the Spirit. So, could it be that when he comes to consider appointments (functions) as the final point of his teaching in this chapter, he is talking about those who operate only in a local church setting? In other words are there local apostles as distinct from the twelve and distinct from the apostles of the church universal?

The problem that we face is one of translation. The Greek *apostolos* (Strong 652) signifies one who is sent forth with orders. He is a delegate or a messenger. Our English apostle transliterates the word and this has tended to create grandiose ideas, which may not have occurred had the word been translated. Peter Wagner and the many Assembly of God and other Pentecostal leaders, such as Brian Houston, Phil Pringle, Mark Conner, John Lewis and Danny Guglielmucci, whom we named in the previous CETF[23] as being some who have jumped on the band wagon of self promotion, have cashed in on this and in so doing have over-looked what Paul had to say about himself and other genuine ambassadors (apostles) of the New Testament church. He calls himself the least of the saints, the greatest of sinners and, as an apostle, one who was set last not first. He was an apostle of the Lord Jesus Christ i.e. one who was sent forth to represent the One who made Himself of no reputation and became obedient to the death of a cross. It is an issue of identification not one of authority.

If all the marks of an apostle as outlined by Paul were applied to those who see themselves as modern day apostles there would be few takers. Yes Paul does speak of supernatural signs (2 Corinthians 12:12) and church planting (2 Corinthians 10:16), but he also points to the things that he suffered and his good example in appointing to office only those who shared his character and humility (2 Corinthians chapters 11 & 12).

On one occasion I told my former colleagues who were touting one of their members as an apostle that he was precluded on account of the character of some whom he appointed as pastors. One was a homosexual and another became a double adulterer. These things do count even though the modern church so readily overlooks them and hides the facts. Apostles don't appoint men of questionable character and conduct as pastors or elders of God's people.

So in summary, while Cessationists may see only one expression of the ministry of apostles and prophets in the NT, there is a strong biblical argument for at least two and possibly three.

Gifts of the Holy Spirit

"But the manifestation of the Spirit is given to every man to profit everyone. For to one is given by the Spirit the word of wisdom; to another the word of knowledge by the same Spirit; To another faith by the same Spirit; to another the gifts of healing by the same Spirit; To another the working of miracles; to another prophecy; to another discerning of spirits; to another different kinds of tongues; to another the interpretation of tongues: But all these work by one and the selfsame Spirit, dividing to every man according to his will"

1 Corinthians 12: 7-11

The biblical word "manifestation"(1 Corinthians 12:7) Greek *phanerosis* (Strong 5321) is derived from *phaneroo* (Strong 5319), which contains the idea of something that "shines forth" as distinct from "fruit" (Galatians 5:22) Greek *karpos* (Strong 2590), which signifies that which grows i.e. the natural product of life. The nine gifts of the Spirit, in their pure expression are manifestations i.e. (the out-shining) of the works of God, of whom the Holy Spirit is the executor. The nine fruit of the Spirit are the natural product of the nature of God, which is love. True manifestations and the real fruit of the Holy Spirit reveal God in His works and in His nature and character. They are complementary and should never be viewed as competitive or mutually exclusive.

Cessationists never question the validity of the fruit of the Spirit at any point in church history, including the present day, so why do they question the gifts of the Holy Spirit? Is there any biblical basis for their denial?

Some point to 1 Corinthians 13:8-13. The argument mainly relates to the statement that "tongues will pas saway" (in the middle voice) i.e. "pass away of themselves". The argument in not convincing as an examination of the passage shows:

"Love never fails: but whether there be prophecies, they shall fail; whether there be tongues, they shall cease; whether there be knowledge, it shall vanish away. For we know in part, and we prophesy in part. But when that which is perfect is come, then that which is in part shall be done away"
(verses 8-10)

Groups like the Strict or Bible Baptists and some Open Brethren have argued that the "perfect", which Paul said would come, is a reference to the completion of the canon of scripture, when prophecies and tongues would cease.

While not naming the denominations, John MacArthur acknowledges,

"Many suggestions have been made as to the meaning of 'the perfect'. Some believe it is the complete New Testament; thus they conclude this passage is saying that tongues would cease when the canon was closed."[24]

But there are huge logical and contextual problems to that idea. Paul says that knowledge will *"vanish away"*. Did this happen with the advent of the canon of scripture? Knowledge far from vanishing has increased enormously. Faced with this problem some cessationists say that the knowledge referred to is the supernatural gift of the word of knowledge mentioned in verse 8 of the previous chapter. If that is so then how do they explain the phrase "we know in part" in the context of their argument? Did the canon of scripture make our knowledge complete? If you reason that Paul and the Holy Spirit are referring to the supernatural "word of knowledge" then logically you must say that the coming of the canon of scripture extended the gift into another dimension. It didn't cause it to cease.

Then they are faced with a further problem when asked to explain the analogy of 1 Corinthians chapter 13 verses 11 and 12,"When I was a child, I spoke as a child, I understood as a child, I thought as a child: but when I became a man, I put away childish things. For now we see through a glass, darkly; but then face to face: now I know in part; but then shall I know even as also I am known".

The completion of scripture does not put anyone of us in a position where we know everything (even as we are known), nor does it ensure that we always put away childish thoughts and ways. The coming of the "perfect" to which Paul refers cannot possibly be a reference to the canon of scripture though we agree that the scriptures are perfect. And yes we agree with many cessationists that it is not our Lord Jesus Christ that he is referring to, though He too is perfect. On the basis of logic and the context of the passage it is quite clear that Paul is talking about a future state, which will eclipse this present church age. He is alluding to the Second Coming of our blessed Lord and Saviour Jesus Christ when the gifts of the Holy Spirit as the early church and the pilgrim church of the ages experienced them will no longer be required. The clause *"then face to face"* (v 12) is the key to WHEN this will be at his second coming.

So what are these gifts and how do they operate? First we must face a prior question what initiates the reception and/or manifestation of the nine gifts of the Holy Spirit?

"In those days came John the Baptist, preaching in the wilderness of Judea, (v2) and saying, Repent for the kingdom of heaven is at hand. (vs 5&6) Then went out to him Jerusalem, and all Judea, and the entire region round about Jordan, and were baptized of him in Jordan, confessing their sins (vs 10-12). And now also the axe is laid to the root of the trees: therefore every tree, which brings not forth good fruit, is hewn down, and cast into the fire. I indeed baptise you with water to repentance: but he who comes after me is mightier than I, whose shoes I am not worthy to bear: he shall baptise you with the Holy Spirit, and with fire: Whose fan is in his hand, and he will thoroughly purge his floor, and gather his wheat into the granary; but he will burn up the chaff with unquenchable fire."

Matthew 3:1-12

According to Hebrews chapter six there is a New Testament doctrine of baptisms (c/f v2) note the plural. In the above scripture John Baptist mentions two:

1) His own baptism in water to repentance; and

2) Baptism by Christ with (into) the Holy Spirit and with fire.

The New Testament mentions three other baptisms:

3) The Baptism of Suffering for Christ and His followers (Luke 12:50 c/f Matt 20:22-23);

4) Christian Water Baptism replacing John's Baptism (Matthew 28 c/f Acts 19:3-5);

5) Baptism by the Holy Spirit into the body of Christ (1 Corinthians 12:13).

Each of these baptisms forms an important part of the third of the six foundational truths spoken of in Hebrews chapter 6 and is worthy of deep study. For the purposes of this article we need to look briefly at the second and the fifth viz baptism by Christ, the Head of the church in or into the Holy Spirit and baptism by the Holy Spirit into Christ i.e. the body of Christ.

In 1 Corinthians 12:13 Paul refers to the Holy Spirit as the subject of the action and the body of Christ as the element into which the believer is immersed. In Matthew 3:11 John the Baptist identifies Christ as the subject of the action and the realm of Holy Spirit as the element into which the followers of Christ would be baptised. There are obvious distinctions so we must conclude that there is a real difference. Can this be confirmed from other Bible passages?

John chapters 14, 15 and 16 contain the major teaching of Christ regarding the Holy Spirit whom He identifies as the comforter, helper, advisor or advocate. His essential work is to replace and represent Christ by *"abide*[ing] *with you forever"* (John 14:16-18), *"teach*[ing] *you all things and bring*[ing] *all things to your remembrance"* (John 14:26), *"testify*[ing] *of Me"* (John 15:26) and *"convict*[ing] *the world of sin, ... righteousness and of judgement."* In achieving this Jesus said to His disciples, *"you know him; for he dwells with you, and shall be in you"* (John 14:17).

In summary our Lord taught that the Holy Spirit is WITH in REVELATION i.e. convincing or convicting of sin, righteousness and judgement. He comes INTO to bring ANIMATION i.e. life at the moment of the new birth or what we call regeneration. This is illustrated when our Lord appeared to His disciples on the day of His resurrection, breathed on them and said, *"Receive the Holy Spirit"* (John 20:22). Such teaching is in complete harmony with Peter's view of the new birth as taught in his epistle,

"Blessed be the God and Father of our Lord Jesus Christ, which according to his abundant mercy has begotten us again to a lively hope by the resurrection of Jesus Christ from the dead"

1 Peter 1:3

"Being born again, not of corruptible seed, but of incorruptible, by the word of God, which lives and abides for ever."

1 Peter 1:23

In the act of regeneration the Holy Spirit enters the life of the believer and applies the Word of God, which is the active life-giving agent. As Paul puts it, *"So then faith comes by hearing, and hearing by the word of God"* (Romans 10:17). The basis of this is not what happened at Pentecost but what happened at the resurrection of Christ.

In Acts chapter one our Lord promised that the Holy Spirit would come upon His disciples to empower them to become witnesses to Him i.e. DEMONSTRATION, see Acts 1:8. In verses 4 and 5 He calls this the Promise of the Father, which He Himself had previously told them about and which He links to the action and statement of John the Baptist see Matthew 3:11. It is very clear that the baptism in or into the Holy Spirit by Christ the head of His church, to which John the Baptist referred and which Christ said would occur *"not many days from now"*, took place on the day of Pentecost as recorded in Acts chapter 2, ten days after Christ's ascension (Acts 1:9).

By comparing scripture with scripture it seems reasonable to say that it is by the entry of the Holy Spirit into a person that he/she is "baptised" (initiated) into the body of Christ and it is by the coming of the Holy Spirit upon the believer that he/she is baptised (initiated) by Christ into the realm of the Spirit. That both may happen simultaneously is possible; that each may be separate in time and occasion is also possible.

The Crux of the Matter

"He that speaks in an unknown tongue edifies himself; but he that prophesies edifies the church. I would that you all spoke with tongues, but rather that you prophesied: for greater is he that prophesies than he that speaks with tongues, except he interpret, that the church may receive edifying."

1 Corinthians 14:4&5

1 Corinthians chapters 12 to 14 contain some of the most difficult and contentious parts of the New Testament.[25] The issue of "speaking with

tongues" has been one of the most divisive. While that is acknowledged, neither the passage of scripture nor the gift of tongues should be ignored. All scripture is inspired of God i.e. God breathed (2 Timothy 3:16) and is therefore vital to us as His people.

In 1 Corinthians 14:4-5 Paul brings together what are often referred to by Pentecostals as the three vocal or inspirational gifts, though both designations are obvious over-simplifications. The context shows that he is teaching the correct public function of these gifts in the local church at Corinth, where he implies all sorts of abuses including the wrong use of the gift of tongues. He tells us that the person who prophesies is greater than the one who speaks in tongues unless that person actually interprets the tongue, which he speaks. The reason being that tongues, on its own does edify the individual but it does not edify the church, while prophecy on its own does edify the church. The basic idea of edify is to build up. Remembering that Paul is teaching the public operation of the gifts for the benefit of the whole church, his meaning is quite clear and, contrary to what has been claimed by some cessationists, he is correcting but not condemning the public use of tongues. In another verse he actually says that he uses the gift of tongues more than anybody and thanks God that he does, but when he is in church he chooses not to speak in tongues, his emphasis being on teaching. (1 Corinthians 14:18-19).

Quite obviously then Paul has in mind a speaking in tongues which is other than public. In verse 15 he writes: *"I will pray with the spirit, and I will pray with the understanding also: I will sing with the spirit, and I will sing with the understanding also"* and links this in verse 18 with speaking with tongues. The argument of verses 4 and 5 see above points very clearly to the idea that all public tongues speaking, whether ordinary speech or in song requires interpretation for the edifying of the church, something which is not required if it is done in private. This is in line with the force of Paul's argument of verses 18 and 19. There is no other satisfactory explanation of this passage of scripture,

"What is it then? I will pray with the spirit, and I will pray with the understanding also: I will sing with the spirit, and I will sing with the understanding also. Else when you shall bless with the spirit, how shall he that occupies the place of the unlearned say Amen at your giving of thanks, seeing he does not understand what you say? For you indeed give thanks well, but the other is not edified. I thank my God, I speak with tongues more than you all: Yet in the church I had rather speak five words with my understanding, that by my voice I might teach others also, than ten thousand words in an unknown tongue." 1 Corinthians 14:15-19

What is the Gift of Speaking with Tongues?

"And when the day of Pentecost was fully come, they were all with one accord in one place. And suddenly there came a sound from heaven as of a rushing mighty wind, and it filled the entire house where they were sitting. And there appeared to them divided tongues like fire, and it sat upon each of them. And they were all filled with the Holy Spirit, and began to speak with other tongues, as the Spirit gave them utterance."

Acts 2:1-4

Those in the upper room the context suggests all 120, not just the 12 apostles spoke forth what the Holy Spirit gave them to articulate. They did not know what to expect. It would be much better if people, who seek the fullness or baptism of the Holy Spirit today didn't know either. Pentecostal specialists, who first instruct then suggest what to articulate, actually degrade the experience to a humanistic and psychological level. This is the result of an undue and unbiblical emphasis on speaking in tongues. That which was a sovereign act of God has been reduced to a human manipulation where men count scalps. How many have "come through" is all too frequent a question on the lips of Pentecostal seekers. Speaking in tongues not the mighty baptism in the Holy Spirit has become the focus and pursuit of many. In Acts 1:8 Jesus promised ability (*dunamis*) to bear witness (become martyrs) not some initial evidence of speaking with tongues. Nonetheless they did (all of them) speak in tongues so what was it or what is it?

"And there were dwelling at Jerusalem Jews, devout men, out of every nation under heaven. Now when this was noised abroad, the multitude came together, and were confounded, because that every man heard them speak in his own language. And they were all amazed and marvelled, saying one to another, Behold, are not all these which speak Galileans? And how is it that we hear every man in our own tongue we were born with? Parthians, and Medes, and Elamites, and the dwellers in Mesopotamia, and in Judea, and Cappadocia, in Pontus, and Asia, Phrygia, and Pamphylia, in Egypt, and in the parts of Libya about Cyrene, and strangers of Rome, Jews and proselytes, Cretans and Arabs, we do hear them speak in our tongues the wonderful works of God. And they were all amazed, and were in doubt, saying one to another, what does this mean? Others mocking said, These men are full of new wine."

Acts 2:5-13

The "other" Greek "*heteros*"[26] (= other than one's own) "tongues" Greek *glossa*"[27] (= languages or dialects) of verse 4 is paralleled by "our tongues" of erse 11. Those identified in verses 1 to 4 spoke in identifiable languages, vhich were recognised by a number of foreign visitors at Jerusalem and not earned or previously known by those who spoke. Some of their audience did ot understand the languages spoken or what was happening. The scoffers ismissed it all as the conduct of drunks, not because there was any suggestion f conduct associated with drunken behaviour, but simply because they didn't nderstand the languages nor what was happening. Each spoke in an unknown ongue.

Six times in 1 Corinthians chapter 14 the KJV translates the word *glossa* by 'unknown tongue" see verses 2, 4, 13, 14, 19 and 27. The fact that there is no Greek equivalent for the English "unknown" does not destroy the significance f the words chosen by the KJV translators. The context of each verse listed bove implies that the language or dialect spoken was unknown to the person peaking and to the body of the church unless what was said was interpreted. In airness when Pentecostals use the word unknown in this context they do not mply that it is not a valid language that was spoken, as some Cessationists ave falsely claimed.

Pentecostal scholar and commentator, Dr Gordon Fee, writes concerning 1 Corinthians 13:1,

"'Tongues of men' would then refer to human speech, inspired by the Spirit out unknown to the speaker, 'tongues of angels' would reflect an understanding hat the tongues-speaker was communicating in the dialect(s) of heaven."[28]

The unknown tongue is a valid language that will be known and spoken somewhere on earth or in heaven.[29] In fairness though I disagree with the use f the expression *ecstatic utterance,* in respect of speaking in tongues, it does ot imply meaningless babble. It simply expresses the attitude and expression f joy of the person speaking.

On account of the bizarre, outrageous and totally absurd claims and conduct f some of my former Pentecostal friends I have, at times, longed to be able to ind an explanation for *speaking in tongues* other than the one which I was aught within the Pentecostal camp, but I can't. The idea that speaking in ongues is simply a linguistic ability just makes nonsense of what Paul says and eaches. It also contradicts what happened on the day of Pentecost as recorded n Acts chapter 2. Both apply *speaking in tongues* to an act of the Holy Spirit, which superseded human knowledge and intelligence,

"And they were all filled with the Holy Spirit, and began to speak with other tongues, as the Spirit gave them utterance."

Acts 2:4

"For he that speaks in an unknown tongue speaks not to men, but to God: for no man understands him; but in the spirit he speaks mysteries."

1 Corinthians 14:2

Why Tongues?

There are four major clear incidents in the book of Acts where we are told about the Holy Spirit filling, falling upon or being received by the people Acts 2, 8, 10 and 19. On three of these occasions speaking in tongues is directly identified. Cessationists say that each is a sort of corporate baptism or initiating the first of the Jews, the second of the Samaritans, the third of the gentiles and the fourth a special case. This is an extra biblical explanation or a dispensational interpretation. There is no basis in scripture itself for the conclusion. It is theologically and logically unacceptable. If there is a need for a corporate baptism of different ethnic groups, which is highly questionable, it still does not account for the Special Case of Acts 19 where, in verse 6 we have the evidence of tongues and prophecy. Some say that in the case of the latter we have a group of people who were not Christians but simply followers of John Baptist. But verse 1 denies this. The word *"disciple"*, unless it is otherwise previously qualified, is consistently applied to Christ's followers in the four gospel narratives and the book of Acts. Consistency demands that it means and implies here what it does elsewhere. The issue in question is not whether these 12 men were followers of Christ but whether they had heard about the Holy Spirit, which then raised the issue of baptism. The question remains if the idea of corporate baptism by the Spirit is a valid one then why the special case?

The only other case that features in scripture is that of Saul of Tarsus who became Paul the apostle,

"Ananias went his way, and entered into the house; and putting his hands on him said, Brother Saul, the Lord, even Jesus, who appeared to you in the way as you came, has sent me, that you may receive your sight, and be filled with the Holy Spirit."

Acts 9:17

Interestingly and to contradict those Cessationists who argue that the filling of the Holy Spirit referred to here was a reference to Saul's conversion, Ananias calls him "brother" and makes no reference to his pending conversion, regeneration or new birth, but simply to his receiving sight and being filled with the Holy Spirit. Saul's unconditional submission to the Lordship of Christ (Acts 9:6) makes it very clear that he was converted on the road to Damascus (c/f 1 Corinthians 12:3) and then later filled or baptised into the Holy Spirit and into water. Later he says to the Corinthians, *"I thank my God, I speak with tongues more than all of you"* (1 Corinthians 14:18).

So of the five cases mentioned in scripture there are no others there are four incidents of speaking in tongues either at the time or subsequently. The one exception is Acts 8, where quite obviously there was some dramatic and immediate supernatural sign that the believers had received the Holy Spirit seeing Simon the sorcerer offered money for the power to impart the Holy Spirit. We do not know what it was and must not argue from silence either for or against tongues. We do know that Simon had witnessed miracles performed by Philip and that he did not make the same offer to him that he later made to Peter and John. So what he saw and/or heard when the Samaritans received the Holy Spirit was obviously quite remarkable and Simon expected similar displays when others received.

The question remains "Why did God choose speaking in tongues?"

Paul applies the prophecy contained in Isaiah 28:11-12 to the New Testament practice of speaking in tongues c/f 1 Corinthians 14:21 and gives one reason for tongues speaking viz a sign to unbelievers (1 Corinthians 14:22). This is what happened on the day of Pentecost and it became at least in part a fulfilment of what Isaiah said would happen. However the force of Paul's words, being in the present tense and the local church setting, is that the sign would be ongoing, but only in a selective way.

"Brethren, do not be children in understanding: but in malice be children, but in understanding be men. In the law it is written, With men of other tongues and other lips will I speak to this people; and yet for all that will they not hear me, says the Lord. So then tongues are for a sign, not to them that believe, but to them that do not believe: but prophesying serves not for them that do not believe, but for those who believe. If therefore the whole church come together into one place, and all speak with tongues, and there come in those that are uninformed, or unbelievers, will they not say that you are mad?"

1 Corinthians 14:2

Paul is not condemning tongues speaking. He is correcting the abuse of it in the local church and regulating its function to the edification of the body. That it is a sign to the unbeliever remains a truth established by testimony (Acts chapter 2) and by doctrine (Paul's teaching). To depart from this is to depart from the Sola Scriptura principle.

"Let all things be done for edification. If any man speaks in an unknown tongue, let it be by two, or at the most by three, and in succession; and let one interpret. But if there is no interpreter, let him keep silence in the church; and let him speak to himself, and to God."

1 Corinthians 14:26-28

We may deduce another reason why God chose tongues from the teaching of James who tells us that no-one is capable of controlling his tongue i.e. his speech (James chapter 3). What happened at Pentecost and in the house of Cornelius and at Ephesus and to Paul and the Corinthian tongues speaking believers all of these are clearly established historic incidents were displays of divine ability to control what no man or woman is able to control unaided by the Holy Spirit. At Pentecost God tamed the human tongue and caused men and women to speak forth the praises of God in languages which they had never learned, thus by-passing the one faculty which tends to make us arrogant and proud our intellect. Could there be any greater reason why God would choose tongues?

However, having said all that, there are two important things to emphasise:

1) God does not arbitrarily overrule man's will, so the control, which is illustrated in the gift of speaking in tongues, is not a permanent feature in respect of human behaviour. It was as the Holy Spirit gave them to articulate at Pentecost and it is as the Holy Spirit distributes as He wills in respect of all of the gifts of the Spirit; and

2) It is unbiblical to seek tongues per se. We should seek the baptism or filling of the Holy Spirit and there's the rub and what I consider to be a major contributing factor to much of the error that has crept into the Pentecostal and charismatic movements. Many Pentecostals have become "tongues" seekers instead of being seekers after God and the mighty baptism into the Holy Spirit.

CHAPTER FOUR

Brief Historic Survey

JOHN WESLEY (1703-1791), who with his brother Charles saw the start of the great world-wide Methodist movement was regularly in dispute with another minister called Conyers Middleton. In response to inquiries about the gift of tongues by Rev Dr Conyers Middleton, John Wesley (JW) said,

"Sir, your memory fails you again: It has undoubtedly been pretended to [ie practised], and that at no great distance either from our time or country. It has been heard of more than once, no farther off than the valleys of Dauphiny. Nor is it yet fifty years ago since the Protestant inhabitants of those valleys so loudly pretended to [ie practised] this and other miraculous powers, as to give much disturbance to Paris itself... He who worketh as He will, may, with your good leave, give the gift of tongues, where he gives no other; and may see abundant reasons so to do, whether you and I see them or not."[30]

On another occasion John Wesley preached,

"It does not appear that these extraordinary gifts of the Holy Ghost were common in the church for more than two or three centuries. We seldom hear of them after that fatal period when the Emperor Constantine called himself a Christian; and, from a vain imagination of promoting the Christian cause thereby, heaped riches and power and honour upon the Christians in general, but in particular upon the Christian clergy. From this time they almost totally ceased; very few instances of the kind were found. The cause of this was not, (as has been vulgarly supposed,) 'because there was no more occasion for them,' because all the world was become Christians. This is a miserable mistake; not a twentieth part of it was then nominally Christian. The real cause was, 'the love of many,' almost of all Christians, so called, was 'waxed cold.' The Christians had no more of the Spirit of Christ than the other heathens. The Son of Man, when he came to examine his church, could hardly 'find faith upon the earth'. This was the real cause why the extraordinary gifts of the Holy Ghost were no longer to be found in the Christian church; because the Christians were turned heathens again, and had only a dead form left."[31]

Today (21/09/00), as I am writing this piece, I received a copy of Edmund Hamer Broadbent's (1861-1945) magnificent book *The Pilgrim Church,* which I first encountered when studying at the AoG Commonwealth Bible College (CBC) in Brisbane, (1957-1959), the city where we have just returned to live. It has been re-published by Gospel Folio Press, PO Box 2041, Grand Rapids, MI 49501, USA and contains a foreword by Dave Hunt. The enthralling record of the faithful remnant church as distinct from the structured (organised) false Christendom, which masquerades as the church, focuses on the persecutions not the incidents of supernaturalism of church history, but nonetheless the author provides convincing evidence of God at work through the gifts of the Holy Spirit. Writing of Christ's declared intention for His church, the author records,

"Each of these consists of those disciples of the Lord Jesus Christ who, in the place where they live, gather together in His Name. To such the presence of the Lord in their midst is promised and the manifestation of the Holy Spirit is given in different ways through all the members (Matthew 18:20; 1 Corinthians 12:7).

Each of these churches stands in direct relationship to the Lord and draws its authority from Him and is responsible to Him (Revelations 2 and 3). There is no suggestion that one church should control another or that any organised union of churches should exist, but an intimate personal fellowship unites them (Acts 15:36).

The chief business of the churches is to make known throughout the world the gospel or glad tidings of salvation. This the Lord commanded before His ascension, promising to give the Holy Spirit as the power in which it should be accomplished (Acts 1:8).

Events in the history of the churches in the time of the Apostles have been selected and recorded in the Book of the Acts in such a way as to provide a permanent pattern for the churches. Departure from this pattern has had disastrous consequences, and all revival and restoration have been due to some return to the pattern and principles contained in the scriptures."[32]

Elsewhere he writes,

"The practice of founding churches where any, however few, believed, gave permanence to the work, and as each church was taught from the first its direct dependence on the Holy Spirit and responsibility to Christ, it became a centre for propagating the Word of Life." [33]

"The growth of a clerical system under the domination of the bishops, who in turn were ruled by "metropolitans" controlling extensive territories, substituted a human organisation and religious forms for the power and working of the Holy Spirit and the guidance of the scriptures in the separate churches."[34]

"In Phrygia, Montanus[35] began to teach (156), he and those with him protesting against the prevailing laxity in the relations of the church to the world. Some among them claimed to have special manifestations of the Spirit, in particular two women, Prisca and Maxilla. The persecution ordered by the Emperor Marcus Aurelius (177) quickened the expectation of the Lord's coming and the spiritual aspirations of the believers. The Montanists hoped to raise up congregations that should return to primitive piety, live as those waiting for the Lord's return and, especially, give to the Holy Spirit His rightful place in the church."[36]

At this point we should acknowledge the possibility of bias and prejudice. I am reminded of the well known statement made by Ken Ham of Answers in Genesis to the effect that we are all biased so we might as well choose the bias with which we are biased. We all read history in the light of our particular mindset. Montanists[37] are viewed by many as heretics, but as Broadbent shows there were several expressions of the movement both within and outside of the RCC.[38]

There are only 16 sayings which are extant that are regarded as coming from Montanists. We are thus relying for our view of the movement as it was seen by its opponents. The only literature we really have on them comes from Eusebius of Caesarea and Epiphanius of Salamis. The indication is that the movement was erratic. The earliest group may have started in the Spirit and like so many present day Pentecostals and charismatics ended in the smoke of confusion and uncorrected excesses, which inevitably express themselves in false doctrine.

A Montanist group seems to have predicted the second coming, with the New Jerusalem descending on Phrygia, which presents us with another interesting parallel between what happened historically and what is happening today. Both the Montanists and the Revival Now people adopt false teaching about the End Times and the Return of Christ. Our only point in referring to the Montanists and to some other groups is to produce historic evidence for our basic biblical premise. We do not in any way endorse the excesses of Toronto and Pensacola, which undoubtedly parallel the heresies of some of the Montanists. There is nothing new under the sun.

IRENAEUS (AD 115-202), pupil of Poly-carp, who was a student of John the apostle wrote: "In like manner do we also hear many brethren in the church, who possess prophetic gifts, and who through the Spirit speak all kinds of languages, and bring to the light for the general benefit the hidden things of men and declare the mysteries of God, whom also the apostles term spiritual."[39]

JUSTIN MARTYR (AD 100-165) "It is possible now to see among us women and men who possess gifts of the Spirit of God."[40]

TERTULLIAN (AD 160-220) invited the heretic Marcion, who was his contemporary, to produce among his followers anything similar to that which was evident among orthodox Christians. "Let him exhibit prophets such as have spoken, not by human sense but with the spirit of God, such as have predicted things to come, and have manifest the secrets of the heart; let him produce a psalm, a vision, a prayer, only let it be by the Spirit in an ecstasy, that is in a rapture, whenever an interpretation of tongues has occurred to him."[41]

PACHOMIUS (AD 292-348). In his book *LIVES OF THE SAINTS* (1756) A Butler refers to Pachomius, who after seasons of prayer was able to speak under the power of the Holy Spirit, the Greek and Latin languages, which he had never learned.[42]

MARTIN LUTHER (AD 1483-1546) In a letter to one of his followers (1545) "When you depart lay your hands upon the man again and say, *'These signs shall follow them that believe; they shall lay hands on the sick and they shall recover.'*"

On the basis of the available evidence one is forced to the conclusion that throughout history there can be discovered incidents, remote at times, but nonetheless there, which prove beyond reasonable doubt that the supernatural manifestations of the power and presence of God through the gifts of the Spirit have occurred and recurred among God's people under God's providence.

The Covenaters and Puritans

Alexander Peden was a Scottish minister who was ejected in 1662. His farewell sermon lasted until midnight! He became a field preacher and had all sorts of experiences where he just escaped arrest through a prophetic word, which warned him of where to go or where not to go.

A strict cessationist would have some trouble with his biography.[43] The book is full of prophetic words, which happened to Peden all through his career.

SAMUEL RUTHERFORD (1600-1661) was a Christian Scottish writer in the seventeenth century, who saw no conflict between an authoritative Bible and the Almighty God giving divine revelation to people outside of the Bible. He records how this has happened through the history of the church:

"There is a revelation of some particular men, who have foretold things to come, even since the ceasing of the Canon of the Lord, as John Husse [John Hus], Wickeliefe [Wycliffe], Luther, have foretold things to come and they certainly fell out, and in our nation of Scotland, M. George Wishart foretold that Cardinall Beaton should not come out alive at the Gate of the Castle of St Andrews, but that he should dye a shamefull death, and he was hanged over the window that he did look out at, when he saw the man of God burnt, M. Knox prophesied of the hanging of the Lord of Grange, M. Ioh Davidson uttered prophecies, knowne to many of the kingdome, diverse Holy and mortified preachers in England have done the like..."[44]

CHARLES HADDON SPURGEON (1834-92) was the prominent Baptist preacher in England during the 19th century, who spoke of a "sermon at Exeter Hall in which he suddenly broke off from his subject, and pointing in a certain direction, said, 'Young man, those gloves you are wearing have not been paid for: you have stolen them from your employer'. At the close of the service, a young man, looking very pale and greatly agitated, came to the room, which was used as a vestry, and begged for a private interview with Spurgeon. On being admitted, he placed a pair of gloves upon the table, and tearfully said, 'It's the first time I have robbed my master, and I will never do it again. You won't expose me, sir, will you? It would kill my mother if she heard that I had become a thief'."[45]

"On another occasion while he was preaching, Spurgeon said there was a man in the gallery who had a bottle of gin in his pocket. This not only startled the man in the gallery who had the gin, but it also led to his conversion."[46]

Spurgeon gives further examples of his prophetic ministry:

"While preaching in the hall, on one occasion, I deliberately pointed to a man in the midst of the crowd, and said, 'There is a man sitting there, who is a shoemaker; he keeps his shop open on Sundays, it was open last Sabbath morning, he took nine pence, and there was four pence profit out of it; his soul is sold to Satan for four pence!' A city missionary, when going his rounds, met with this man, and seeing that he was reading one of my sermons, he asked the question, 'Do you know Mr Spurgeon?' 'Yes,' replied the man 'I have every reason to know him, I have been to hear him; and under his preaching, by God's grace I have become a new creature in Christ Jesus. Shall I tell you how it happened? I went to the Music Hall, and took my seat in the middle of the place: Mr Spurgeon looked at me as if he knew me, and in his sermon he pointed to me, and told the congregation that I was a shoemaker, and that I kept my shop open on Sundays; and I did, sir. I should not have minded that; but he also said that I took nine pence the Sunday before, and that there was four pence profit; but how he should know that, I could not tell. Then it struck me that it was God who had spoken to my soul through him, so I shut up my shop the next Sunday. At first, I was afraid to go again to hear him, lest he should tell the people more about me; but afterwards I went, and the Lord met with me, and saved my soul.'"[47]

How does Spurgeon explain this prophetic ministry?

"I could tell as many as a dozen similar cases in which I pointed at somebody in the hall without having the slightest knowledge of the person, or any idea that what I said was right, except that I believed I was moved by the Spirit to say it; and so striking has been my description that the persons have gone away, and said to their friends, 'Come, see a man that told me all things that ever I did; beyond a doubt, he must have been sent of God to my soul, or else he could not have described me so exactly.' And not only so, but I have known many instances in which the thoughts of men have been revealed from the pulpit. I have sometimes seen persons nudge their neighbours with their elbow, because they had got a smart hit, and they have been heard to say, when they were going out, 'The preacher told us just what we said to one another when we went in at the door.'"[48]

OS GUINNESS

"Speaking once at Essex University, I saw sitting in the front row a strange-looking girl with an odd expression on her face. Remembering an incident the previous night when a radical had tried to disrupt the lecture, I spoke on but also prayed silently that she would create no trouble. She remained quiet the whole evening but came up as soon as it was finished with a very troubled look and asked me what spell I had cast to keep her quiet. She told me she was part of a spiritist circle in the south of England and that the spirits had ordered her to travel to Essex, where she had never been before, to disrupt a series of lectures beginning that week. The curious sequel to this was that when I arrived back in Switzerland someone else in the community, far from a fanciful visionary, asked me what had happened in the Essex lectures. Praying for them one morning, she had seen in a vision, as real as waking reality, the lecture hall and the strange girl about to disrupt the meeting. Having prayed for her, she was convinced that nothing had happened, but she wondered if it was just her imagination. The presence of a Christian praying in the power of the Holy Spirit is always enough to render the occult inoperable."[49]

19th and 20th Centuries

Contrary to what is generally perceived, modern Pentecostalism finds its roots not at the beginning of the 20th century at Azusa Street, Los Angeles but in the revival towards the end of the previous century. Men such as Charles Finney, Dwight L. Moody and R.A. Torrey stirred the hearts of many towards God. There are reports particularly during the ministry of Moody of people speaking in tongues.[50] For example the American evangelist in 1873 conducted a campaign in Sunderland, England. Robert Boyd was a journalist who visited the services and reported,.

"When I got to the rooms of the YMCA I found the meeting on fire. The young men were speaking in tongues and prophesying. What on earth did it mean? Only that Moody had been addressing them that afternoon."

F B MYER comments on his visit to the Baltic provinces of Russia: "It is very remarkable at a time when the Lutheran Church of this land has lost its evangelistic fervour .... The gift of tongues is heard quite often in the meetings ..."

In addition to these facts one has to take into account the impact of the Welsh revival of 1904 upon Pentecostalism. Jesse Penn Lewis classic WAR ON THE SAINTS points to excesses and the counterfeits, which seem to always accompany true revivals. But the thing about the early Pentecostals is that they quickly discerned the false. My late father told me how he stood against a man in Cardiff who sought platform position at their new Pentecostal church and how God showed him up as a spiritualist medium. One night God led Dad through the streets of Cardiff to a hall where the man in question was performing a séance. The early Pentecostals were people with discernment who quickly purged out the excesses and the counterfeit. Sadly this no longer applies in respect of many of their modern counterparts.

Classic Pentecostals agree with moderate Cessationists that some of the events associated with Methodist minister Charles Parham and holiness preacher W J Seymour surrounding the Topeka Bible college and Azusa stable revival in Los Angeles were not biblical. Where they differ is regarding the perceived impact of Parham and Seymour, who in reality had limited effect upon what happened in the eventual spread of the revival. In UK, Pentecostalism developed out of the Welsh revival not from Azusa Street. What occurred in Wales and later in England, Scotland and Ireland impacted upon Scandinavia, Europe and far away India and Australia with a feedback into the USA helping to bring a balance with a strong emphasis on biblical doctrine.

CORRIE TEN BOOM (Born 1892 Amsterdam, Holland died on her 91st birthday in 1983 in the USA.[51] The Nazis sent this godly Dutch woman to a concentration camp for protecting Jews. She tells of an incredible supernatural happening in the prison:

"The vitamin bottle was continuing to produce drops. It scarcely seemed possible, so small a bottle, so many doses a day. Now, in addition to Betsie, a dozen others on our pier were taking it. My instinct was always to hoard it Betsie was growing so very weak! But others were ill as well. It was hard to say no to eyes that burned with fever, hands that shook with chill. I tried to save it for the very weakest but even these soon numbered fifteen, twenty, twenty-five...

"And still every time I tilted the little bottle, a drop appeared at the tip of the glass stopper. It just couldn't be! I held it up to the light, trying to see how much was left, but the dark brown glass was too thick to see through.

'There was a woman in the Bible,' Betsie said, 'whose oil jar was never empty.' She turned to it in the book of Kings, the story of the poor widow of Zarephath who gave Elijah a room in her home: 'The jar of meal wasted not, neither did the cruse of oil fail, according to the word of Jehovah which he spoke by Elijah.'

"Well but wonderful things happened all through the Bible. It was one thing to believe that such things were possible thousands of years ago, another to have it happen now, to us, this very day. And yet it happened, this day, and the next, and the next, until an awed little group of spectators stood around watching the drops fall onto the daily rations of bread."[52]

However, as soon as more vitamins became available from the hospital, this supernatural source ceased. Corrie explains:

"That night, no matter how long I held it upside down, or how hard I shook it, not another drop appeared."[53]

CHAPTER FIVE

In Conclusion

I FEEL that I have laboured the topic somewhat and yet at the same time sense that there are areas that have not been fully covered. Many on both sides Cessationists and Classic Pentecostals have opposed the bizarre and strange displays and doctrines of what has been variously called The Toronto-Pensacola, Revival Now and River Revival movements. Some of us have stood shoulder to shoulder in our opposing the frightening ecumenical drift towards Rome. One of my purposes in writing this article is to try to build a bridge across which some will walk to join forces in our mutual efforts to earnestly contend for the faith once delivered to the saints. You may not agree with me on all points, but what I have presented is honestly believed and I think it is biblically based. Further I think church history supports the view that I have presented.

Sola Scriptura and let us all recognise and remember,
"It's not by might nor by power but by MY Spirit says the Lord".

FOOTNOTES:

[1] Wayne Grudem, *Systematic Theology*. Leicester, England: Inter-Varsity Press, 1994, p1031.

[2] In quoting Jack Deere, here and elsewhere in this article, we do not intend to give the impression that we endorse his extreme charismatic position. We consider he is correct in what we have quoted.

[3] Jack Deere, *Surprised by the Spirit*. Grand Rapids, Michigan: Zondervan Publishing House, 1993, pp55-56.

[4] Peter Masters, *The Healing Epidemic*. London: The Wakeman Trust, 1988, p69-70.

[5] J.G.S.S. Thomson and W. A. Elwell, "Spiritual Gifts," in Walter A. Elwell (ed.), *Evangelical Dictionary of Theology*. Grand Rapids, Michigan: Baker Book House, pp1045-1046).

[6] "The New Testament prophetic gift (Rom. 12:6; 1 Cor 12:10) primarily has to do with declaration, not revelation. The New Testament prophet 'speaks to men for edification and exhortation and comfort' (1 Cor 14:3). He is a preacher, not a source of ongoing revelation. His task is one of forth-telling, not foretelling. That is, he proclaims already revealed truth; he is not generally a conduit for new revelation" (John MacArthur, *Charismatic Chaos*. Grand Rapids, Michigan: Zondervan Publishing House, 1992, p81).

[7] Thomson & Elwell, *Evangelical Dictionary of Theology*, p1045.

[8] Jack Deere, *Surprised by the Voice of God*, p274.

[9] H.C. Waetjen, "Biblicism, Bibliolatry," in Walter A. Elwell (ed.), *Evangelical Dictionary of Theology*. Grand Rapids, Michigan: Baker Book House, 1984, p152).

[10] Alec Motyer, *Isaiah* (Tyndale Old Testament Commentaries). Leicester, England: Inter-Varsity Press, 1999, pp86-87).

[11] "Verse 20. Slogans abound in this portion of the prophet's message. Verse 16 is a slogan which describes the course necessary for the present: 'bind up the testimony...' Verse 19 describes a slogan against the following of which men are to be warned. 'Consult the mediums...' Verse 20 again gives the best slogan of all, in the very concise form: 'To the law and to the testimony'. It is true that 'law' means 'instruction'. It is also true that from an early date the Mosaic law was regarded as a primary instance of such instruction. 'Testimony' again was another synonym for the 'law'. Apparently then the two terms together imply that men should turn back to all instruction oral or written (emphasis added), that may have been brought to their attention at any time. Such instruction may have been largely ignored. It was important then. It is important now. In fact, the giving heed to it is the most important issue of the day. It could therefore be aptly paraphrased: Let the nation turn back to that basic instruction which has come to it from God in the past; to do so is their only hope" [H.C. Leupold, *Exposition of Isaiah: Volume 1, Chapters 1-39* (one vol. edition) Grand Rapids, Michigan: Baker Book House, 1971, p177].

[12] In commenting on vv. 18-19, Robert H. Mounce writes: "The book [of Revelation] draws to a close with a severe warning against adding to or taking away from its prophetic message... It is best to take the passage in a straightforward manner as a severe warning to the hearers not to distort the basic message revealed through John" [Robert H. Mounce, *The Book of Revelation* (The New International Commentary on the New Testament, F.F. Bruce, ed.). Grand Rapids, Michigan William B. Eerdmans Publishing Company, 1977, pp395-96].

[13] MacArthur, *Charismatic Chaos*, pp192-193.

[14]. Jack Deere, *Surprised by the Spirit*, p55.

[15] Benjamin Breckenridge Warfield, *Counterfeit Miracles*.Edinburgh: Banner of Truth Trust, 1918, reprint 1983, p6, in Deere, *Surprised by the Spirit*, n9, p268.

[16] Jack Deere, *Surprised by the Voice of God*. pp88-89.

[17] John MacArthur, *Charismatic Chaos*, pp202-203.

[18] Ibid., pp205-206.

[19] Wayne Grudem, *Systematic Theology*, p1077.

[20] C. Peter Wagner, *Praying with Power*. Ventura, California: Regal Books, 1997, p44.

[21] Some versions render this as 'Junias' which is masculine.

[22] Grudem, *Systematic Theology*, p909.

[23] CETF Vol 6.1 (April 2000) page 4.

[24] John MacArthur, *Charismatic Chaos*, p389.

[25] It also includes the sublime chapter on love.

[26] Strong 2087

[27] Strong 1100

[28] Gordon D. Fee, *The First Epistle to the Corinthians*. Grand Rapids, Michigan: William B. Eerdmans Company, 1987, p630.

[29] My personal view is that 1 Cor 13:1 is an hyperbolic reference to the power of oratory. It does not prove or disprove the idea of angelic languages. In scripture angels always communicated in the local dialect.

[30] John Wesley, "A Letter to the Reverend Doctor Conyers Middleton Occasioned by his late 'Free Inquiry,'" in *The Works of John Wesley* (3rd. Edition, Complete and Unabridged), Vol. X, "Letters, Essays, Dialogs, Addresses. Grand Rapids, Michigan: Baker Book House, 1872 edition, reprinted 1978, p56.

[31] John Wesley, Sermon LXXXIX, "The More Excellent Way, " in *The Works of John Wesley* (3rd. Edition, Complete and Unabridged), Vol. VII, "2nd, 3rd, 4th & 5th Series of Sermons." Grand Rapids, Michigan: Baker Book House, 1872 edition, reprinted 1978, pp26-27.

[32] *The Pilgrim Church* page 26

[33] ibid page 27

[34] ibid page 32

[35] *Encyclopaedia Britannica,* Article, Montanus.

[36] *The Pilgrim Church* - page 35

[37] Dr Barry Chant of Tabor Bible College wrote to Philip Powell, *"What Broadbent says of the Montanists is substantially correct. See FF Bruce, The Spreading Flame for some good evangelical stuff on them."*

[38] *The Pilgrim Church* pages 35, 36

[39] *Against Heresies, V:6:*1

[40] *Dialogue with Trypho,* 82, 88

[41] *Against Marcion* see also *On The Soul,* 9

[42] I have misplaced the exact reference to Pachomius and the following one to Martin Luther. Would one of our readers be able to assist me with the exact bibliography and quotes?

[43] *Alexander Peden: The Prophet of the Covenant* by John C. Johnston Mourne Missionary Trust,1988

[44] Samuel Rutherford, *A Survey of the Spirituall Antichrist, Opening the Secrets o Familisme and Antinomianisme in the Antichristian Doctrine of John Saltmars*h.. London: no pub., 1648, p42, in Jack Deere, *Surprised by the Voice of Go*d, p85.

[45] Susannah Spurgeon and Joseph Harrald (compiled by, rev. ed.), *C. H. Spurgeon Autobiograph*y: Vol. 2, *The Full Harves*t. Edinburgh: The Banner of Truth Trust, 1973 p60. I was alerted to this incident by Jack Deere, *Surprised by the Voice of Go*d, p89.

[46] F.Y. Fullerton, *Charles H. Spurgeo*n. Chicago: Moody, 1966, p206, in Jack Deere, *Surprised by the Voice of Go*d, p89.

[47] Charles H. Spurgeon, *The Autobiography of Charles Spurgeo*n (Vol 2). Curtin & Jenkins, 1899, pp226-227, in Jack Deere, *Surprised by the Voice of Go*d, pp89-90.

[48] Ibid, in Jack Deere, *Surprised by the Voice of Go*d, pp90-91.

[49] Os Guinness, *The Dust of Deat*h. Downers Grove, Illinois: InterVarsity Press p299.

[50] I have misplaced the exact reference to the ministry of Moody and tongues, but I think it was in Michael Harper's *As At The Beginning*. Would one of our readers be able to assist me with the exact bibliography and quotes? I have also misplaced references to the quotes below by Robert Boyd and F B Myer.

[51] "Heroes of History," at http://www.heroesofhistory. com/page59.html, spotted 26 October 2000.

[52] Corrie ten Boom with John and Elizabeth Sherrill, *The Hiding Place*. Minneapolis, Minnesota: A Chosen Book (Special Crusade Edition), Billy Graham Evangelistic Association, 1971, p202.

[53] Ibid., p203. I was alerted to this example of God's supernatural power available today by Jack Deere, *Surprised by the Voice of Go*d, pp87-88.

ABOUT THE AUTHOR:

PHILIP POWELL was born in Wales and migrated to New Zealand aged twelve, with his sister and brother and their Welsh parents. His late father was an AoG pastor. Philip has ministered internationally and trans-denominationally. In his capacity as National General Secretary of AoG in Australia he took a stand for sound biblical doctrine, values and practices, resigning in 1992. On the basis of this conviction he launched Christian Witness Ministries (CWM) in 1994 and established the first CWM Fellowship in February 2001 in Brisbane. Philip has been married to Kathleen for almost 36 years. They have three sons and a daughter and five grandchildren

SECTION III

Chapter One

Tony Pearce

Out of the Sixties

'This is brinkmanship. We could be on the brink of a third world war.'

The year was 1962. The place was a classroom in Bedford School. The event in question was the Cuban missile crisis when the United States and the Soviet Union confronted each other over the Soviet intention to put nuclear missiles on Cuba. I was 16 years old, studying for my 'A' Levels and we were having a lesson called 'World Affairs.' Our teacher, Mr Eyre, walked in and began his lesson with this dramatic announcement.

As I sat there a flood of thoughts rushed through my brain. Could there really be a nuclear war? If so what chance had we got of survival? What kind of a crazy world is it in which the whole future of the human race can be decided by a handful of politicians over whom ordinary people like me have no control at all? What is the point of my studying to pass these exams and get on in the world if someone I don't know can press a button and blow us all up in a moment of time? Above all, what is to be done about it?

From that moment on a change came over my thinking. The possibility of doomsday entered my mind and I began to look for some way to make sense of the world, which had become so threatening to my future. Two thoughts began to take root one to experience as much as I could of life and two to try to change the world. The results pushed me towards the counter culture of the sixties. I hitch hiked round Europe and beyond in the summer holidays, getting as far as Istanbul, Turkey one year and Tangier, Morocco the next year. I listened to music by The Beatles and Bob Dylan and agreed that 'All you need is love' and 'The times they are a'changin.' The new road of a world without war and competition beckoned to me with its promises of peace, love and socialism.

By 1967 I was studying Modern Languages (French and German) at Cambridge University. French existentialist writers like Jean Paul Sartre and Albert Camus appealed to my way of thinking, although their philosophy led to the depressing conclusion that life has no real meaning. I had also spent some time in Germany. While I was there one of the big questions which came to me, as I stayed with a German family, was, 'How was it possible that these people who seemed so ordinary and not so different from us could have followed a madman like Hitler?' When I asked my hosts this question, the mother of the family said, 'You have no idea what it was like to stand in one of Hitler's rallies and feel the power that came out from his eyes.'

The question of Nazi Germany raised another question I was grappling with. 'Why do people always pick on the Jews? What is it about these people that causes such hatred?' At school and at university I had Jewish friends and felt sympathy towards Jewish people. In May 1967 I was revising for my second year exams when the news came through of the build up of Arab forces on the borders of Israel. The newspapers were predicting a war against Israel and I read of Nasser of Egypt threatening to drive the Jews into the sea. I felt deeply involved in the issue and for some reason, which I could not quite explain, I wanted to help Israel.

One day I hitch hiked down to London and went to an Israeli agency and offered to go out to help Israel if there was a war. My parents naturally were horrified at this idea and as it turned out, when war did break out in June, Israel did very well in 6 days without any help from me. As the Israelis went into Jerusalem I knew that something very important had happened, although I did not know why. In fact from the point of view of the left wing ideology I was moving towards, I was on the wrong side.

By 1969 I had finished my studies and was now working as a teacher. I had changed my course in my final year at Cambridge and graduated with a degree in English. I ended up teaching English at a Grammar School in Retford, Nottinghamshire, a place I had never heard of before and after a few weeks of living there I wished I had never heard of it at all. There seemed to be nothing of any interest happening there and as I knew no-one in the town I became quite lonely. But I had so much work to do preparing lessons and marking books that I really did not have time for much else except the job.

I had an 'A' level English class to teach and found some outlet for my interests in using my lessons to inject a bit of Marxist philosophy into these boys. There were two boys who were quite resistant to my ideas however. They annoyed me greatly by coming into class wearing little badges, which said, 'Jesus lives.' It turned out they went to a local Pentecostal church, which I concluded must be some kind of a weird cult as I had never heard people from the Anglican church I had been to in my youth going on about Jesus in the way these boys did.

One day I set the class an essay to write on any book that had influenced them. I had not thought this one through, because what I got from these two boys was two long essays full of quotations from the Bible. Things like: 'All have sinned and come short of the glory of God' and 'The wages of sin is death but the gift of God is eternal life' and 'You must be born again.'

'This is serious,' I thought. 'These guys are trying to convert me. Never mind, I know what to do. I have been to university and studied all kinds of thinkers and writers. I'll soon cure them of this infantile delusion of believing in God. We'll have a debate in the library and I'll show them why they should not believe.'

I really don't remember what I said at the debate, but I do remember that about half way through the proceedings I had a sinking feeling that I did not know what I was talking about. One of the boys, Alec, said how he had come to know God personally through faith in Jesus Christ and how he communicated with God in prayer. Suddenly it came to me that they had been brainwashed into this by their parents and so I said, 'That's just your subjective experience. There is no objective evidence for the existence of God.'

They then said that the Bible is full of prophecies which cannot be explained without the supernatural foreknowledge of God and that there were even prophecies being fulfilled today relating to the second coming of Christ.

'Oh yeah? Like what?' I asked sceptically.

'It says in the Bible that the Jews will go back to Israel and that there will be a lot of trouble over Jerusalem and then Jesus will come back.'

Israel, Jerusalem, the Jews. My mind raced back two years to the 1967 Six Day War and I wondered if that was the reason I had felt that there was something so important about that event. Without admitting it to the boys I knew that I had lost this debate and had to get myself better informed about why I should not believe the Bible. What better way to do this than buy a Bible and start reading it to be better able to say why it is a collection of fairy tales?

This event happened towards the end of the summer term. In the summer holidays it so happened that I had fixed up to go on a international youth conference organised by the Quakers in Sheffield at which there would be delegates from Britain, the USA and the Soviet Union. The idea was to do some work on a youth club in a deprived area and also to have political discussions about world peace. I did not have much time to read the Bible before I was pitched into high powered discussions with the group about world events and how to create peace and a better world for the future.

We talked about the big political events of the time and I was really in my element telling both the Americans and the Soviets how they needed to sort out their countries and get their troops out of Vietnam and Czechoslovakia respectively. Before long I had established myself on the left politically which made me interesting to some of the Soviet delegation. They were all good Communists because at that time it was impossible to get a visa to travel outside the Soviet Union without the approval of the Communist authorities.

A very attractive Russian girl called Lara was openly flirting with me and on one occasion when we were alone, she asked me, 'Do you believe in God, Tony?'

'I'm not sure,' I answered.

'In the Soviet Union all progressive young people do not believe in God,' she replied. 'To make a better world we have to do it without God and religion.'

I felt a battle going on inside me. During the three weeks of this conference I found myself increasingly moving away from God and the Bible and beginning to commit myself to Communism. I remember sitting in a park in Sheffield on my own and renouncing God in favour of the revolution.

Because I had found Retford such a boring place, I had already handed in my notice at the school there and got myself a job at a Comprehensive School

in west London. This school was much more multi racial than the school i
Retford with many Asian pupils. I hoped they would be more receptive to m
left wing ideas and that they would realise that the answer to racial prejudice i
a socialist society. I went to lectures on world revolution at London Universit
and joined demonstrations about Vietnam and South Africa and was excited a
the prospect of really getting involved in the radical left scene in London.

But however hard I tried to get away from God, I found that he kep
popping up all over the place. One day I was going home from work on th
underground and in front of me was a poster with a Bible verse on it. It said
'But know this, that in the last days perilous time will come; for men will b
lovers of themselves, lovers of money, boasters, proud, blasphemers
disobedient to parents, unthankful, unholy, unloving, unforgiving, slanderers
without self control, brutal, despisers of good, traitors, headstrong, haughty
lovers of pleasure, rather than lovers of God' (2 Timothy 3.1-4).

Again thoughts went racing through my mind. 'In the last days! And that'
a pretty good description of people today. Suppose Jesus is coming back and
don't believe in him. What will happen to me? Suppose he comes back whil
I'm riding in this underground train. Don't be stupid. Of course Jesus isn'
coming back. It's a fantasy. Forget it.'

But the thought would not go away. I went to a demonstration about th
Vietnam War outside the US Embassy in Grosvenor Square, London. I wa
standing there with a placard saying, 'US Imperialists out of Vietnam!' when
girl went by giving out leaflets. Not an unusual occurrence as these demo
were places where all kinds of groups were handing out information trying t
get you to join their faction working for the great and glorious revolution. Bu
this leaflet was a bit different. It began with a quote from the South America
Marxist icon of the 60s, Che Guevara:

'Hasta la Victoria Siempre' 'Until the Everlasting Victory'

We must uproot all injustice, hatred, greed and bitterness …. in ourselves.
The revolution must begin where the problems begin …. in human hearts.
Marx says change society and people will change as a result.
Jesus says, 'You must be born again', not physically but spiritually, for:
'If anyone is in Christ Jesus he is a new creation, the old has gone, the ne
has come'. (2 Corinthians 5.17).

Think about it. Decide for yourself who is right.

Viva la Victoria Siempre.'

I did not say anything to this girl but as I read this leaflet I knew deep down that it was true. The communist experiment had been a miserable failure, promising to free people from the chains of 'hatred, greed and fear' but in fact binding those chains ever more tightly around the people in dictatorships which crushed and oppressed the people and gave power to the clique who gained control of the Communist Party.

At the time I had just been reading a book, called 'The New Class' by a Yugoslav writer called Milovan Djilas, who helped to bring the Communists to power in Yugoslavia after the war and for a time was second in command to Tito. Then he fell from favour and became a dissident protesting at the corruption of power in the Stalinist Communist regimes of Eastern Europe. The basic idea of his book was that in power the Communists transformed themselves from being a revolutionary movement working for the rights of the people into a selfish bureaucracy concentrating power and wealth in their own hands and passing on their privileges to their children. In fact they became the new ruling class. He pointed to there being something flawed in human character, which means that we cannot attain our ideals, and end up corrupting ourselves and everything we touch because of human selfishness.

As I read this leaflet and thought about the book by Djilas, I realised that this is what the Bible says is the problem - what is inside of us, a basic selfishness and tendency to corruption which is defined by the old fashioned and very unpopular word 'sin.' I also realised that the Christians I had met claimed they had found a solution to this problem in the person of Jesus Christ. For the next two months a huge battle was going on inside me. I knew in my heart that I could not get away from Jesus, and yet I did not want to become a Christian. The battle came to a head on New Year's Eve 1969. I spent the last evening of the Sixties at a very decadent party at which I got drunk and ended up in bed with a girl I hardly knew.

The next day I woke up with a hangover and a bad conscience and an amazing feeling that Jesus was in the room with me. The story of the Prodigal Son, which I remembered from my childhood came back to me, and I saw myself eating the pig food of my generation and now in a state of despair. I felt that Jesus was saying to me, 'Now you have to make a choice to carry on down the road you are going which will lead to destruction or to turn to me and find the way to life.' I prayed there and then asking God to forgive me for all the wrong things I had done and to change my life.

It was New Year's Day 1970 and I knew that the first day of the new decade had brought me to a new life. Almost immediately I felt peace and I knew that I had experienced what Christians call being born again. I went up to Retford and told Alec, one of the boys at the school what had happened. He told me that they had been praying for me for the past six months at his church.

I decided to see whether prayer worked and so I prayed that I would meet the girl who had given me the leaflet at the demonstration in Grosvenor Square. A couple of weeks later, I went to a meeting in central London and she was there giving her story about how she had come out of the Communist Party and the Lord had told her to go and give out leaflets and talk to people at demonstrations like the one I had been on. I went and told her how I had received one of her leaflets and now become a Christian and she was delighted.

Her name was Nikki and we started going out together to Speakers' Corner in Hyde Park and other places in central London to give out leaflets. (A bit later we got married and enjoyed 27 years together until Nikki became ill with Multiple Myeloma, a form of leukaemia and died in 1998).

I began to read the Bible seriously. As I read it through I became convinced of three things:

1. That the Bible is the Word of God.
2. That Jesus is the Messiah and only mediator between humans and God.
3. That Jesus is coming back again and the signs of his return are happening now.

I have now believed this for more than 30 years and nothing has happened to change my view on these three issues. The purpose of this book is to look at number three on this list the second coming of Jesus!

Chapter 2

Birth pangs.

'But concerning the times and the seasons, brethren, you have no need that I should write to you. For you yourselves know perfectly that the day of the Lord so comes as a thief in the night. For when they say, 'Peace and safety!' then sudden destruction comes upon them, as labour pains upon a pregnant woman.' (1 Thessalonians 5.1-3)

When will Jesus come again? The date is unknown and anyone who claims to know it is deceiving you and rejecting Jesus' own words, 'But of that day and that hour, no one knows, not even the angels of heaven, but my Father only' (Matthew 24.36). Someone once sent me a book with the title '40 reasons why Jesus is coming again in 1988'. The book was not a best seller in 1989. Date setters (especially the Jehovah's Witnesses) have done great harm to this teaching, making it the subject of ridicule when the supposed date of the second coming comes and goes with nothing happening.

In fact if we could work out the date then one of the main points of the teaching would be lost. Suppose we could work out that Jesus is coming back in June 2007. Many people would think, 'Well I can carry on living the way I am until May 2007 and then I'll repent of my sins and be ready for the second coming of Jesus.'

Because we don't know the date we are to be ready all the time, as John wrote in his letter 'Everyone who has this hope in Him purifies himself, just as He is pure' (1 John 3.3). If we believe that Jesus could come at any time we want to be ready to meet him all the time and won't want to be caught out in doing something sinful at the time of his return. The thief does not ring us up to say, 'I'm coming round to rob your house at midnight tomorrow.' Because we know there is always a possibility that a thief could come to rob us, we take precautions all the time to keep our property secure as far as we are able.

If a thief does break in, there are some things he will take and some things he will leave behind. If we leave a £50 note or a gold ring lying around, he will take them. But he will not take our dirty socks or old toothbrush. He takes what has value to him and leaves behind what has no value. Jesus is coming to take what has value to Him those who have accepted Him as Saviour and leave behind those who have not. So perhaps the most important thing anyone reading this book can do is make sure that you are saved and ready for Jesus to take you when he returns. If you are not sure about this turn to the back of the book now and read through the section on how to be ready.

Despite the fact that we do not know the exact time of the Lord's return, there are a number of signs he has given us in the Bible of conditions on the earth at the time of his return. What is amazing about our time is that they are all happening now. So when these things beginning to happen, Jesus says, 'Look up and lift up your heads, because your redemption is drawing near.' (Luke 21.28). In other words when you see the things he has described as associated with his second coming beginning to happen, you know that the main event, the second coming itself, is going to happen. So we need to identify what are the signs given in the Bible for the second coming. These are some of the major ones we shall be looking at in this book:

1. The Jewish people back in Israel and a time of trouble centring on that land, especially focussing on the status of Jerusalem.
2. Globalisation causing the emergence of a one world political system, which will ultimately be controlled by the Antichrist.
3. A falling away from the truth within professing Christendom, leading to a coming together of world religions in a religious system described as the 'whore of Babylon'.
4. The collapse of moral values and the breakdown of family life bringing with it all kinds of related evils drug abuse, violence, sexually related diseases, etc.
5. An increase in wars and conflicts within nations, also famines and plagues, causing people to be afraid of what is coming on the earth.
6. A massive invasion of the earth from the demonic realm causing people to become involved in the occult and to mock and blaspheme the God of the Bible.
7. Dramatic increase in natural disasters as human mismanagement of the planet brings us all to the brink of destruction.
8. Increased scientific knowledge bringing about the technology needed to control the world by the Antichrist.
9. A false peace process which appears to bring a solution to the problems

of the world, but in fact leads to a time of trouble unlike any other, which without divine intervention would lead to the end of all life on earth.

10. The message of the Gospel reaching all nations despite opposition and persecution.

In the verses from Paul's letter to the Thessalonians quoted at the beginning of this chapter, there is reference to the woman in labour. This is a picture, which is used in both the Old and New Testaments for the last days of this age. Three observations can be made about the woman in labour. When a woman goes into labour a process begins which cannot be reversed until the child is born. She experiences a series of shocks, known as contractions, which become more intense as she gets nearer to the birth of the child. When the child is born she quickly forgets the sorrows of the labour she has been through for joy at the birth and the new life that has come into the world.

This picture applies very much to the end times in Bible prophecy. The birth of the child corresponds to the main event, the return of the Lord Jesus Christ in power and glory. Then he will bring an end to the present age of sin and wickedness and establish the Millennial reign of peace and justice on the earth, which will cause people to forget the former time of trouble. The birth pains of the woman in labour are the sorrows which the world will go through before this event, which will become more and more intense the nearer we get to the end.

The birth pains are certainly underway right now in human events and have been for some time now. In some ways we could say the period began to take off with the First World War, which gave rise to a number of developments leading up to the end time scenario: the League of Nations, the first attempt to bring the nations together in the cause of peace, the Bolshevik Revolution, the humiliation of Germany, leading to the rise of the Nazis, the Balfour Declaration and the British taking the Mandate for Palestine, being the main ones.

Out of these events were set in motion the Second World War and the Nazi holocaust; the spread of Communism, leading to the Cold War and then, following the collapse of the Soviet Union, the push towards the 'New World Order'; the development of the United Nations and acceleration of the 'globalisation' process; the establishment of the State of Israel, together with the discovery of oil in the Gulf region bringing Israel and the Islamic Middle

East into the centre of the frame of world attention. The massive social upheavals of the First and Second World Wars also speeded up the breakdown of traditional moral and religious values in much of society.

Once a woman goes into labour no one can reverse the process, which will ultimately lead to the birth of the child. Similarly, once the labour pains of the last days have been set in motion (and they have!), no religious or political leader is going to be able to reverse them. They may take some positive measures to slow them down or some harmful measures to speed them up, but no one will be able to prevent events moving towards the final conclusion prophesied in the Bible.

The only thing, which will stop the catastrophic process now at work in the world, is the second coming of the Lord Jesus. Some people say to me, 'If Jesus comes again, won't people do to him what they did the first time?'

They won't have that option. When Jesus came the first time, he voluntarily humbled himself and took on himself 'the form of a servant' (Philippians 2.7). He submitted himself to rejection and the unjust verdict of wicked men, in order to die as the sacrifice for the sins of the world and rise again to give eternal life to all believers. When he comes again he will appear as 'King of Kings and Lord of Lords' (Revelation 19.16) with all the power of God at his disposal to 'destroy those who destroy the earth' (Revelation 11.18) and set up his rule from Jerusalem (Isaiah 2.1-4). Then the wicked will have to submit to him and suffer eternal judgement unless they repent and believe in Him.

As Paul told the people in Athens: 'The times of ignorance God overlooked, but now he commands all people everywhere to repent, because he has appointed a day on which he will judge the world in righteousness by the man he has ordained. He has given assurance of this by raising him from the dead.' Acts 17.30-31.

Before we look at some of the signs of the second coming of Jesus there is one difficult area which needs to be cleared up.

Chapter 3

Sorting out the different views.

'You know how to discern the face of the sky, but you do not know how to iscern the signs of the times.' (Matthew 16.3).

I spend a lot of my time travelling around the country speaking on issues relating to the end times. I can almost guarantee that after such a talk someone will come up to me and say, 'We never hear about this in our hurch.' Perhaps one reason why many pastors do not like to speak about this ssue is that they know that there will probably be a number of different views n the subject in the church and they do not want to create controversy. But esus was never bothered about creating controversy and if we delete the ubject for this reason, we have given Satan the victory and shut up about one uarter of the Bible!

The two major issues which divide Christians are the Millennium and the apture of the Church. The questions are:

1. 'Will there be a literal 1000 year reign of Jesus Christ on the earth after is second coming?'
2. 'Will the believing church go through the Great Tribulation or be taken ut before it begins?'

By the 'Great Tribulation' I mean the period which will precede the second oming of Christ which according to Jesus himself will be a unique period of rouble on the earth: 'For then there will be great tribulation, such as has not een since the beginning of the world until this time, no, nor ever shall be. nd unless those days were shortened no flesh would be saved' (i.e. there vould be an end to all life on earth). Matthew 24.21-2. This period is escribed in more detail in Revelation 6 19. During this time a world ruler nown as the Beast, or Antichrist will come to power. At the beginning people vill think he is bringing 'peace and safety' but in fact he will bring in the most atastrophic series of events the world has ever seen.

The Millennium.

The controversy about the Millennium centres on the question of Chapter 2 in the Book of Revelation and a number of passages in the Old Testament. Th word Millennium is in fact taken from two Latin words, 'mille', meaning 100 and 'annus', meaning year. According to Revelation 20 this is the 1000 yea period when Satan will be bound (unable to influence the world) and Jesus wi reign on the earth (along with true believers who will be resurrected at thi time): 'Blessed and holy is he who has part in the first resurrection. Over suc the second death has no power, but they shall be priests of God and of Messiah and shall reign with him a thousand years.' (Revelation 20.6)

During this time there will be the fulfilment of Messianic passages in th Hebrew Prophets such as Psalm 2, 72, Isaiah 2.1-4, 11-12, Ezekiel 40-48 Daniel 7.13-14 and Zechariah 14. Messiah will come in the clouds of heave with all the power of God at His disposal to destroy all that opposes His rule All international conflicts will cease and there will be world peace in whic even the animal kingdom will be at peace with itself. His dominion will reac to the ends of the earth and all nations will come up to worship Him and lear from Him at the rebuilt Temple in Jerusalem. Israel will be regathered and a last know peace and safety as Jewish people recognise Yeshua (Jesus) as th promised Messiah.

The question is 'Should these passages be taken literally as events whic will take place on earth, or are they allegorical of the life of the believin church on the earth now or of the future life in heaven?'

Perhaps the main view in the church today is 'a-millennialism' meaning tha there is no millennium (a is the Greek prefix meaning 'no'). For those wh take this view the second coming is the end of the world and the beginning o heaven and hell (i.e. there is no time when Jesus reigns in person on the earth) If one takes this line there are a number of passages in scripture, which have t be taken allegorically rather than literally. So when Isaiah says that 'Natio will not lift up sword against nation' this means that, for example, an Israe Jew and a Palestinian Arab who come to faith in Jesus are reconciled an become friends not enemies, not that the conflict itself will cease. In this vie the second coming itself seems to be a bit of a wasted journey a walk throug the ruins of a shattered world after the time of great tribulation, only to blow u the planet and make a new one. God could do this without Jesus having t leave heaven at all.

Another view is called 'post millennialism' which means that the second coming happens after (post) the church has succeeded in establishing the kingdom on the earth through a great revival which some people claim will convert all the nations to Christianity. Dave Mansell wrote in Restoration Magazine (January 1991) 'A new order is emerging in purity and power - the kingdom of God. The people of God, united in love and submission to Jesus Christ, will fill the earth as they take the kingdom and as all nations are brought beneath the feet of King Jesus.' John Giminez wrote: 'We believe it's God's will that the righteous should reign on this earth, and we're seeing people preparing themselves to be lawyers, doctors, generals, admirals, presidents, and congressmen. The righteous will rule and the people will rejoice.' ('New Wine Magazine' January 1986). The evidence of this happening on this side of the second coming of Christ is thin to say the least. Jesus taught that good and evil will coexist until the end of this age (Matthew 13.24-43) and according to Revelation 13 the second coming will be preceded by the vast majority of people turning to Antichrist not Jesus Christ.

I believe the pre millennial view, which means that Jesus comes back pre (before) the Millennium. Jesus comes back in person to the earth at the time of the Great Tribulation, and then establishes the glorious reign of the true Messiah, showing how the world should be run under God's authority.

The pre-millennial view was the expectation of the early church, as is testified by a number of sources. Edward Gibbon (1737-1794), author of 'The History of the Decline and Fall of the Roman Empire', stated, 'The ancient and popular doctrine of the Millennium was intimately connected with the second coming of Christ. ... It was inferred that this long period of labour and contention would be succeeded by a joyful Sabbath of 1000 years; and that Christ, with the triumphant band of saints and the elect who had escaped death, or who had been miraculously revived, would reign upon earth till the time appointed for the last and general resurrection. Though it might not be universally received, it appears to have been the reigning sentiment of the orthodox believers.' Gibbon was a historian trying to uncover the facts and was not sympathetic to Christianity, so his comments do not come with any bias of his own belief.

In his writing 'Dialogue with Trypho', Justin Martyr, who lived from approximately 100 to 165 AD, stated, 'But I and others, who are right minded Christians on all points, are assured that there will be a resurrection of the dead, and a thousand years in Jerusalem, which will then be adorned, and enlarged as the prophets Ezekiel and Isaiah and others declare. ... And further there was a certain man with us, whose name was John, one of the apostles of Christ, who prophesied, by a revelation that was made to him, that those who believed in our Christ would dwell one thousand years in Jerusalem; and that thereafter the general and in short the eternal resurrection and judgement of all men would take place.' Justin's use of the phrase 'right minded Christians on all points' indicates that this view of the Millennium was the prevailing one in his day.

This view began to lose influence in the third century of the Christian era with the teachings of Origen who adopted an allegorical method of interpreting the prophets. In other words he taught that instead of speaking about a time when Jesus would literally rule the earth from Jerusalem and swords would be beaten into ploughshares, the prophecies indicate a spiritual kingdom in which Jesus would reign from heaven in the hearts of believers and there would be peace in their relationships with each other. One of Origen's disciples, called Dionysius, went so far in opposing the idea of a literal reign of Messiah on earth that he influenced the Greek Church to remove the Book of Revelation from the New Testament. It was not restored until the late Middle Ages.

The major influence on the western church, Augustine, also rejected the idea of a literal reign of the Messiah on the earth. In his book 'City of God' he wrote that the abyss into which Satan is cast in the Millennium (Revelation 20.1-3) is not a literal location. Instead he said, 'By the abyss is meant the countless multitude of the wicked whose hearts are unfathomably deep in malignity against the Church of God.' He said that the binding of Satan in the abyss 'means his being unable to seduce the church.' He was convinced that this binding of Satan in the abyss is a reality in this present Church age. This teaching led into the rise of Roman Catholicism as the Church ruling and reigning for Jesus in this age and the Pope as the Vicar of Christ on earth enforcing His will (i.e. 'binding' or preventing the influence of evil). Unfortunately far from being 'unable to seduce the church', by the Middle Ages, Satan was more or less running the show, with the true Gospel suppressed and real Christians ruthlessly persecuted, along with Jews and others who stood in the way of the so-called 'Church Triumphant.'

With the Reformation there came a renewed interest in studying the Bible, but end time prophecy was not high on the agenda of the Reformers. They tended to take on board the Roman Catholic view that the Millennium should be applied to the spiritual reign of Christ in the Church, not a future event to take place after His second coming. That is why today belief in the literal Millennium remains a minority view among Christians.

Fortunately what will happen does not depend on what we believe, but on what God decrees. He is not going to let Satan have the last word in the affairs of this planet by making the reign of Antichrist and the Great Tribulation the end of the world. Rather He will show through the glorious thousand year reign of the Messiah just how wonderful life on this planet can be when God, not Satan and human sin, are in control. This prelude to the eternal state (Revelation 21-22) is something to look forward to as the days of this age become darker and the forces of evil become stronger.

Satan will have his brief day in the coming Great Tribulation (7 years), but the Lord Jesus will rule and reign for 1000 glorious years on earth and then for eternity in heaven. The choice to the human race is whether to join the loser in his eternal doom or to get on the winning side and believe in the Messiah who is coming again in triumph.

The Rapture.

There is another aspect of the teaching on the end times which is controversial amongst Bible believing Christians. This is the teaching of the Rapture of the Church ('rapture' is the Latin form of the Greek 'harpazo' to catch up or seize away). This event is described in the verses from 1 Thessalonians 4.13-5.11: 'For the Lord Himself will descend from heaven with a shout, with the voice of an archangel, and with the trumpet of God. And the dead in Christ will rise first. Then we who are alive and remain shall be caught up to meet the Lord in the air. And thus we shall always be with the Lord.' In this passage the Lord comes for the saints (i.e. the true believers in Jesus) and meets them in the air. In other passages in scripture (Zechariah 14.5, Jude 14-15 and Revelation 19.14) the Lord comes with the saints to the earth for his millennial (1000 year) reign.

The question is, 'Does this event coincide with the coming of the Lord to the earth or is it separated in time by a period of years (in the most common understanding of this view, the period is seven years)?' In other words, 'Is the Second Coming of Christ in two stages?' The view that the second coming is in two stages is known as the pre-tribulation rapture, because this event is said to precede the final seven years of the Great Tribulation described in Matthew 24.15-31 and in Revelation 6-19. Critics of this view say that the second coming is all one event and that the idea of a separation in time between the two stages of the second coming is a 'novel idea' which the early church knew nothing of.

The usual criticism is that the pre-tribulation rapture theory originated around 1820, ascribed either to Emmanuel Lacunza (1812), Edward Irving (1816), Margaret Macdonald (1830) or John Darby (1820). Dave MacPherson in 'The Incredible Cover Up' stated: 'Margaret Macdonald was the first person to teach a coming of Christ that would precede the days of Antichrist. Before 1830 Christians had always believed in a single future coming, that the catching up of 1 Thessalonians 4 will take place after the Great Tribulation of Matthew 24 at the glorious coming of the Son of Man when He shall send His angels to gather together all of His elect.'

However there is evidence of an understanding of the coming of the Lord in two stages in the early church. The writer Ephraem the Syrian was a major theologian of the early Byzantine Church. He lived from 306 to 373. In his work 'On the Last Times, the Antichrist and the End of the World', he wrote 'For all the saints and elect of God are gathered prior to the tribulation that is to come, and are taken to the Lord lest they see the confusion that is to overwhelm the world because of our sins.'

Ephraem's text shows a literal method of interpreting scripture and teaches the pre-millennial return of Christ. It reveals a clear statement about the Lord returning before the tribulation to take his elect saints home to be with him to escape the coming tribulation. In addition Ephraem declares his belief in a personal Antichrist who will rule the Roman Empire during the last days, a rebuilt Temple, the two witnesses and a literal Great Tribulation lasting 1260 days.

Ephraem's writing concludes: 'And there will be a great tribulation, as there has not been since people began to be on the earth … and no one is able to sell or buy of the grain of the harvest, unless he is the one who has the serpentine sign on the forehead or the hand. And when the three and a half years have been completed, the time of the Antichrist, through which he will have seduced the world, after the resurrection of the two prophets, in the hour which the world does not know and on the day which the enemy or the son of erdition does not know, will come the sign of the Son of Man, and coming orward the Lord shall appear with great power and much majesty, with the ign of salvation going before him, and also even with all the powers of the eavens with the whole chorus of the saints.'

So the teaching that the second coming is in two stages was not unknown to he early church. It may have been little known and understood, but that is not bar to it being true. At the time of the first coming of the Messiah Jesus, it vas not understood even by his closest disciples that there were to be two tages in his Messianic mission, the first to suffer and die as a sacrifice for sin in fulfilment of prophecies such as Isaiah 53), the second to rule and reign ver the redeemed earth (in fulfilment of Isaiah 2.1-4 and other prophecies). After the Day of Pentecost they understood the truth, that there was to be a time gap between his first and second coming during which time they were to evangelise the world (see Acts 1.6-8).

So too the literal understanding of the prophecies demands that there is a ime gap between the first and second stage of the second coming of Christ. The first stage, the rapture of the church happens unexpectedly, as a thief in the night. Even from the point of view of the writers of the New Testament it could happen at any time:

'You also be patient, brethren. Establish your hearts, for the coming of the Lord is at hand.' (James 5.8) See also 1 Corinthians 1.7, 16.22, 1 Thessalonians 1.10, Titus 2.13, Hebrews 9.28, James 5.7-9, 1 Peter 1.13, Jude 21, Revelation 3.11, 22.7,12,17,20. If the rule of Antichrist, the Great Tribulation and the Mark of the Beast system had to come first it would be mpossible for Christ to come at any time as was the expectation of the early Christians. In the passage from 1 Thessalonians 5 quoted in the previous chapter, people are saying 'Peace and Safety' at the time of the Lord coming as a 'thief in the night.' They will hardly be saying this after all the plagues of Revelation have been poured out and as the armies of the world gather at Armageddon.

Expecting Jesus to come at any time means that we as believers should keep our lives in continual readiness for this event as John taught in his epistle: 'We know that when he is revealed, we shall be like him because we shall see him as he is. And everyone who has this hope in him purifies himself, just as he is pure.' (1 John 3.2-3). This is also a tremendous hope for those who are suffering in this body: 'For our citizenship is in heaven from which we eagerly wait for the Saviour, the Lord Jesus Christ, who will transform our lowly body that it may be conformed to his glorious body. … The Lord is at hand.' (Philippians 3.20, 4.5)

Chapter Four

Israel Accident of History or Fulfilment of Prophecy?

'At Basel I founded the Jewish State. If I were to say this today, I would be greeted with universal laughter. In five years, perhaps, and certainly in fifty, everyone will see it.' So wrote Theodor Herzl in his diary on August 29th 1897 after the conclusion of the First Zionist Congress at Basel. On November 29th, 1947 the General Assembly of the United Nations passed by 33 votes to 13, with 10 abstentions (including the British), the resolution to partition Palestine, which led to the creation of the State of Israel in May 1948.

Is this an accident of history or the fulfilment of prophecy? To answer this question we have to look back over events, which happened over a period of nearly 4000 years, recorded in the Bible. So we will look at this subject as a foundation for the next chapter, which will deal with what is happening in Israel today.

Back in Genesis God made a covenant with Abraham, making him two amazing promises:

'Look now toward heaven and count the stars if you are able to number them. So shall your descendants be.' (Genesis 15.5)

'I am the Lord, who brought you out of Ur of the Chaldeans to give you this land to inherit it.' (Genesis 15.7)

Concerning the first promise Abraham believed the Lord 'accounted it to him for righteousness' (i.e. He confirmed the promise on the basis of Abraham's faith). Today a vast number of people claim descent in some form from Abraham. Jews claim him as their physical father, Christians claim him as their spiritual father and Muslims too claim that Abraham was their father (more on this later).

Concerning the second promise God did something, which we would find hard to understand, but Abraham would have had no problem understanding.

He told Abraham to take some animals, 'a three year old heifer, a three year ol
female goat, a three year old ram, a turtledove and a young pigeon' and to cu
them in two and leave a path between the pieces of the divided animals. Ther
'there appeared a smoking oven and a burning torch that passed between thos
pieces.' The smoking oven and burning torch represent the presence of God
which passes between the divided animals. Abraham does not pass betwee
the divided animals.

'On the same day the Lord made a covenant with Abram saying, 'To you
descendants I have given this land, from the river of Egypt to the great river
the River Euphrates.' (Genesis 15.17-18)

What was all this about? In Abraham's culture if two parties were making
land deal, they did not go to the estate agent and the solicitor. They cut animal
in two, passed between the divided animals and said in effect, 'May God (o
the gods) to us as we have done to these animals if we do not keep our word.
Now it was not the best day in the life of those animals when they were cut i
two, so they were invoking a curse upon themselves if they did not keep thei
word. By passing between the divided animals and not causing Abraham t
pass between them God was communicating something very important. Thi
covenant, by which He was giving the title deeds of ownership of the land t
Abraham and his descendants, depended on God's faithfulness not theirs.

The major problem from Abraham's point of view was that he did not hav
even one descendant, let alone a multitude, and his wife Sarah was barren an
past childbearing age. So Sarah suggested that Abraham had a child by Haga
her maid, which he did. So Ishmael was born, but God told Abraham that thi
son would not inherit the promise. Instead Sarah would have a so
supernaturally and this child was to be called Isaac:

'Sarah your wife shall bear you a son, and you shall call his name Isaac;
will establish my covenant with him for an everlasting covenant and with hi
descendants after him. As for Ishmael, I have heard you. Behold I hav
blessed him, and will make him fruitful and will multiply him exceedingly. H
shall beget twelve princes and I will make him a great nation.' (Genesi
17.19-20)

God says that the covenant relating to the land applies to Isaac and hi
descendants and not to Ishmael and his descendants. Ishmael will become

great nation, but the covenant will be with Isaac. Today the conflict over the land of Israel involves the Jewish people who claim descent from Isaac and the Arab people who claim descent from Ishmael. In Islam, the dominant religion of the Arabs, Abraham is believed to be a prophet of Islam and the promised son is believed to be Ishmael and not Isaac. Therefore the promises given to Abraham go to Ishmael and his descendants, the Arabs and not to the Jews.

A few years ago I visited the burial place of Abraham, the Machpelah in Hebron, and saw a large impressive mosque, where Muslims were praying with a section separated off for Jews to pray at, heavily guarded by Israeli soldiers. Is it a coincidence that one of the major flashpoints of tension in the conflict today is the site of Abraham's burial place?

The promise given to Abraham was repeated to Isaac (Genesis 26.2-5) and to Jacob (Genesis 28.13-15). It was the basis on which God called Moses to lead the Israelites out of Egypt into the Promised Land (Exodus 6.6-8). But as they made their way through the wilderness God gave them the Torah (Law / commandments) and told them to live by these. According to Deuteronomy 28 if they obeyed the commandments they would enjoy the land with good harvests, peace and prosperity, and they would defeat their enemies and be a light to the surrounding nations. But if they worshipped other gods and disobeyed the commandments a series of disasters would come upon them as a judgement, with the final judgement being removal from the land:

'You will be left few in number, whereas you were as the stars of heaven in multitude, because you would not obey the voice of the Lord your God. And it shall be that just as the Lord rejoiced over you to do you good and multiply you, so the Lord will rejoice over you to destroy you and bring you to nothing; and you shall be plucked off the land, which you go to possess. Then the Lord will scatter you among all peoples from one end of the earth to the other.' (Deuteronomy 28.62-64)

In these verses we see the reversal of the promise given to Abraham. However even if this most severe judgement took place, the removal of the people of Israel from the land would not be permanent:

'If any of you are driven out to the farthest parts under heaven, from there the Lord your God will gather you and from there he will bring you. Then the Lord your God will bring you to the land which your fathers possessed, and you shall possess it.' (Deuteronomy 30.4-5).

These verses also say that the return to the land will be accompanied by a return to the Lord, which is actually more important because God is much more interested in where we are spiritually than where we are physically.

Much of the Old Testament can be seen as the outworking of these principles. At times when Israel was faithful to the Lord they were blessed in the land and overcame their enemies. At the height of Israelite power under King David they reached for a brief while the promised boundaries of the land with dominion as far as the Euphrates (2 Samuel 8.3). But more often disobedience to the Lord and the worship of other gods caused Israel to be diminished by the surrounding nations, and eventually to suffer deportation from the land (2 Kings 17, 24-5).

Jeremiah was the prophet who God raised up to speak to the generation before the deportation of the Jewish people to Babylon. As a prophet he did three main things:

1. He told them what was going to happen.
2. He gave a reason for it.
3. He gave a promise of restoration.

For forty years Jeremiah warned his generation that the Babylonians were going to invade and destroy Jerusalem and the Temple and take them into captivity unless they repented of their sins. The reason why it was going to happen was the worship of idols and the breaking of God's commandments:

'Behold you trust in lying words that cannot profit. Will you steal, murder, commit adultery, swear falsely, burn incense to Baal, and walk after other gods whom you do not know, and then come and stand before me in this house which is called by my name and say 'We are delivered to do all these abominations'?' (Jeremiah 7.8-10)

Far from repenting, Jeremiah was mocked and rejected as the people preferred false prophets who said they were going to have peace and safety. But Jeremiah was not just a prophet of doom. He also promised a return from Babylon:

'For thus says the Lord: After seventy years are completed at Babylon, I will visit you and perform my good word toward you, and cause you to return to this place. For I know the thoughts that I have towards you says the Lord, thoughts of peace and not of evil, to give you a future and a hope.' (Jeremiah 29.10-11).

This promise was fulfilled when the Persians overthrew the Babylonian Empire and the Persian Emperor Cyrus issued a decree that the Jewish people should return to the Promised Land and rebuild the Temple in Jerusalem (Ezra 1.1-4). In this way the covenant was being fulfilled as the descendants of Abraham returned to the land God promised to Abraham.

Jeremiah also looked beyond the return of the Jewish people to a time when God would make a new covenant with the house of Israel. The terms of this covenant would be different from the covenant God made with Israel when he brought them out of Egypt:

'This is the covenant that I will make with the house of Israel after those days, says the Lord: I will put my law in their minds and write it on their hearts: and I will be their God and they shall be my people. No more shall every man teach his neighbour and every man his brother saying 'Know the Lord' for they shall all know me from the least of them to the greatest of them says the Lord. For I will forgive their iniquity and their sin I will remember no more.' (Jeremiah 31.33-34).

The new covenant points to the Messiah who was to come to deal with the problem of the sin nature, which causes us all to break God's commandments. According to Isaiah 53 this one would be a suffering servant of the Lord:

'He is despised and rejected of men, a man of sorrows and acquainted with grief. And we hid as it were our faces from him: He was despised and we did not esteem him. Surely he has born our griefs and carried our sorrows: Yet we esteemed him stricken, smitten by God and afflicted. But he was wounded for our transgressions, he was bruised for our iniquities; the chastisement of our peace was upon him, and by his stripes we are healed. All we like sheep have gone astray; we have turned every one to his own way and the Lord has laid on him the iniquity of us all.' (Isaiah 53.3-6)

When Jesus came in fulfilment of this and many other prophecies he was bringing in the new covenant, through dying as a sacrifice for the sins of the world at the time of the Passover. At the time that the Jewish people were offering the Passover lambs to remember the blood of the lamb which protected them from the Angel of Death (see Exodus 12) Jesus was put to death by crucifixion in fulfilment of Psalm 22, Daniel 9.26 and Zechariah 12.10. He was the 'lamb of God who takes away the sin of the world' (John 1.29).

Did the coming of the new covenant mean that God was finished with the Jewish people and that the covenant made with Abraham no longer applied? Much of the church actually teaches this in so called 'replacement theology' which means that the promises to Israel are now given to the church. But it is significant that after Jeremiah gives his promise of the new covenant he says that as long as the sun, the moon and the stars exist, so long will Israel be a nation before the Lord (Jeremiah 31.35-36).

If we look carefully at Jesus' words we discover that in relation to Israel, Jesus too functioned in the same prophetic way that Jeremiah did.

1. He warned of the coming catastrophe.
2. He gave a reason for it.
3. He gave a promise of restoration.

As Jesus was riding into Jerusalem at the beginning of the week which would lead up to his crucifixion and resurrection he stopped half way down the mount of Olives and wept over the city. He said:

'If you had known even you especially in this your day the things that make for your peace! But now they are hidden from your eyes. For the days will come upon you when your enemies will build an embankment around you, surround you and level you and your children within you to the ground; and they will not leave on you one stone upon another, because you did not know the time of your visitation' (Luke 19.41-44).

Jesus prophesied the coming destruction of Jerusalem and the Temple by the Romans in 70AD. He told those who believed in him to flee from the city when they saw the armies gathering, because this was going to lead to a time of terrible slaughter and destruction:

'For there will be great distress in the land and wrath upon this people. And they shall fall by the edge of the sword and be led away captive into all nations. And Jerusalem will be trampled by Gentiles until the times of the Gentiles are fulfilled.' (Luke 21.20-24)

In these verses Jesus warns of the coming destruction of Jerusalem, and the dispersion of the Jewish people into the lands of the Gentiles. He also gives a reason for it: 'because you did not know the time of your visitation'. In other words because the people did not recognise in Jesus the promised Messiah, the one who can bring peace. Of course there were many Jewish people who did recognise Jesus as Messiah and went out into the world to preach the Gospel, but the religious leadership rejected his claim and continued to offer the animal sacrifices for sin in the Temple, even after Jesus had come as the final sacrifice for sin.

For this reason Jesus said, 'Your house (the Temple) is left to you desolate; for I say to you (i.e. Jerusalem), you shall see me no more until you say 'Blessed is he who comes in the name of the Lord.' (Matthew 23.28-9). 'Blessed is he who comes in the name of the Lord' is not just any old phrase. In Hebrew it is 'Baruch ha ba be shem adonai', the traditional greeting for the coming Messiah.

In this verse as in Luke 21.24 quoted above, Jesus is pointing to a time when the desolation of Jerusalem will be reversed and the city will no longer be 'trodden down of the Gentiles'. What will cause this to happen will be the recognition of Jesus as the Messiah and the resulting outpouring of the Holy Spirit on those who call on His name.

A number of Old Testament prophecies tie in with this. In Ezekiel 36-37 there are prophecies of both a physical restoration of Israel, from being a barren land, denuded of its trees and with its cities forsaken, to becoming a fertile land 'like the Garden of Eden.' But more importantly there is also a prophecy of the spiritual restoration of the people:

'For I will take you from among the nations, gather you out of all countries and bring you into your own land. Then I will sprinkle clean water on you and you shall be clean; I will cleanse you from all your filthiness and from all your idols. I will give you a new heart and put a new spirit within you; I will take the heart of stone out of your flesh and give you a heart of flesh. I will put my

Spirit within you and cause you to walk in my statutes, and you will keep my judgements and do them. Then you shall dwell in the land that I gave to your fathers; you shall be my people and I will be your God.' (Ezekiel 36.24-28)

This passage points to Israel being born of the flesh and then born of the spirit, the very process which Jesus spoke to Nicodemus about when he said 'That which is born of the flesh is flesh and that which is born of the spirit is spirit. Do not marvel that I said unto you. 'You must be born again.' (John 3.6-7).

Several scriptures point to the method by which God is going to bring Israel to this point of spiritual rebirth a time of unique trouble (Jeremiah 30, Ezekiel 38-9, Daniel 12, Joel 2-3, Zechariah 12-14, Matthew 24, Luke 21, Revelation 6-19). This time known as the time of Jacob's trouble (Jeremiah 30.7) and the Great Tribulation (Matthew 24.21-22) immediately precedes the event known in the Old Testament as the Day of the Lord and in the New Testament as the Second Coming of Christ.

During this time of trouble all the nations of the world become involved and Israel signs a 'peace settlement' with the coming world ruler who is considered by some to be the which turns out to be a 'covenant with death' (Isaiah 28) leading to Israel being persecuted and brought to the brink of annihilation (Daniel 9.27, 11.29-12.1, Zechariah 12-14, Revelation 12, 16).

Amazingly Zechariah tells us that the focal point of this time of trouble will be the status of Jerusalem, a question, which will not just affect the countries of the region, but the whole world:

'And it shall happen in that day that I will make Jerusalem a very heavy stone for all peoples; and all who would heave it away will surely be cut in pieces, though all nations of the earth are gathered against it.' Zechariah 12.3.

From God's point of view this time of trouble is permitted to come upon Israel to correct something, which Israel has got wrong (Jeremiah 30.11). What could this be? Jesus said there would be no peace for Jerusalem while he is rejected as the Messiah. Therefore what is going to bring peace to the people and the land of Israel will be the acceptance of Jesus as the Messiah, which is precisely what is pointed to in all these scriptures. What needs to be corrected is Jewish rejection of Jesus as Messiah. Zechariah gives one of the most amazing prophecies of both the first and second coming of Messiah when he says that at the time of worldwide conflict over Jerusalem:

'I will pour on the house of David and on the inhabitants of Jerusalem the Spirit of grace and supplication; then they will look on me whom they have pierced and mourn for him as one mourns for his only son.' Zechariah 12.10.

The revelation of the 'only son' who has been 'pierced' points to the Messiah who came the first time to be pierced, dying by crucifixion, in order to redeem the world, and who comes the second time to judge the world according to how we have responded to his message. At this point Israel will recognise that 'God so loved the world that he gave his only begotten son that whoever believes in him should not perish but have everlasting life.' (John 3.16). They will welcome Jesus as Messiah and so know real peace and safety.

Chapter 5

The Battle for Israel.

'Hear the word of the Lord, O nations, and declare it in the isles afar off and say, 'He who scattered Israel will gather him and keep him as a shepherd does his flock.' Jeremiah 31.10.

From the last chapter we should expect to see the following sequence o events taking place regarding Israel.

1. The Jewish people scattered from the land of Israel and dwellin amongst the Gentile nations of the earth.
2. The Jewish people keeping their identity in the lands of dispersion an regathering to Israel.
3. This regathering to be in unbelief.
4. A time of trouble taking place during which the nations of the worl gather against Israel.
5. A false peace plan.
6. Out of this time of trouble a spiritual rebirth to take place as a result c which the remnant of Israel calls on the name of Yeshua (Jesus) for salvation.
7. The physical return of Jesus the Messiah to the earth to rule and reig from Jerusalem during the Millennium (Messianic Age).

Today we see the stage being set for all this to happen. The Jewish peopl have been scattered to the nations of the world, where for the most part the have been treated shamefully, especially by those who claimed to b Christians, but by their deeds denied everything that Jesus stood for. Whethe it was in Islamic lands or in Christendom they kept their identity and never los their desire to go back to the land of Israel. Each year at Passover they end th meal with the words 'Le shana ha ba b'irushalayim', 'Next Year in Jerusalem In Russia and Poland, for long the home of the majority of Jews, they woul remember the New Year of Trees in January. There is not much chance c planting trees in the snowy lands of the north in January, but they were remembering the time when trees were planted in the Holy Land. By such reminders the desire to return to the land of Israel was kept alive through the long years of exile.

According to Ezekiel 36 during the time of Jewish exile from the land, it would become a land of 'desolate wastes' and 'cities that are forsaken' (Ezekiel 36.4). This was exactly the condition Mark Twain, the American author of 'Tom Sawyer' and 'Huckleberry Finn', found when he visited Palestine in 1867 and described it in his book, 'The Innocents Abroad': 'Of all the lands there are for dismal scenery, I think Palestine must be the prince ... It is a hopeless, dreary, heart broken land ... Palestine sits in sackcloth and ashes. Over it broods the spell of a curse that has withered its fields and fettered its energies. ... Palestine is desolate and unlovely.' Of Jerusalem he wrote: 'Rags, wretchedness, poverty and dirt abound, lepers, cripples, the blind and the idiotic assail you on every hand. Jerusalem is a mournful, dreary and lifeless. I would not desire to live here'.

By the late 19th century Zionist pioneers, mainly from Russia and Ukraine, began to immigrate into Palestine and to purchase land from absentee Arab landlords. They drained the swamps and planted trees and began the process of turning the barren land into a fertile place. The population of Jerusalem swelled from about 15,000 in 1865 to 45,472 in 1896, of whom 28,112 were Jews. The prophecy of the physical rebirth of Israel was beginning:

'But you, O mountains of Israel, you shall shoot forth your branches and yield your fruit to My people Israel, for they are about to come. For I am indeed for you and I will turn to you and you shall be tilled and sown. I will multiply men upon you, all the house of Israel, all of it; and the cities shall be inhabited and the ruins rebuilt.' Ezekiel 36.8-10.

Herzl dreamed of an orderly return to Zion from the nations of the world. In fact the return and the establishment of the State of Israel in 1948 came through the agony of the Holocaust and the destruction of one third of the world Jewish population in the worst atrocity yet committed in history. It also came in the teeth of fierce opposition from the Arab world and from the British government, which had the Mandate for Palestine at that time. Despite all this, the United Nations took the decision to partition Palestine and allow the establishment of a tiny Jewish state on a fraction of the land originally promised by the British government through the Balfour Declaration.

The immediate and continuing response of the surrounding Arab nation was to seek to eliminate the Jewish state in fulfilment of the words of Psalı 83.4, 'Come let us cut them off from being a nation, that the name of Israe may be remembered no more'. In verses 6-8 there is a list of nations, whic can be identified with Jordan, Egypt, Lebanon, Gaza, Syria and Iraq. In 194 1967 and 1973 Israel has had to fight wars for survival against superior armie from these countries bent on pushing the Jewish state into the sea.

In 1964 the Palestine Liberation Organisation (PLO) was set up with th intention of 'liberating' Israeli lands and returning them to Arab control. Th Palestine National Covenant, the Charter of the PLO, calls for the 'liberation c Palestine' from the 'Zionist invasion' by 'armed struggle' and 'aims at th elimination of Zionism in Palestine' (i.e. the destruction of Israel). It denie that the Jews are a nation or that they have 'historical or religious ties wit Palestine.' It states that only 'the Jews who normally resided in Palestine unt the beginning of the Zionist invasion will be considered Palestinians.'

Therefore it denies Israel's right to exist in any form and commits th organisation to a programme aiming at the replacement of Israel with Palestinian State from which the majority of Jewish citizens would be expelle Article 33 of the Covenant states that: 'This Charter shall not be amended sav by a vote of a majority of two thirds of the total membership of the Nation Congress of the PLO taken at a special session convened for that purpose Despite claims to the contrary such a meeting has never taken place an therefore the Charter remains the guiding principle of the PLO. To further it aims, the PLO initiated the tactics of terrorism, which have been copied b other terrorist organisations throughout the world.

In spite of all that has been thrown against her Israel has survived an through victories won in 1948 and 1967 ended up with control of mor territory. The Six Day War in 1967 brought the whole of the West Bank (Jude and Samaria), the Gaza Strip and the Golan Heights under Israeli control. I 1968 Israel offered to return these territories in return for peace and recognitio by the Arab world, but the response of the Arab nations at the Khartou Conference was: 'No negotiations, no recognition, no peace with Israel.'

For Jewish people the capture of the West Bank meant the regaining of th most significant places in their history from a biblical point of view Hebro 'ablus (Shechem), Bethlehem, Jericho and of course the Old City of erusalem. From 1948 to 1967 Jerusalem had been a city divided by a wall 'ith barbed wire and checkpoints as Berlin was. The new part of the city, 'here the Knesset (Israeli parliament) is housed, was under Israeli control. he historic Old City was under Jordanian control. Here were the holy places, acred to Jews, Christians and Muslims, the Church of the Holy Sepulchre, the 'ia Dolorosa, the Temple Mount (Dome of the Rock and Al Aqsa mosques) nd the Jewish Quarter with the Western (Wailing) Wall. During the entire eriod of Jordanian rule all Jews were expelled from the Old City and unable to ray at the Western Wall.

When the Israelis entered the Old City of Jerusalem on June 6th 1967, the hief of Staff of the Israeli Defence Force, Moshe Dayan, stood at the Western Vall and said, 'We have regained our holiest place, never again to depart.' srael adopted an open policy to all the holy places for all faiths. At the same me the Jewish Quarter was resettled and became the centre for study centres or Orthodox Jews and the focus of worship of Jewish people world wide at the Vestern Wall. However the most holy place for Jewish people, the Temple Iount, remained under Islamic control.

As a result of this the stage was set for the end time conflict described in the Bible. Jerusalem became the 'burdensome stone' of Zechariah 12.3, the rresolvable point of conflict, which involved not just Israel and the Arab vorld, but 'all nations'. For the Arab world any solution, which left the Old City of Jerusalem in Jewish hands, was not acceptable. For the Jewish world, erusalem became the indivisible capital of Israel and could not be handed back o the Arabs.

By virtue of its significance to Jews, Christians and Muslims millions of eople Jerusalem became the focal point of world attention. Another factor in his is the fact that the Middle East is the main oil-producing region in the vorld and the economies of all nations depend on the free flow of oil. Therefore any war over Israel affects all people whatever their faith or lack of t. The easy accessibility of Jerusalem and the whole of Israel to the world's nedia also means that any flare up of violence in this city will almost nevitably be flashed across TV screens around the world. At the time when Zechariah wrote his prophecy the idea that a conflict over Jerusalem could be a ubject of concern to the whole world would have seemed ridiculous. In our ime it is a reality.

The Six Day War also increased the outrage and radicalisation of the Islamic world. In Islamic thinking the world is divided into the 'Dar al Islam' (abode of Islam, meaning territories governed by Muslims) and the 'Dar al Harb' (abode of war, meaning those lands not under Muslim control). The 'Dar al Harb' is the object of 'Jihad' until the Day of Judgment, with the aim being to bring it under Muslim control, either by means of converting the population to Islam or using force to impose Islam. Of particular concern is any land, which has once been Muslim and for some reason ceases to be controlled by Muslims.

For this reason Israel and the Zionist movement has been the object of Jihad in the aggressive sense from the very beginning. For Islam a Jewish state has no place in the Middle East, being situated on territory conquered by the Muslims in 638 AD, and containing sites holy to the Muslims, in particular the Dome of the Rock and Al Aqsa Mosques in Jerusalem. According to Islamic thinking Allah was diminished when his territory was taken by non-Muslims, and it must be reclaimed by the Muslim community. Any Jewish claims to the land based on the covenants of the Bible are discounted because according to the Muslims the Jews and Christians 'changed the books' (i.e. our Bible is not the original message given by God). The only solution from a Muslim point of view is the elimination of Israel and its replacement with a Palestinian Arab state ruled by Muslims. In this state Arab Christians and a remnant of the Jewish community would be permitted to live as 'dhimmis' (subject people to the Muslims).

For the Muslim world the Israeli victory in 1967 was not just a military defeat, but also a reversal of the march of history and a stain on Islam, which must be avenged. In 1968 there was a conference to discuss the implications of the Six Day War at al-Azhar University in Cairo, the main intellectual centre of the Islamic world. The general conclusion was that this defeat was a kind of judgement of Allah on the Muslim world because they had been taking on board influences from Western Capitalism and from Soviet Communism. The answer was to return to pure Islam and so defeat Israel.

This led to the radicalisation of the Islamic world, the overthrow of the Shah in Iran in 1979 in Khomeini's Islamic Revolution, and the spread of fundamentalist Muslim groups like Al Qaeda and Hamas, often willing to use terror and extreme violence to gain their ends. Suicide terrorism has been used with devastating effect in the events of September 11th 2001 in America and in terrorist attacks in Israel. Muslim preachers in the Palestinian areas, in Saudi Arabia and throughout the Islamic world regularly issue blood-curdling threats against Israel and the Jewish people.

Although not explicitly mentioned in the Koran, there is a Hadith, which gives a detailed series of events connected with the second coming. (A Hadith is a saying or tradition, not part of the Koran but given importance in Islamic thinking). It speaks of Jesus (who is considered to be a prophet in Islam) going to Jerusalem with a lance in his hand with which he will kill a false Messiah. Then he will kill the pigs, break the cross, demolish churches and kill Christians except those who believe in him (i.e. in the Muslim sense as a prophet not as the Son of God). Then he will remain on the earth for as long as Allah wills - perhaps for 40 years. Then he will die and the Muslims will pray over him and bury him.

Many Muslim preachers are speaking today of an apocalyptic scenario involving a great war with the Jewish people over Jerusalem. This will be the first stage of the planned Islamic conquest of the whole world. They are confident of victory and see no need for any compromise with Israel or the west. The following is an extract from a sermon given by Imam Sheikh Ibrahim Madhi in Gaza on April 12th 2002 and broadcast live on Palestinian TV. It is typical of the kind of incitement being given in mosques throughout the Islamic world.

'We are convinced of the [future] victory of Allah; we believe that one of these days, we will enter Jerusalem as conquerors, enter Jaffa as conquerors, enter Haifa as conquerors, and all of Palestine as conquerors, as Allah has decreed...'Anyone who does not attain martyrdom in these days should wake in the middle of the night and say: 'My God, why have you deprived me of martyrdom for your sake? For the martyr lives next to Allah'...'

'The Jews await the false Jewish messiah, while we await, with Allah's help... the Mahdi and Jesus, peace be upon him. Jesus' pure hands will murder the false Jewish messiah. Where? In the city of Lod, in Palestine. Palestine will be, as it was in the past, a graveyard for the invaders. A reliable Hadith [tradition] says: 'The Jews will fight you, but you will be set to rule over them.' What could be more beautiful than this tradition? 'The Jews will fight you' that is, the Jews have begun to fight us. 'You will be set to rule over them' Who will set the Muslim to rule over the Jew? Allah… Until the Jew hides behind the rock and the tree. But the rock and tree will say: 'Oh Muslim, oh servant of Allah, a Jew hides behind me, come and kill him.'

'We believe in this Hadith. We are convinced also that this Hadith heralds the spread of Islam and its rule over all the land…Oh beloved, look to the East of the earth, find Japan and the ocean; look to the West of the earth, find [some] country and the ocean. Be assured that these will be owned by the Muslim nation, as the Hadith says… 'from the ocean to the ocean…''

In the coming days there is no doubt that the spirit of hatred being inspired by such sermons will bring the Muslim nations into all out war aimed at Israel's destruction as described in Psalm 83 quoted above. In this Psalm there is a reference to Zeba and Zalmunna, who said, 'Let us take for ourselves the pastures of God for a possession' (v 12). We find reference to Zeba and Zalmunna in Judges 8. They were kings of Midian, leaders of the army, which came against Israel in the days of Gideon. In Judges 8.21 we read: 'Gideon arose and killed Zeba and Zalmunna and took the ornaments that were on their camel's necks'. The Hebrew word used for 'ornaments' is 'ha saharonim', an unusual word, which is correctly translated in the New King James Version as 'crescent ornaments'. The crescent ornament showed dedication to the moon god of paganism.

Today there is a world religion, which uses the crescent as its symbol Islam. Islam embodies everything spoken of in this Psalm in its attitude towards Israel. It is the dominant religion of the countries, which surround Israel. Those countries have made an alliance against Israel aiming at the elimination of the Jewish state. While they propose a treaty, which offers 'peace', which we will look at in the next chapter, their real aim is the destruction of Israel.

They wish to take possession of the land of Israel, which is considered to be part of the Dar al Islam (house of Islam). The Bible says Israel is the land, which God gave to Abraham in a covenant, which he confirmed with Isaac and Jacob (Genesis 15, 26.2-5. 28.3-4). Islam has changed the message to make Ishmael not Isaac the inheritor of the covenant, which contradicts the Bible (Genesis 17.19-21). Therefore in their view Muslims as descendants of Abraham and Ishmael should rule over Jews, the descendants of Abraham, Isaac and Jacob. For this reason it does not matter how many concessions

Israel makes, Islamic militants will not make a real peace with Israel. Their hostility has nothing to do with the way Israel treats the Palestinians. It is based on the fact that Israel exists.

Chapter 6

Peace, Peace.

There is another side to Islam and to the whole situation, which appears to be running in the opposite direction to what I have written in the previous chapter. In an interview for 'Newsweek' (3/12/01), Tony Blair said, 'True Islam is immensely tolerant and open'. Many western leaders promote the idea that there is a moderate form of Islam, which wants to make peace with Israel and the western world.

On this basis Israeli Prime Minister Rabin and PLO Chairman Arafat signed the Oslo Accords in September 1993, announcing, 'It is time to put an end to decades of confrontation and conflict ... and to strive to live in peaceful coexistence and mutual dignity and security.' The hope was that by an Israeli withdrawal from territories captured by Israel in the Six Day War and an Arab renunciation of violence against Israel, the way could be made for a comprehensive Middle East peace plan.

At the time I wrote in Light for the Last Days (October 1993) that the agreement would break down over Jerusalem. Even as it was being signed the leaders were making mutually exclusive claims on the city. Rabin said, 'Jerusalem remains under Israeli sovereignty and our capital.' But Arafat said, 'Whoever would relinquish an inch of Jerusalem is not an Arab or a Muslim.'

Seven years later the Oslo Agreement did break down primarily over the issue of Jerusalem. In July 2000 at talks for a final peace deal in the USA, Israeli Prime Minister Barak offered Arafat far more than anyone, including US President Clinton, expected. There was agreement on most of the territorial issues and even on the contentious issue of refugees. The sticking point was Jerusalem. Barak offered Arafat half of the Old City of Jerusalem and control of the Arab neighbourhoods both in the city and surrounding it (something Rabin had refused to offer in 1993). He agreed that the Palestinian State would have authority over the Temple Mount, that they could fly their flag there and that Arafat could have his office on the Temple Mount. He has even spoken of two capitals, one called Jerusalem as capital of Israel and the other called Al Quds as capital of Palestine.

Arafat rejected this offer to the dismay of Clinton, refusing to compromise over the Palestinian demand for sovereignty over the whole of the Old City of Jerusalem. As this includes the Jewish Quarter and Jewish holy places, there was no way Barak could accept this demand, without provoking total rejection from the Israeli population. At the meeting of the Islamic Conference Organisation in Morocco a month later in August, Arafat declared, 'Our struggle will continue and we won't concede even an inch of the city.' Jerusalem remained the 'burdensome stone' just as Zechariah prophesied 2500 years ago.

Out of that rejection came the bloody uprising, which has claimed thousands of lives on both sides. The threat of the situation spiralling out of control and sparking a general war in the Middle East has focussed the minds of politicians all around the world. 'It is clear that American mediation efforts have failed and we need new mediation before the Israel-Palestinian conflict balloons into an all out regional war,' said European Commission President Romano Prodi.

The European Union has begun to play a much larger role in looking for a peace settlement. The Arab world prefers European mediation to American because the Americans are considered to be too sympathetic to Israel. In Chapter ? we shall consider the prophetic significance of the rise of the EU.

In March 2002 Saudi Prince Abdullah launched a new initiative calling for 'full normalisation of relations with Israel' in exchange for 'withdrawal from all the occupied territory in accordance with UN resolutions, including in Jerusalem.' This proposal demanded much greater concessions from Israel than were previously put forward in the Oslo Accords, but it has now become the main proposal on the table. If accepted it would mean Israel withdrawing from all of the West Bank and Gaza, the Golan Heights and the whole of the Old City of Jerusalem. It would leave Israel perilously exposed with Syria regaining the Golan Heights in the north and coming right down to the northern shore of the Lake of Galilee and with the Palestinians in control of areas vital to Israel's defence along the Jordan Valley and the heights of Samaria.

In return Israel would have a peace treaty with the Arab nations. How mu would this peace treaty be worth? From past experience not much. Wh Yasser Arafat shook hands with Yitzhak Rabin on the White House lawn September 1993 he pledged to seek a peaceful solution to the conflict a renounce terrorism. Since that time he has done nothing of the kind.

A reason for this is to be found in the strategy, which was agreed on by t PLO in 1974. Known as the '10 Points Phased Doctrine' this strategy aimed set up a mini-state as the first step in 'liberating Palestine'. The statement the Palestine National Council said, amongst other things: 'Once it established, the Palestinian national authority will strive to achieve a union the confrontation countries, with the aim of completing the liberation of Palestinian territory and as a step along the road to comprehensive Arab unity In other words this state would be a springboard for the final goal, which is t elimination of Israel.

When Arafat was criticised by some of his own side for making a trea with Israel he replied that this was the phased policy which had already be agreed on. He also referred on several occasions to the Truce of Hudaybiyy which Mohammed made with the residents of Mecca at the beginning of h conquest of Arabia. In this treaty Mohammed made peace with the Mecca (who rejected his claim to be a prophet) and withdrew his forces to Medina. the time of making the peace treaty the Meccans were stronger th Mohammed's forces. Within two years Mohammed's forces were stronger th the Meccans, so he abandoned the peace treaty and made war, defeating t opposition to Islam in Mecca and imposing it by force.

This made a precedent for Islam in which you can make an armistice wi an enemy while he is stronger than you and if the armistice is good for t Islamic community. But when your enemy is perceived to be weaker, war imperative and is demanded by the Koran. You are no longer bound by t peace treaty you made previously.

It is interesting that in 1995 the Mufti of Saudi Arabia, Sheikh Abdel Az Bin-Baz, handed down a religious ruling to the effect that Islamic law does n rule out peace with Israel. However he went on to explain that 'peace wi Israel is permissible only on condition that it is a temporary peace, until t Moslems build up the [military] strength needed to expel the Jews.' By th logic the 'peace plan' is merely a trick to weaken Israel in order to deliver t ıal blow when the Islamic forces are strong enough.

In Psalm 83 the countries which are seeking the destruction of Israel 'have ›nsulted together with one consent. They form a confederacy against you.' other words they have a hidden agenda. They may say words of peace to ›ose who want to hear that message (primarily the leaders of the USA and EU) ıt their real aim is the opposite one. As a result of this Israel is pushed into gning a 'covenant with death', an 'agreement with hell'. The aim of this ;reement is to protect Israel from the 'overflowing scourge' (invasion and ›struction), but it is based on deception and so will not stand: 'For we have ade lies our refuge and under falsehood we have hidden ourselves' (Isaiah 3.15). All of this ties in very much with the present scenario in which a peace an is being proposed.

Apart from the Islamic dimension there is also a link in this process to ome. The key scripture making this connection is Daniel 9.26-7: 'And after e sixty two weeks Messiah shall be cut off but not for himself; (i.e. the ıcrificial death of the Messiah Jesus) and the people of the prince who is to ›me shall destroy the city and the sanctuary (the destruction of Jerusalem and ; Temple in 70 by the Romans, 40 years after the crucifixion and resurrection ' Jesus). The end of it shall be with a flood and till the end of the war ›solations are determined (following the first coming of Messiah there will be prolonged period of wars and the desolation of Jerusalem). Then he (i.e. the ince who is to come) shall confirm a covenant (peace agreement) with many r one week (7 years see Genesis 29.27); but in the middle of the week he ıall bring an end to sacrifice and offering. And on the wing of abominations ıall be one who makes desolate, even until the consummation which is ›termined is poured out on the desolate.'

This prophecy indicates that 'the prince to come', the one who will make e covenant with Israel will come out of the area of the Roman Empire. The ›ople who destroyed the Temple were the Romans, so the 'prince to come' ill also have a connection to Rome. He will offer peace but will turn out to be deceiver who will break his word to Israel and instead bring desolation until › meets his appointed end at the return of the Messiah.

Both Israel and the Palestinians have made representations to Rome and the atican. The papacy is very concerned for the 'holy places' in Jerusalem. 'hile not supportive of Israel's claim on the city, they are worried that a dical Islamic control of it would shut them out of these most important shrines of Christendom. Therefore the proposal has been made that the city should be internationalised.

When the Pope visited Damascus in May 2001 he said, 'We know that real peace can only be achieved if there is a new attitude of understanding and respect between the three Abrahamic religions, Christianity, Islam and Judaism. ... There is a need for a new spirit of dialogue and cooperation between Christians and Muslims. Together we must proclaim to the world that the name of God is a name of peace and a summons to peace.' The Pope's efforts to reconcile Roman Catholicism and Islam complemented his visit to Jerusalem the previous year when he called for reconciliation with Judaism.

There have been a number of moves to increase the involvement of the Vatican, the Italian government and the European Union in the peace process. The end of the standoff at Bethlehem's Church of the Nativity in May 2002 was mediated through a deal made by Israeli foreign minister, Shimon Peres, through talks with Italian Prime Minister, Silvio Berlusconi and top Vatican officials.

The possibility has been put forward of holding an international peace conference, involving representatives from the UN, USA, EU, Russia, Arab League and Israel. Israel has said that it favours Italy as the venue for such a conference. Both Prime Minister Sharon and Shimon Peres have expressed interest in Rome being the venue. Sharon said: 'We have excellent relations with Rome and my personal relations with Prime Minister Berlusconi are great.'

Berlusconi also has good relations with the Palestinians, as Italy has proposed a 'Marshall Plan' to help revive the Palestinian economy. Rome mayor Walter Veltroni offered the Eternal city as a possible location for the talks, saying, 'If a peace conference for the Middle East is held, then Rome would be the ideal venue.'

From the point of view of biblical prophecy it is highly likely that some kind of peace deal will emerge involving Rome and the European Union acting as mediators rather than the Americans. Whether that involves the characters in power at the time of writing this remains to be seen, but in many ways we see the stage being set for a peace treaty, which will tie in with the prophecies of the Bible. It is interesting that the Oslo Accords broke down exactly seven years after the signing ceremony in Washington. Instead of a final peace ceremony, the world's TV screens were filled with images of Israeli soldiers fighting with Palestinians on the Temple Mount, as the Al Aqsa Intifada began. Oslo was a kind of dry run of the final peace treaty, which is coming, which will end up seven years later with the armies of the world gathering at Armageddon!

SECTION IV

Typology of the Temple

JACOB PRASCH

SOMEONE ASKED ME, "WHEN IS THE Temple going to be rebuilt?" There are archaeological excavations that have been carried on by the Department of Antiquities of Hebrew University for some years. Dr. Kauffman of Hebrew University has done archaeological explorations beneath the Temple Mount. He actually went up on the Temple Mount to take measurements, with a view to rebuilding it. There is a movement to rebuild the temple. I would be very surprised if it was not rebuilt eventually, but this is a complicated subject. To understand it, we have to begin at the beginning.

Words for 'Temple'

There are at least three main words in Hebrew for tabernacle or temple, and three main words in Greek. In Hebrew the words are *mishkan,* which means 'tabernacle' or 'dwelling place,' *beit*, which means 'house,' and *haikhol*, 'a temple'. Different terms are used in different contexts.

The first Greek word is *oikos*, which simply means 'house.'

The second is *naos*, which means 'shrine.'

The third is *hieron*, which means 'temple.'

They are used in different contexts, in different verses in the New Testament. The most important thing in understanding the temple, or the tabernacle, is this: it is the holy place where God dwells.

The word *Shekinah* refers to the Holy Spirit, manifested in the cloud and in the fire. The word comes from the Hebrew root *shekhan*, 'to dwell.' That is where we get the word *mishkan*, 'God's dwelling place,' one of the words used for the temple.

The Tabernacle

John chapter one says, 'He dwelt among us.' The Greek word is kataskenoo, meaning 'to pitch a tent,' alluding to the Jewish idea of 'the dwelling.' There are at least seven major tabernacles in the Bible.

The first tabernacle is the one we call in Hebrew ha ohel, 'the tent of meeting.' It was a dynamic tabernacle, designed to be portable by the Levites who would move it. When it was pitched at night, the tribes of Israel would, in a configuration, camp around it according to their tribes (Numbers 2:1-31); the tribes, of course, being those of the patriarchs, the twelve sons of Jacob, the New Testament equivalent of the twelve apostles.

The second tabernacle is the First Temple, the temple of Solomon.

The third is the Second Temple, the temple of Zerubbabel, later called Herod's Temple when he expanded it. He actually used Ezekiel's vision of a temple as the blueprint to expand it along Greco-Roman lines to impress the Romans.

The fourth temple is the one that Ezekiel saw which, to the best of my under-standing, is probably a millennial temple.

Jesus spoke of His physical body as a temple (John 2:19-21) – the fifth temple.

The sixth tabernacle or temple is our body. Do you not know that you are a temple of God, and that the Spirit of God dwells in you? (1 Corinthians 3:16).

The seventh, and final, tabernacle is the church. In at least seven places in the New Testament 1 Corinthians 3:16,17; 6:19; 2 Corinthians 6:16; Ephesians 2:21; Rev-elation 13:6; 21:3 – the church is called the tabernacle of God. Each of the seven tabernacles follow this pattern: it is constructed as a box, within a box, within a box. There is the sanctum sanctorum, or the 'holy of holies.' In Hebrew it is called ha kodesh kodeshim. Then there is the outer chamber and a third chamber. It's sort of like a box, within a box, within a box.

The structure of the Temple

Do you not know that your body is a temple of the Holy Spirit who is in you? (1 Corinthians 6:19).

The Outer Court or the Court of the Gentiles corresponds to our physical bodies.

It is what everyone sees and everyone has contact with. At the inside edge of the Outer Court during Jesus' time there were signs warning Gentiles not to go any further. Then there is the Holy Place. The Holy Place was entered by the Levites for sacrificial purposes. Then there is the Holy of Holies, where God's Spirit dwells.

The 'innermost man'

It is important to understand this. If the Outer Court that everyone can see is our physical body, then the Holy Place is our soul: our emotions, our mind, our intellect. The Hebrew word is nephesh.

Then inside our soul is another box. That is our spirit, our 'innermost man'. The New Testament usually alludes to it by the metaphor of 'the heart'; the Old Testament uses the term 'kidneys'.

'Demonized' Christians?

"Can Christians be demonized?" is a question that is often asked. The answer depends on what you mean by 'demonized'. Christians can be demonized in the Outer Court. Demons can afflict the bodies of Christians. They can affect our emotions, our minds. Christians can be oppressed, but a demon can never come into the innermost man. Only unsaved people can be possessed. The only way a Bible believing Christian can have the innermost man entered by a demon is if he backslides beyond a terrible point, the way Saul did. Unfortunately, some people involved in deliverance do not make these distinctions and they wind up convincing Christians that they are demon possessed. There is a difference between oppression and possession. There is a limit to how far Satan can go in dealing with a believer.

Walls of partition

The temple followed a pattern of a box, within a box, within a box. There were things called 'walls of partition.' Sin brings separation. The most important wall of partition was the curtain between the Holy Place and the Holy of Holies, which was torn from top to bottom when Jesus was crucified (Matthew 27:51).

There was a wall of partition at the place where the priests entered, another at the place where the men entered, and another at the court of women. Women were separated from men by a physical barrier. The clergy were separated from the men by a barrier, and the high priest was separated from the rest of the priests by a physical barrier. Around all of this there was a peripheral wall of partition, separating Jew from Gentile.

These divisions between Jew and Gentile, men and women, the clergy and the lay people and divisions between the ordinary clergy and the high priest are all a result of the division between a holy God and unholy men.

Abraham's children

The Jews thought that they were special because they were physically descended from Abraham. Jesus told them that God could raise up Abraham's children out of the stones. Midrashically speaking, He was saying that He could make Gentile believers, Christians, into Abraham's descend-ants. On Palm Sunday the Jews cried out,"Hosanna, hosanna, to the Son of David".

And some of the Pharisees in the multitude said to Him, "Teacher, rebuke Your disciples." And He answered and said, "I tell you, if these become silent, the stones will cry out" (Luke 19:39-40). He was saying, "If the Jews don't recognize me as the Messiah, the Christians will".

Bricks cemented together

You also, as living stones, are being built up as a spiritual house for a holy priest-hood (1 Peter 2:5).

We are the stones. The Hebrew word for 'fellowship' comes from the ver chabar, meaning 'to join together.' The reference is to bricks that have bee cemented together. It is one thing to come to church, but it is very different t come to fellow-ship. If you come to church, you temporarily sit together. If yo come to fellowship, you are cemented together.

A building with bricks missing here and there is what a church is like i people are only coming to church and not to fellow-ship. There is a bi difference.

God's building

For we are God's fellow workers; you are God<'s field, God's building (Cor. 3:9). This is a Greek text, but Paul is drawing on the Hebrew idea c binyon, 'what God has built,' We are God's structure, God's building, God' temple.

So then you are no longer strangers and aliens, but you are fellow citizen with the saints, and are of God's household, having been built upon th foundation of the apostles and prophets, Christ Jesus Him-self being the corne stone, in whom the whole building, being fitted together is growing into a hol temple for the Lord; in whom you also are being built together into a dwellin of God in the Spirit (Eph. 2:19-21).

Notice that the word skenoo in Greek, 'dwelling,' is the same root as th Hebrew word mishkan or shekinah, meaning God in the Spirit.

The church is to be the temple where God dwells. Never say there is n temple. There is a temple.

Christians are the stones, Jesus is the corner stone and the apostles an prophets are the foundation stones.

The stone which the builders rejected is become the chief cornerston (Psalm 118:22). Jesus is the cornerstone of this temple, the apostles an prophets are the foundation stones, and we are built on that.

postles

There are five kinds of apostles in the Bible. 'Apostle' in Hebrew is olakh, the one who is 'sent' to establish a church. The Greek word is postolos, meaning the same thing, one who is 'sent.

First, Jesus is called the Apostle, the One who was sent, with the definite rticle. He is unique. All other apostolic authority must come from Jesus.

Second, there is the unique case of the twelve apostles. The twelve apostles orrespond to the twelve patriarchs, or the twelve sons of Jacob in the Old 'estament. As all the people of Israel were the descendants of the twelve tribes f Jacob, we, in some way, are the spiritual descendants of the twelve apostles.

The apostles are the foundation upon which the church is built. Jesus is the postle, and then there are the twelve apostles. Even Paul did not have all the ualifications of the original twelve. He affirmed that he was not the least of e apostles; his authority was coequal with theirs (2 Corinthians 11:5). Yet he aid he was the least because he had persecuted the church. In Revelation hapter 4, you see the twenty four elders. They are mentioned twice in evelation. An educated guess as to who they are would be that they are the welve patriarchs and the twelve apostles. It is an eternally fixed number of hich Paul is not a part.

Third, when they looked for a replacement for Judas, they had to pick omeone who has been around from the baptism of John (Acts 1:15-26).

After the twelve apostles, there is the al-most unique case of Paul. He is omeone who had the same authority as they did, but did not match all of their equirements in every sense – not having been around from the baptism of ohn.

Fourth, in 1 Corinthians we see that there were other apostles. Paul was ealing with the problem of party spirit. He rebuked it, saying, Now I mean is, that each one of you is saying, "I am of Paul," and "I of Apollos," and "I f Cephas," and "I of Christ" (1 Corinthians 1:12).

There is Jesus, who is totally unique. There is Cephas (Peter), who was one of the twelve. There is Paul. And then there is Apollos, a fourth kind. He was not like Paul, and he was certainly not like the twelve, but he had an apostolic ministry.

Fifth, there are apostles today in the sense of church planting missionaries. They are not pastors. Once the church is established, they need to go somewhere else and establish another church. They are not very good pastors usually, but they are very good at planting churches.

Apostolic authority

In the context of Ephesians, the foundation stones mainly mean the twelve apostles, Paul, the apostles in the early church who wrote the Bible, and the Old Testament prophets.

The same process holds true. If a church is planted, its foundation is going to be the apostle who planted it. In that sense apostolic authority can exist, but remember, the main New Testament thrust of apostolic authority is doctrine.

Does apostolic authority in the sense of the apostles exist today? Yes it does – in the New Testament.

The teaching of the apostles; that is apostolic authority. It is not heavy shepherding. It is not, "You do this and you do that." It is doctrine.

Be careful of people in Restorationism who are appropriating to themselves the title of 'Apostle,' thinking themselves to be somehow foundational, and assuming an authority that the Word of God or the Spirit of God gives to nobody. The only kind of apostles we have today are church planting missionaries.

Apostolic authority as the apostles had it is preserved in the doctrine of the New Testament; it was always concerned with doctrine, not with politics. Secondly, it was always plural, unlike the house churches, with their heavy shepherding and their leaders who claim to be "the apostle."

The Holy Spirit said, "Set apart for me Barnabas and Saul for the work to which I have called them" (Acts 13:1). Jesus sent the apostles out in pairs (Mark 6:7). In the book of Acts, when they wanted to see what was happening n Samaria, they sent two apostles (Acts 8:14). Not only that but there was a mutual submission to the general council in Acts 15.

Be careful of people who appropriate to themselves the title of 'Apostle.' This mentality exists in the house churches and, unfortunately, has come into much of Pentecostalism, but it is not Biblical.

The Body of Christ

But speaking the truth in love, we are to grow up in all aspects into Him, who is the Head, even Christ, from whom the whole body being fitted together by that which every joint supplies, according to the proper working of each individual part, causes the growth of the body for the building up of itself in love (Ephesians 4:15-16).

Ephesians combines the language of architecture with the language of anatomy and structure. We are the body of Christ - bones, flesh, eyes, feet, etc.

How lovely on the mountains are the feet of him who brings good news, who announces peace and brings good news of happiness, who announces salvation and says to Zion, your God reigns (Isaiah 52:7).

"How lovely on the mountains are the feet of him." That is what Paul is drawing on in Ephesians.

having shod your feet with the preparation of the gospel of peace (Ephesians 6:15). We are the body of Christ. Who are the feet? They are the evangelists. The lamp of your body is your eye; when your eye is clear, your whole body also is full of light (Luke 11:34). The eye sees. The eye is the teacher.

Good conduct is very important, but do you know what? The New Testament exhorts Christians to right doctrine twice as much as it exhorts them to right conduct. Why? Because if you do not have right doctrine, you won't know what right con-duct is.

Tabernacle of David

"After these things I will return, and I will rebuild the tabernacle of David which has fallen, and I will rebuild its ruins, and I will restore it, in order that the rest of mankind may seek the Lord, and all the Gentiles who are called by My name", says the Lord, who makes these things known from of old (Acts 15:16-18). This prophecy is taken from Amos 9:11.

"After these things I will return and I will rebuild the tabernacle of David which has fallen, and I will rebuild its ruins, and I will restore it." Before the temple was built by Solomon, David's tabernacle was the tent that was in Shiloh. David's tabernacle was dynamic. It was meant to be transported, even though it was usually found in Shiloh.

Amos predicted that the tabernacle of David would be restored. Somehow we would go from a fixed building back to something dynamic. Acts 15 shows that the dynamic structure which fulfills this prophecy is the church. The church is the mobile tabernacle of David.

Pillars of apostolic authority

And recognizing the grace that had been given to me, James and Cephas and John, who were reputed to be pillars, gave to me and Barnabas the right hand of fellowship, that we might go to the Gentiles, and they to the circumcised (Galatians 2:9).

The original twelve apostles recognized the apostolic ministry of Paul and Barnabas, but the twelve apostles were said to be 'pillars.' There were two pillars in the temple, "Boaz" and "Jakin" (1 Kings 7:21). Boaz means 'in His strength,' and Jakin means 'he will establish' or 'Yahweh will establish.' Pillars hold the roof up. If the pillars go, the roof collapses. If apostolic authority goes, the building will collapse.

Unfortunately, apostolic authority is going. Why? Because the church is departing from the teaching of the apostles into Restorationist Theology, with its false concept of apostolic authority.

Notice that physical components of the temple are identified with different kinds of Christians.

He who overcomes, I will make him a pillar in the temple of my God. (Revelation 3:12).

There is no temple in the eternal city. There is a tabernacle because Jesus is there; the whole place is a tabernacle, but not a building, not a temple as such. This has something to do with the church because there is no temple in heaven: a tabernacle, yes, but not a temple (Revelation 21:22). The people who overcome will be the pillars.

To be a real apostle, to be a real church planter, you have to be somebody who is, above all things, an overcomer. Look at the lives of the apostles. They faced terrible opposition, persecution, heresy, and betrayal, but they overcame.

Raising up the temple

In so many places, over and over, the New Testament defines the church, or identifies the church, as the tabernacle. God has always had a tabernacle, ever since the first one, but now it is us.

Jesus spoke of His body as the temple. "Destroy this temple and I will raise it again in three days" (John 2:19). But the church is the body of Christ. What happens to Him, happens to us.

The Hebrew language is usually dependent on three letters, sometimes two but usually three, called the shoresh, which means 'root.'

When any two words have the same root, they are connected etymologically, and they are often connected theologically. The root of Hosea, Hoshea (DVYU), is shin (V). Isaiah is Yeshiyahu (YUWDVW). Joshua is Yehoshua (DYVVYUW). Jesus is Yeshua (DVW). Whenever the sh sound occurs in Hebrew, it means something to do with salvation.

He will revive us after two days; He will raise us up on the third day that we may live before Him (Hosea 6:2).

His resurrection is replayed, or recapitulated, in the experience of the church in the last days. Jesus said, "Destroy this temple and I will raise it again in three days" (John 2:19). That happened to His temple – His body, and somehow it also happens to us. This is very important when you read Matthew 24.

They were marvelling at the stones of the Herodian temple, and He said, "not one stone will be thrown down upon another." Jesus was referring to the prophecies of the prophet Daniel. The Messiah would have to come and die before the second temple would be destroyed.

Somehow that destruction of the temple is a type of what happens to the church at the end. The stones are thrown down, but then resurrected in glory to an eternal temple, the way His body was.

Marriage and temple typology

When you understand temple narrative and the temple typology, you understand the reasons why God said that marriage is to be held sacrosanct and to let the marriage bed remain undefiled.

If you are a Christian and you have a wife, her body is a temple of the Holy Spirit. You do not enter God's temple irreverently. It does not mean that it is not erotic. It does not mean that it is not fun. It does mean that it is not to be with sin.

Sexuality in marriage is like the high priest going into the temple, or it is Jesus going inside His bride, the church, causing the church to be fruitful. We are made in His image and likeness. Sex replays spiritual things. "Keep the marriage bed undefiled." "Don't you know that you are a temple of the Holy Spirit?" Hassidic Jews understand this idea. They say that the Shekinah dwells over the marriage bed when a couple is making love. They understand that there is this spiritual aspect to it and that God's Spirit hovers over it.

Partnership between Jew and Gentile

Now Hiram [who was a Gentile] king of Tyre sent his servants to Solomon, when he heard that they had anointed him king in place of his father, for Hiram had al-ways been a friend of David (1 Kings 5:1). Right here there is a picture of camaraderie between Jew and Gentile. Remember that David is usually a type of Jesus. Jesus is called Yeshua ben David (Jesus the Son of David).

Then Solomon sent word to Hiram, saying, "You know that David my father was unable to build a house for the Name of the Lord his God because of the wars which surrounded him, until the Lord put them under the soles of his feet. But now the Lord my God has given me rest on every side; there is neithe adversary nor misfortune. And behold, I intend to build a house for the name of the Lord my God, as the Lord spoke to David my father, saying, 'Your son, whom I will set on your throne in your place, he will build the house for my Name.'

Now therefore, command that they cut for me cedars from Lebanon, and my servants will be with your servants; and I will give you wages for your servants according to all that you say, for you know that there is no one among us who knows how to cut timber like the Sidonians" (1 Kings 5:2-6).

Notice that: nobody knows how to cut down trees like the Gentiles.

And it came about when Hiram heard the words of Solomon, that he rejoiced greatly and said, 'Blessed be the Lord today, who has given to David a wise son over this great people.' So Hiram sent word to Solomon, saying, 'I have heard the message which you have sent me; I will do what you desire concerning the cedar and cypress timber. My servants will bring them down from Lebanon to the sea, and I will make them into rafts to go by sea to the place where you direct me, and I will have them broken up there, and you shall carry them away. Then you shall accomplish my desire by giving food to my household' (1 Kings 5:7-9). [Remember that the Phoenicians were very good sailors.] So Hiram gave Solomon as much as he desired of the cedar and cypress timber (1 Kings 5:10).

David had left the gold and silver that Solomon needed to build the temple. He received from his father that which he needed, but then he used the Gentiles to bring in more of what he needed to build this temple.

Solomon then gave Hiram 20,000 kors of wheat as food for his household, and twenty kors of beaten oil; thus Solomon would give Hiram year by year. The Lord gave wisdom to Solomon, just as He promised him; and there was peace between Hiram and Solomon, and the two of them made a covenant (1 Kings 5:11-12).

Solomon is the son of David who caused peace between Jew and Gentile. But lasting peace between Jew and Gentile was something that would only come from Jesus, the Son of David.

Minerals of redemption

And now send me a skilled man to work in gold, silver, brass and iron, an in purple, crimson and violet fabrics, and who knows how to make engravings to work with the skilled men whom I have in Judah and Jerusalem, whon David my father provided (2 Chronicles 2:7).

The colors and the precious minerals have special significance. The furthe into the temple you went, and the closer you drew to the Holy of Holies, th greater the cost of the minerals with which it was constructed. The progressio was from brass to silver to gold.

Brass has to do with fire. The brazen al-tar was made of brass and was type of the cross. The only way we can get to God is through the cross, whic makes atonement for sin.

The brazen altar was made from the mirrors of women (Exodus 38:8). The did not have glass in those days. Mirrors were made from a kind of coppe which was polished until you could see your face reflected in it. The idea wa that they gave their own vanity over to the Lord's service. They used the thing that would exalt them to make a type of the cross.

Silver always has to do with the price of redemption. Jesus was betrayed fo thirty pieces of silver (Matthew 26:15). The Levites had to redeem their firs born with silver (Numbers 18:15-16).

Then, in the innermost, is gold. An excellent wife is the crown of he husband (Proverbs 12:4). Gold is godliness. The diamonds are forged with fire When we sing the hymn, "Crown Him with many crowns," it is the churc crowning Jesus.

The church is supposed to be the glory of Jesus, like the crown is to a king' head – the gold inset with precious stones that have been forged by fire. That i one of the reasons why we go through trials. It is the fire that perfects th stones.

Solomon needed people who knew how to work these things.

Send me also cedar, cypress and algum timber from Lebanon, for I know at your servants know how to cut timber of Lebanon; and indeed, my servants ill work with your servants, to prepare timber in abundance for me, for the ouse which I am about to build will be great and wonderful.

Now behold, I will give your servants, the woodsmen who cut the timber, 0,000 kors of crushed wheat, and 20,000 kors of barley, and 20,000 baths of ine, and 20,000 baths of oil (2 Chronicles 2:8-10).

Trees, grain, water, oil, wine

Let's begin with the trees. Jesus healed the blind man, who said that he saw en "like trees, walking about" (Mark 8:24).

The trees of the field [the mission field] will clap their hands (Isaiah 55:12). /e shall be called "trees of righteousness" (Isaiah 61:3). A good tree cannot roduce bad fruit, nor can a bad tree produce good fruit (Matthew 7:18). Trees epresent different things in the Bible in different places. Here they represent od's people.

Our grain is the word of God; it is our spiritual food. "Cast much bread pon the water." "The bread that I give you." Different liquids represent the oly Spirit in different aspects. Jesus said that He would give the woman at the ell "living water" (John 4:10). Isaiah 44:3 shows us that "living water" is od's Spirit. Wine is the joy of the Spirit. Oil is the anointing of the Holy pirit. The Holy Spirit is typified, or represented, by different liquids in ifferent contexts in Scripture.

ifferent skills and resources

So look at what we have here. There is peace between Jew and Gentile and ey are building this immense structure together. They are going to build a ouse for the Lord.

Stones, pillars, trees. Different components of the temple represent different inds of Christians. The Jews had the blueprint. David gave the blueprint to his on, as the Father gave the blueprint to His Son (both are the 'Son of David').

The Jews had the grain. The Jews had the oil. The Jews had the precious stones. The Jews had the gold. Jews had the silver. The Jews had the fabric.

The Gentiles had the numbers. The Gentiles had the 'know how.' The Gentiles had the manpower.

The temple never could have been built by the Jews alone. The Gentiles alone never could have built it. There had to be reconciliation between Jew and Gentile to build this temple. The Jews could not do it without the Gentiles, and the Gentiles could not do it without the Jews. They were mutually dependent upon each other. Nobody knows how to cut down trees like the Gentiles. Who are the biggest soul winners in history? Since the early church almost all of them have been Gentiles. The great evangelists: Spurgeon, Billy Graham, D.L. Moody, the Wesleys, George Whitefield – nobody knows how to cut down a tree like a goy (Gentile).

The foundation is Jewish

Not only that, but they floated the trees on the sea. The earth usually corresponds to Israel, but the sea corresponds to the nations. The Gentiles brought the trees to Jerusalem. Cedars of Lebanon and cypress trees are types of Gentile Christians. Most of the structure of the temple was made up of these trees. The biggest part of the temple was Gentile, but its foundation was built by Jews.

The foundation is under the ground. My grandparents were from the north of England. I was born in New York where they have skyscrapers: more than one thousand of them in Manhattan alone. The tallest London building would not be considered impressive in Manhattan. When they build a skyscraper, they display a picture of what it is going to look like on the boards they put around the construction site. Then they dig through the rock, deeper and deeper. This goes on for months. You start to think that the building will never be completed.

Then, suddenly, the girders are up, practically overnight, and next thing you know, there is the building. How did it get there so fast? The most important thing was getting the foundation right. You cannot construct a one hundred story building without a deep, solid foundation.

God dealt with the Jews for two thousand years to give birth to the church. It took a very long time but, once that foundation was there, what happened on ıe day of Pentecost? Bang! There it was. There was the building.

You do not see the foundation stones. They are under the ground. But, when ou see a hundred story building, you know that there must be a very strong, eep foundation. Even though you do not see it, the building could not exist vithout it. The church is no different. It has a very strong and a very deep oundation, built by the Jews. It is similar to the argument in Romans chapter 1. You do not see the roots, but they are there. If the roots were not there, the ree would die. If God is finished with the Jews, He must also be finished with ne church. It does not matter what the Restorationists tell you.

'he 'mystery' of the gospel

Jews and Gentiles working together. The Gentiles had the 'know how,' the ;entiles had the manpower and the ability to bring the trees by sea to erusalem – a type of the heavenly Jerusalem.

What did the Jews give the Gentiles? The blueprint, the grain, and the oil the Holy Spirit was poured out on the Jews on the day of Pentecost).

Remember Jeremiah 31. "I will make a new covenant with the house of srael and the house of Judah"– not with the Baptists, not with the Pentecostals. 'he new covenant is made with the Jews.

The Jews gave the Word of God to the Gentiles. The Jews gave the lueprint. The Jews provided the foundation, but then the Gentiles built the uilding.

That was God's plan from the beginning. Paul called it the "mystery" of the ;ospel – peace and reconciliation between Jew and Gentile in order to build a emple to our God. That was always His plan, right from the beginning.

Vhen the new one was ready, the old one came down

The church is also called the 'tabernacle of David,' from Amos. It is to be lynamic. The "coming out of Egypt" spoke of the church coming out of the vorld on its way to heaven, with the Holy Spirit leading them. The Egyptians ;ave them the materials that were later used in constructing the tabernacle. God akes the things of the world and uses them for His glory.

Will the temple be rebuilt? Over and over the Bible teaches that the church is the temple. In the book of Acts they were meeting in Solomon's Portico. The temple was under the sentence of death because of Daniel 9. But while this temple was under the sentence of death, God was already rebuilding another one right next to it: the church.

When the new one was ready, the old one came down.

It had to come down. Why? The Holy Spirit is signifying this, that the way into the holy place has not yet been disclosed, while the outer tabernacle is still standing (Hebrews 9:8).

The destruction of the physical temple, as predicted by Daniel, happened in 70 A.D.. It was reiterated by Jesus in the Olivet discourse (Matthew 24, Luke 21). The destruction of the physical temple was simply a natural reflection of the destruction of Jesus' body. After Jesus had been nailed to the cross for our sins, the temple had to be destroyed.

The Talmud tells us that on Yom Kippur, the Day of Atonement, a scarlet thread was hung before the Holy of Holies. If the people's sins were forgiven, the scarlet thread would turn white. If the people's sins were not forgiven, the thread would remain crimson. For forty years before the temple was destroyed (in other words, from the time that Jesus was crucified), the scarlet thread did not turn white, the people's sins were not forgiven under the law.

The temple had to be destroyed because as long as it stood it represented the separation of sinful man from holy God, the separation of the high priest from the clergy, the separation of the clergy from the people, the separation of men from women, the separation of Jew from Gentile.

Saved to serve

For we are His workmanship, created in Christ Jesus for good works, which God prepared beforehand, that we should walk in them (Ephesians 2:10).

You were not only saved to go to heaven; you were saved to do something in this world.

You are like one of Solomon's workers if you are Jewish, or like one of

Hiram's workers if you are Gentile.

God has some work for you to do in building this temple.

The book of Nehemiah has the same idea – different groups of people worked together rebuilding the walls of Jerusalem. You were saved to build something in this temple. If you do not put that brick in, God will have to get somebody else to do what He had for you to do.

Before you were born again, before the world was created, there was something that God had in mind for you to do in building this temple. There is no born again Christian in the world that God does not have something for them to do. You are saved to serve.

The commonwealth of Israel

Therefore remember, that formerly [that is, under the old covenant] you, the Gentiles in the flesh, who are called "Uncircumcisionn" by the so-called "Circumcision," which is performed in the flesh by human hands – remember that you were at that time separate from Christ, excluded from the commonwealth of Israel, and strangers to the covenants of promise, having no hope and without God in the world. But now in Christ Jesus

['Christ Jesus' is different to 'Jesus Christ.' 'Christ Jesus' always has to do with Him after He has been glorified] you who formerly were far off have been brought near by the blood of Christ. For He Himself is our peace, who made both groups into one, and broke down the barrier of the dividing wall, by abolishing in His flesh the enmity, which is the Law of commandments contained in ordinances, that in Himself He might make the two into one new man, thus establishing peace, and might reconcile them both in one body to God through the cross, by it having put to death the enmity (Ephesian 2:11-16).

There is no way into the Holy Place when the outer one is standing. Because Jesus' body was destroyed, the temple had to be destroyed. The temple represents the division between Jew and Gentile. When He died, He got rid of that division, so the temple, which was designed to teach people about it, went as well.

He is our peace

And He came and preached peace to you who were far away [that is, th Gentiles], and peace to those who were near [that is, the Jews]; for throug Him we both have our access in one Spirit to the Father. So then you are n longer strangers and aliens, but you are fellow-citizens with the saints, and ar of God's household, having been built on the foundations of the apostles an prophets, Christ Jesus Himself being the cornerstone, in whom the whol building, being fitted together is growing into a holy temple in the Lord; i whom you also are being built together into a dwelling [drawing on the sam He-brew idea, mishkan from the Hebrew, kataskenoo from the Greek] of Go in the Spirit (Ephesians 2:17-22).

Because of sin, these barriers are here. Jesus said, "Destroy the temple and will raise it up," speaking of His body. The old temple was destroyed; the nev one, the church, meeting in Solomon's Portico, was raised up in its place.

Jesus' body was crucified, but His glorified body was created in its place The church at the end will be crucified, but then resurrected to victory. Whe Jesus died, the natural temple had to be destroyed be-cause Gentile would n longer be separated from Jew, and therefore the natural wall of partition had t be knocked down.

He is our reconciliation. He is our peace. We shall be one. In Jerusalem even in the midst of the Intifada and the hatred, you can see meetings with Jev and Arab together, singing in Hebrew, in Arabic, and in English, "He is ou peace."

The barrier between men and women had to go

The orthodox Jews pray, "Thank God I was not born a dog or a Gentile or woman."

There are differences between men and women, different functions, but b the standards of the ancient world, the Jews gave women a much higher plac than Gentiles did.

You still see this in the Middle East. If you want to see what women wer like outside of Judaism, or in the pre-Christian Middle East, look at th Moslem culture. Nobody says anything about the way little girls are abused b their brothers. In a place like rural Egypt, in the villages, a man will have camel whip up on his wall. Is that for his camel? No. It is for his wife. He can divorce her and get the kids under Islamic law and she has no claim to anything. All he has to do is say three times, "I divorce you," and she is legally finished. These guys make their wives strip and they beat them. That is how women were treated in much of the ancient world.

The Jews gave women rights under Halachah that were not found outside of the Jewish context, usually, in the ancient world. Then Christianity was almost like feminism – with Paul saying that women are coequal in Christ, and coheirs in Christ, and Peter saying, "Submit to one other in love." This does not mean that the husband is not the head, but it does mean that a wife is a coheir.

The Jewish idea gave women a much higher status than most of the Gentile ideas of what women were supposed to be like. But then the church brought something totally, radically different again.

The husband is the head of the wife

The Greek idea was that every man should have three women. He should have a concubine – who would basically be a sex object, he would have a mistress – for intellectual compatibility, and he would have a wife – who would be the mother of his children.

Now in the Christian design, the same woman would fulfil all three functions. It went totally against the Greek idea and it went against the Jewish idea, which was already superior to the Gentile one. The wall of partition is broken down.

That does not mean that I believe in women pastors. I do not.

We are still living in a fallen world, and men and women are both under the curse of the fall. Women are very vulnerable to spiritual seduction, more so than men. They are very sensitive and can hear the voice of the Holy Spirit more easily than men can. When a husband and wife pray together, it will usually be the wife that God speaks through. When a husband and wife get saved, it is usually the wife who gets saved first.

But because women are more sensitive and it is easier for them to hear the voice of the Holy Spirit, it is also easier for them to hear the voice of another spirit. The serpent beguiled the woman. Women are much more vulnerable by nature to spiritual seduction. That is the idea of headship.

God's idea of headship is protection, not domination or dominion.

A husband is head of the wife as Christ is head of the church.

A husband is expected by God to give himself for his wife, the way that Christ laid His life down for the church. On the other hand, she has to recognize his responsibility and authority. It is a protective model, it is not master-slave. That is the world's mentality.

So the wall of partition between Jew and Gentile has to go. And then the one between men and women has to go.

The barrier between clergy and laity had to go

But then the wall that separates the clergy from the lay people has to go. We are all priests. The Body of Christ is a kingdom of priests.

Before Satan paganised the church, he Judaized it. Roman Catholicism is based on two corruptions of the church: Judaization and paganization.

The paganization came later, after Constantine mainly. The Judaization came first. Instead of a priesthood of all believers, they reintroduced a separate priesthood, going back under the law in a way that Paul warned against in Galatians.

The whole Church of England is split over the question of women priests. The question is not, "Should we have women priests?" The question is, "Why should we have 'priests' at all?"

The whole issue is superfluous, yet people leave the Church of England over it.

When an Anglican bishop denied the resurrection of Jesus Christ, and denied the virgin birth, when Anglican clergymen openly stated that they were homosexual, when George Carey rejected the petition of Evangelicals to stop Hindu, Moslem and witchdoctor worship in Canterbury Cathedral, we did not ee anyone walking out. They are only willing to walk out over something that s not Biblical. ("Don't mess with my religion!")

Before Satan paganised the church, he Judaized it. Instead of having a abernacle like David's, where God's Spirit moves, the Catholics say that He is n the church building in a little box on the 'altar' called the 'tabernacle' where hey put the 'Eucharist'. They say, "That is where He dwells". It is a return to he Law.

Roman Catholicism is a Judaization and a paganization of Christianity. You oolish Galatians, who has bewitched you? (Galatians 3:1). This false teaching ias to go because it separates the clergy from the people.

'he veil had to go

Then the veil had to go. It separated holy God from sinful man. Jesus ecame our righteousness. We are counted righteous through repentance and aith in Him. So the separation between man and God goes. Jesus died to break own the wall of partition between Jew and Gentile, between men and women, etween clergy and lay people and, ultimately, between holy God and sinful nan.

When Jesus died, the temple veil was torn from the top to the bottom. Jotice that it began internally. God always begins on the inside and works utward. The world does the opposite: it goes from the outside and tries to vork inward. Even when God gave the blueprint for building the tent of neeting, He began on the inside and worked outward.

Jesus has raised up a new temple where Jew will no longer be separated rom Gentile, men no longer separated from women, clergy no longer separated rom lay people, and sinful man no longer separated from a holy God.

etting up the abomination of Desolation

Will another temple be built, based on second Thessalonians? The kelihood is

that it will, but remember that when the physical temple was destroyed in 70 .D., fulfilling the prophecies of Daniel, it was only a reflection of the deeper spiritual truth that you read about in Hebrews chapter 9.

Access to the innermost Holy of Holies was not possible while the outer one, of which it was a type, was still standing. It says directly in Hebrews that this temple is a copy of things in the heavens. The destruction of this physical temple was only a reflection of something spiritual.

When the veil before the Holy of Holies was torn, a physical event happened in the physical temple, which was only a reflection of a deeper spiritual truth: that sinful man was no longer separated from holy God, because Jesus paid the price.

If the physical temple is rebuilt, and an abomination of desolation is set up, it will only reflect a deeper spiritual truth. When you see the Archbishop of Canterbury involved in "interfaith worship" in a Christian church, the abomination of desolation has already begun.

When you see homosexual clergy, that is the abomination of desolation. When you see a bishop denying the resurrection of Jesus Christ, and two thirds of the other bishops defend him, that is the abomination of desolation.

I have no doubt in my mind that the Antichrist will be worshipped in Christendom. If the physical temple is rebuilt, with an image set up in it, that will only be a reflection of what is really going on.

When you see the archaeologists from Hebrew University digging underneath the Mosque of Omar, looking to rebuild the temple, it is simply a reflection of what is happening in Canterbury Cathedral, or in St. James, Piccadilly, or any of the other New Age churches.

Will the temple be rebuilt? The temple has already been rebuilt: it is us. It is not the building of a physical temple that concerns me, but the abomination of desolation already being set up in the temple.

SECTION V

Communicating the Gospel

a look at some New Testament methods

Philip Foster

Part 1 - letters of Christ

2 Cor 2:14-4:10

14 But thanks be to God, who always leads us in triumphal procession in Messiah and through us spreads everywhere the fragrance of the knowledge of him.

15 For we are to God the aroma of Messiah among those who are being saved and those who are perishing.

16 To the one we are the smell of death; to the other, the fragrance of life. And who is equal to such a task?

17 Unlike so many, we do not peddle the word of God for profit. On the contrary, in Messiah we speak before God with sincerity, like men sent from God.

Ch.3.

1 Are we beginning to commend ourselves again? Or do we need, like some people, letters of recommendation to you or from you?

2 You yourselves are our letter, written on our hearts, known and read by everybody.

3 You show that you are a letter from Christ, the result of our ministry, written not with ink but with the Spirit of the living God, not on tablets of stone but on tablets of human hearts.

4 Such confidence as this is ours through Messiah before God.

5 Not that we are competent in ourselves to claim anything for ourselves, but our competence comes from God.

6 He has made us competent as ministers of a new covenant- not of the letter but of the Spirit; for the letter kills, but the Spirit gives life.

7 Now if the ministry that brought death, which was engraved in letters on stone, came with glory, so that the Israelites could not look steadily at the face of Moses because of its glory, fading though it was, 8 will not the ministry of the Spirit be even more glorious?

9 If the ministry that condemns men is glorious, how much more glorious is the ministry that brings righteousness! 10 For what was glorious has no glory now in comparison with the surpassing glory.

11 And if what was fading away came with glory, how much greater is the glory of that which lasts! 12 Therefore, since we have such a hope, we are very bold.

13 We are not like Moses, who would put a veil over his face to keep the Israelites from gazing at it while the radiance was fading away.

14 But their minds were made dull, for to this day the same veil remains when the old covenant is read. It has not been removed, because only in Messiah is it taken away.

15 Even to this day when Moses is read, a veil covers their hearts.

16 But whenever anyone turns to the Lord, the veil is taken away.

17 Now the Lord is the Spirit, and where the Spirit of the Lord is, there is freedom.

18 And we, who with unveiled faces all reflect the Lord's glory, are being transformed into his likeness with ever-increasing glory, which comes from the Lord, who is the Spirit.

CHAPTER 4

1 Therefore, since through God's mercy we have this ministry, we do not lose heart.

2 Rather, we have renounced secret and shameful ways; we do not use deception, nor do we distort the word of God. On the contrary, by setting forth the truth plainly we commend ourselves to every man's conscience in the sight of God.

3 And even if our gospel is veiled, it is veiled to those who are perishing.

4 The god of this age has blinded the minds of unbelievers, so that they cannot see the light of the gospel of the glory of Christ, who is the image of God.

5 For we do not preach ourselves, but Jesus Messiah as Lord, and ourselves as your servants for Jesus' sake.

6 For God, who said, "Let light shine out of darkness," made his light shine in our hearts to give us the light of the knowledge of the glory of God in the face of Christ.

7 But we have this treasure in jars of clay to show that this all-surpassing power is from God and not from us.

8 We are hard pressed on every side, but not crushed; perplexed, but not in despair; 9 persecuted, but not abandoned; struck down, but not destroyed.

10 We always carry around in our body the death of Jesus, so that the life of Jesus may also be revealed in our body.

We shall look later on at various words used in the New testament for spreading the Gospel: *Persuade/convince, Debate and argue, Proclaim/declare, Preach and teach.*

But I want first to look at Paul's word to Corinth: "We are the aroma of Christ, we are a letter to people written in our hearts and lives."

This makes clear something that should undergird all that we do: that our lives speak volumes. How we live is both a witness to men and our service to God - our spiritual worship.

In Leviticus we read:

(Lev 1:13 NIV)

13 He is to wash the inner parts and the legs with water, and the priest is to bring all of it and burn it on the altar. It is a burnt offering, an offering made by fire, an aroma pleasing to the LORD.

Now our lives are a whole offering to the Lord.

3 You show that you are a letter from Christ, the result of our ministry, written not with ink but with the Spirit of the living God, not on tablets of stone but on tablets of human hearts.

We are a letter from Christ to those to whom we go with the gospel. It is not exactly that 'deeds speak louder than words' - which might be construed from this passage. But it is true that unless our lives genuinely, not hypocritically, show Christ's nature, then much of what we say may be dismissed.

But a letter does SPEAK: that is that 'good lives' are NOT a substitute for words, but rather 'the paper on which the words are written'. There can be no words written unless they are written on paper (or I suppose today - on a computer screen): in other words, unless our lives ARE changed by Christ, through New birth by the Spirit of God .... [and the allusion to Ezekiel is intended I think. (Ezek 36:2627 NIV) *26 I will give you a new heart and put a new spirit in you; I will remove from you your heart of stone and give you a heart of flesh. 27 And I will put my Spirit in you and move you to follow my decrees and be careful to keep my laws.]* .... then the words will be illegible.

(1Cor 13:1 NIV)

1 If I speak in the tongues of men and of angels, but have not love, I am only a resounding gong or a clanging cymbal.

But equally, if all we offer people is a nice clean sheet of paper without words on it, then though the paper may be admired for its cleanness, it conveys no clear and specific message. We MUST speak of a our faith, we must tell people of the gospel and not be frozen into silence by fear of being accused of inconsistency.

Letters received in those days were always of importance - there was n junk mail.

Our lives are changed - are being changed. When we meet others they see brief sample of what is a process: our sanctification. For, as Paul says:

4 Such confidence as this is ours through Christ before God.

5 Not that we are competent in ourselves to claim anything for ourselve but our competence comes from God. 6 ***He has made us competent*** *a ministers of a new covenant- not of the letter but of the Spirit; for the lett kills, but the Spirit gives life.*

God has given us the competence to do this. It is not our doing.

Now the English of our translation appears to makes a play on words whic is not in the Greek.

"We are Christ's letter [*epistole*], we are ministers of a New covenant - n of the letter [*gramma*] but ..."

Now this particular verse has suffered from misuse in certain circles. It suggested that this contrasts the written Word of the Bible with 'the life of th Spirit'. This is totally to misunderstand Paul's contrast.

He is contrasting the Old Mosaic covenant of the Torah and the Te commandments - written on stone in Hebrew letters - to the New Covena whereby this SAME Word is now written in our hearts by the living Holy Spir of God. At Pentecost, the Jews, amongst other things, celebrated the giving the Torah to Moses. It is fitting that this Festival marks the giving of the Ho Spirit to the apostles: the Spirit who takes God's word and writes it upon ou hearts:

13 But when he, the Spirit of truth, comes, he will guide you into all trut He will not speak on his own; he will speak only what he hears, and he will te you what is yet to come. 14 He will bring glory to me by taking from what mine and making it known to you.

The Holy Spirit IS the teacher of the Word.

What we need to grasp is the that the Holy Spirit is inseparable from th Word of God. The Holy Spirit inspired the Word. As Peter points out in h second epistle:

1:19 And we have the word of the prophets made more certain, and you w do well to pay attention to it, as to a light shining in a dark place, until the d dawns and the morning star rises in your hearts.

20 Above all, you must understand that no prophecy of Scripture came about by the prophet's own interpretation.
21 For prophecy never had its origin in the will of man, but men spoke from God as they were carried along by the Holy Spirit.

Thus the Word and the Spirit are inseparable. The Spirit interprets the Word of God to us: this was what Jesus was saying to the disciple, that He will lead them into all truth [in part because they would need to be writers of Scripture themselves, but we must not take to ourselves in quite the same way these words: ie WE must NOT think that God will give us extra revelations and teaching beyond Scripture: that was specific to the Apostles.] We have the Holy Spirit in us to apply Scripture in our lives. This fulfils God's promise to Jeremiah that:
31:33 'This is the covenant that I will make with the house of Israel after that time,' declares the LORD. 'I will put my law in their minds and write it on their hearts. I will be their God, and they will be my people.
34 No longer will a man teach his neighbour, or a man his brother, saying, 'Know the LORD,' because they will all know me, from the least of them to the greatest,' declares the LORD. 'For I will forgive their wickedness and will remember their sins no more.'
7 Now if the ministry that brought death, which was engraved in letters on stone, came with glory, so that the Israelites could not look steadily at the face of Moses because of its glory, fading though it was, 8 will not the ministry of the Spirit be even more glorious?

The letter in the context means the LAW which brings condemnation,whereas the Holy Spirit coming to us through the gospel, as we put our faith in Jesus, gives life and imparts the New Covenant as promised by Jeremiah, where the Word is written on our heart, and we are washed clean by the blood of the Lamb and by the Word of God.

Thus The Holy Spirit teaches us the Word. He does for us what Jesus did for the apostles when He 'opened their minds to understand the Scriptures.'
Thus without the Holy Spirit we cannot really understand, be taught or teach effectively the Scriptures.
He will not speak on his own; he will speak only what he hears.

Without the Scriptures the Holy Spirit cannot easily teach.
I will not say cannot teach, because in the extreme situations of persecution, God's Spirit has I think taught believers who did not have the written Word.
The Holy Spirit then does not teach 'new truths' that are not in Scripture. This is one of the reasons why Roman Catholicism is in error: it claims that the

Holy Spirit goes on revealing new truths not found in scripture through t teachers of the church. This cannot be. Scriptures contain the whole couns of God for our salvation.

Romans 15:4 For everything that was written in the past was written teach us, so that through endurance and the encouragement of the Scriptur we might have hope.

1 Cor 4:6 *'Do not go beyond what is written.'*

And as our Reformers in the Church of England stated:

Article VI. Of the Sufficiency of the holy Scriptures for salvation.

HOLY Scripture containeth all things necessary to salvation : so th whatsoever is not read therein, nor may be proved thereby, is not to required of any man, that it should be believed as an article of the Faith, or thought requisite or necessary to salvation.

1 Therefore, since through God's mercy we have this ministry, we do n lose heart.

2 Rather, we have renounced secret and shameful ways; we do not u deception, nor do we distort the word of God. On the contrary, by setting for the truth plainly we commend ourselves to every man's conscience in the sig of God.

As I hope to show later Paul never suggests a silent witness, but the need s forth the truth plainly, not diluted, but backed up by lives that show the gosp is effective in changing our lives.

Parents, more than any, know that word and life go together. It would b strange parents who never spoke to their child, but hoped the child wou merely imitate their actions? Yes we want that, (when we are behaving well but we need words too or they might grow up dumb!

To live AND speak the word is no guarantee of success of course:

3 And even if our gospel is veiled, it is veiled to those who are perishing.

4 The god of this age has blinded the minds of unbelievers, so that the cannot see the light of the gospel of the glory of Christ, who is the image God.

5 For we do not preach ourselves, but Jesus Christ as Lord, and ourselve as your servants for Jesus' sake.

6 For God, who said, "Let light shine out of darkness," made his light shin in our hearts to give us the light of the knowledge of the glory of God in th face of Christ.

7 But we have this treasure in jars of clay to show that this all-surpassing ›wer is from God and not from us.

Part 2

Convince & persuade

2 Corinthians CHAPTER 5

1 Now we know that if the earthly tent we live in is destroyed, we have a uilding from God, an eternal house in heaven, not built by human hands.

2 Meanwhile we groan, longing to be clothed with our heavenly dwelling, 3 ·cause when we are clothed, we will not be found naked.

4 For while we are in this tent, we groan and are burdened, because we do ›t wish to be unclothed but to be clothed with our heavenly dwelling, so that hat is mortal may be swallowed up by life.

5 Now it is God who has made us for this very purpose and has given us the ›irit as a deposit, guaranteeing what is to come.

6 Therefore we are always confident and know that as long as we are at ›me in the body we are away from the Lord.

7 We live by faith, not by sight.

8 We are confident, I say, and would prefer to be away from the body and at ›me with the Lord.

9 So we make it our goal to please him, whether we are at home in the body · away from it.

10 For we must all appear before the judgment seat of Christ, that each one ay receive what is due to him for the things done while in the body, whether ›od or bad.

11 Since, then, we know what it is to fear the Lord, we try to persuade men. hat we are is plain to God, and I hope it is also plain to your conscience.

12 We are not trying to commend ourselves to you again, but are giving you ı opportunity to take pride in us, so that you can answer those who take pride what is seen rather than in what is in the heart.

13 If we are out of our mind, it is for the sake of God; if we are in our right ind, it is for you.

14 For Christ's love compels us, because we are convinced that one died for l, and therefore all died.

15 And he died for all, that those who live should no longer live for emselves but for him who died for them and was raised again.

16 So from now on we regard no-one from a worldly point of view. Though we once regarded Messiah in this way, we do so no longer.

17 Therefore, if anyone is in Christ, he is a new creation; the old has gone, the new has come! 18 All this is from God, who reconciled us to himself through Messiah and gave us the ministry of reconciliation: 19 that God was reconciling the world to himself in Christ, not counting men's sins against them. And he has committed to us the message of reconciliation.

20 We are therefore Christ's ambassadors, as though God were making his appeal through us. We implore you on Christ's behalf: Be reconciled to God.

21 God made him who had no sin to be sin for us, so that in him we might become the righteousness of God.

Convince & persuade: both are from the greek word: *PEITHO*: to persuade, obey, yield to, be confident in.

Notice that in the ancient world if you were persuaded or convinced you DID something - you obeyed that you were convinced of. ie you repented - changed you mind and acted differently as a direct consequence. Today we are whisked away from such results. Always on the look out for something new to be startled by, but not to have to act upon: only in Athens - where the high brow hung out do we find attitudes approaching this modern viewpoint.

Some examples of the word being used:

(Lk 16:31 NIV)

31 *"He said to him, 'If they do not listen to Moses and the Prophets, they will not be convinced even if someone rises from the dead.'"*

(Acts 19:26 NIV)

26 And you see and hear how this fellow Paul has convinced and led astray large numbers of people here in Ephesus and in practically the whole province of Asia. He says that man-made gods are no gods at all.

(Acts 28:2327 NIV)

23 They arranged to meet Paul on a certain day, and came in even larger numbers to the place where he was staying. From morning till evening he explained and declared to them the kingdom of God and tried to convince them about Jesus from the Law of Moses and from the Prophets.

24 Some were convinced by what he said, but others would not believe.

(Rom 8:3839 NIV)

38 For I am convinced that neither death nor life, neither angels nor demons, neither the present nor the future, nor any powers, 39 neither height or depth, nor anything else in all creation, will be able to separate us from the ove of God that is in Christ Jesus our Lord.

(Phil 1:2125 NIV)
21 For to me, to live is Christ and to die is gain.
22 If I am to go on living in the body, this will mean fruitful labour for me. et what shall I choose? I do not know! 23 I am torn between the two: I desire depart and be with Christ, which is better by far;
24 but it is more necessary for you that I remain in the body.
25 Convinced of this, I know that I will remain, and I will continue with all f you for your progress and joy in the faith,

(2Tim 1:12 NIV)
12 That is why I am suffering as I am. Yet I am not ashamed, because I know vhom I have believed, and am convinced that he is able to guard what I have ntrusted to him for that day.

[Rom 4:21] *being fully persuaded that God had power to do what he had romised.*

(2Tim 3:1215 NIV)
12 In fact, everyone who wants to live a godly life in Christ Jesus will be ersecuted,
13 while evil men and impostors will go from bad to worse, deceiving and eing deceived.
14 But as for you, continue in what you have learned and have become onvinced of, because you know those from whom you learned it,
15 and how from infancy you have known the holy Scriptures, which are ble to make you wise for salvation through faith in Christ Jesus.

Interestingly the word is most often used in the passive sense of being onvinced.

Now it is clearly of enormous importance that if we are going to ommunicate the gospel to others that we ourselves are convinced.

We often talk about Christian 'faith' or 'belief': the world in its ignorance ometimes talks of 'faith communities' etc.
To be strictly accurate to the NT, they proclaimed a Christian ONVICTION.
let us look at the times this mentioned in the NT: The word 'proofs' egarding the resurrection for example:

(Acts 1:3 NIV)

3 After his suffering, he showed himself to these men and gave many convincing proofs that he was alive. He appeared to them over a period of forty days and spoke about the kingdom of God.

We are reminded that the world always seeks to dull the edge of this dramatic reality. The Gospel is God's truth and our conviction, not our opinion, and we can only hope to convince and persuade others if we ourselves ARE convinced.

'He, The Spirit will convict the world...' We are not alone in our own convictions -The Holy Spirit brings that conviction to the world.

No one wants to hear your or my opinion about anything until they know us well enough to assess its weight, but with the gospel message we may not have that time span. We may have but one opportunity.

Thus we must learn to avoid certain assumptions in the world around us, saturated as it is by Hegelian dialectic. Balance and compromise have a place in certain areas of human life, but today the balanced position is between what is right and wrong, between good and evil - and it is the death of us.

Christians can be very good at studying post-modernism or whatever -ism is the latest fad. I doubt this is often very profitable.

> 'I suppose there are two views about everything,' said Mark [to Hingest].
> 'Eh? Two views? There are dozens of views about everything until you know the answer. Then there's never more than one.' (*That Hideous Strength* C.S.Lewis)

If we present the serious message of repentance and faith in Christ tentatively, as an option, as an opinion held by certain people, then people will simply wait for a more amenable opinion to come along: and like buses, they come in bunches.

Dare I say it, if we invite people to a discussion group, we are in danger of 'using underhand methods' that Paul refers to. For we are purporting to let them give their opinion, even purporting to accept that opinion as valid, only to spring it on them that ultimately we have an agenda we want them to conform to. That is actually being, unwittingly maybe, deceitful!

I read nowhere in the New Testament of Jesus or the apostles having 'discussion groups'. He is always totally above board when talking with people: with the Samaritan woman (in John ch.4) Jesus didn't waste much time on her 'cherished' opinions - he dismisses them.

It is also grossly unfair to ask someone to give an opinion about Christ or Christianity when they are likely to be pig ignorant of it anyway.

"Total war is more humane in the long run" - Clauswitz.

Unfortunately it is because we have let the world's mindset steadily erode the God given conviction of the gospel, that we avoid straightforward imparting of gospel data.

For how can people believe unless they hear...

(Rom 10:1415 NIV)

14 How, then, can they call on the one they have not believed in? And how can they believe in the one of whom they have not heard? And how can they hear without someone preaching to them?

15 And how can they preach unless they are sent? As it is written, "How beautiful are the feet of those who bring good news!"

I'll be dealing with **argument** later, but argument must be informed and 98% of people we meet are likely to be misinformed, disinformed, or plain uniformed.

Here we must, like Paul, have a clear conviction that: *the gospel is the power of God ....*

Of course there ARE matters where we may give an opinion - and this must always be made crystal clear when we do this.

But never must we give God's Word out as being a matter of mere opinion.

That is always FACT - ETERNAL fact.

For let also remember that as Paul says, 2 Cor 5:11 *Since, then, we know what it is to fear the Lord, we try to persuade men.*

We fear God, as Ezekiel feared God:

(Ezek 3:1920 NIV)

19 But if you do warn the wicked man and he does not turn from his wickedness or from his evil ways, he will die for his sin; but you will have saved yourself.

20 "Again, when a righteous man turns from his righteousness and does evil, and I put a stumbling-block before him, he will die. Since you did not war him, he will die for his sin. The righteous things he did will not be remembere and I will hold you accountable for his blood.

We fear God's judgment on those to whom we speak. We also know c God's redeeming love to them, which they cannot receive unless first the discover that God's wrath lies upon them: yet that is the evidence that He love them enough to care that they are doomed: a point, in our politically correc world, frequently ignored.

Part 3
Argue and debate.

2 Corinthians 10

1 By the meekness and gentleness of Christ, I appeal to you- I, Paul, who ar "timid" when face to face with you, but "bold" when away! 2 I beg you tha when I come I may not have to be as bold as I expect to be towards som people who think that we live by the standards of this world.

3 For though we live in the world, we do not wage war as the world does.

4 The weapons we fight with are not the weapons of the world. On th contrary, they have divine power to demolish strongholds.

5 We demolish arguments and every pretension that sets itself up against th knowledge of God, and we take captive every thought to make it obedient t Christ.

6 And we will be ready to punish every act of disobedience, once you obedience is complete.

7 You are looking only on the surface of things. If anyone is confident tha he belongs to Christ, he should consider again that we belong to Messiah jus as much as he.

8 For even if I boast somewhat freely about the authority the Lord gave u for building you up rather than pulling you down, I will not be ashamed of it.

9 I do not want to seem to be trying to frighten you with my letters.

10 For some say, "His letters are weighty and forceful, but in person he i unimpressive and his speaking amounts to nothing."

11 Such people should realise that what we are in our letters when we ar absent, we will be in our actions when we are present.

12 We do not dare to classify or compare ourselves with some wh commend themselves. When they measure themselves by themselves an

ompare themselves with themselves, they are not wise.
13 We, however, will not boast beyond proper limits, but will confine our oasting to the field God has assigned to us, a field that reaches even to you.
14 We are not going too far in our boasting, as would be the case if we had ot come to you, for we did get as far as you with the gospel of Christ.
15 Neither do we go beyond our limits by boasting of work done by others. ur hope is that, as your faith continues to grow, our area of activity among ou will greatly expand, 16 so that we can preach the gospel in the regions eyond you. For we do not want to boast about work already done in another an's territory.
17 But, "Let him who boasts boast in the Lord."
18 For it is not the one who commends himself who is approved, but the one hom the Lord commends.

We come to the words argue and debate.

3 For though we live in the world, we do not wage war as the world does.
4 The weapons we fight with are not the weapons of the world. On the ontrary, they have divine power to demolish strongholds.
5 We demolish arguments and every pretension that sets itself up against the nowledge of God, and we take captive every thought to make it obedient to hrist.

Both of these are now words of mostly pejorative meaning.
'Stop arguing.'
'It's silly to argue over religion.'

'That's very debatable.'

'That mere rhetoric': meaning words without substance etc.

The World has been very effective in neutralising these biblical means of communicating truth.

One of the main symptoms of it is TV and radio, but the heart of it is what can be best crystallised by the word sloth or mental laziness.
(*Amusing ourselves to death,* by Neil Postman is well worth reading.)

100 years ago, ordinary people would think nothing of listening to public speakers debating for two hours each! They knew that if you wanted to be

informed you had to commit time and mental energy to it.

Even Newspapers 100 years ago were mostly print not pictures.

'A Picture is worth a thousand word':' well yes - the more's the pity for picture saves mental effort.

Jesus used **words** for the parables not pictures: yes, the words 'painted picture' but did so by employing the mental energy and mind of the hearer: " *who has ears to hear let him hear"*. Even 'seeing' was primarily as understanding.

Pictures, particularly moving pictures, bypass the higher faculties a manipulate the brain far more directly. That is why the Bible is Word n pictures.

Today, the sound bite replaces thought. TV is worst, but radio is a go runner up: issues which are genuinely serious are given short shrift: fi minutes at most until the broadcaster says "we've run out of time".

We are told no one can listen for more than 20 minutes, so we must nev talk for more than this.

Yet Jesus would teach for a whole day: now of course we are not Jesus, b none the less we must not be put off by these 'worldly' ideas.

If the above were really true, then how is that the real evangelic awakenings of the 18th and 19th cent. occurred? Any of Wesley's Whitfield's sermons lasted a good hour and they were preached for the mc part to illiterate working people!

If you aim low you will always fall lower.

We do not wage war as the world does.

The second way the world deludes us is with variety. 'Don't think too lo about anything':

> Before I knew where I was I saw my twenty years' work beginning to totter. If I had lost my head and begun to attempt a defence by argument I should have been undone. But I was not such a fool. I struck instantly at the part of the man which I had best under my control and suggested that it

was just about time he had some lunch. The Enemy presumably made the counter-suggestion (you know how one can never quite overhear what He says to them?) that this was more important than lunch. At least I think that must have been His line for when I said "Quite. In fact much too important to tackle at the end of a morning", the patient brightened up considerably; and by the time I had added "Much better come back after lunch and go into it with a fresh mind", he was already half way to the door. Once he was in the street the battle was won. I showed him a newsboy shouting the midday paper, and a No. 73 bus going past, and before he reached the bottom of the steps I had got into him an unalterable conviction that, whatever odd ideas might come into a man's head when he was shut up alone with his books, a healthy dose of "real life" (by which he meant the bus and the newsboy) was enough to show him that all "that sort of thing" just couldn't be true.

Screwtape letters by C.S.Lewis

God's word is the objective truth against which we stub our mental toes.

We do not wage war as the world does.

We are afraid to 'get into an argument'. We are urged we must be 'good steners' - of course there situations where this is vital; but not usually when esenting the gospel: the unredeemed mind *cannot understand the things of od.* But Words can help to unblock this misunderstanding.

The World seeks to disarm those who would challenge its ways: consensus ot confrontation. Consensus with regard to truth is **lethal**. It talks of seeking eas where we all agree and not therefore challenging the areas where we are odds. Yet these are often the MAIN issue!!

Remember James? (Jas 2:19 NIV)

19 You believe that there is one God. Good! Even the demons believe that nd shudder.

Or the demons acknowledging Jesus.

(Mk 1:2326 NIV)

23 Just then a man in their synagogue who was possessed by an evil spirit ied out,

24 "What do you want with us, Jesus of Nazareth? Have you come to estroy us? I know who you are the Holy One of God!"

25 "Be quiet!" said Jesus sternly. "Come out of him!"

26 The evil spirit shook the man violently and came out of him with a shriek.

There will always be areas of agreement!

The Jewish leaders believed in 'God', but they did not know him.

But today this is where we are so easily swept along with modern thought.
Because we agree on certain things, mostly because they are common to most of humanity, we are assumed to want to concentrate on these matters!
Yet what teacher would spend time getting a student simply to practice the bits he already fully understands? Surely, a good teacher will confront the area the students does NOT understand.

'The devil is in the detail'. So is the Truth!!
The Gospel is clear and **detailed**: right from the start it was under attack not only from unbelievers, but from those who thought they had a 'better' version.

"Students of popular religion are apt to say: Christianity and Buddhism are very much alike - especially Buddhism!" (G.K.Chesterton: *Orthodoxy*)

We are involved in a war, Paul says, the war of words and ideas.

This is prime spiritual warfare - not binding spirits of this and that - but argument and debate using the Word of God.

We face the problem I raised earlier: ignorance. For debate in NT times meant a careful presentation of a coherent case.

One reason why there could be 3000 converts in one day at Pentecost was that the people there were not ignorant of the data. Each one had learned the Jewish Scriptures from the age of 5.

When Paul argued he had a framework to use with his fellow Jews. Even among some gentile groups there was such a knowledge:
James' comment in Acts 15 :21
21 For Moses has been preached in every city from the earliest times and is read in the synagogues on every Sabbath."

We must not let ourselves be muzzled, but argue and debate, laying out clearly the basis of our arguments.
The gospel requires the use of reason: Jesus is the Logos: the Word, Reason, people must be enabled to see the reasons for their need of the Gospel.

Yet again this weapon has been weakened by modern thought - 'mere logic', chopping logic' etc. People honestly think that if something requires careful easoning, it must be wrong! The truth ought to be 'lying out on the surface' ccessible without the least mental effort.

This, in passing, may be why Darwinian Evolution as a hypothesis has been o successful!

It is a biological slight of hand: usually 'well we are here so it must have appened!' And slough over the annoying facts of geology etc which get in the vay. Indeed it has become in biology like an unnecessary layer of management o which every 'department' has to submit its work. A form of political orrectness, yet remove Evolution from the life sciences and no one would ctually notice the difference, all the genuine experimental science would ontinue, freed from the need to force every discovery into the Evolutionary traight-jacket.

On the wider issue of the gospel, we must not ourselves be trapped by the vorld's thinking.

But perhaps also, we need to watch out for arguing over the wrong ground! Thus it may be unwise to tackle say Creation/ Evolution debate if you are uniformed. These matters are seldom central anyway.

What we say will, initially jar, run counter to PC thinking.

1. The ultimate good is perceived to be the preservation of the planet, it jars people to be told that God has fixed a day for its destruction:

elements burned up 2 peter.

(2Pet 3:1013 NIV)

10 But the day of the Lord will come like a thief. The heavens will disappear vith a roar; the elements will be destroyed by fire, and the earth and everything in it will be laid bare.

11 Since everything will be destroyed in this way, what kind of people ought you to be? You ought to live holy and godly lives

12 as you look forward to the day of God and speed its coming. That day will bring about the destruction of the heavens by fire, and the elements will melt in the heat.

13 But in keeping with his promise we are looking forward to a new heaven and a new earth, the home of righteousness.

2. It jars the world to hear that they are accountable not to human 'values', but to God's judgement.

3. It jars the world to hear that God views them as sinners deserving Hell.

4. It jars the world to hear that they are powerless to save themselves, despite all our learning and civilisation.

5. It jars the world to hear that all their religions are worthless, and their gods are '*shedim*' - demons.

(Deut 32:17 NASB'77)

17 " They sacrificed to demons who were not God,
To gods whom they have not known,
New gods who came lately,
Whom your fathers did not dread.

No *we do not wage war as the world does.*

5. It jars the world's thinking to be required to repent, change their minds and way of living.

Ultimately it jars the world to hear that only Jesus' death on the Cross is the way of salvation.

Let us not be ashamed to argue and debate the Gospel with people.

6. Lastly, do not be anxious if you appear to 'lose' the argument, God's Truth is never wasted: most of us I think will remember, before we became Christians, when we thought we had 'won' an argument against a Christian.

(Is 55:1012 NIV)

10 As the rain and the snow
come down from heaven,
and do not return to it
without watering the earth
and making it bud and flourish,
so that it yields seed for the sower and bread for the eater,
11 so is my word that goes out from my mouth:
It will not return to me empty,
but will accomplish what I desire
and achieve the purpose for which I sent it.
12 You will go out in joy
and be led forth in peace;
the mountains and hills
will burst into song before you,
and all the trees of the field
will clap their hands.

Part 4

Declaring and proclaiming

Isaiah CHAPTER 40

1 Comfort, comfort my people, says your God.

2 Speak tenderly to Jerusalem, and proclaim to her that her hard service has been completed, that her sin has been paid for, that she has received from the LORD's hand double for all her sins.

3 A voice of one calling: "In the desert prepare the way for the LORD; make straight in the wilderness a highway for our God.

4 Every valley shall be raised up, every mountain and hill made low; the rough ground shall become level, the rugged places a plain.

5 And the glory of the LORD will be revealed, and all mankind together will see it. For the mouth of the LORD has spoken."

6 A voice says, "Cry out." And I said, "What shall I cry?" "All men are like grass, and all their glory is like the flowers of the field.

7 The grass withers and the flowers fall, because the breath of the LORD blows on them. Surely the people are grass.

8 The grass withers and the flowers fall, but the word of our God stands for ever."

9 You who bring good tidings to Zion, go up on a high mountain. You who bring good tidings to Jerusalem, lift up your voice with a shout, lift it up, do not be afraid; say to the towns of Judah, "Here is your God!" 10 See, the Sovereign LORD comes with power, and his arm rules for him. See, his reward is with him, and his recompense accompanies him.

11 He tends his flock like a shepherd: He gathers the lambs in his arms and carries them close to his heart; he gently leads those that have young.

12 Who has measured the waters in the hollow of his hand, or with the breadth of his hand marked off the heavens? Who has held the dust of the earth in a basket, or weighed the mountains on the scales and the hills in a balance?

13 Who has understood the mind of the LORD, or instructed him as his counsellor?

14 Whom did the LORD consult to enlighten him, and who taught him the right way? Who was it that taught him knowledge or showed him the path of understanding?

15 Surely the nations are like a drop in a bucket; they are regarded as dust on the scales; he weighs the islands as though they were fine dust.

16 Lebanon is not sufficient for altar fires, nor its animals enough for burnt offerings.

17 Before him all the nations are as nothing; they are regarded by him a worthless and less than nothing.

18 To whom, then, will you compare God? What image will you compar him to?

19 As for an idol, a craftsman casts it, and a goldsmith overlays it with gol and fashions silver chains for it.

20 A man too poor to present such an offering selects wood that will not ro He looks for a skilled craftsman to set up an idol that will not topple.

21 Do you not know? Have you not heard? Has it not been told you from th beginning? Have you not understood since the earth was founded?

22 He sits enthroned above the circle of the earth, and its people are lik grasshoppers. He stretches out the heavens like a canopy, and spreads then out like a tent to live in.

23 He brings princes to naught and reduces the rulers of this world t nothing.

24 No sooner are they planted, no sooner are they sown, no sooner do the take root in the ground, than he blows on them and they wither, and whirlwind sweeps them away like chaff.

25 "To whom will you compare me? Or who is my equal?" says the Hol One.

26 Lift your eyes and look to the heavens: Who created all these? He wh brings out the starry host one by one, and calls them each by name. Because o his great power and mighty strength, not one of them is missing.

27 Why do you say, O Jacob, and complain, O Israel, "My way is hidde from the LORD; my cause is disregarded by my God"?

28 Do you not know? Have you not heard? The LORD is the everlastin God, the Creator of the ends of the earth. He will not grow tired or weary, an his understanding no-one can fathom.

29 He gives strength to the weary and increases the power of the weak.

30 Even youths grow tired and weary, and young men stumble and fall; 3 but those who hope in the LORD will renew their strength. They will soar o wings like eagles; they will run and not grow weary, they will walk and not b faint.

1Jn 1:12

1 That which was from the beginning, which we have heard, which we hav seen with our eyes, which we have looked at and our hands have touched thi we proclaim concerning the Word of life.

2 The life appeared; we have seen it and testify to it, and we proclaim to yo the eternal life, which was with the Father and has appeared to us.

Declaring and proclaiming feature a huge amount in both the old and th new Testaments.

Primarily they differ from the others in that these words are about telling people things they could not know for themselves.

A government makes a declaration or proclamation that 'X' is going to happen:
(Lk 2:1 NIV)
1 In those days Caesar Augustus issued a decree that a census should be taken of the entire Roman world.
Something no ordinary person could expect to anticipate or to know.

Declaring and proclaiming are about imparting DATA and demands.

One of the problems I've touched upon earlier has been the problem that many people (through no particular fault of their own in some cases) are simply ignorant of the DATA of the Christian gospel.

Now there is the Good News both in the old and the new:
Comfort, comfort my people, says your God.
2 Speak tenderly to Jerusalem, and proclaim to her that her hard service has been completed, that her sin has been paid for, that she has received from the LORD's hand double for all her sins.

But Good News only makes meaningful sense if there has been bad news first. I know we now live in a world of spin, where everything has to be portrayed as good news, so the point I'm making may seem obscure.

But 'bad news, good news' is essentially part of the human condition.

But it's not much use merely proclaiming the 'good' bit unless people are first aware of the bad bit!

Look at the passage in Isaiah we read.
6 A voice says, "Cry out." And I said, "What shall I cry?" "All men are like grass, and all their glory is like the flowers of the field.
7 The grass withers and the flowers fall, because the breath of the LORD blows on them. Surely the people are grass.
8 The grass withers and the flowers fall, but the word of our God stands for ever."
9 You who bring good tidings to Zion, go up on a high mountain. You who bring good tidings to Jerusalem, lift up your voice with a shout, lift it up, do not be afraid; say to the towns of Judah, "Here is your God!" 10 See, the Sovereign LORD comes with power, and his arm rules for him. See, his reward

is with him, and his recompense accompanies him.

First, the bad news: *all flesh is as grass.* We are all going to die, we a only here for an instant in time.

Now this 'bad news' has not changed in 2.8 thousand years! We are still going to die, but we spend a very large proportion of our lives trying not think about it. Up to a point this is sensible enough, or we becon hypochondriacs - as indeed has become the situation with regard to safety work for example - the current tend is the way of madness... but equally it very foolish to live thinking you are not going to die - and yet in fact millio do live like this today: millions are not even thinking about preparing for old age: young people are not investing in pensions! Maybe they think th will not grow old! We'll see a little more about this later.

How much less then are people even thinking about eternity.

So this is the first part of our declaration: to remind people that they a mortal. But this is of course not 'news' in one sense. "Death and taxes" on two certainties!

But there is another and crucial piece of bad news that people genuinely a ignorant of:

(Deut 5:17 NIV)
1 Moses summoned all Israel and said:
Hear, O Israel, the decrees and the laws I declare in your hearing toda Learn them and be sure to follow them.
2 The LORD our God made a covenant with us at Horeb.
3 It was not with our fathers that the LORD made this covenant, but with u with all of us who are alive here today.
4 The LORD spoke to you face to face out of the fire on the mountain.
5 (At that time I stood between the LORD and you to declare to you th word of the LORD, because you were afraid of the fire and did not go up th mountain.) And he said:
6 "I am the LORD your God, who brought you out of Egypt, out of the lan of slavery.
7 "You shall have no other gods before me......

God is a righteous and holy God who cannot look on iniquity.
People need to grasp the fact that they are sinners. Unless people hear th they are sinners, they will see no need for responding to the Good News.

Wesley was reputed to say that he preached 80% law and 20% grace.

(Ps 19:7 KJV)
7 The law of the LORD [is] perfect, converting the soul: the testimony of the RD [is] sure, making wise the simple.

[Ps 19:1] *The heavens declare the glory of God;...*

The fact that God would judge the world, and it's best to get sorted before t terrible day can be illustrated from numerous passages in Scripture:
(Mal 3:12 NIV)
1 "See, I will send my messenger, who will prepare the way before me. Then ddenly the Lord you are seeking will come to his temple; the messenger of covenant, whom you desire, will come," says the LORD Almighty.
2 But who can endure the day of his coming? Who can stand when he pears? For he will be like a refiner's fire or a launderer's soap.

(Acts 17:3031 NIV)
30 In the past God overlooked such ignorance, but now he commands all ople everywhere to repent.
31 For he has set a day when he will judge the world with justice by the man has appointed. He has given proof of this to all men by raising him from the ad."

But how can we achieve this first part when the message is initially so comfortable? First acknowledge that we ourselves are no different, we are ners saved by grace.

(Ps 51:1013 NIV)
10 Create in me a pure heart, O God,
and renew a steadfast spirit within me.
11 Do not cast me from your presence
or take your Holy Spirit from me.
12 Restore to me the joy of your salvation
and grant me a willing spirit, to sustain me.
13 Then I will teach transgressors your ways,
and sinners will turn back to you.

Second, remember that the Holy Spirit is with us and in us and
(Jn 16:711 NIV)
7 But I tell you the truth: It is for your good that I am going away. Unless I

go away, the Counsellor will not come to you; but if I go, I will send him to you.

8 When he comes, he will convict the world of guilt in regard to sin and righteousness and judgment:

9 in regard to sin, because men do not believe in me;

10 in regard to righteousness, because I am going to the Father, where you can see me no longer;

11 and in regard to judgment, because the prince of this world now stands condemned.

Sometimes to be specific: have you never lied?, never hated? etc...

Point them to to Jesus' words in the Sermon on the Mount:
(Mt 5:2126 NIV)

21 "You have heard that it was said to the people long ago, 'Do not murder, and anyone who murders will be subject to judgment.'

22 But I tell you that anyone who is angry with his brother will be subject to judgment. Again, anyone who says to his brother, 'Raca,' is answerable to the Sanhedrin. But anyone who says, 'You fool!' will be in danger of the fire of hell.

23 "Therefore, if you are offering your gift at the altar and there remember that your brother has something against you,

24 leave your gift there in front of the altar. First go and be reconciled to your brother; then come and offer your gift.

25 "Settle matters quickly with your adversary who is taking you to court. Do it while you are still with him on the way, or he may hand you over to the judge, and the judge may hand you over to the officer, and you may be thrown into prison.

26 I tell you the truth, you will not get out until you have paid the last penny.

Once people understand something of their predicament, THEN the Good News becomes really good news:

.... but the word of our God stands for ever."

9 You who bring good tidings to Zion, go up on a high mountain. You who bring good tidings to Jerusalem, lift up your voice with a shout, lift it up, do not be afraid; say to the towns of Judah, "Here is your God!" 10 See, the Sovereign LORD comes with power, and his arm rules for him. See, his reward is with him, and his recompense accompanies him.

11 He tends his flock like a shepherd: He gathers the lambs in his arms and carries them close to his heart; he gently leads those that have young.

God Himself has come to rescue the sheep, even though they have gone astray, Jesus has laid down His life for the sheep, that they may not perish, but have eternal life.

The problem we all face perhaps is how humanly speaking we can break through the crust of virtual reality most people live in today and see the dire situation that is reality. Jesus was not afraid to puncture the virtual reality of the Pharisees in their day:

(Mt 23:27 NIV)

27 "Woe to you, teachers of the law and Pharisees, you hypocrites! You are like whitewashed tombs, which look beautiful on the outside but on the inside are full of dead men's bones and everything unclean.

Paul himself knew that the power of the Law of God was not to save, but to expose sin:

(Rom 7:711 NIV)

7 What shall we say, then? Is the law sin? Certainly not! Indeed I would not have known what sin was except through the law. For I would not have known what coveting really was if the law had not said, "Do not covet."

8 But sin, seizing the opportunity afforded by the commandment, produced in me every kind of covetous desire. For apart from law, sin is dead.

9 Once I was alive apart from law; but when the commandment came, sin sprang to life and I died.

10 I found that the very commandment that was intended to bring life actually brought death.

11 For sin, seizing the opportunity afforded by the commandment, deceived me, and through the commandment put me to death.

Is 40:8 The grass withers and the flowers fall, but the word of our God stands for ever."

This very passage Peter uses to new believers to explain how, by the Word of God, we become immortal.

(1Pet 1:2325 NIV)

23 For you have been born again, not of perishable seed, but of imperishable, through the living and enduring word of God.

24 For,
"All men are like grass,
and all their glory is like the flowers of the field;
the grass withers and the flowers fall,
25 but the word of the Lord stands for ever."
And this is the word that was preached to you.

Then we can declare the wonders of God's super-abundance of grace and goodness to those who believe. Do you remember I said young people are not buying pensions because they think they won't grow old?

They are mistaken in the sense we mean that, but God genuinely offers us 'eternal youth'. We may think that the world is passing us by, getting on with amassing fortunes, get cosmetic surgery etc etc, but God has given us unspeakable riches in Christ, not least will be eternal Youth in New heaven and the new earth, where we won't need pensions!

27 Why do you say, O Jacob, and complain, O Israel, "My way is hidden from the LORD; my cause is disregarded by my God"?
28 Do you not know? Have you not heard? The LORD is the everlasting God, the Creator of the ends of the earth. He will not grow tired or weary, and his understanding no-one can fathom.
29 He gives strength to the weary and increases the power of the weak.
30 Even youths grow tired and weary, and young men stumble and fall; 31 but those who hope in the LORD will renew their strength. They will soar on wings like eagles; they will run and not grow weary, they will walk and not be faint.

So, with such good news to offer:

[Ps 22:23] *I will declare your name to my brothers; in the congregation I will praise you.*

[Ps 96:3] *Declare his glory among the nations, his marvellous deeds among all peoples.*

And so...

(Eph 6:1920 NIV)
19 Pray also for me, that whenever I open my mouth, words may be given me so that I will fearlessly make known the mystery of the gospel,
20 for which I am an ambassador in chains. Pray that I may declare it fearlessly, as I should.

(1Pet 2:9 NIV)
9 But you are a chosen people, a royal priesthood, a holy nation, a people belonging to God, that you may declare the praises of him who called you out of darkness into his wonderful light.

(Acts 20:2021 NIV)

20 You know that I have not hesitated to preach anything that would be helpful to you but have taught you publicly and from house to house.

21 I have declared to both Jews and Greeks that they must turn to God in repentance and have faith in our Lord Jesus.

1Jn 1:12

1 That which was from the beginning, which we have heard, which we have seen with our eyes, which we have looked at and our hands have touched this we proclaim concerning the Word of life.

2 The life appeared; we have seen it and testify to it, and we proclaim to you the eternal life, which was with the Father and has appeared to us.

Part 5

Preach & teach

1 After Jesus had finished instructing his twelve disciples, he went on from there to teach and preach in the towns of Galilee.

2 When John heard in prison what Messiah was doing, he sent his disciples 3 to ask him, "Are you the one who was to come, or should we expect someone else?"

4 Jesus replied, "Go back and report to John what you hear and see: 5 The blind receive sight, the lame walk, those who have leprosy are cured, the deaf hear, the dead are raised, and the good news is preached to the poor.

6 Blessed is the man who does not fall away on account of me."

7 As John's disciples were leaving, Jesus began to speak to the crowd about John: "What did you go out into the desert to see? A reed swayed by the wind?

8 If not, what did you go out to see? A man dressed in fine clothes? No, those who wear fine clothes are in kings' palaces.

9 Then what did you go out to see? A prophet? Yes, I tell you, and more than a prophet.

10 This is the one about whom it is written: "'I will send my messenger ahead of you, who will prepare your way before you.' 11 I tell you the truth: Among those born of women there has not risen anyone greater than John the Baptist; yet he who is least in the kingdom of heaven is greater than he.

12 From the days of John the Baptist until now, the kingdom of heaven has been forcefully advancing, and forceful men lay hold of it.

13 For all the Prophets and the Law prophesied until John.
14 And if you are willing to accept it, he is the Elijah who was to come.
15 He who has ears, let him hear.
16 "To what can I compare this generation? They are like children sitting in the market-places and calling out to others: 17 "'We played the flute for you, and you did not dance; we sang a dirge, and you did not mourn.' 18 For John came neither eating nor drinking, and they say, 'He has a demon.' 19 The Son of Man came eating and drinking, and they say, 'Here is a glutton and a drunkard, a friend of tax collectors and "sinners".' But wisdom is proved right by her actions."
20 Then Jesus began to denounce the cities in which most of his miracles had been performed, because they did not repent.
21 "Woe to you, Korazin! Woe to you, Bethsaida! If the miracles that were performed in you had been performed in Tyre and Sidon, they would have repented long ago in sackcloth and ashes.
22 But I tell you, it will be more bearable for Tyre and Sidon on the day of judgment than for you.
23 And you, Capernaum, will you be lifted up to the skies? No, you will go down to the depths. If the miracles that were performed in you had been performed in Sodom, it would have remained to this day.
24 But I tell you that it will be more bearable for Sodom on the day of judgment than for you."
25 At that time Jesus said, "I praise you, Father, Lord of heaven and earth, because you have hidden these things from the wise and learned, and revealed them to little children.
26 Yes, Father, for this was your good pleasure.
27 "All things have been committed to me by my Father. No-one knows the Son except the Father, and no-one knows the Father except the Son and those to whom the Son chooses to reveal him.
28 "Come to me, all you who are weary and burdened, and I will give you rest.
29 Take my yoke upon you and learn from me, for I am gentle and humble in heart, and you will find rest for your souls.
30 For my yoke is easy and my burden is light.

We come to two more words connected with spreading the Gospel: **Preach and teach.**

Don't preach! How often have you been told that? Yet preaching is mentioned over 120 times in the Bible!

We have already looked at subsets of communicating convincing and persuading: pointing out that unless we are convinced we will not convince!

Ve have looked at arguing and debating: we have looked and declaring and roclaiming: imparting necessary information which is either unknown - as in ne case of Gentiles or forgotten or obscured as in the case of Jews, who knew ne OT.

Obviously there is overlap in these words and also obviously we don't think n terms of "Today I'll convince, tomorrow I'll debate": the very cut and thrust f any serious conversation on Christian issues will contain all these elements n an infinite variety of 'mixes'.

But let us look at these two words, beginning with Preach: It is a word ssociated very much with our last two: declare and proclaim: two greek roots re used angelio (from which we get angel): and keruxo: both, like declare and roclaim are announcements of a message.

It is interesting to reflect that Jesus did a lot of this! And that he seldom ersuaded or even argued - and frequently he was castigating them:

20 Then Jesus began to denounce the cities in which most of his miracles ad been performed, because they did not repent.
21 "Woe to you, Korazin! Woe to you, Bethsaida! If the miracles that were erformed in you had been performed in Tyre and Sidon, they would have epented long ago in sackcloth and ashes.
22 But I tell you, it will be more bearable for Tyre and Sidon on the day of udgment than for you.
23 And you, Capernaum, will you be lifted up to the skies? No, you will go lown to the depths. If the miracles that were performed in you had been erformed in Sodom, it would have remained to this day.
24 But I tell you that it will be more bearable for Sodom on the day of udgment than for you."

Of course he is the Word made flesh, he himself did not need to be onvinced of his message - He was His message: He was both its origin, writer nd proclaimer. In that regard He is different to us.

He, perhaps unlike us, did not doubt the message. Even John the baptiser ould doubt:
(Mt 11:26 NIV)
2 When John heard in prison what Christ was doing, he sent his disciples
3 to ask him, "Are you the one who was to come, or should we expect omeone else?"
4 Jesus replied, "Go back and report to John what you hear and see:

5 The blind receive sight, the lame walk, those who have leprosy are cured the deaf hear, the dead are raised, and the good news is preached to the poor.
6 Blessed is the man who does not fall away on account of me."

He had preached the message of the Coming of the Lord, and yet it seemed as if his message was not coming true in Christ.

We, who have believed can and should try to persuade and convince those who, as yet, do not believe. In this respect we share something with our fellow sinners: we both know what it is to be 'far away'. Something that Jesus never was.

There are times, like with John, when we can wonder whether we are right in insisting that God has entrusted us with His gospel, how could God be relying on such feeble vessels? It may seem fine to try and convince or debate but preach?
(1Cor 1:2125 NIV)
21 For since in the wisdom of God the world through its wisdom did not know him, God was pleased through the foolishness of what was preached to save those who believe.
22 Jews demand miraculous signs and Greeks look for wisdom,
23 but we preach Christ crucified: a stumbling-block to Jews and foolishness to Gentiles,
24 but to those whom God has called, both Jews and Greeks, Christ the power of God and the wisdom of God.
25 For the foolishness of God is wiser than man's wisdom, and the weakness of God is stronger than man's strength.

But remember it is God's message we preach, not our own opinions however worthy they may seem: 'Christ Crucified and ourselves your servants for Christ's sake.'

Teaching:

1 "All this I have told you so that you will not go astray.
2 They will put you out of the synagogue; in fact, a time is coming when anyone who kills you will think he is offering a service to God.
3 They will do such things because they have not known the Father or me.
4 I have told you this, so that when the time comes you will remember that I warned you. I did not tell you this at first because I was with you.
5 "Now I am going to him who sent me, yet none of you asks me, 'Where are you going?' 6 Because I have said these things, you are filled with grief.
7 But I tell you the truth: It is for your good that I am going away. Unless I

go away, the Counsellor will not come to you; but if I go, I will send him to you.

8 When he comes, he will convict the world of guilt in regard to sin and righteousness and judgment: 9 in regard to sin, because men do not believe in me; 10 in regard to righteousness, because I am going to the Father, where you can see me no longer; 11 and in regard to judgment, because the prince of this world now stands condemned.

12 "I have much more to say to you, more than you can now bear.

13 But when he, the Spirit of truth, comes, he will guide you into all truth. He will not speak on his own; he will speak only what he hears, and he will tell you what is yet to come.

14 He will bring glory to me by taking from what is mine and making it known to you.

15 All that belongs to the Father is mine. That is why I said the Spirit will take from what is mine and make it known to you.

16 "In a little while you will see me no more, and then after a little while you will see me."

13 But when he, the Spirit of truth, comes, he will guide you into all truth. He will not speak on his own; he will speak only what he hears, and he will tell you what is yet to come. 14 He will bring glory to me by taking from what is mine and making it known to you.

The Holy Spirit is the teacher of the Word. The first thing we need to grasp is the The Holy Spirit is inseparable from the Word of God. The Holy Spirit inspired the Word. As Peter points out in his second epistle Ch. 1:

19 *And we have the word of the prophets made more certain, and you will do well to pay attention to it, as to a light shining in a dark place, until the day dawns and the morning star rises in your hearts.*

20 Above all, you must understand that no prophecy of Scripture came about by the prophet's own interpretation.

21 For prophecy never had its origin in the will of man, but men spoke from God as they were carried along by the Holy Spirit.

Thus the Word and the Spirit are inseparable. The Spirit interprets the Word of God to us: this was what Jesus was saying to the disciple, that He will lead them into all truth (in part because they would need to be writers of Scripture themselves, but we must not take to ourselves in quite the same way these words: ie We must NOT think that God will give us extra revelations and teaching beyond Scripture: that was specific to the Apostles. We have the Holy Spirit in us to apply Scripture in our lives:

This fulfils God's promise to Jeremiah that:

31:33 "This is the covenant that I will make with the house of Israel afte that time," declares the LORD. "I will put my law in their minds and write on their hearts. I will be their God, and they will be my people.

34 No longer will a man teach his neighbour, or a man his brother, saying 'Know the LORD,' because they will all know me, from the least of them to th greatest," declares the LORD. "For I will forgive their wickedness and wi remember their sins no more."

The Holy Spirit teaches us the Word. He does for us what Jesus did for th apostles when He opened their minds to understand the Scriptures. Thu without the Holy Spirit we cannot really understand, be taught or teac effectively the Scriptures.

'He will not speak on his own; he will speak only what he hears,'

The Holy Spirit then does not teach 'new truths' that are not in Scripture This is one of the reasons why Roman Catholicism is in error: it claims that th Holy Spirit goes on revealing new truths not found in scripture through th teachers of the church. This cannot be. Scriptures contain the whole counse of God for our salvation.

Thus when we teach, just as when we preach, we bring people God's Wor not our opinions. New believers, as pray God we may receive into ou fellowship, need the teaching:

(Acts 2:42 NIV)

42 They devoted themselves to the apostles' teaching and to the fellowship to the breaking of bread and to prayer.

Now remember these people were all Jews or proselytes, already instructe in the OT. If they needed teaching, how much more do those today who com to saving faith in Christ?

What is one of the best ways? One to one teaching: And because of that depending on how things go, we will need people willing to do this. Rea Mark, John and read Romans as starters!

(Prov 22:6 NIV)

6 Train a child in the way he should go, and when he is old he will not turn from it.

But the Word is there to teach us about the future ***and he will tell you wha is yet to come.***

This little statement is easily overlooked. It also can understandably be a ource of embarrassment which picture in our minds of "the End is Nigh" etc.

1. It is not, of course about what I might call future voyeurism. Every uman being would like to know what lies around the corner for them: to :now the future in that rather cheap sense of the astrologers etc. Look at the ascination with time travel fantasies etc.

But none the less the Holy Spirit, through the Word, will teach us about vhat is to happen. It is no coincidence that the NT contains the book of Revelation, plus many other sections that deal with the future.

Why then does God's Word teach about the future? Because we have a job o do: You and I are called to warn and tell people that they must repent and ut their trust in Jesus. Not so that we can sit back (like Jonah did) and wait for he bang! It is always an urgent necessity to witness for Jesus, but never more o than when the future as predicted in the Bible begins to take on the nature of he present.

The OT teaches us by reciting history that a nation (Israel) heads for udgment as it disobeys God. So too does a church and the nation in which it as been called to be a witness. God gives times of respite, windows of special pportunity. We must not miss them.

We must be taught by the Spirit the Word so that we may teach. Remember hat Jesus commanded

Mt 28:*19 Therefore go and make disciples of all nations, baptising them in he name of the Father and of the Son and of the Holy Spirit, 20* ***and teaching hem to obey everything I have commanded you.*** *And surely I am with you lways, to the very end of the age."*

Part 6

A Sample conversation

JOHN 4

4 Now he [Jesus] had to go through Samaria.

5 So he came to a town in Samaria called Sychar, near the plot of groun Jacob had given to his son Joseph.

6 Jacob's well was there, and Jesus, tired as he was from the journey, sc down by the well. It was about the sixth hour.

7 When a Samaritan woman came to draw water, Jesus said to her, "Wi. you give me a drink?"

8 (His disciples had gone into the town to buy food.) 9 The Samarita. woman said to him, "You are a Jew and I am a Samaritan woman. How ca. you ask me for a drink?" (For Jews do not associate with Samaritans.) 1 Jesus answered her, "If you knew the gift of God and who it is that asks you fo a drink, you would have asked him and he would have given you living water.'

11 "Sir," the woman said, "you have nothing to draw with and the well i deep. Where can you get this living water?

12 Are you greater than our father Jacob, who gave us the well and dran from it himself, as did also his sons and his flocks and herds?"

13 Jesus answered, "Everyone who drinks this water will be thirsty agair. 14 but whoever drinks the water I give him will never thirst. Indeed, the water give him will become in him a spring of water welling up to eternal life."

15 The woman said to him, "Sir, give me this water so that I won't ge thirsty and have to keep coming here to draw water."

16 He told her, "Go, call your husband and come back."

17 "I have no husband," she replied. Jesus said to her, "You are right whe you say you have no husband.

18 The fact is, you have had five husbands, and the man you now have is no your husband. What you have just said is quite true."

19 "Sir," the woman said, "I can see that you are a prophet.

20 Our fathers worshipped on this mountain, but you Jews claim that th place where we must worship is in Jerusalem."

21 Jesus declared, "Believe me, woman, a time is coming when you wi worship the Father neither on this mountain nor in Jerusalem.

22 You Samaritans worship what you do not know; we worship what we d know, for salvation is from the Jews.

23 Yet a time is coming and has now come when the true worshippers wi orship the Father in spirit and truth, for they are the kind of worshippers the ather seeks.

24 God is spirit, and his worshippers must worship in spirit and in truth."

25 The woman said, "I know that Messiah" (called Christ) "is coming. 'hen he comes, he will explain everything to us."

26 Then Jesus declared, "I who speak to you am he."

We would all like a situation to witness which was well rehearsed! But of ourse this is simply not possible. Real people have a curious habit of not ollowing an imagined script (Winnie the Pooh and the Heffalump trap?). 'I'll ay this.' then 'they'll say that.' usually breaks down at about line two!!

The passage in John is probably the most extensive dialogue of its kind in e Scriptures. Here is a 'chance' encounter as we indeed may get at any time. arely do we get, "What must I do to be saved? We are more likely to be in e John 4 situation. Now of course we are not Jesus! But none the less we are lled by His Spirit and so we needn't totally despair!

First, Jesus is where a good Jew would not feel at all comfortable! In amaria. Now we need to understand that it is one thing to be where 'good' eople would not go, it is another to be there and to be absorbed into it ie to go to a nightclub to reach someone for Christ is quite different from going in to e seen as 'one of the lads' - 'I'm no different from you' sort of thing. If we e believers, whether we like it or not, we ARE or should be different! "You RE the light of the world..." "no one after lighting a light puts it under a ushel." "If the world hates me it will hate you also."

Second, as at mid day a women comes to the well, Jesus breaks another boo (nearly three actually) he talks with her - indeed opens the conversation: e is a women (good Jewish men would not be seen talking to women in ublic - not of course in the Law) she is a Samaritan - an impure race, third she almost certainly even an outcast in her own already 'tainted' society. The ery fact that she has come at midday means she wishes to avoid the other omen in the town who would naturally come early to the well before it got ot. She is therefore a woman with a 'reputation'. I mention this point in that e often think we cannot have the insights Jesus had into people's lives - well deed we may not, but we can use our renewed minds and our logic in order to ring a relevant message to a household or person.

Once when I talked to a Muslim friend of my son's at Oxford, I talked about e fact that Saul (Paul), before his conversion, could not believe that God's Messiah could be killed - because Muslims think that about Jesus.

Of course we must not jump to conclusions, but we shouldn't miss clue: Evidence of drinking or drugs. Or it may simply be an elderly person who ha serious difficulties looking after themselves or whatever. We must observe an if possible act to help. Pure religion 'looks after the fatherless and the widow and the weak in mind etc.

Thirdly it is not wrong to use a means to get to the heart of the gospel. Jesu asks for a drink, he **was** thirsty, but he had an ulterior motive behind th request which took him straight to the opportunity he needed: 'If you knew th gift of God... living water'.

What does he mean? Exactly what woman asks herself! What gift, wha water? Her curiosity is aroused.

She does NOT understand but is genuinely drawn into debate.

We are sometimes told we must keep it simple, don't ever use religiou words that ordinary people might not understand. There is some wisdom i that but equally we do not need to be over concerned, after all the Word of Go comes from the Spirit of God who convicts the World of Sin, righteousness an judgment: many 'religious' words are not that difficult: SIN, DEATH MERCY, LOVE, FAITH.

'What do you think will happen to you when you die?'

She clings to what she does know: 'Our father Jacob... etc.'

'Go call your husband' - he needs to know this too! Why? Because wer she to be married, they are one flesh.

I'll not forget once instance of visiting: 'Oh, you're from the church, I'll ge the wife'!

But this request brings an admission! Which Jesus well knew of course (an we might have guessed) - his further comment is of course something we coul not know, but lays bear her problem! SIN.

Indeed she could not receive the gift of God or the Water of Life unless thi happens.

Today we tend to think that Sin is something people have little idea about. am very much less certain than I was about that. And for a number of reasons:

1. God says His Spirit will convict the world... The Spirit of God will sho

eople their sin, just as Jesus did that woman. Do we believe that?

2. All have what has always been called a conscience which condemns them ıowever fitfully) when they sin and thereby highlights their nature.

3. It is of course obvious that people can speak for hours about the evils of ıe world - of politicians etc etc, of horrible neighbours - so much so that TV rogrammes are now devoted to this kind of public slandering and abuse.

It can indeed become a topic of conversation, next perhaps only to the veather, when strangers meet at a bus stop or in the pub. "Isn't it all dreadful? Vhat is the world coming to?" etc.

Now although getting into such a conversation can be time wasting and nprofitable, we can actually turn it to something much more direct. I would trongly recommend that you read Romans chs 1 and 2. Because that is just hat Paul does (amongst other things of course). In the latter part of chapter ne he lists and describes a whole host of personal and social evils, and oubtless has his readers nodding in agreement, tut tutting:

ROMANS 1

29 They have become filled with every kind of wickedness, evil, greed and epravity. They are full of envy, murder, strife, deceit and malice. They are ossips, 30 slanderers, God-haters, insolent, arrogant and boastful; they invent ays of doing evil; they disobey their parents; 31 they are senseless, faithless, eartless, ruthless.

32 Although they know God's righteous decree that those who do such hings deserve death, they not only continue to do these very things but also pprove of those who practise them.

One can imagine his readers yelling their 'amens' of approval....

THEN:

CHAPTER 2

1 You, therefore, have no excuse, you who pass judgment on someone else, or at whatever point you judge the other, you are condemning yourself, ecause you who pass judgment do the same things.

2 Now we know that God's judgment against those who do such things is ased on truth.

3 So when you, a mere man, pass judgment on them and yet do the same hings, do you think you will escape God's judgment?

Paul is right on the button, right on target - now his readers have not a leg to tand on!

Could we dare do this? Well, I think, with God's help, we can! After all ne thing the Holy Spirit gives us is boldness is witness. Of course be careful to make clear that we are sinners too!!!

Coming back to the original conversation - the effect of this direc confrontation is interesting - and very like what you might expect today ir many ways. A diversion into the general (it has got rather too uncomfortable for the woman): 'You Jews worship at Jerusalem, we here on this mountain whose right?'

"Well, I believe in all religions, or I'm a catholic or a hindu." This can be again a tricky moment in a conversation! Accept this as in some sense 'OK' and humanly speaking the opportunity is gone. Here we again must be as direct as Jesus was. He says "You Samaritans are wrong and the Jews are right!" He may be in Samaria and talking to a Samaritan, but the truth stil sticks in the throat! How very un-PC!

Hinduism, catholicism etc are wrong which can be hard to say in the curren climate!

I believe that this topic is important to all of us - not just missionaries. We all live now in what is called the post Christian Age. Most of our fellow citizens are not Christians. Yet most of them (~ 70%) "believe in God", but the God they believe is not the God of Israel and the God and Father of our Lorc Jesus Christ: if they did then they would be with us (or others) worshipping and witnessing.

Identification

What was very common in the Ancient World when one nation conquerec another was to identify their gods with the gods of the local people. The Greeks did it, the Romans did it. Thus Zeus = Jupiter. Venus = Astarte = Asherah etc. Saturn = Chronos etc.

Things that look similar may possibly be the same. But equally they may well be subtly different.

Israel was warned not to make this identification: something they DID do when they committed the apostasy of the Golden Calf.

The confusion of Yahweh with the god of the Calf is obvious in Ex 32:4-5.

4 He took what they handed him and made it into an idol cast in the shape o a calf, fashioning it with a tool. Then they said, "These are your gods, O Israel who brought you up out of Egypt." 5 When Aaron saw this, he built an altar ir front of the calf and announced, "Tomorrow there will be a festival to the LORD."

Only once in the history of God's dealings with Abraham and his escendants is there any example of Identification. It occurs in Genesis 4:18-19.

18 Then Melchizedek king of Salem brought out bread and wine. He was riest of God Most High, 19 and he blessed Abram, saying, "Blessed be Abram y God Most High, Creator of heaven and earth.

And of course Melchizedek is a type of Christ (as the letter to the Hebrews nake clear).

Paul expands on v17 in Romans chs1-2 in particular 1v18

18 The wrath of God is being revealed from heaven against all the odlessness and wickedness of men who suppress the truth by their wickedness, 9 since what may be known about God is plain to them, because God has nade it plain to them.

But this danger of identification - or another word for the process - yncretism - is very much with us today.

Thus we hear talk of the 'three great monotheistic religions': Christianity, udaism and Islam.

The implication of this is that the God of each is in some sense the same. But this is not in fact true: they are either worshipping the true God or they are nti-christ: one test from the Bible's point of view is given in 1 John 4:2-3.

2 This is how you can recognise the Spirit of God: Every spirit that cknowledges that Jesus Messiah has come in the flesh is from God, 3 but very spirit that does not acknowledge Jesus is not from God. This is the spirit f the antichrist, which you have heard is coming and even now is already in he world.

We must not concede too much ground before we reach the good news. What do I mean? Paul tells us that no other foundation can any man lay than hat which is laid: which is Jesus Christ (1 Cor 3:11). If instead we try to lay a oundation say on a supposed shared belief in 'one god' we can be in deep rouble from the start.

Let us look at the Samaritan woman. Her religion was not true Judaism of esus' day. If we go back a few hundred years to the time of Ezra:

4:*1 When the enemies of Judah and Benjamin heard that the exiles were building a temple for the LORD, the God of Israel, 2 they came to Zerubbabel and to the heads of the families and said, "Let us help you build because, like you, we seek your God and have been sacrificing to him since the time of*

Esarhaddon king of Assyria, who brought us here."

3 But Zerubbabel, Jeshua and the rest of the heads of the families of Israe answered, "You have no part with us in building a temple to our God. We alone will build it for the LORD, the God of Israel, as King Cyrus, the king of Persia, commanded us."

6: 21 So the Israelites who had returned from the exile ate it, together with all who had separated themselves from the unclean practices of their Gentile neighbours in order to seek the LORD, the God of Israel.

22 For seven days they celebrated with joy the Feast of Unleavened Bread because the LORD had filled them with joy by changing the attitude of the king of Assyria, so that he assisted them in the work on the house of God, the God of Israel.

The issue here was identification: "we seek God" yes, but which god? Joshua and Zerubbabel discerned that the god was NOT the same God. This was not just nationalistic arrogance, it was spiritual discernment based on their practice. Later, others 'from the land' who had separated themselves were welcomed at the Passover.

Jesus first of all clears up any possible misunderstandings she might be harbouring: The Jews were right, the Samaritans wrong'. For long before, as we have seen the Samaritans had syncretised their religion.

But for most people we meet who 'believe in god' we need to be very clear about the fact that the true God is not their God, however 'like' him their god appears to be. They are often using their god to suppress the truth about the true God. "The god I believe in wouldn't do this or would allow that..." that is indeed the religion of antichrist. A god who makes people feel good about themselves, who does not condemn, but is so loving...

"If you knew the Gift of God" - you wouldn't follow these man made religions.

Firstly salvation is from the Jews - it is specific and in that sense exclusive - there is only One Way to be saved and it is entirely of God's making and entirely of God's grace.

But there needs to be a definite change:

23 Yet a time is coming and has now come when the true worshippers will worship the Father in spirit and truth, for they are the kind of worshippers the Father seeks.

24 God is spirit, and his worshippers must worship in spirit and in truth."

And this cannot happen unless first, they repent and then can receive the Gift of God, the Messiah and His Holy Spirit - Living Water - who will lead a person into all truth and give grace to worship God as He requires.

"But are there not other ways - easier ways - to be saved?" That is part of what the woman's remark is implying: "I'll wait for a second opinion."

Now today that is a problem: there are now so many competing voices, competing 'offers' that a person might indeed be forgiven for wanting to get a few more estimates!!! 'There will be another one along shortly.'

Whereas we must not pressurise or bully, the New Testament DOES encourage us to persuade.

(Acts 18:4 NIV)

4 Every Sabbath he [Paul] reasoned in the synagogue, trying to persuade Jews and Greeks.

(2Cor 5:11 NIV)

11 Since, then, we know what it is to fear the Lord, we try to persuade men. What we are is plain to God, and I hope it is also plain to your conscience.

We live in an age that has nearly forgotten how to argue and to reason: we see it as unseemly even to debate and argue - but this should not be so. Again with the boldness of the Holy Spirit we can persuade. We speak, He convicts.

(2Cor 10:35 NIV)

3 For though we live in the world, we do not wage war as the world does.

4 The weapons we fight with are not the weapons of the world. On the contrary, they have divine power to demolish strongholds.

5 We demolish arguments and every pretension that sets itself up against the knowledge of God, and we take captive every thought to make it obedient to Christ.

For of course the truth is there is no other 'opinion' but God's and He has made it plain.

Ultimately it is of course the Holy Spirit who will open people's eyes, but He uses us to be the means. Not all of us can do all these things - but we can do some and maybe more than we think!

Whereas we are to lead people to Jesus, we can make opportunities for a more lengthy presentation of the gospel (as Paul did in the Hall of Tyrannus in Ephesus). To lead someone to faith in Christ on the spot is most unusual (but it has happened!) and then requires effective follow up: Paul said to the Philippian Jailer

"Sirs, what must I do to be saved?"

31 They replied, "Believe in the Lord Jesus, and you will be saved- you and your household."

32 Then they spoke the word of the Lord to him and to all the others in his house.

v31 was the bullet point but it needed full exposition v32 before the Jailer was ready:

33 At that hour of the night the jailer took them and washed their wounds; then immediately he and all his family were baptised.

INTRODUCTION

The study of the history and archaeology of the New Testament and its contemporary world is the work of a lifetime and this is not to be seen as a substitute for such study.

However, many people need to be assured that the *data* contained in the New Testament is genuine and has been transmitted without distortion. For some, the lack of such basic knowledge has been a stumbling block to belief in Messiah Jesus.

This booklet is simply a brief sample of some source material, but it may help to remove genuine intellectual questions which can hinder the Gospel.

Below is a very brief book list which may be useful if a person wants to pursue further studies in this fascinating area.

Books:

Rekindling the Word, *Carsten Thiede*
The Jesus Papyrus, *Carsten Thiede and Matthew D'Ancona*
Redating the New Testament, *J.A.T.Robinson*
A New Eusebius, *Edited by J.Stevenson*
New Testament History, *F.F.Bruce*
Archaeology of the New Testament, *R.K.Harrison*
The Jewish War, *Flavius Josephus (translations available)*

Historical and Archaeological Sources concerning the New Testament

This leaflet contains several extracts plus photographs of material which is relevant to the New Testament and provides corroborative evidence for the context of New Testament writings.

Non-Biblical Source material

1. Roman

Tacitus:

THE NERONIAN PERSECUTION

The Great Fire of Rome took place in July 64. Only four of the fourteen wards of the city escaped damage. Nero was suspected of having caused the fire. Of our ancient authorities Tacitus is non-committal, while Pliny the Elder, Suetonius, and Dio Cassius attribute the fire to the agency of the Emperor. Whatever the truth, the Emperor found the accusation awkward, particularly at a time when through his crimes and follies his own popularity was at a low ebb.

(Tacitus, Annals, XV.44.2-8.)

But all human efforts, all the lavish gifts of the emperor, and the propitiations of the gods, did not banish the sinister belief that the conflagration was the result of an order. Consequently, to get rid of the report, Nero fastened the guilt and inflicted the most exquisite tortures on a class hated for their abominations, called Christians by the populace. Christus, from whom the name had its origin, suffered the extreme penalty during the reign of Tiberius at the hands of one of our procurators, Pontius Pilatus, and a deadly superstition, thus checked for the moment, again broke out not only in Judaea, the first source of the evil, but also in the City, where all things hideous and shameful from every part of the world meet and become popular. Accordingly, an arrest was first made of all who confessed; then, upon their information, an immense multitude was convicted, not so much of the crime of arson, as of hatred of the human race. Mockery of every sort was added to their deaths. Covered with the skins of beasts, they were torn by dogs and perished, or were nailed to crosses, or were doomed to the flames. These served to illuminate the night when daylight failed. Nero had thrown open his gardens for the spectacle, and was exhibiting a show in the circus, while he mingled with the people in the dress of a charioteer or drove about in a chariot. Hence, even for criminals who deserved extreme and exemplary punishment, there arose a feeling of compassion for it was not, as it seemed, for the public good, but to glut one man's cruelty, that they were being destroyed.

The evidence of Tacitus is not contemporary, but dates from about 50 years after the event. By that time Christians must have increased considerably in numbers, and Tacitus, as governor of Asia c.112, must have been perfectly familiar with them. As can be seen from the above passage, he regards them as scum.

Suetonius adds:

Punishment was inflicted on the Christians, a class of men given to a new and wicked superstition. *(Suetonius, Life of Nero, XVI.2.)*

Suetonius: **Expulsion of the Jews from Rome c49**

Since the Jews constantly made disturbances at the instigation of Chrestus, he [Claudius] expelled them from Rome ..
(Life of Claudius XXV.4) (cp Acts 18:2)

THE CHRISTIANS IN BITHYNIA: PLINY'S DILEMMA, c.112

(Pliny, Epp. X.96.)

Pliny was sent to Bithynia, instead of the usual Senatorial governor, c.112 by Trajan to reorganize the affairs of the province, particularly those of the self-governing cities, which had fallen into a deplorable state through the mismanagement of "local authorities". The extant correspondence between him and the Emperor shows Pliny to be "upright and conscientious, but irresolute, pedantic, and totally unable to think and act for himself in any unusual circumstances." The Christians were one of the 'unusual circumstances'.

It is my custom, lord emperor, to refer to you all questions whereof I am in doubt. Who can better guide me when I am at a stand, or enlighten me if I am in ignorance? In investigations of Christians I have never taken part; hence I do not know what is the crime usually punished or investigated, or what allowances are made. So I have had no little uncertainty whether there is any distinction of age, or whether the very weakest offenders are treated exactly like the stronger; whether pardon is given to those who repent, or whether a man who has once been a Christian gains nothing by having ceased to be such; whether punishment attaches to the mere name apart from secret crimes, or to the secret crimes connected with the name. Meantime this is the course I have taken with those who were accused before me as Christians. I asked them whether they were Christians, and if they confessed, I asked them a second and third time with threats of punishment. If they kept to it, I ordered them for execution; for I held no question that whatever it was that they admitted, in any case obstinacy and unbending perversity deserve to be punished. There were others of the like insanity; but as these were Roman citizens, I noted them down to be sent to Rome.

Before long, as is often the case, the mere fact that the charge was taken notice of made it commoner, and several distinct cases arose. An unsigned paper was presented, which gave the names of many. As for those who said that they neither were nor ever had been Christians, I thought it right to let them go, since they recited a prayer to the gods at my dictation, made supplication with incense and wine to your statue, which I had ordered to be brought into court for the purpose together with the images of the gods, and moreover cursed Christ – things which (so it is said) those who are really Christians cannot be made to do. Others who were named by the informer said that they were Christians and then denied it, explaining that they had been, but had ceased to be such, some three years ago, some a good many years, and a few even twenty. All these too both worshipped your statue and the images of the gods, and cursed Christ.

They maintained, however, that the amount of their fault or error had been this, that it was their habit on a fixed day to assemble before daylight and recite by turns a form of words to Christ as a god; and that they bound themselves with an oath, not for any crime, but not to commit theft or robbery or adultery, not to break their word, and not to deny a deposit when demanded. After this was done, their custom was to depart, and to meet again to take food, but ordinary and harmless food; and even this (they said) they had given up doing after the issue of my edict, by which in accordance with your commands I had forbidden the existence of clubs. On this I considered it the more necessary to find out from two maid-servants who were called deaconesses, and that by torments, how far this was true: but I discovered nothing else than a perverse and extravagant superstition. I therefore adjourned the case and hastened to consult you. The matter seemed to me worth deliberation, especially on account of the number of those in danger; for many of all ages and every rank, and also of both sexes are brought into present or future danger. The contagion of that superstition has penetrated not the cities only, but the villages and country; yet it seems possible to stop it and set it right. At any rate it is certain enough that the almost deserted temples begin to be resorted to, that long disused ceremonies of religion are restored, and that fodder for victims finds a market, whereas buyers till now were very few. From this it may easily be supposed, what a multitude of men can be reclaimed, if there be a place of repentance.

TRAJAN'S REPLY TO PLINY (Pliny, Ep. X.97.)

You have adopted the proper course, my dear Secundus, in your examination of the cases of those who were accused to you as Christians, for indeed nothing can be laid down as a general ruling involving something like a set form of procedure. They are not to be sought out; but if they are accused and convicted, they must be punished – yet on this condition, that whoso denies himself to be a Christian, and makes the fact plain by his action, that is, by worshipping our gods, shall obtain pardon on his repentance, however suspicious his past conduct may be. Papers, however, which are presented unsigned ought not to be admitted in any charge, for they are a very bad example and unworthy of our time.

THE NAZARETH STONE

The inscription, which is in Greek, but was probably composed originally in Latin, bears the heading 'Decree of Caesar'. It suggests that the Resurrection story may have caused a local 'scare' of some kind. It runs as follows:

It is my pleasure that sepulchres and tombs, which have been erected as solemn memorials of ancestors or children or relatives, shall remain undisturbed in perpetuity. If it be shown that anyone has either destroyed them or otherwise thrown out the bodies which have been buried there or removed them with malicious intent to another place, thus committing a crime against those buried there, or removed the headstones or other stones, I command that against such person the same sentence be passed in respect of solemn memorials of men as is laid down in respect of the gods. Much rather must one pay respect to those who are buried. Let no one disturb them on any account. Otherwise it is my will that capital sentence be passed upon such person for the crime of tomb spoliation.

THE ROTAS-SATOR SQUARE

This intriguing palindromic letter square reads the same in all horizontal and vertical directions:

Of this word square seven examples which date from Roman times have been found, two at Pompeii, one at Cirencester, and four at Dura-Europos in Mesopotamia. These are not formal inscriptions, but are scratched on walls or pillars. The Pompeian examples must date from before 79, when the city was overwhelmed in the great eruption of Mount Vesuvius, and the other examples belong to the third century A.D., those at Dura being anterior to 256 when the city was destroyed by the Persians. The meaning, if any, of the words is difficult to determine ('Arepo, the sower, holds the plough with care' has been suggested), but the square as a whole must have a further meaning.

Two suggested 'solutions' to the cryptic meaning of the Square.

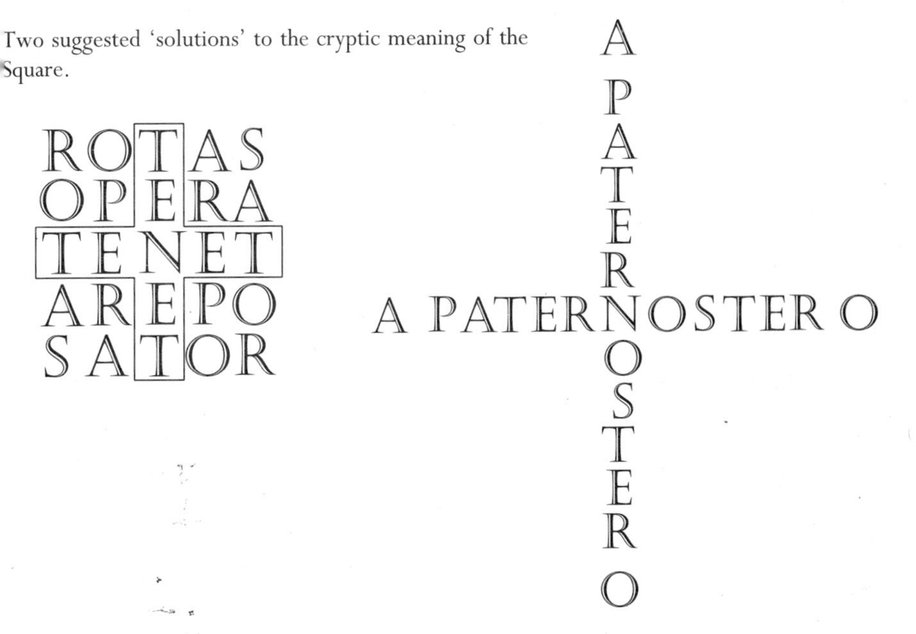

If these or similar interpretations are correct the interesting problem is raised of Christians who, before 79, used Latin, A (Alpha) O (Omega) as a description of God, and a cryptic rendering of the Cross as a Christian symbol. TENET means "He holds" which could also describe what Christ does: he holds those who believe.

FLAVIUS JOSEPHUS

A Jew, born 37AD sadly excelled himself as a toady to the Romans after the Jewish War of 6
73AD. However we are indebted to him for his Histories: "Jewish Antiquities" and "the Jew
War", which latter was written to put the Romans in the best possible light. In passing
mentions John the Baptist, Herod, Pontius Pilate, Annas, Caiaphas and Jesus in some det
(nearly half a page on John the Baptist!). Below is an emended text on Jesus (it is thought th
the unemended version had been tampered with by later Christian editing.)

Now there arose about this time *a source of further trouble* in one Jesus, wise man who performed surprising works, a teacher of men who glad welcome *strange things*. He led away many Jews, and also many of th Gentiles. He was the *so-called* Christ. When Pilate, acting on informatic supplied by the chief men among us, condemned him to the cross, thos who had attached themselves to him at first did not cease *to cause troubl* and the tribe of Christians, which has taken this name from him, is no extinct even today.

NATIVITY PICTURE pre 79AD

This painting, now in the Museum at Naples, came originally from a vill near Herculaneum, destroyed along with Pompeii during the eruption c Vesuvius in 79AD.

Known in the catalogu simply as '*unknown mytho logical subject*', it is almos certainly a nativity scene Mary and child in a cav (the stable was in fact cave), a manger and tw shepherds. This does no mean the villa owner wa necessarily a Christian, bu it does indicate that th story of Jesus' birth had become current among th decorating craftsmen o the period.

ew Testament Information

here is increasing evidence to suggest that the whole New Testament as completed before 70AD, the year the Romans took Jerusalem and estroyed the Herod's Temple. Some of the dates below can be deduced retty accurately – those of the Pauline letters which can be worked out om the book of Acts and internal evidence. Other dates are necessarily ore uncertain. *(Based on "Redating the New Testament" by J.A.T.Robinson)*

Date of Crucifixion / Resurrection	*29 / 30AD*
Conversion of Saul	*32 / 33AD*
James	c.47-8
I Thessalonians	early 50
II Thessalonians	50-1
I Corinthians	spring 55
I Timothy	autumn 55
II Corinthians	early 56
Galatians	later 56
Romans	early 57
Titus	late spring 57
Philippians	spring 58
Philemon	summer 58
Colossians	summer 58
Ephesians	later summer 58
II Timothy	autumn 58
Mark	c.30s-60
Matthew	c.40-60+
Luke	-57-60+
Jude	61-2
II Peter	61-2
Acts	-57-62+
II, III and I John	c. 60-65
I Peter	spring 65
John	c.-40-65+
Hebrews	c.67
Revelation	late 68(-70)

New Testament Manuscripts (MSS)

The quantity of MSS evidence for the N.T. is greater by orders of magnitude than that for other writings from the period. This was due to the urgent desire by Christians to spread the message of the gospel by all possible means.

Papyrus fragment **p52** c110
diagrammatic
reconstruction of the text

εἰπεν αὐτῳ οἱ Ἰουδαιοι ἡμιν οὐκ ἐξεστιν
ἀποκτειναι οὐδενα ἱνα ὁ λογος του Ἰησου
πληρωθηὁ νεἰ πεν σημαιων ποιῳ θανατῳ
ἡμελλενἀπο θνησκειν εἰσελθεν οὐν παλιν
εἰς τοπραιτωριονὁ Πιλατος και ἐφωνησεν
του Ἰησουν και εἰπεν αὐτῳ Συ εἰ ὁ βασιλ
ευς των Ἰουδα ιω ν;

The Jews said to him, We are not able to put anyone to death. This was in order that the word of Jesus might be fulfilled which he said showing by what death He had to die. Again therefore Pilate came into the Praetorium and called Jesus and said to him, Are you the King of the Jews?

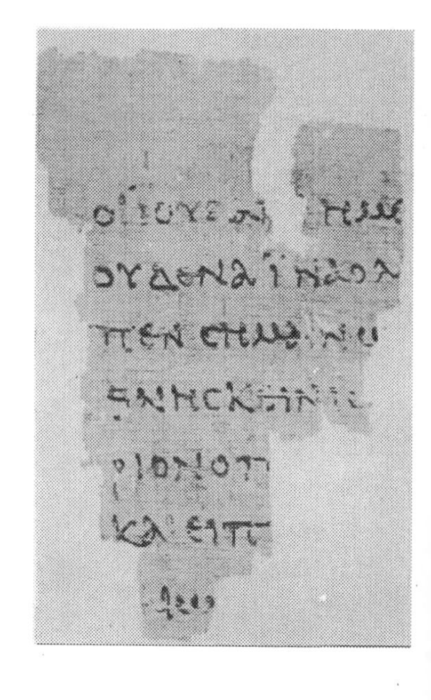

Papyrus fragment **p52**
c110AD
John 18:31-32

ore recent MSS discoveries, in particular fragments of the gospel of atthew *(from Luxor and given to Magdalen College, Oxford at the turn of the ntury)* and the sensational discovery of a fragment of Mark's gospel elow) in one of the Dead Sea Caves *(abandoned in 68AD)*, make it very ear that these gospels were well known long before that date and onfirming the dating on pages 325, 340.

Q5 from the Qumran Caves – earlier than 68AD

Research work carried out by
Dr Carsten Thiede and Matthew D'Ancona
Below: diagrammatic reconstruction of text.

The crucial letter N *(nu)* whose existance was demonstrated using a special laser scanning microscope

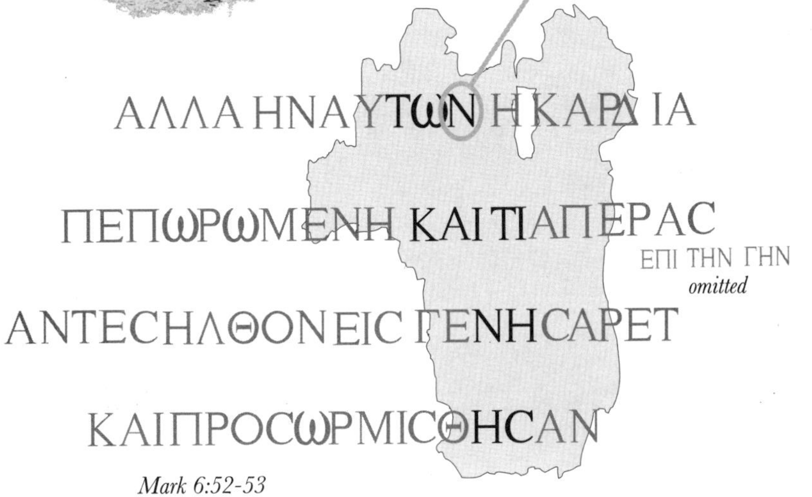

ΑΛΛΑ ΗΝ ΑΥΤΩΝ Η ΚΑΡΔΙΑ

ΠΕΠΩΡΩΜΕΝΗ ΚΑΙ ΤΙΑΠΕΡΑC

ΕΠΙ ΤΗΝ ΓΗΝ
omitted

ΑΝΤΕCΗΛΘΟΝ ΕΙC ΓΕΝΗCΑΡΕΤ

ΚΑΙ ΠΡΟCΩΡΜΙCΘΗCΑΝ

Mark 6:52-53
But their heart was
hardened. And when they had crossed over they came [to the land of]
Genesaret and moored to the shore

ΕΠΙ ΤΗΝ ΓΗΝ
omitted

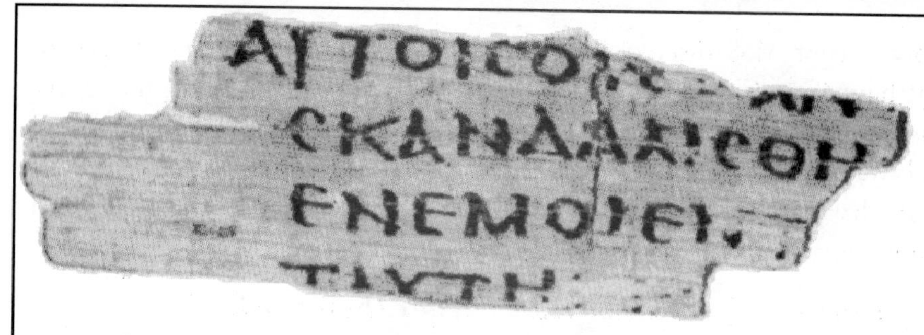

.. which she poured on his head as he was reclining at the table. When the disciples saw this, they were indignant. "Why this waste?" they asked. *Mt 26:7-8*

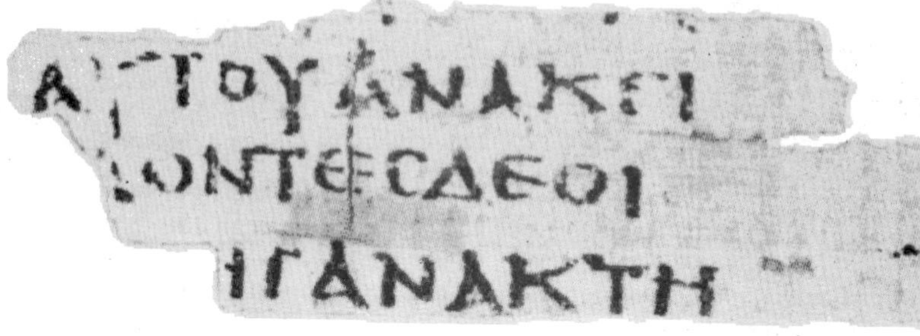

Then Jesus told them, "This very night you will all fall away on account of me, for it is written: "'I will strike the shepherd, and the sheep of the flock will be scattered.' *Mt 26:31*

But after I have risen, I will go ahead of you into Galilee." Peter replied,.. *Mt26:32-33*

Jesus said to them, "Why are you bothering this woman? She has done a beautiful thing to me *Mt26:10*

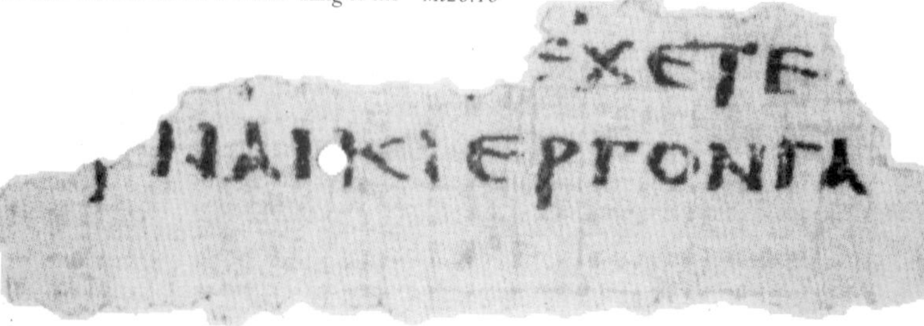

The Magdalen papyri: two fragments (front & back) of Matthew's gospel, 50s AD.

Codex Sinaiticus, a greek Codex containing the old Testament and the New in Greek. This is Psalm 20:-24:5.

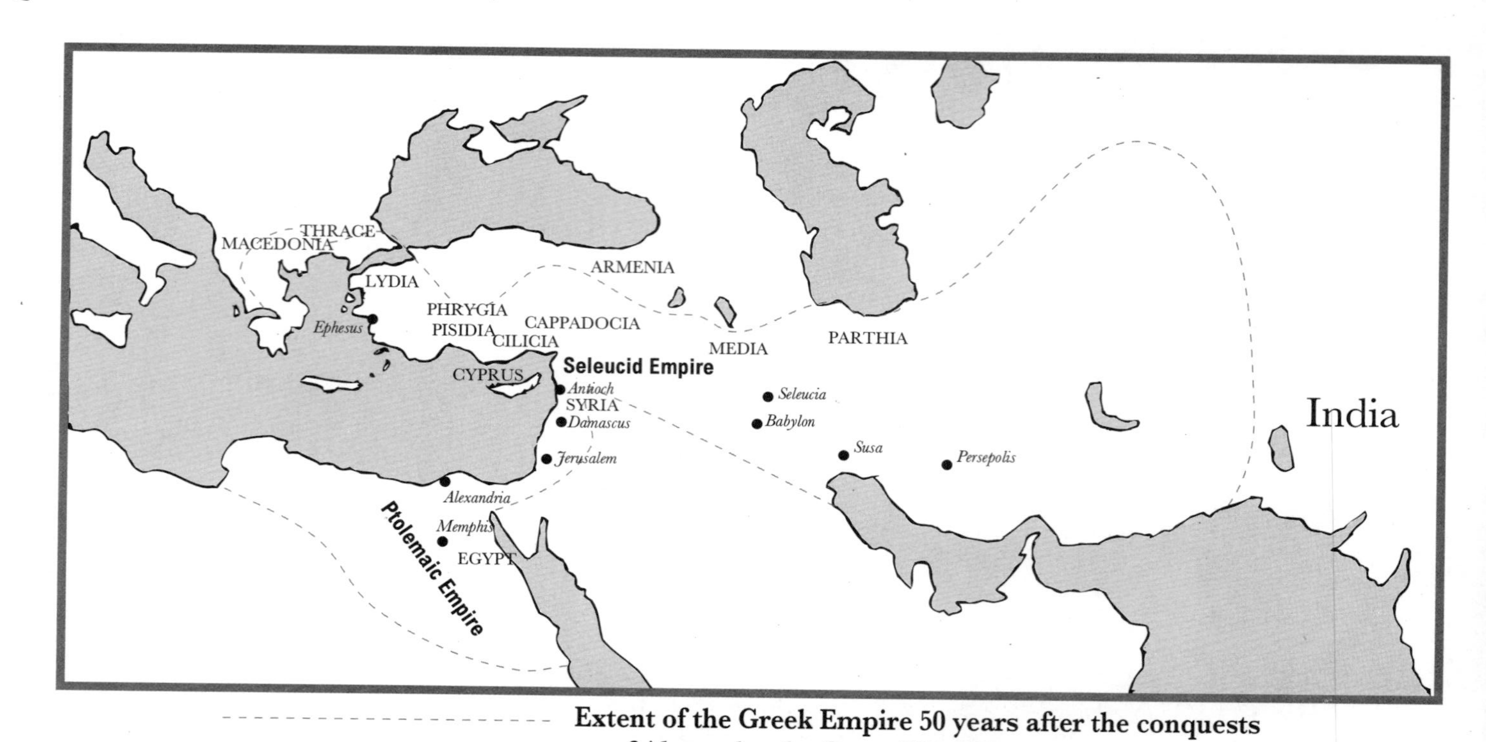

Extent of the Greek Empire 50 years after the conquests of Alexander the Great (334-323)

Reliability of the NT

1. Some wider questions. Perhaps some disillusions!

A brief summary of the Roman World.

1. Society.

A world in some ways very like our own: relatively prosperous but beginning to face inflation as the Empire's boundaries reached their zenith. Conquest was prosperity: retrenchment meant rising costs!

2. Transport

Both by road and sea movement was relatively easy. Eg five days from Rome to Alexandria.

3. language

The spread of Greek as a language was due to the conquests and subsequent empire of Alexander the Great. When Alexander died, his empire was divided among his generals who became dynastic rulers: the Ptolemies in Egypt and the Seleucids in Palestine and the Middle East – for example Cleopatra was a Greek not an Egyptian!]

A brief summary of the Jewish World

Society: the NT reflects the society very accurately

Education: all Jewish boys were educated up till 15. A village without a school should be destroyed according to the Talmud!

The New Testament itself.

The problem being seen as how:

(a) the actual originals were transmitted
(b) how reliable are the originals, &
(c) and why they were selected.

Starting with the first half

(a) How did we receive the present day Bible?

Firstly it is a translation (obvious point!) from the original language which it was written - Koine Greek, that is "pigeon Greek" a version Greek known throughout the East as a second language, in which t authors of the NT, for that very reason, chose to write.

How do we now have what they wrote over 1900 years ago - how has been transmitted?

BY HAND COPYING until the invention of printing. (c1450)
Two methods used:

(1) Sight copying, one at a time,
(2) Dictation to a group, "mass production".

So, we have a long chain of copies of copies of copies etc back to th original.

This raises one important issue: **ERRORS.**

As copies were made errors would creep in and so, like Chine whispers, would not the "final" version be wildly different from th original? Fortunately (or rather by God's Providence), the answer to th is NO:

(1) Copying was always considered a very special task (the OT Jewi copiers would have to destroy a scroll if they made a mistake!), it w regarded as a sacred duty to ensure perfect transmission. (This is or part of the significance of the Dead Sea Scrolls; they illustrate, for th OT, the accuracy of transmission). Now, of course, mistakes still did g in - but they are relatively few, and there are otherway we can chec these errors.

(2) The Checksum!

God's Algebra?

There are twenty two letters in the Hebrew Alphabet (or more correctl 'Alephbet' א, ב being the first two letters), each letter*
represents a number, thus: א=1, ב=2, ג=3, ד=4, ה=5, ו=6, ז=7,

’=8, ט=9, י=10, כ *or* ך=20, ל=30, מ *or* ■=40, נ *or* ן=50, ס=60, ע=70,
or ף=80, צ *or* ץ=90, ק=100, ר=200, ש=300, ת=400.

ome letters have two forms

ut the method I want to describe involves numbers (and was called
phrim in Hebrew). You may have seen an ancient Hebrew manuscript:
olumns of neat Hebrew script like this one below of *Leviticus 5:18-6:5*
Vhen a copier (called a scribe) made a copy, he kept the same column

widths and lengths. After he had completed a copy of each line of text, he would then check it, not just by sight, but by adding up the number values of each letter first in the original and then in his copy. If the sum was the same then he could continue, but if it was different he then had to check for his mistake. Have a look at the example in the box below.

Curiously a similar method is used today in barcodes - the 'checksum' at the end (the last number) is calculated from the other numbers - and if it is wrong it
ows the main code is also wrong and the barcode invalid. Truly 'there
nothing new
ıder the sun'!

> The Hebrew of Genesis ch.1:1 reads: *its sum is:*
> בְּרֵאשִׁית בָּרָא אֱלֹהִי■ אֵת הַשָּׁמַיִ■ וְאֵת הָאָרֶץ׃=2701
> Now suppose the scribe actually copied this as:
> בְּרֵאשִׁית בָּרָא אֱלֹהִי■ אֵת חַשָּׁמַיִ■ וְאֵת הָאָרֶץ׃=
> Can you spot the difference?
> If you do the sum for this line you will get 2704.
> [the mistake is in הַשָּׁמַיִם where the scribe has written חַשָּׁמַיִם]

) We do not just rely on the end of a chain.
'e can go way back down the chain of transmission - because many of
e links in the chain have been preserved, either deliberately or by
cident.

There are in fact an amazing number of early versions of the NT - ranging from whole Bibles (using the Greek OT, the LXX) to tiny papyrus fragments dug up in Egyptian rubbish dumps - literally hundreds of them (It is a curious fact that no other ancient text that we know today has anything like the MSS evidence that the NT has!)

A couple of examples:

A. Textus Sinaiticus - (p329) now in the British Museum. It is actually the whole Bible (Old LXX & New) in Greek and dates from the 4th Century ie 300 perhaps 270 years after the originals.

B. p52 (see page 328) is a fragment of papyrus unglamourous named - and contains bits of Jn ch18vv31-33 as this picture shows - this can be dated around 110AD - that is 50 years after the original, and it fits exactly!

C. More recent material:

The work of Carsten Thiede and others has brought to light fragments that are even earlier:

The Magdalen papyri.

The first (page 328) are dated by style of writing to mid 50s AD. Found in Luxor at the end of the 19th Century they were overlooked for many years.

1. Scholars assumed that it took years for MSS to get from say Israel to Luxor in Egypt/

Why? It reality it would take only a matter of weeks!

7Q5 (page 327)

By direct dating must be pre 68AD when we know that the Qumran caves were abandoned.

It is a fascinating question to know what it was doing there in first place!

There is little evidence to suggest that the Qumran groups were ever Christian. Part of the answer may lie in the respect that these (and indeed all religious) Jewish groups had for 'Scriptures' which contained the Divine Name in any form. The NT certainly does and there is a reference in the Babylonian Talmud to Christian Scrolls in Jewish ssession because they contained the Divine Name, but that 'they were t to be saved in the event of fire!' [reference: *Sabbat 16,1* and *Sabbat 6a*]

ıis fragment contains all of 20 letters! It was suggested as early as the 70s that this was an extract of Mark, but dismissed by many scholars as possible: but they were assuming a late date both for Mark and for the ıer gospels. However Thiede has shown convincingly that it is indeed ragment from Mark.

ımmary

using all the fragments, their place in the chain can be reasonable ›rked out - then where there are "variations" it can usually be deduced ıich version predated which - hence the general text can be revised in : light of these discoveries and conclusions.

ıis picture I have given is somewhat simplified, it is not always possible decide which variation is correct on the basis of date alone, other :hniques have to be employed (the science of textual criticism). But a r conclusion from all this study is THAT THE TEXT WE USE)DAY FOR OUR TRANSLATIONS IS PROBABLY THE MOST :LIABLE SINCE THE EARLY CENTURIES OF THE CHURCH.!

›elieve God has deliberately planned this, so that a scientific and mewhat testing age can be presented with the more accurate version.

›w to the second question:

ıe reliability of the originals.

In what they tell us,

› in who told us.

Records like the NT must be allowed to speak for themselves. The iters of letters had little idea they were "writing" scripture. Paul for tance, was dealing with real situations and real people and perhaps was ssfully unaware that we would still be reading "over his shoulder". In :m there is no room for "invention, myth or any other trick of deceptive writing" - people don't do that in letters. I believe they speak for themselves and the Spirit speaks straight through them. Their content, almost artlessly, backs up that other major segment of the NT - the gospels.

The gospels have frequently been attacked as "propaganda" and therefore to be suspect. ie they are fiction purporting to be fact to bolster the new movement etc... It must of course be admitted that they were written "that you may believe in that Jesus is the Messiah and have life in His Name." But that does not follow they are therefore invention. For one thing the ancient world did not have "novels" - that literary device was unknown, and indeed would remain unknown for centuries. They wrote poetic saga and myth, they wrote histories etc, but not novels.

An extract from C.S.Lewis, 'Fern Seed and Elephants' p108:

> Then turn to John. Read the dialogues: that with the Samaritan woman at the well, or that which follows the healing of the man born blind. Look at its pictures: Jesus (if I may use the word) doodling with his finger in the dust; the unforgettable ῆν δε νυξ *(and it was night)* 13:30. I have been reading poems, romances, vision-literature, legends, myths all my life. I know what they are like. I know that not one of them is like this. Of this text there are only two possible views. Either this is reportage ... pretty close up to the facts; nearly as close as Boswell [*to Johnson*]. Or else, some unknown writer in the second century, without known predecessors or successors, suddenly anticipated the whole technique of modern, novelistic, realistic narrative. If it is untrue, it must be narrative of that kind. The reader who doesn't see this has simply not learned to read. I would recommend him to read Auerbach.*
>
> [*Erich Auerbach's *Mimesis: The Representation of Reality in Western Literature*, translated by Willard R. Trask (Princeton, 1953).]

The gospels are unique in that they are like nothing else, they portray a

Person and they betray time and again those personal touches of eyewitness accounts: "there was much green grass", "there ***is*** in Jerusalem", "they could not even eat etc." Perhaps most significant from the point of view of date: Mark ch.15v7 "the uprising" suggesting an event very close in time to the writing down of the event. Might we postulate Mark (who was clearly around at the time of the passion – witness Mk14:52 – what is the point of *this* incident unless it was autobiographical?) making notes, knowing the importance of the events he was at least a part witness of, and when he comes to put together his fuller version, incorporating his notes in this respect at least, unaltered?

We are dealing with records as near to the events as a say 5-25 years after. It is now thought that we can date all of the NT before AD70 (see p.339).

The argument behind this is well laid out in detail in *Redating the NT* by J.A.T Robinson. But to put it simply: there is nothing in the NT to suggest that the writers knew that the Temple had been destroyed: such a cataclysmic event for Jews – whether believers or not in Jeshua – would have been mind numbing: like the destruction of Westminster Abbey or the Monarchy. Yet all the writers write as if it were still there: John, 'there is in Jerusalem' (John 5:2). Hebrews assumes the sacrifices are continuing. Paul anyway, for other reasons, was writing before 70AD. The Pauline letters can be dated with considerable precision.

Luke who wrote a two part (two Scroll?) gospel and sequel (Acts) concludes part 2 with Paul in Rome under house arrest awaiting his appeal to Caesar – why? Surely every reader would be asking the obvious question: "what happened to Paul?" answer: "we do not know yet!" It is reasonable certain Paul was martyred in 64AD during the Neronian persecution.

Corroborative evidence (cross bearings).

Historians like, quite properly to get cross bearings. There are several references to Christians in contemporary material: Roman and Jewish.

From various Roman historians and writers we know there were Christians in Rome. (pp 319-320) It looks very much as if the Lukan nativity story had reached Pompeii (the 'Southend' of Rome) p324. Indeed nothing is more probable: we know from Acts that Paul met existing Christians in Italy.

Priscilla and Aquila (p2) Acts 18:1-3

1 After this, Paul left Athens and went to Corinth.

2 There he met a Jew named Aquila, a native of Pontus, who had recently com from Italy with his wife Priscilla, because Claudius had ordered all the Jews t leave Rome. Paul went to see them, 3 and because he was a tentmaker as the were, he stayed and worked with them.

Acts 28:13 *From there we set sail and arrived at Rhegium. The next day th south wind came up, and on the following day we reached Puteoli.*

14 There we found some brothers who invited us to spend a week with them. An so we came to Rome.

15 The brothers there had heard that we were coming, and they travelled as far a the Forum of Appius and the Three Taverns to meet us. At the sight of these me Paul thanked God and was encouraged.

16 When we got to Rome, Paul was allowed to live by himself, with a soldier t guard him.

Josephus had things to say both about Jeshua (p6) and John the Baptise and about James (the Lord's brother)

> *Ant. xviii. 116-19*
>
> Some of the Jews thought that Herod's army had been destroyed by God as a just punishment for his treatment of John called the Baptist. Herod killed him, though he was a good man and commanded the Jews to practise virtue, by exercising justice towards one another and piety towards God, and to come together to baptism. For the baptism would be acceptable to God if they used it, not for the putting away of certain sins, but for the purification of the body, the soul having previously been cleansed by righteousness. Now when the rest crowded together to him (for they were greatly moved by hearing his words) Herod was afraid lest John's great influence over the people might lead to a revolt;

for they seemed ready to do anything he advised. He therefore thought it much the better course to anticipate any rebellion that might arise from him by destroying him, than be involved in difficulties through an actual revolution and then regret it. So John, a victim to Herod's suspicion, was sent to Machaerus (the fortress mentioned above), and there killed.

Ant. xx. 200
Ananus *(son of Annas)* therefore, being of this character, and supposing that he had a favourable opportunity on account of the fact that Festus *(Acts 24:27f)* was dead, and Albinus *(who took office in 62AD)* was still on the way, called together the Sanhedrin, and brought before them the brother of Jesus, the so-called Christ, James by name *(Acts 15:13, 1 Cor 15:7, Gal 2:12, epistle of James)*, together with some others, and accused them of violating the law, and condemned them to be stoned.

Lastly, the Canon itself:

This occurred naturally, "by common consensus". By AD190 we know that the Church in Rome considered all the books in the NT except for 2 Peter, Jude, 3John and James as authoritative. Later church Councils ratified this.

The Canon was completed by 400AD but there had never been much argument except over the more peripheral areas, eg whether to include the Didache, the Shepherd of Hermas etc.

Alexander the Great conquers Palestine	*333BC*
Ptolemies rule	*300BC*
Seleucids rule	*200BC*
Maccabean revolt	*167BC*
Temple rededicated (Chanukkah)	*164BC*
Hasmoneans rule	*100BC*
Romans capture Jerusalem (under Pompey)	*63BC*
Herod the Great	*37-4BC*
Jesus' birth	*5/6BC*

Date of Crucifixion / Resurrection	*29/30AD*
Conversion of Saul	*32/33AD*
James	c.47-8
I Thessalonians	early 50
II Thessalonians	50-1
I Corinthians	spring 55
I Timothy	autumn 55
II Corinthians	early 56
Galatians	later 56
Romans	early 57
Titus	late spring 57
Philippians	spring 58
Philemon	summer 58
Colossians	summer 58
Ephesians	later summer 58
II Timothy	autumn 58
Mark	c.30s-60
Matthew	c.40-60+
Luke	-57-60+
Jude	61-2
II Peter	61-2
Acts	-57-62+
II, III and I John	c. 60-65
I Peter	spring 65
John	c.-40-65+
Hebrews	c.67
Revelation	late 68(-70)
Jewish revolt	*66*
Fall of Jerusalem & destruction of Temple	*70*
Fall of Massada	*73*

Dateline for Bible and Church History

ate	Person/Event	Books of the Bible/events
00	Abraham	Genesis*
00	Exodus/Moses	Exodus-Deuteronomy *(*written down by Moses)*
00	Entry into Canaan	Job(?), Judges† Ruth
00	David	1-2 Samuel†, 1 Chronicles†
		Psalms *begun*
0	Solomon	1 Kings†, 2 Chronicles†
	1st Temple built	Song of Songs, Proverbs *begun,* Ecclesiastes
	Divided Kingdom (922)	1-2 Kings†, 2 Chronicles†, Joel, Jonah,
0	Fall of Samaria (721)	Isaiah, Amos Hosea, Micah, Obadiah(?)
		Zephaniah
0	Fall of Jerusalem (586)	Jeremiah, Nahum, Habakkuk, Lamentations
	Babylonian Exile	Ezekiel, Esther, Daniel
		†completed during the Exile in Babylon
0	Return	
5	Temple rebuilt *(2nd Temple)*	Haggai,
8	Walls Rebuilt	Zechariah, Malachi, Ezra,
0	Alexander the Great	Nehemiah
3	Greek conquest	
0	Antiochus/Maccabees	*rededication of the Temple defiled by Antiochus:*
		Festival of Chanukkah. (lights)
	Roman Occupation	
-4	Herod the Great	*major refurbishment of 2nd Temple begun*
8	Birth of Jesus	**BC**

		AD
	Crucifixion/Resurrection of Jesus	
	Conversion of Saul = apostle Paul	*New Testament written:*
		Mark, Matthew, Luke, John,
	Jewish War	Acts, Romans - Revelation
	Fall of Jerusalem	
	destruction of 2nd Temple.	
	2nd Exile	*Canon of Scripture closed*
		Beginnings of 'modern' Judaism
0	Constantine	'Christianity' becomes the 'official state religion of the Roman Empire.
0		Emergence of the papacy in the West
		Rise of Islam in the East
00		Schism between Eastern and Western 'Christendom'
00	Reformation	
48	Israel restored	